Dem. Argyriades

CAPITAL CORRUPTION

Capital Corruption

The New Attack on American Democracy

Amitai Etzioni

New Introduction by the Author

Transaction Books
New Brunswick (USA) and Oxford (UK)

Library of Congress Catalog Number: 87-25572
ISBN 0-88738-708-X
Printed in the United States of America

Library of Congress Cataloging-in-Publication Data

Etzioni, Amitai.
    Capital corruption: the new attack on American democracy/Amitai Etzioni.
        p.   cm.
    Originally published: San Diego: Harcourt Brace Jovanovich. © 1984.
    Includes bibliographical references and index.
    ISBN 0-88738-708-X
    1. Corruption (in politics)—United States. I. Title.
JK2249.E89   1987   87-25572   320.973—dc19

For Willi and Gertrude Falk,
my parents,
who taught me there is a
better way of making it:
observe the rules; work harder.

"I can't be bought," responded Representative John Breaux to allegations of corruption in Congress, "but I can be rented."

"Free and untrammeled representation of the public is possible only when men and women in high office are not indebted to special interests for financial donations." Senate bill 3242, 84th Congress.

CONTENTS

A PERSONAL NOTE

"Washington is corrupt to the core," I wrote in *The New York Times,* in conclusion of a study of American society in November 1982. The conclusion still shocks me, although five years of traversing the corridors of power in the nation's capital, including one year in the White House, and observing politicians at work and on the take should make anyone immune to shock.

In response to the *New York Times* article, John W. Nichols (USNR-Ret) wrote to me: "What *country* are *you* from??? Cuba? USSR? Bulgaria? You've got a G——D——d nerve. . . . You, sure as hell, are *no American* Patriot!" He could not be more in error. I *chose* to live in this country. (My profession allows me to practice and live comfortably in any free country.) I have the highest respect for the U.S. Constitution, history, and potential. Indeed, this book is an expression of my concern for, and dedication to, American democracy.

Some may say these are the words of a bigot, typically trying to refute my arguments by my alleged origins—rather than by disproving what others and I have found. Nevertheless, his reaction should not be dismissed out of hand. His is but an uncouth expression of a feeling many Americans share. They see in criticism of the American government an act of disloyalty. They may well agree that most politicians are "crooked," but they attribute their corruption to weakness of the flesh or character, not to the American political system: "The American Constitution is the greatest in the world." They perceive corruption either as an inevitable part of human nature, or as a problem to be treated by changing the set of characters in office—"throw the rascals out"—but not by introducing changes in the system.

Fortunately for the American democracy and for those of us who feel compelled to call things the way we see them, the basic American constitutional structure is not infested. However, the problems are quite pervasive enough. A whole set of laws has been passed that has

xi

opened the floodgates to special interests, undermining the representative system. As a result, shoring up American democracy now requires much more than a change of the people in office.

In a sense this whole book is an attempt to share with my fellow citizens a learning experience I had. When I started checking up on reports about political corruption in the nation's capital, I thought that the press was, as is often the case, exaggerating the bad news. By the time I finished, I had become convinced that, for once, the problems have not been overplayed.

FIVE KEY QUESTIONS

The daily news carries allegations of political corruption. Representative Henry Helstoski was accused of selling to illegal immigrants private bills that would prevent their deportation. Senator Paul Laxalt is reported to have received campaign contributions from major figures in the underworld of organized crime while he was serving as chairman of the Senate Judiciary subcommittee which drafts criminal laws. Campaign contributions by the auto dealers' political-action committee (PAC) have urged Congress to veto a regulation that would have prevented the dealers from knowingly selling a "lemon." Congress passed a bill prohibiting all candidates for public office from converting "surplus" campaign funds for personal use—except those who were members of Congress on January 8, 1980, the day the bill was enacted.

Such news items raise five basic questions this book seeks to address:

1. *What is the scope of political corruption?* Are there a few isolated incidents—or is it fairly widespread? And who is at fault—some unscrupulous individuals, or is there a serious fault in the system by which we are governed?

2. After reviewing the evidence, a collation from numerous sources plus additional bits of my own digging, I have found that political corruption is both pervasive and endemic. The book then turns from a review of symptoms to a cardinal question of diagnosis: Many countries have known political corruption and learned to "live with it." *Why is corruption particularly debilitating to our political system, to American democracy?*

3. Some experts on the American political scene, people who have

devoted a lifetime of study to the subject, maintain that political corruption is not undercutting American democracy. On the contrary, they argue, it provides a form of representation that adds to and supplants the electoral process. How can they possibly reach such a conclusion? *Where did the experts go wrong?*

4. The nation has been wracked by bouts of political corruption before. *What does our history, especially the Progressive Era, teach us about the sources of the problem and what might be done?*

5. Last, but most important: Reforms have been tried before, in the wake of Watergate and earlier. *How can we marshal a more effective drive to clean up American politics?*

A. E.
Washington, D.C.
March 1984

INTRODUCTION TO THE TRANSACTION EDITION

RISING CONCERN ABOUT PACed CORRUPTION

Political corruption, as measured by campaign contributions of special interests to elected officials, increased significantly in the few years since the first publication of *Capital Corruption*. The number of PACs rose from 2,551 in 1980 to 4,157 by 1986. The percentage of PAC contribution of total campaign costs increased from 31.4 percent in 1980 to 41.9 percent (House) and 24.5 percent to 27 percent (Senate) in 1986. The number of Congressional races in which PACs contributed more than 50 percent of the funds in 1986 was 163, almost one-third of both houses (44 percent of House members). The tilt to incumbents over challengers, which ossifies the system and retards change, first documented in the first edition of *Capital Corruption,* has intensified: PACs gave incumbents 4.6 times more than to challengers in 1984; in 1986 it was six times. *Ninety-eight percent of all challengers not supported by PACs lost in the 1986 House races.*

Supreme Court decisions, difficult for non-lawyers to fully comprehend, at least this one, let stand various limits on campaign contributions on behalf of a candidate, but removed all limits on spending *against* a candidate and on so-called "independent" spending (by groups not affiliated with the candidate). The net effect has been, in effect, to remove all limits on campaign contributions. For example, in the Senate race in Illinois an out-of-state affluent individual, Michael Goland, spent more than $400,000 against Senator Charles H. Percy. (The limit on individual contributions for a candidate is $1,000).

The tidal wave of private funds, many directed by special interests in their efforts to either buy an election of a representative (see chapter 2) or to gain specific items of legislation (see chapter 3), reached such flood-levels that even the receipt-politicians have been expressing growing unease with the PACed polity. Senator Thomas Eagleton of Missouri (since retired) in referring to the Capitol, states "there is the stench of money around this building." Eagleton elaborated, concerning PAC contributions, ". . . they expect something for the money. And when you receive that money, you know those folks have an expectation. You're not blind." Senate Majority Leader Byrd described the private fund raising process of elections as the "poison arrow aimed at the heal of representative democracy."

The growing concern about the role of PACs is further reflected in the introduction and drafting, but so far not enactment, of several items of legislation that seek to curb the PAC's scope and/or introduce public financing of election campaigns to Congress as they are in place for the presidency. (Both measures recommended in the first edition of *Capital Corruption*.)

Current efforts to curb PACs differ from previous ones in that they are introduced by major legislative figures such as Senator David L. Boren (Democrat from Oklahoma) and Senator Daniel P. Moynihan (Democrat from New York) and Senators George J. Mitchell (D from Maine) and Max Baucus (Democrat from Montana). The Boren bill (S.2), which has the widest support, is co-sponsored by 29 other senators. It calls for a voluntary system of spending limits, partial public financing of Senate general election campaigns, and to further limitations of contributions by PACs. (A similar bill has been introduced into the House.) The other bills under consideration have less following. Indeed a previous amendment to curb PACs by Senator Boren won Senate approval by 69 to 30 in August of 1986. However it died when the bill it amended was not enacted. In earlier sessions of Congress such bills were sponsored largely by maverick liberals with comparatively little following.

Despite the enhanced support, passage of the Boren bill is not assured. Furthermore, even if enacted, because of its partial mandate, it will only curb or modify the problem, but not stop the flood of private money into politics, although public financing (as distinct from various new limitations on PACs, such as the suggested reduction of contributions they can make to a candidate from $5,000 to $3,000) would have a significant effect. (The rationale for this conclusion is provided below.)

The problem is not limited to campaign contributions. Another way private interests pay members of the House and the Senate is by providing them with "lecture" fees, given even, as Senator Proxmire put, if one merely reads the phone book, and not to the best speakers but to the most powerful members of committees of interest to the providors of fees. In recent years, honoraria were up: $7.2 million in 1986, up from $5.4 million in 1984. Leading sources include Chicago Commodity trades, whose intellectual needs may not exceed those of other groups, but who actively sought to keep special tax rules for their trading profits; tobacco companies, fighting excise taxes; and billboard companies who defeated attempts to remove roadside advertising.

The amount of fee a Congress member can accept ethically (according to Senate and House rules) is calculated as a percentage of their salary. Since Congress has given itself a very hefty raise in 1987, it increased the amount members can earn on the side. Before 1987 representatives earned $75,100 a year and could earn from fees up to an additional 30 percent of their salary (or $22,530) to a total income of $97,630. Senators earned $75,100 and could earn up to an additional 40 percent of their salary, leading to a total of $105,140. Now, representatives earn $86,283 a year and can earn up to an additional 30 percent of their salary to a total of $112,108, while senators earn $87,483.30 a year and can earn up to $122,476. (Senators find ways to go even higher. For instance, Senator David F. Durenberger (Republican from Minnesota) found a way around the limit by directing a group to pay a $10,000 fee due him—to his publisher, to cover costs of promoting his book.)

In approving its raise, Congress did not follow our suggestion, nor was it pressed by public interest lobbies, to tie the raise to a prohibition on accepting fees, honoraria, and other income from special interest and other private sources. Maybe it will come around to it, when a next raise is considered.

Attempts to curb lobbying made next to no progress in the period that passed. Even a bill to limit lobbying by former federal officials (following the Deaver scandal) failed to win congressional approval.

The machinery to enforce whatever rules and regulations are in place, most important the requirement to disclose contributions, was weakened as part of the general thrust of deregulation during the Reagan ascendancy. The Federal Election Commission, a politically appointed body, of three Republicans and three Democrats, has disregarded in recent years a whole series of recommendations made by its legal and auditing staff. In the process it expanded old loopholes and opened new ones. For example, it allowed Vice President George Bush to make major expenditures in the Michigan primary without counting them against the limit imposed on presidential candidates, and it decided neither to investigate nor to rule on the use of "soft money" (which flows in the millions via state party committees).

Statistical studies, of the kind previously reported here, continued to be issued. For example, an independent analysis shows that in predicting how senators will vote on military spending, money from military-related political action committees (PACs) is a far better indicator than the extent of home-state Defense Department contracts or payroll. An eleven-month study by the nonpartisan Military Spending Research Services found a "strong and consistent" relationship between votes for higher military spending and contributions from PACs formed by defense contractors. Researchers determined after analyzing 68 key votes from 1979 through 1984 that senators in the top one-fifth of contractor PAC recipients were almost twice as likely to support higher military spending than those in the bottom one-fifth.

PACs on state and local levels were not studied in this volume. They remain a much under-studied subject. Press reports suggest that in many localities across the U.S.A. political corruption in all forms is even more rampant than in Washington, D.C. Some reform attempts have been sprouting locally. In Arizona, a coalition of citizens groups collected 100,000 signatures and put on the ballot in November 1986, a Clean Government Initiative, to greatly limit PAC contributions. Dubbed Proposition 200, it passed with 65 percent of the vote. However, by and large, state and local PACing is rarely covered in systematic studies or much affected by reform groups.

SPECIAL INTERESTS AND DEMOCRATIC THEORY

PACs, as the author sees it, are but a tool—new, potent, but not more than one instrument—of special interest groups. The real problem is the loss of balance between group-M*eism* and commitment to the commons. That is, the essence of a democratic society is not pluralism but pluralism within unity; the fragmenting forces must be balanced by unity building; the I with the We. Moreover, it is argued that in the U.S.A., in the last decades, fragmenting forces rose while those that sustain the commons weakened. (This was a major thesis of the first edition, see Chapter 14; it has also been advanced by Robert Bellah, et. al., in *Habits of the Heart,* and George Lodge and Ezra Vogel in *Ideology and National Competitiveness.*)

There are signs galore that special interest continued to push around Congress and dominate the country. One major recent example is the passage, in 1987, of the $88 billion highway bill, chock full with "pork", while the economy was straining under the weight of a huge deficit and the fear of inflation was being rekindled. However, in recent years the ability to enhance the commons, to act in the public interest, despite the powerful special interest, was dramatically demonstrated by the passage of the 1986 tax reform act. The act closed numerous loopholes in the tax code, practically all concessions to one special interest of another. The bill is no panacea. It allowed some loopholes to stand (For example, independent oil producers kept their allowance for depletion of reserves and their ability to "expense" all intangible drilling costs.) It even opened some new loopholes of its own. (The first batch is to be found in the so-called "transition rules" that will cost taxpayers an estimated $5.6 billion. These rules either exempt an industry from a new tax rule or defer its application for a number of years. Among the beneficiaries are chicken farmers, pen manufacturers, timber growers, and oil and gas investors.) And, interest groups are hard at work to fashion new ones. Nevertheless, given its size and sweep, it shows that the polity and Congress, when the pendulum swings too far toward the special interests, have the capacity to push it back in the public interest. Most observers were much less sanguine and did not expect the tax reform bill to pass. Another major bill, the immigration act, for fifteen years stalemated by conflicting interest groups, passed in 1986.

From the viewpoint of the democratic theory developed in this book (see parts II and III) these developments are encouraging; They speak to the ability of the American democracy to correct at least major imbalances, even if they are long overdue, and even if the corrections are only partial. To fully assess the significance of these corrections it remains to be seen if they will hold. Will the reformed tax code be riddled with new concessions to special interests, or will the code be further reformed? Will the main provisions of the immigration act, especially employer sanctions on the hiring of illegal immigrants, be enforced?

Reforms do not spring into being from thin air. Why did the reforms, such as they are, take place in 1986 to 1987? are they isolated events or part of a general trend, and what propels them, are questions that remain to be answered.

GENERAL MORALITY AND CONCERN

When *Capital Corruption* was published, following hard on the footsteps of *Politics and Money* by Elizabeth Drew, a book on the same subject, neither created much of a stir. Neither did other books about PACs (Larry Sabato's *PAC Power* for example). One reason may have been that the country was in a very upbeat mood, at the height of the Reagan, feeling good, patriotic, high. Reports about corruption and need for major reform did not quite suit. Since then the mood has changed considerably, especially late in 1986 and 1987 following the insider trading scandals on Wall Street, the Iran-Contra scandal, and the continued weak performance of the economy. Still much attention is paid to various individual "apples" rather than to the structure of the barrel that may cause many apples to rot, a tendency reported previously in these pages. For example, early during the insider trading scandal a *Businessweek* reporter called the author to ask him about the special background of those caught. The author suggested that there was nothing unique about them, that insider trading and other transgressions were extremely common. The reporter's response was "You must be a socialist!" Since then, *Businessweek* itself published a study showing that out of 172 mergers studied, "unusual" stock run-ups occured in 172 cases.

Additional evidence is included in a study of the 500 leading U.S. industrial corporations. The conduct of corporations was examined for ten years (1975 through 1984) rather than covering their full track record or their behavior over the last generation or so. Only incidents on record were covered; no investigative work was undertaken to uncover new incidents. And yet, 62 percent of all the Fortune 500 corporations were involved in one or more of the incidents involving significant illegal activity during the period; 42 percent in two or more. Fifteen percent were involved in five incidents or more. "Corruption" for the purpose of the study, was defined as acts that are illegal. Acts that are unethical by prevailing community standards but not illegal were not included. The largest category of incidents (17 percent) involved pricing violations. These include price fixing and overcharging. Nine percent involved violation of environmental regulations; another 12 percent, violation of antitrust laws; 9 percent concerned domestic and foreign bribes; 8 percent, fraud or deception (falsification of tax records to conceal political contributions, deceptive advertising, or bookkeeping), 15 percent, various violations of market regulation (patent infringement, violation of securities and exchange regulation); 15 percent, an assortment of others.

It continues to be clear that a major, multi-faceted reform, one that will encompass politics, business, and other sections of the society, lifting them to a higher standard of legality and morality, will not occur until the need for such a reform becomes the core theme of a major social movement—the way environmental issues were in the 1970s and civil rights were in the 1960s. Such reforms were the theme of the Progressive movement between 1900 and 1917 (see pp. 150*ff*). Without such a movement the public support needed to achieve a major reform will be lacking. The moral level of a polity, a society, is not an ephemeral thing; a matter subject to individual tastes and preferences. It is based on what the community at large supports and will not tolerate. At this stage, concern about political corruption and the wider social malaise have caught the attention of some intellectuals and investigative reporters but are not an issue on which the public has been seriously aroused. A Progressive social political movement continues to be as much needed as it is absent.

REFERENCES

Elizabeth Drew. 1983. *Politics and Money: The New Road to Corruption*. New York: Macmillan.

Larry Sabato. 1984. *PAC Power: Inside the World of Political Action Committees*. New York: Norton.

Robert N. Bellah, et. al. 1985. *Habits of the Heart: Individualism and Commitment in American Life*. Berkeley: University of California Press.

George C. Lodge and Ezra F. Vogel, eds. 1987. *Ideology and National Competitiveness: An Analysis of Nine Countries*. Boston: Harvard Business School Press.

PART I

CORRUPT WAYS: The Problem

CHAPTER ONE

THE NEW PLUTOCRACY IN AMERICA

POLITICAL CORRUPTION

America is not a plutocracy—at least not yet. Certainly it is not a full-fledged one. But there were, from day one, plutocratic tendencies, persons and groups who commanded wealth—or other forms of economic power—and who sought to use it to corrupt the democratic government. Now the country is subject to a strong new bout of the same. Interest groups, most of which reflect concentrations of economic power, have found new, effective ways of undercutting the American government.

At issue is nothing less than who has the power to guide the government. If you believe that in contemporary America it is the people, each person having an equal say, as in "one person, one vote," you probably also believe in the tooth fairy. There have always been select groups within society that used their power to make government heed them more than the rest of the people. When the select group is the church, we talk about a "theocracy." When the power behind the public scenes is a titled, closed group of owners of large estates, we refer to a "landed aristocracy." When the powers that be are those who command economic power, and when they use it to wreak their will on those in office, the appropriate label is "plutocracy."

Plutocrats in a democracy work by corrupting public life. They seek to turn a government of, by, and for the people into one in tow

3

of the wealthy. Corruption, the dictionary says, is evil or wicked behavior. To corrupt is to change a sound condition to an unsound one. However, the corruption that is my subject is not regular garden-variety corruption, but the special species rampant in Washington, D.C.—corruption of a political system. The unsound condition I deal with is the use of public office for private advantage. This statement may seem to imply that the abuse at hand is something public officials do. Indeed they do, but usually in close collaboration with private parties. Political corruption is typically perpetrated, we shall see, by private interests seeking illicit public favors and finding quite willing elected officials. The change of the government's condition from sound to unsound often involves at least one public and one private partner.

WHERE THE POWER LIES

Plutocracy does *not* assume one ruling class, or one power elite, as the Marxists would have us believe. America's power wielders include a variety of groups—corporations and labor unions, big business and associations of small businesses, oil companies and farm associations and banks. They do not all pull in the same directions and they are not in cahoots with one another, like one well-organized, tidy bunch. On the contrary, each interest group seeks to tilt the system its own way, so that the riches on the table will roll into its own pockets. Cumulatively, however, they do prevent the government from discharging its appointed duties, from serving the public first and foremost.

While there are a fair number of private power wielders who tug and pull, the government's serving them all does not, as some would have it, amount to a new form of democracy, an interest-group state, a government system by which everyone is served because all are represented by one plutocrat or another. There are many who go unrepresented, and more who go underrepresented. In the interest-group state, the government works overtime only for the strongest interest groups. The rest are cut in as second cousins—if they are not cut out. Thus, while the country is not run by a single power elite, a military-industrial establishment, neither is it governed by a large variety of more or less coequal interest groups, more or less embracing all.

What we have in America is a *power profile* of powerful groups, less powerful ones, and the unrepresented. The power elite evokes the image of a pyramid; pluralism, a room filled with balloons; and the power profile, the image of a Manhattan skyline, with some overpowering skyscrapers, some high-rise buildings, and quite a few slums.

SOMETHING OLD, SOMETHING NEW: PACed INTEREST GROUPS

There are those who say that political corruption, private power, interest groups have been with us forever. In the Federalist Papers, published in 1787–88, James Madison bemoaned their influence. (He called them "factions." Latter-day terms include "lobbies" and "pressure groups.") Others zero in on the new PACs (political-action committees) as if bringing money to bear on American politics were a new, unprecedented phenomenon.

PACs are a mechanism for raising political money; they collect money from a bunch of individuals and their directors decide to whose election campaigns to contribute the funds. In legal terms, PACs are "non-party," "multi-candidate" political committees that maintain a separate, segregated fund for political contributions: "non-party" because they are set up by interest groups, not by political parties; "multi-candidate" because they must distribute their largesse to at least five candidates ("political contributions" only; no charity to be mixed in here).

What corrupts American democracy most these days is *PACed interest groups,* the old interest groups equipped with a new set of computer-age tools for cracking public safes. While interest groups have haunted American democracy since its inception, only recently have they acquired the legal right to amass, openly, the resources needed to elect (or defeat) the nation's lawmakers.

There are now PACs for most interests, from bootmakers to dairy farmers, from defense contractors to those who favor abortion-on-demand. However, the largest concentration of PACs serves corporate America. Of the 3,371 PACs plying their trade on January 1, 1983, 1,467 (or 43.5 percent) were working for American corporations, their list reading like a *Who's Who* in American business, from AT&T to the Zapata Corporation. In addition, trade associations representing various segments of the business community have PACs, which are some of the largest and most powerful, such as the American Bankers Association PAC (BankPAC) and the Realtors PAC.

Professionals such as doctors, lawyers, and dentists have PACs, of which the largest is AMPAC, that of the American Medical Association. Farm organizations also grow PACs. Dairy farmers, for example, are represented by the Committee for Thorough Agricultural Political Education (sponsored by Associated Milk Producers), Special Political Agricultural Community Education (sponsored by Dairymen, Inc.), and several others. Labor unions have organized some 380 PACs, of which the largest is the Voluntary Community Action Program of the United Auto Workers.

Some PACs represent a mixture of economic interest and ideological perspective. For example, several Southwestern oilmen have formed PACs to promote right-wing conservative, anti-big-government viewpoints, as well as oil interests. Others are purely ideological —for example, liberal PACs such as ProPAC, the Progressive Political Action Committee. But most PACs by far, more than 75 percent, express first and foremost an economic interest.

The amounts of money mobilized and applied to politics are quite substantial. Some of the larger PACs raise as much as $8 or $9 million in a two-year congressional-election cycle that typically includes a primary, general elections, and, possibly, a run-off. During the 1981–82 congressional-election campaign, for example, Senator Jesse Helms's archconservative PAC, the National Congressional Club, raised $9.7 million. The total raised by PACs for the 1981–82 congressional campaign was $199 million.

The PACs basically reflect the distribution of economic power in society. Corporations, the mainstay of a modern economy and the bases of economic power within the community, raised 24 percent ($47.2 million) of the total PAC money in the 1981–82 campaign. Large corporations had sizable PACs of their own, as well as participating in trade associations' PACs. Most small businesses have no PACs, or only puny ones. They can rely only on their trade associations.

Trade, membership, and health organizations raised 22 percent ($43.2 million) of the $199-million total. This category contains disparate groups, such as the PACs of the auto dealers, AMA, and trial lawyers, but is one of the general categories in which the Federal Election Commission tallies the relevant data.

Labor unions, less powerful than corporations—especially recently, following years of decline in membership and clout (although set on a comeback)—raised 19 percent ($37.4 million) of the PAC money in the same period.

Weaker groups, such as the poor, unemployed, and senior citizens, or less well organized groups, such as consumers, either have weak PACs or none at all. For instance, two Senior PACs, advocating the interests of older people, raised only $176,536 between them in 1981–82.

While the majority of PACs have clear economic bases and represent economic interests, some are not piggybacked on a corporation, trade association, or labor union, but rely fully on their own resources. These atypical PACs are much more likely to advance a political philosophy, whether conservative or liberal, than a specific economic interest.

Four Views of the Impact of PACs

There are four viewpoints regarding the seriousness of the challenge PACs pose to American democracy. One savvy Washington observer expects "a major political money scandal," à la Watergate, to break out any moment (Mark Shields of *The Washington Post*). Another equally keen Washington correspondent (Elizabeth Drew of *The New Yorker*) believes "that scandal may already be occurring. It takes the form not of one explosive event but of many often undramatic, everyday events." Political scientist Herbert Alexander suggests that PACs merely "supplement" interest groups. Finally, political scientist Michael Malbin sees PAC corruption as "business as usual," little more than a new expression of an age-old problem.

Closer examination suggests that these viewpoints are not as divergent as they seem at first. Shields may well be right that a particularly blatant incident of legislation-buying will capture the attention of the media and the public sometime in the near future, and will come to symbolize what Drew accurately reports as happening daily in the nation's capital.

Malbin is correct in suggesting that political corruption plagued the United States before PACs. There surely were serious bouts of corruption in earlier generations. Its precise scope, after the Progressive cleanup early in this century, is difficult to assess, because up to the new reform wave of 1974, private "contributions" to politicians were largely under the table. Since the take-off of PACs, in recent years, the main contributions have been in the open, which makes them more evident, but not necessarily more abundant. At the same time PACs now involve such a cross-section of the country's lawmakers, corporations, labor unions, and other organizations that it is difficult to imagine they would all have been involved in bribery and illicit donations in previous eras. We shall see some compelling reasons why, following the breakdown of seniority in Congress and the decline of political parties, interest groups (or lobbies) seem to have more power today than they had, say, a generation ago. But even if it is true that present-day corruption is merely as massive as before, this does not suggest at all that it does not deserve close attention.

PACs in Historical Perspective

While PACs are the latest contrivances that interest groups use to pressure elected officials, other recent developments have contributed to the new plutocratic attack on American government. Until not long ago a number of factors held back the interest groups. The Progressive cleanup (roughly 1900–17), followed by increased involvement of the public in politics; the spread of high-school and later college education (tending to enhance the public's political sophistication); the rise of the electronic village (first radio, then TV, and, with them, the public's political awareness); relatively strong political parties—all helped to contain the interest groups. As a result, interest groups after 1900 were relatively reserved compared with, say, their brazen predecessors in American politics before 1900. There was also, after World War II, a relatively strong commitment to the shared community. Although this did not stop interest groups from pursuing their ends, it seems to have kept many of them from going whole-hog.

During the early to middle sixties, three major developments unleashed the interest groups. First, the general decline of American institutions and ethics (spelled out in my recent book, *An Immodest Agenda*) resulted in personal, and group-level, me-ism, a mentality that encouraged each person and group to watch out for number one to the disregard of all others. Interest groups started punching with both fists, rather than keeping one tied behind their backs. Their natural proclivity toward self-service was now blessed by a social climate that celebrated self-interest. In the realm of business, for instance, this was reflected in the growing rejection of various social demands, from helping the poor to enhancing equality between the sexes. Now the catchphrase "the business of business is business" was widely endorsed. Other groups, from labor to the professions, behaved similarly: My group—and who else?

Second, a whole slew of new politically active constituencies— blacks, Hispanics, women, senior citizens—entered power politics, a development often referred to as the revolution of rising expectations. For a while the groups that more traditionally had been active— business, professionals, conservatives—were shell-shocked, especially in the liberal era of the New Frontier and the Great Society. Even in the early seventies, practically no major group spoke up against environmentalists. However, in the mid-seventies these establishmentarian groups found their voices, regained their political will and muscle, and joined the fray. They drew both on reinvigorated interest groups (such as the Chamber of Commerce) and on new ones (such as the Business Roundtable). With both establishmentarian groups and social and environmentalist groups in the arena, interest-group activities reached a new peak.

Both liberal and conservative advocates object to the preceding view, which sees the unleashing of interest groups of all stripes as a source of trouble for American democracy. Liberals feel that one cannot lump together groups representing the underprivileged with lobbies of the fat cats. Conservatives argue that the new groups are often nothing but ungrateful "troublemakers," or good people duped by agitators. I will have much to say about the differences among interest groups, but one thing needs to be clearly introduced here: more interest groups make for more confrontation and group me-ism, whatever the background of the groups or the merits of their causes.

It was in the mid-seventies that interest groups gained a new political tool that magnified their power by allowing great concentrations of private money to be injected into politics. This was the advent of PACs. True, PACs have existed since the 1930s; however, they were so few and so ineffective that as recently as the early seventies most books on campaign financing made no reference to political-action committees. It was in 1974 that they emerged as a force.

PACs came into their own in response to the Watergate scandals. During the Watergate investigations it was established that corporations were making large illegal campaign contributions, in violation of the 1907 (Progressive Era) Tillman Act. Contributions were either delivered in large bundles of hard-to-trace cash or "laundered" via the corporations' foreign subsidiaries.

Various post-Watergate investigations and hearings revealed that specific favors were granted in return for the contributions. The dairy industry pledged $2 million to President Nixon's re-election campaign. Soon thereafter the administration pledged to support increases in prices and subsidies for the industry. A few weeks after the Amerada Hess Corporation, an independent oil company, gave $250,000 in corporate and subsidized individual contributions, the Department of the Interior ended a wide-ranging investigation of the company's oil-refinery operations in the Virgin Islands without taking any action. Presidential lawyer Herbert Kalmbach, like Mark Hanna in the *pre-*Progressive days, actively solicited contributions from corporations and promised special treatment in exchange.

In addition, very large contributions to Nixon's re-election efforts were made by individual millionaires, including Robert Vesco ($200,000), Howard Hughes ($100,000), Mellon heir Richard Scaife ($1 million), and top insurance executive W. Clement Stone ($2 million and change). Such donations, which were not illegal at the time, were as a rule nevertheless concealed—to avoid unfavorable publicity and, at least in two instances, because illicit favors were reportedly sought. Hughes's donation was set up as a special trust fund in Bebe Rebozo's Florida bank. The account channeled funds for the President's private use. In return, the White House intervened in the IRS investigations of Rebozo and of individuals connected to Hughes. Frederick Malek, an aide to Nixon, led a "responsiveness" program that sought to enlist various parts of the executive branch to help the President's supporters and punish his enemies. The program attempted to channel federal grants, contracts, loans, and subsidies to political contributors and groups that endorsed Nixon's re-election.

Campaign-law reforms in 1974 sought to prevent this flow of large amounts of money—and, with it, concentrated private power—into the public realm. Efforts were made to strengthen the prohibition on corporate contributions, a job that fell to the newly created Federal Election Commission (FEC). PAC contributions were limited to $5,000, individual donations to $1,000. Campaign expenditure limits, later declared unconstitutional, were established. Requirements that candidates disclose the sources of their funds were tightened. Much more public financing was made available for presidential elections, including primaries.

Private power was stemmed for a brief while. Soon, however, the floodgates were reopened as a result of a change sought by labor unions. At their suggestion, the 1974 Federal Election Campaign Act had repealed the provision prohibiting entities that engage in government contracts from making campaign contributions through PACs. Because many corporations have or seek government contracts, this provision had served as an effective ban on corporate PACs—especially for larger corporations. After the ban was lifted, corporations still hesitated. But when the FEC ruled, in response to a request by a PAC of Sun Oil, that corporations and unions could use their treasury funds to establish, administer, and solicit contributions for PACs, the green light was on. Within six months of the SunPAC ruling in 1975, the number of corporate PACs more than doubled, from 139 to 294. The total number of PACs increased from 608 in 1974 to 3,371 as of January 1, 1983. Overall PAC spending increased from $21 million in the 1974 election to $190 million in the 1982 election, an increase of 805 percent. Contributions to candidates for House and Senate seats also increased dramatically, from $12.5 million in 1974 to $83.1 million in the 1982 election, more than a sixfold increase.

Growing Need for Campaign Funds

PACs are the most convenient way for a politician to raise the funds needed to run for office, or to retain office once elected. The amount of campaign funding a candidate needs has skyrocketed in the last decade, a troubling factor in itself.

Campaign resources take many forms. They may include volunteers, arrangements for free transportation, legal consultations with a company's or a labor union's lawyer; an invitation to make a campaign appearance where a large audience is likely—say, at a large factory; help from a national figure, such as a pop singer or a visiting president. But money—the most flexible, universal, easy to amass and apply— is pivotal, the most widely used and most consequential resource. The essence of politics in a mass society is the ability to amass the support of a large number of individuals. Although there are several ways to gain such aggregation, under most circumstances money is by far the most effective. Volunteers help, but they are fickle and unreliable, and they themselves require organizing. They cannot be aggregated in large numbers, stored, shifted around, readily shipped across the country. Money obviously can. It is highly liquid, convertible, and nonperishable. (Indeed, it grows if saved; volunteers grow stale.)

In short, whoever can *aggregate* large amounts of money has a considerable advantage over those who cannot. Sometimes, in fact, potential opponents will not run against a candidate who has a large money chest. True, money does not *guarantee* an election. Millionaire Lewis Lehrman spent some $8 million of his own money to finance his 1982 campaign to become governor of New York State; oilman William Clements spent some $14 million in Texas. Both lost. And $7 million did not secure a Senate seat to shopping-center tycoon Mark Dayton in Minnesota. Other factors, from the candidate's personality to his social philosophy, do play a role. But money—especially a big pile—can make a significant difference.

In the 1982 elections, twelve senators each spent more than $2 million on their campaigns. Of these, nine won. The three who lost faced others who were able and willing to spend more than $2 million. In the House, the median winner spent $203,831; the median loser, $86,397. Of course, those who look as if they will lose will draw less money. In short, those who say, "You cannot buy an election" are only technically correct: usually one cannot buy a victory against all odds, but one can substantially improve one's chances.

These days, most candidates for public office need large quantities of money for their campaigns. The amounts are great in the House, in which one barely pays last year's election debts before one must run again. They are great in the Senate, in which one runs every six rather than every two years, but where one must cover a whole state, not merely a district. They have increased sharply in recent years, especially with the growing reliance on television campaigning, mass mailings, computers, public-opinion polls, and political consultants.

The cost of primary and general congressional elections ran up rapidly from 1972 to 1982. The total amount raised for all House campaigns rose from $38.9 million in 1972 to $214.1 million in 1982; for Senate campaigns it went from $23.3 million to $142.6 million. The increases represent a 450-percent jump and a 512-percent jump, respectively—three times as great as the increase in the Consumer Price Index, the widely used measure of inflation. And inflation was rising during much of this period. In 1982, the average amount spent by Democratic candidates for Senate seats in the general election was $1.8

million; by Republicans, $1.6 million. In the House, the averages were $202,962 for Democratic candidates and $221,256 for Republican candidates.

These average figures understate the cost of contested seats in Congress, where of course the role of money is more pronounced. Included in the averages are quite a few "safe" seats, for which candidates, because of personal popularity or party domination, need spend very little to be elected or re-elected. New Jersey Representative Peter Rodino, Jr., in the spotlight during the Watergate hearings, spent only $27,000 in 1976 and $46,000 in 1978, and each time was re-elected with over 80 percent of the vote. Representative Tom Bevill, from a sleepy district in southern Alabama, spent only $8,000 in 1978 and $16,000 in 1980. Bevill had to double his spending in 1980 to fight off some tough competition: his share of the vote declined from 100 percent to 98 percent.

In contrast, winning or holding on to a contested seat can run up quite a bill. In 1980, for example, Representative Robert Dornan spent nearly $2 million defending his House seat against Democrat Carey Peck, son of movie star Gregory Peck. (Peck spent only $559,315, but his name was a distinct advantage; Dornan won by only 51 percent to his 47 percent.) Senator John Tower spent $4,324,601 in 1978 against Democratic challenger Bob Krueger, who spent the not-so-paltry sum of $2,428,666. Tower won by one-half of one percentage point. A more typical example of expenditures for an open or a contested seat in the Senate is the $1,688,499 spent by Democrat Bill Bradley to defeat Republican Jeffrey Bell in 1978. Bell spent $1,418,931 in his attempt to win the Senate seat. In the House, Ed Weber spent $380,673 in 1980, more than three times the House average that year, to upset Democratic incumbent Thomas Ashley, who spent $254,264. All these monies must be raised from private pockets.

While campaign costs have been increasing, PAC contributions to congressional candidates have grown faster, rising as a proportion of total general-election campaign funds from 15.7 percent in 1974 to 26.2 percent in 1982.*

---

*Joseph E. Cantor of the Congressional Research Service notes that the final 1982 figure will probably be higher, perhaps as high as 27 percent, when the FEC completes the adjustments of the data.

And—Fees

The second channel through which private interests reach elected officials is fees paid to members of Congress. Fees are comparatively small, a maximum of $2,000 a shot, but the freedom with which they can be used contrasts favorably with campaign contributions.

Campaign contributions go into specially set-aside chests. They are meant to be used for campaign expenditures only, and are subject to some scrutiny. It is clear, however, that campaign chests are not watertight: members of Congress do use them for what surely seem like personal expenses. For instance, Representative Robert E. Badham used $3,380 of his campaign funds to pay his wife's way to accompany him overseas, and $1,369 for her dresses. Charles Rangel spent $1,782 on a trip to Hawaii for himself and his wife. Still, the most direct way to enhance the personal wealth of members of Congress is for the same interest groups that provide campaign contributions also to provide fees, which go directly to the recipients' pockets.

Senators and representatives receive fees for addressing conventions, board meetings, luncheons, and so on, as well as travel expenses. The expenses of a spouse may also be covered. Senator James A. McClure and his wife were flown to Hawaii at the expense of the National Association of Realtors. Senator Robert Packwood and his wife had their way paid to Tel Aviv by the American Jewish Congress. The speeches may be long, detailed addresses, but they may just as easily be ten-minute off-the-cuff remarks. "If you're chairman of the Banking Committee," says Senator William Proxmire, "you don't have to speak at all. . . . You can read the phone book, and they'll be happy to pay your honoraria."

After the tightening of campaign contribution laws in 1971 and in 1974, the frequency and amounts of such fees increased. As a result, Congress came under pressure from public opinion to limit honoraria. The 1976 amendments to the Federal Election Campaign Act placed a $25,000 ceiling on the amount members of Congress could earn from honoraria.

In 1977, Congress got around to tackling a perennial political football and gave itself a $12,900 raise. In an attempt to soften the political reaction, both the House and the Senate wrote a stricter limit on income from honoraria into their new ethics codes, which were being formulated at about the same time. But wait. The limit, which would have allowed income from honoraria to be no more than 15 percent of a member's salary (or $8,625), was set to take effect in the future, in 1979. And in March of 1979, as the time for the imposition of the limit drew near, the Senate voted to suspend it for four years. This action left standing the 1976 limit of $25,000. In 1981 this in turn was removed. Thus, in 1981 Senator Robert J. Dole was able to collect $66,650 on the lecture circuit. Senator Jake Garn collected $48,000 in speaking and writing fees, many from groups affected by the Banking Committee, which he chairs. On the Democratic side, Senator Alan Cranston received $30,600, Henry Jackson $56,250. All in all, twenty-five senators received more than $25,000 each in 1981, though several of these turned over parts of their fees to charity.

In 1982, the first full year without a limit, there was a substantial increase in the amount senators earned from speeches before private groups. Fifteen senators earned over $50,000 each. Senator Dole, who earned $134,000, passed along $51,000 to charity, which left $83,000 to supplement his salary (an amount greater than his $60,662 public salary). Senator Ernest F. Hollings earned $92,000 and kept it all.

Representatives, who generally receive less in honoraria than senators, did not delay implementation of the 1977 limit of 15 percent. However, on December 15, 1981, the House doubled the limit to 30 percent, or about $18,000, without a recorded vote. During the lame-duck session of Congress in December 1982, the House gave its members a $9,000 raise, and kept the 30-percent limit on honoraria. But the Senate, fearing the political backlash, instead of giving itself a pay raise during a recession, voted not to reimpose the $25,000 limit in January of 1983 as they had pledged to do when suspending it in 1981.

In June 1983, this exercise was repeated with a slightly new twist. The senators voted themselves a pay raise, and set a limit of 30 percent, or $20,800, on the amount of outside fees they could legally accept. However, while the raise was to take effect immediately (July 1, 1983), the limit on accepting fees was set for a future date (January 1, 1984). It remains to be seen whether that deadline will not be further extended.

Meanwhile, there is no effective limit on fees. Senators can rake in all they wish, and members of the House, all they can get. Since representatives are less in demand than senators, for the most part they cannot earn as much from speeches as they are allowed.

Several of the highest recipients were committee chairmen: Budget Committee Chairman Senator Pete Domenici, $83,450; Energy Committee Chairman McClure, $60,000; and Banking Committee Chairman Garn, $76,000. In all, senators collected $2.4 million in speaking fees in 1982. D'an Rostenkowski, chairman of the House Ways and Means Committee, got $52,600 in fees in 1981, though he had to give most of it to charity because the House limit at the time was $18,200. Members of key committees, such as Ways and Means and Energy and Commerce, received disproportionately large amounts in speaking fees, whereas members of such committees as Judiciary and Foreign Affairs received much less. As Martin Tolchin of *The New York Times* pointed out, this indicates that "it was a senator's power rather than his speaking ability that really earned those fees."

Members of Congress fly almost weekly for a tour arranged by the Chicago Board of Trade and by the Mercantile Exchange. Aside from a visit to the facilities and lunch with executives, they make some remarks. Fees range from $1,000 to $2,000 (and expenses). However, one representative, Martin Russo, got three times the standard fee, not because his talk was longer or better. In 1981, Russo worked hard in favor of special tax-deferral arrangements for commodity traders.

Larger fees than the legal limit are arranged by the members of Congress appearing several times within a day. In this way Avco, with a keen interest in the MX missile, paid an MX advocate, Representative William Chappell, $4,000 for one day.

And—"Independent Expenditures"

A third tool used by interest groups is known as "independent expenditures." These are expenditures, on behalf of a candidate, incurred by a PAC or individual not approved by the candidate. Often they take the form of attacks on the favored candidate's opponent. In 1974 Congress sought to limit the amount of independent expenditures, because it was widely recognized that large amounts spent in behalf of a candidate cannot escape the candidate's notice, and can obligate the candidate in much the same way as other contributions. But the Supreme Court, in a ruling discussed below, struck down the limits on independent expenditures, and they are now without limit. PACs, thus, can make contributions directly or indirectly, either by paying for a candidate's campaign expenses or by enhancing that candidate's income outright.

COMMON MISCONCEPTIONS: "NORMAL" LOBBYING AND PERSONAL CORRUPTION

Public Inattention

Despite numerous reports on network TV (especially a courageous series by Bill Moyers on CBS), cover stories in magazines (especially one in *Time* on October 25, 1982), excellent articles by Elizabeth Drew and by Mark Green, numerous front-page stories, and Common Cause's "War on PACs," the usual response to reports about the lobbies' grip on the government is the intellectual equivalent of a big yawn. Indeed, as a sociologist who has studied the American society for twenty-five years, I do not find it easy to spell out the reasons the public has not been as outraged by special interests as it has been by, say, environmental abuses. The problem has failed to draw wide, active public concern and involvement. Such involvement is essential if major correctives are to be introduced.

The Game, Not the Players

The ultimate check on politicians is the voting public. Theoretically, the voters could throw corrupt politicians out of office and vote in a clean bunch. But a major obstacle is that American voters focus their attention on the wrong kind of corruption. Although many Americans agree that most politicians are crooked and that special interests have too much power, they tend to attribute the flaws to the deficient character of individual members of Congress.

They look, for instance, at how Representative Wilbur Mills was consumed by alcohol and neglected his duties to follow a stripper named Fanne Foxe around, ending up—with her—on a striptease stage. People are titillated by the somewhat duplicitous Representative Robert E. Bauman, who represented himself as a staunch supporter of traditional values, yet later admitted to being an alcoholic and a homosexual. Representative George Hansen, not at all a rich man, did quite a bit better with the help of silver multimillionaire Nelson Bunker Hunt. Hansen's wife made $87,000 in three days on an "unusual" silver futures deal, arranged with Hunt's help. And Hunt provided the Hansens with a loan of over $61,000, made in Mrs. Hansen's name. Another loan to Mrs. Hansen, this one $50,000, was also guaranteed by Hunt. About the same time, her husband, a member of Congress, led a drive in Congress to authorize the government to buy silver, even though the nation was already overstocked. Hunt had a keen interest in supporting the price of silver, of which he had amassed a few billions' worth. Hansen was indicted for failure to disclose these and other financial dealings, as required for all members of Congress.

An official of the Department of Justice (who asked not to be identified) confided to a visitor that members of Congress frequently dip into "counterpart funds" when they travel on junkets overseas. These funds are generated when the U.S. government sells under-developed countries some of its products but the country is unable to pay in dollars, or seeks to husband its foreign currency for other purposes. The United States then accepts, instead, funds in the local currency, with the understanding that they must be spent in the partic-ular country. Members of Congress, who vote on the allocation of these funds, use them, the Justice Department official said, to "buy thousands of dollars worth of trinkets, to take home."

In recent years, since Watergate—and Abscam—have heightened the public's concern, Americans have voted out of office most politi-cians found corrupt, obviously hoping to start a cleanup of politics by removing dirty politicians from office. However, such a change of persons has little discernible effect on the government's integrity, because individuals are not the main problem. The main problem is one of "structure," not personalities. *The problem lies in the American political system, because certain key elements of it—especially those that legalize PACs—foster corruption on the part of lawmakers.* Until this point is better understood by the public, the needed changes in the system are unlikely. Instead, muckraking zeal and cries of "Throw the rascals out" will continue to distract the public's quest for a government that is responsive to the populace and more resistant to special interests.

There are three main reasons the public's attention is focused on individual political crooks rather than on the corrupt setup: the misleading personality cult in the media; Americans' proper pride in our form of government; and a failure to recognize that the beneficiaries of corruption have managed to legalize most of it. Only if these factors are brought clearly into the open, into public awareness and consciousness, can the ground be readied for valid correctives.

DISTRACTING FACTORS

The Personality Cult

Time is credited with having invented, decades ago, the kind of reporting in which public issues are personalized, treated as they are reflected in the life of one person—not an average person, but a "personality." Thus, a typical cover story about civil rights deals not with relations between blacks and whites, or even with the lives of some black students bussed into a white school, but with the tribulations of Martin Luther King, Jr. The status of American science is treated by a report on a Nobel Prize winner or, better yet, a scientist/media personality such as Carl Sagan. World War II is dramatized as a struggle among Hitler, Roosevelt, Churchill, and Stalin.

The great success of *Time* has spawned numerous imitators and a very commonly used style of reporting. Often a news story leads off like a personal diary; several personal anecdotes are sure to follow. All this keeps eyes *off* the system.

On a deeper level, Americans—as a society that celebrates individualism and long ago rejected the European system of estates and classes—tend to think about American society and government in terms of individuals. The personalities of movie stars or heads of government agencies (Henry Kissinger as secretary of state, or John Foster Dulles before him; J. Edgar Hoover as head of the FBI) play in American public life the central role played in continental society by the titled aristocrats.

Above all, the personal qualities of the President are considered all-important. He is expected to be able to heal the economy, solve social issues, protect the nation, and so on. But in the public eye and through TV, radio, and large-circulation magazines and newspapers, there is very little discussion of political systems and societal structures. No wonder Americans dwell much more on the integrity of their politicians than on the integrity of the American system.

Loyalty to the Constitution

The dominant American opinion as to where corruption lies, and what its root causes are, is further clouded by a deep-seated loyalty to the basic American form of government, above all to the Constitution. Hence, the same Americans who are quick to observe that politicians are crooked find it hard to accept the statement that much of the American government has been captured by special interests. Indeed, most Americans feel that, despite widespread lapses in integrity and competence, ours is the best system of government in the world. Nor do most Americans wish to seek a superior form of government.

Everett Carll Ladd, a widely recognized expert on public opinion, writes about Americans' view of their own status, national performance, and the nation's underlying institutions:

> Available poll data have made it evident that Americans distinguish sharply among these three. Over the past fifteen years they have criticized soundly immediate national performance and the leaders responsible for it. But they . . . have not withdrawn support for "Americanism" or altered their basic attachment to the nation and its institutions.

Hence, Americans may find it easy to be quite critical of the people who "staff" the government—the members of Congress, the bureaucrats, even the chief executive—but they do not extend these criticisms to the institutional structure of the presidency or the Congress, as if these were almost as sacrosanct as the Constitution itself.

Fortunately, although there are some serious flaws in the contemporary American political system—flaws that must be corrected if corruption is to be cut back—none of them requires a constitutional change. They do require changes in laws and institutional setups, not merely, or first, in people.

"It's Legal"

Most confusing to the public is the fact that the newest, most damaging, and most prevalent forms of corruption in contemporary America are legal. The corruption that currently permeates American public life is of a very different kind from that with which the public seems most concerned. References to corruption in Washington conjure scenes of Abscam, of Congress members calmly stuffing their pockets with bribe money, embarrassed only by their pockets' not being deep enough to accommodate the day's take.

A 1983 *New York Times* article asks, "Is Post-Watergate Government Morality Slipping?" The article deals with transgressions by a list of individuals: Richard V. Allen's acceptance of $1,000 from a Japanese magazine that had been granted an interview with Nancy Reagan;

William J. Casey's failure to list his holdings before he became head of the CIA; Thomas C. Reed's profit from trading options, drawing on inside information; and other questionable practices. PACs are not even mentioned.

Columnists and investigative reporters perpetuate the images of politicians going on junkets overseas, being wined and dined by lobbyists, carousing on yachts or in hunting lodges, plied by hookers procured by special interests. Jack Anderson mentions all of the following, in *one day's* column: The National Association of Broadcasters paid for "mini-vacations" for thirty-two members of Congress by inviting them, all expenses paid, to participate in the NAB's convention in Las Vegas and in Dallas. Entertainment included Bob Hope, Steve Allen, *and* Rich Little. Seventeen of the guests were members of House or Senate committees that consider legislation to deregulate the industry. In 1981–82, the National Association of Home Builders took eighteen members of Congress to Las Vegas, including thirteen from key committees. Further, the National Association of Realtors took members of Congress they care about to San Francisco and Miami. The Distilled Spirits Council took others to Marco Island, Florida, and Palm Springs.

From other media sources: Senator Charles Grassley, his wife, and his daughter were given a ten-day trip to Taiwan and Japan, worth about $9,200, by a Taiwanese trade group. Senator Daniel Inouye spent five days in Hong Kong as a guest of R. J. Reynolds Industries. Cost: about $3,300. One newsmagazine mentioned a clock (valued at $525) given to Representative Charles Stenholm as an award for outstanding service, and two handmade quilts ("value unknown") for Representative Paul Simon.

Other press reports titillate the public with alleged sex-for-votes scandals. Reports published in 1981 featured Paula Parkinson, a registered lobbyist who later posed naked for *Playboy*. Three congressmen allegedly shared a Florida vacation house with Ms. Parkinson in January 1980, and later voted against a crop-insurance bill that Parkinson opposed in her capacity as a lobbyist. The three, Representatives Tom Railsback and Thomas Evans, Jr., and Senator Dan Quayle, denied that the weekend had any effect on their votes, or that anything improper had occurred, though they did admit spending time with Parkinson at the house in which she was staying.

While all this does happen, the picture that emerges is highly misleading. The main problem in contemporary Washington is not illicit sexual favors or bribes, in exchange for which politicians sell their votes to private interests—and in the process their offices, in violation of the public will and trust and the law. As far as I can determine, regardless of individual transgressions—far from unknown—most members of Congress do *not* accept cash illicitly; they can have all the sex they want without consorting with the hucksters and groupies provided by lobbyists; and they will not trade their votes for expensive dinners, nor a trip to Hawaii.

Most members of Congress will not violate their sworn duty to represent the public for bribes in cash or in kind, not because of their integrity but because there is a much higher payoff—one they can rake in quite legally. They have written the laws to legalize the collection of resources that election and re-election require, and personal fees to boot. Why would you climb into a house through the back window when you have the keys to the front door and it stands wide open?

SIZABLE CONTRIBUTIONS ARE
NEITHER ETHICAL NOR DEMOCRATIC

Why do I consider sizable aggregated campaign contributions and fees basically a form of *legalized corruption?* If they are legal, how are they corrupt—and if corrupt, how are they legal? The answer is that what is ethical is not always legal, and vice versa. Racial segregation by force of law, which used to exist in the South, was widely considered unethical. And while it is not illegal under most circumstances for persons to lie, it obviously is unethical. In short, each law must be examined as to its ethical standing, especially when it directly benefits those who enact it.

As citizens we must judge laws by a set of values we cherish. The mere fact that members of Congress put their seal of approval on a legal text—especially when it directly concerns their pocketbooks and power—does not make it right. Joseph J. Senturia, writing in the *Encyclopedia of the Social Sciences,* defines political corruption as "the misuse of public power for private profit." He adds:

> But neither the question of formal legality nor that of the sufferance of the act by the mass of the people is of the essence of the concept. Where the best opinion and political morality of the time, examining the intent and setting of an act, judge it to represent a sacrifice of public for private benefit, it must be held corrupt.

Political scientist Lester Milbrath uses the term "dirty," which he describes as violating "the rules of the game for personal or private ends," to connote corrupt conduct. What is dirty, he adds, depends on the rules of the game, which are defined socially. (Legal prescription is only one kind of statement of a social rule.)

Sizable campaign contributions (and fees) are basically unethical and undemocratic, because they make members of Congress focus on the sources of funds rather than on the electorate, and all too often lead them to violate their sworn duty. As I shall detail, the flow of private money into legislators' campaign chests frequently leads them to vote not what they believe is morally right and in line with their public mandate, but what has been underwritten with private-interest dollars.

The term "bought" is increasingly used with reference to the lawmakers of the land. Michael Barone, an editorial-page writer of *The Washington Post,* writes, "It certainly looks as if a lot of lobbies went over to Congress and, in an aggregate, *bought* legislative action they wanted." Former Representative Millicent Fenwick entitled her November 9, 1982, editorial in *The Washington Post,* "In Congress: *Buy* Your Seat or Sell Your Vote." Representative James A. S. Leach uses a fancier word with the same meaning: "A government of the people, by the people, and for the people cannot be a government where influence is purchasable through large, private campaign contributions."

Technically, the term "bought" is inaccurate. Members of Congress are not swayed by money alone; other considerations enter, especially on matters to which the public is attentive (these are relatively few), or issues of special moral significance (no PAC monies will buy Senator Jesse Helms's vote *for* abortion). But the term does correctly capture the capital's climate and tendencies. Money plays far too cardinal a role in our government. The government is not quite a plutocracy, but it is leaning much too far in that direction.

CHAPTER TWO

THE WAYS PRIVATE POWER PENETRATES

Both members of Congress and spokespersons for PACs deny that sizable campaign contributions by private interests violate the democratic system. Therefore, I turn now to describe the main avenues by which private interests using PACs have tunneled into the public realm, to show that they indeed corrupt the system, and to spell out how it is accomplished, so that when we discuss correctives this information will be at hand.

RETAIL VERSUS WHOLESALE

Private money influences national politics in two main ways. First, it seeks to gain, from lawmakers already in office, specific favors—or, from a candidate, a specific commitment should he or she win. The favor sought may be a vote for or against an item of legislation, a tax exemption, a subsidy, or the like. Since the process seems to resemble an item-by-item sale, the image of retail business seems sadly appropriate.

The second main avenue is to seek to *elect*—by the use of massive funds—representatives who will be cooperative, or to defeat those who seem unlikely to be compliant. If successful, such a drive secures payoffs across the board, not merely for one item of legislation. If you type a lot, and want a secure supply of paper, purchase it by the carload, not a ream at a time. Buy wholesale. "We came to a decision some time ago," says Harold Scroggins, an oil-industry lobbyist, "that the only way we could change the political fortunes of the petroleum industry was to change Congress."

A measure of the scope of such efforts is found in a study commissioned by *Business Week* in 1982. Pollster Lou Harris quizzed six hundred corporate leaders, representing the nation's largest corporations. Findings: "More than two-thirds of the respondents said business is much better organized now than five years ago to deal with politics. In many cases, that condition results from the work of a PAC . . . organized by a company to assist in the election of candidates who favor the company's interests."

One may ask whether the wholesale approach, which attempts to elect cooperative lawmakers, is more or less detrimental to the democratic process than the item-by-item gaining of favors. On deliberation, it seems clear that each approach has its own unique detrimental effects. The wholesale approach causes *un*representativeness, since a typical interest group will tend to promote the election of a candidate who is unrepresentative of his or her constituency, not only on issues of direct interest to the lobby, but on many others.

Let us assume that the real-estate lobby, working to be sure a representative will support its various demands, throws its money in to support a conservative candidate in a district that is relatively liberal. If its effort succeeds, not only will the real-estate interests be served, which the district might otherwise oppose, but on many scores of other issues—ones about which the real-estate lobby *per se* does not care, although its individual members may—the elected representative will thus be unrepresentative of his or her district. In this sense, the wholesale approach is much more detrimental than the retail one. To stay with the example at hand: under the retail approach, a liberal member could represent the district faithfully on all issues but those the real-estate PAC insisted upon.

On the other hand, promoting election of a candidate favorable to an interest group must be done largely in the public eye, while retail deals are typically struck out of sight. This distinction is not total. Wholesale support can also be concealed, or at least camouflaged. For instance, Southwestern oil money appears in Northeastern election campaigns as "independent expenditures" that happen to support archconservative candidates. And a representative's retail votes in favor of a special interest—for instance, used-car dealers—can be called to the attention of his or her district by his or her opponents, even when no one can demonstrate with full certainty *why* the lawmaker is so favorable to the dealers. But, practically speaking, it is very difficult to keep track and tie contributions to the hundreds of specific votes each member of Congress casts; it is relatively easier to trace wholesale PAC support when it must surface in efforts to win public support.

But the main point is not what is the right answer—that question is inappropriate. It matters little which approach is more detrimental to the democratic government. Both violate it in significant, albeit different, ways. It is a bit like asking someone whether he would like to be raked over coals or have his head held under water. Either way, democracy is mangled.

THE IMPACT OF THE WHOLESALE APPROACH

To what extent do the PACs affect elections? The question is not as easy to answer as one might wish, because the role of PACs changes from election to election. For example, there were relatively few liberal PACs in 1980; quite a few more were active in the 1982 campaign.

Furthermore, there are different ways to measure the PAC effect; each way results in a different reading. If one focuses on the money that PACs raise and spend, rather than on the money they contribute to candidates for federal office, one gains a rather different picture. For instance, Senator Jesse Helms's archconservative PAC, the National Congressional Club, raised and spent over $9.7 million in 1981–82. However, it contributed only $135,264 to federal candidates during that period; most of his PAC money was dedicated to building up the club itself. Typical corporate PACs, on the other hand, spend much of what they raise on contributions to federal candidates. For example, the PAC of General Dynamics raised $304,758 and contributed $172,440 in 1981–82. Across the board, corporate PACs contributed 62 percent of what they raised to federal candidates, while ideological PACs provided only 17 percent of their funds to such candidates. Despite all these differences, however, general tendencies *can* be gleaned.

More Clout per Buck Than Yours or Mine

The power of PACs has grown constantly. They provided 26.2 percent of the money raised by congressional candidates in the 1982 election, up from 15.7 percent in 1974.

Yet these often cited figures underestimate the role of PACs. PACs have a better batting average than the public. They have provided more money to candidates who ended up winners (their future allies–debtors) than to losers. In 1982 in the House, winners got 35 percent of all the money they raised from PACs, up from 31 percent in 1980 and 28 percent in 1978.

Almost one-fourth of the 1982 winners received *more than half* of their financing from PACs. Especially favored were key House leaders and committee chairmen. These included Speaker of the House Tip O'Neill and James Jones, chairman of the Budget Committee. House Ways and Means Committee Chairman Rostenkowski, a Democrat, received 56 percent ($290,425) of his campaign funding from PACs; House Minority Leader Robert Michel obtained 68 percent ($476,637) from PACs. John Dingell, chairman of the House Energy and Commerce Committee, gained 58 percent from PACs, the majority of which represented business groups.

By contributing more to winners than to losers, and more to powerful chairmen and leaders than to the rank-and-file, *PACs buy significantly more clout for their dollar than the public, which contributes proportionately more to losers and to the rank-and-file.* If you ever bet on racehorses or dogs, you'll have no difficulty in seeing the full significance of the difference.

Most candidates much prefer to raise money from PACs rather than from individuals. Getting it from individuals involves large expenditures of funds, while raising money from PACs exacts little or no cost in time and energy, or indignity. Most politicians, a wit has suggested, would rather have root-canal work done than pass the hat among individuals. Thomas E. Cronin, who lost in Colorado's 5th District to a better PACed candidate, explains: "Constant trips to raise money [from well-off individuals] eat you up and get in the way of talking about issues and meeting voters." Since PACs are organized in packs, a "good" presentation before a leading PAC, or a PAC coordinator, can generate much of what a candidate needs, though usually several visits are required.

Senator Gary Hart found that he had to spend a lot of time in states like New York and California to raise money for his presidential campaign from individuals, and as a consequence reduced the time he could spend in the early-primary states of Iowa and New Hampshire, states that require considerable "hands-on" campaigning. It hardly helped his prospects.

Senator Alfonse M. D'Amato believes he will need more than $6 million to run his 1986 Senate re-election campaign. Because he wants to raise as much as possible of this amount from individual donors, he has been hitting the fund-raising road—as early as 1983. Fund-raising is almost a weekly part of his routine. A good portion of what he raises goes to pay for raising more. For instance, he spent $219,461 of the $613,393 he raised between June 1981 and December 1982 on transportation, entertainment for volunteers, headquarters expenses, etc. No wonder candidates are under pressure to lean on PACs.

PACs tend to target their monies better than the public, more often directing funds where they may swing the outcome of a close race. PAC money also comes in *late,* when money is frequently badly needed and difficult to raise from the grass roots. In such times it is particularly appreciated. A liberal PAC, the National Committee for an Effective Congress, raised $70,000 in late September 1982 for contributions to a list of close-running liberals. Late in the 1982 campaign, when many Republican incumbents faced strong challenges because of poor economic conditions, "a tidal wave of . . . corporate campaign-committee cash" helped to limit their losses. One inter-PAC newsletter, published by Business-Industry PAC, is specifically designed to spot tight races or potential surprise winners.

It is sometimes said that money is decisive for only about 2 percent of the vote, and that party affiliation, reputation, and issues account for the rest. What is ignored here is the fact that one needs money to advance the other factors. Nor should one underestimate the importance of *2 percent* at the margin. In 1982, a switch of only seventy thousand votes in five Senate races would have given these seats—and hence a Senate majority—to the Democrats.

In 1982, the GOP lost twenty-six seats in the House. Several political analysts have estimated that, had it not been for the large infusion of money, the GOP might have lost another fourteen seats in the House, and some Senate seats as well. The loss of forty seats would have been considered a definitive rejection of Reagan's policies, forcing him to change course because he would have lost control over the House. Loss of twenty-six seats was a much more ambiguous signal; it reduced Reagan's control but did not abolish it. As Deputy Assistant to the President for Political Affairs Lee Atwater put it, "I think the story of this off-year election is that we've marshalled our resources and bought one or two Senate seats and fifteen to twenty House seats, and that's really good."

Many PACs keep their own "win" scores to assess their impact, based on how many of the candidates they support were elected (or how many of those they opposed lost). These are not scientific measures but attempts to play up the PACs' power. They count support given to candidates who were likely to have won anyhow. But since the names of the candidates PACs seek to elect are announced *before* the elections, the PACs' high or low scores serve as an indication of their power.

On average, the "win" record reported is considerable. In 1982, for example, 64 percent of the candidates supported by labor won; in 1982 only 45 percent of the Chamber of Commerce candidates won, but 70 percent won in 1980. The National Abortion Rights Action League won 66 percent in the Senate, 71 percent in the House in 1982. Home-builders, who in the same year gave $1.5 million, scored 90 percent. In short, PACs had a considerable impact.

Aside from actually tipping the balance in marginal elections, PACs have many subtle effects on candidates, which are more difficult to measure statistically. PACs tend to draw the candidates' positions in the direction most PACs are pulling. In 1982, Representative Fortney H. (Pete) Stark, a liberal Democrat from California, anticipated a difficult re-election campaign. It was to be "one that would cost more money than was likely to come from his loyal constituents or his friends in labor. So Stark swallowed his populist rhetoric and asked corporate lobbyist Tom Boggs for help."

On the face of it, Stark should never have needed expensive top-drawer fund-raiser Boggs. Stark was about to start serving on a subcommittee that writes selective revenue measures and attracts corporate PACs better than honey brings out bears. However, Stark had an "anti-business" voting record, so Boggs arranged for a series of dinners at the congressman's house. At these Stark convinced corporate lobbyists that he, as Boggs reported, "wouldn't let his personal views interfere" with the corporate needs. Soon the money was flowing.

Stark is reported to be one of about twenty-five senators and representatives for whom Boggs came through in 1982, including New York Democrat Thomas J. Downey and New Jersey Democrat James J. Florio. Others he had helped, in previous years, include Senators Wendell Ford and Patrick Leahy, and Representatives Tony Coelho, Charles Rangel, and Thomas Luken. Typical case: Tom Luken ended up supporting the candy-makers' fight to prevent the regulation of TV commercials aimed at children. Boggs served, at the time, both as Luken's fund-raiser and as lobbyist for the candy corporation Mars, Inc.

Most PACs Favor the Status Quo

At first blush it might seem that PACs pull in all directions and that the effects will therefore average out. Some PACs' first priority is serving the pecuniary interests of their members; ideology comes second. These include corporate, trade, professional, farm, and labor PACs. Labor is often seen as pulling toward moderates and liberals and favoring Democrats, whereas the other PACs are perceived as pulling toward conservatives and the GOP. (The latter group is often referred to awkwardly as "business and business-related PACs." Because of their sociological base and political predisposition, I use instead the term "establishment" PACs.)* Similarly, there are ideological PACs, including both conservative ones (NRA Political Victory Fund) and liberal ones, such as the Nuclear Weapons Freeze Voting Power PAC. Thus, it may seem that there is a PAC on each side of at least the major economic and ideological dividers.

However, if the effects of all PACs are totaled up, *they strongly favor incumbents over challengers.* In 1980, corporate PACs gave 57 percent of their contributions to federal candidates to incumbents, 32 percent to challengers, and 11 percent to candidates for open seats. Trade and professional associations' PACs distributed 65 percent of their contributions to incumbents, while only 23 percent went to challengers and 12 percent to candidates for open seats. PACs formed by farmers' cooperatives, such as dairy PACs, channeled 81 percent of

---

*Neither of these categories is completely precise, since some nonbusiness PACs are included in both, because we must draw on the categories in which the data are reported by the FEC.

their contributions to incumbents, while 8 percent went to challengers and 12 percent to open-seat contestants. Labor granted 71 percent to incumbents, 17 percent to challengers, and 11 percent to open.

Only ideological PACs favored challengers, sending 50 percent of their contributions to challengers, 32 percent to incumbents, and 18 percent to open-seat contestants. However, their money is only a small portion (9 percent in 1980) of the total of PACs' contributions to federal candidates.

Altogether, 61 percent of the total PAC money, from all sources, went to incumbents, 27 percent to challengers, and 12 percent to candidates for open seats. Since there is a challenger for practically every contest, challengers were disadvantaged 2.3 to 1.

In 1982, PAC contributions favored incumbents even more. All PACs combined gave 67 percent of their contributions to federal candidates to incumbents, 19 percent to challengers, and 14 percent to open-seat candidates. Thus, incumbents enjoyed a 3.5 to 1 advantage in PAC funding for the 1982 election. Corporations gave 74 percent of their funds to incumbents and labor gave 57 percent, compared with 13 and 28 percent to challengers, respectively. Trade and professional groups gave 75 percent of their funds to incumbents and only 13 percent to challengers, while farmers' groups and other cooperatives gave 83 percent to incumbents and only 7 percent to challengers. Even the ideological PACs, which favored challengers in 1980, sided with incumbents in 1982: 46 percent of their funds went to incumbents and 35 percent to challengers. (In 1982 there were more conservative incumbents to support than in 1980, and conservatives are the candidates whom most of these PACs favor.)

PACs thus reinforce the system's tendency to promote the incumbent, already fostered by other factors, such as franking privileges and easier access to free time on news programs. By promoting incumbents, PACs make the American political system further resistant to new groups and new needs—and more establishmentarian.

Republicans Gain More PAC Money Than Democrats

Taken together, the PACs' impact favors the Republican over the Democrat. This seems to contradict the conventional wisdom, which holds that "Democrats . . . continue to receive more PAC money than Republicans," as the *National Journal* put it. True, the Democrats received 52.3 percent of the PAC money distributed to congressional campaigns for the 1980 election, and 54.0 percent in 1982. However, these figures are misleading, because there were significantly more Democratic than Republican incumbents seeking re-election in 1980 and in 1982. Incumbents of *both* parties drew more PAC money than challengers, on average. It is hence necessary to compare the same *types* of candidates—challenger versus challenger, incumbent versus incumbent, open-seat candidate versus open-seat candidate—in the House and in the Senate. In an analysis of FEC data for the 1980 election cycle, I found that, on average, Republicans got more PAC support than Democrats in five out of the six comparisons.

In the Senate, the Republican incumbents received an average of $70,000 more than was received by their Democratic counterparts: $408,562 versus $338,405. PAC money to challengers went overwhelmingly to Republicans: $49,891 as compared with $13,411. And PACs awarded Republican candidates for open seats (perhaps the truest test of party preference, because no one had the advantage of incumbency) an average of two and a half times that of Democrats: $57,386, as opposed to $22,672.

In the House, incumbent Democrats had on average a small advantage over incumbent Republicans: $65,810 to $61,029. This reflects the fact that the powerful committee chairmen, in whose direction money gushes, are Democrats. In contrast, Republican challengers for House seats got more than two and a half times as much as Democratic challengers ($12,832 to $4,909). And PACs gave on average nearly twice as much to Republican candidates for open seats as to Democrats ($22,581 to $12,182). Thus, when the figures are analyzed per Democrat and per Republican, the result is a strong advantage for all Republicans except the incumbents in the House. Furthermore, in the only situation in which the Democrats came out ahead, their margin was small, as compared with the five situations in which Republicans came out on top, where the margin was considerable.

Add to this the fact that PAC independent spending (awarded without consulting or coordinating with the candidate) favors Republicans over Democrats by hefty margins. Of the $16 million spent independently in 1980 (largely by PACs of the ideological type), $13 million was spent *for* Republicans (including presidential candidates), $2 million *against* Democrats, $440,000 for Democrats, and $120,000 against Republicans. Of the $2,340,000 spent independently in congressional races, 84 percent was spent either against Democrats or for Republicans.

It is sometimes said that labor PACs support Democrats much more heavily than business, trade, farm, and professions' PACs support the GOP. Indeed, in 1980, labor PACs gave 94 percent of their contributions to Democrats, while corporate PACs favored GOP candidates 64 percent to 36 percent. In all, the establishment PACs gave 59 percent to Republicans, 41 percent to Democrats.

However, labor does less well for Democrats than business and other establishment PACs do for Republicans because labor raises less money. In 1980, labor PACs contributed $13.2 million to congressional candidates, of which $12.4 million went to Democrats. Corporate PACs contributed $19.2 million, of which $12.3 million went to GOP candidates. Trade and professional PACs gave $15.9 million, of which GOP candidates got $8.9 million. In other words, while labor PACs contributed a larger *proportion* of their funds to Democrats, the total *amount* they gave Democrats was little more than half the amount the establishment PACs contributed to GOP candidates: $12.4 million compared with $21.9 million.

But that's not all. Except for labor's contributions, most of the PAC money that does flow to Democrats is what is called "access" money, used to gain a favor for a corporation, trade association, profession, or farm lobby. It goes largely to those most likely to win anyhow, because only winners, whatever their party, can serve the special interests. Hence it is relatively "wasted" as far as impact on the election goes. As *Wall Street Journal* reporters Brooks Jackson and Dennis Farney report: "Much of the Democratic money is going to incumbents who don't need it—for example, $298,601 through June 30 [1982] to House Ways and Means Chairman Dan Rostenkowski of Illinois, who has only a token GOP opponent."

Although GOP incumbents also draw "access" money, which is equally wasted when the incumbent is not seriously opposed, there have been significantly more Democratic incumbents, so that a larger proportion of the money Democrats get from PACs has been "wasted" than the money Republicans receive. In 1982, 218 Democrats in the House sought re-election, compared with 168 Republicans. (The remainder of the seats were open, and a few incumbents were thrown into a race against each other by redistricting.) Though Republicans outnumber Democrats in the Senate, in 1982 more of the incumbent Democratic senators were up for re-election and chose to run: nineteen Democrats versus eleven Republicans.

When it comes to supporting candidates for open seats (where the better-financed candidate won 81 percent of the races in 1980), or challengers—PACs have a strong preference for Republicans. Business, trade, and independent PACs show overwhelming support of Republicans in their donations to nonincumbents.

Funds from other, non-PAC, sources were not enough to make up the difference. Once again, the conventional wisdom that the Democrats have consistently raised more money than the Republicans masks the advantage Republicans hold on a candidate-by-candidate basis (in five of six categories), as can be seen in the table below.

Campaign Funds from All Sources—1980
Average per Candidate by Type

	House		Senate	
	Democrats	Republicans	Democrats	Republicans
Incumbents	$170,786	$197,095	$1,411,011	$1,276,665
Challengers	33,336	62,302	201,036	287,323
Open-Seat	74,118	105,972	266,482	379,356

In 1982 the Democrats were expected to pick up many congressional seats. It was an off-year election, in which the party not holding the White House usually does well; there was a severe recession; and the President's coattails were weaker than in 1980. Given the preference of most PACs for winners—those who will be in a position to help them with favorable legislation—one would have expected more PAC funds than usual to flow to Democrats. Although there was in 1982 some moderation of the 1980 split between the parties, the pattern remained essentially the same. In four of the six candidate types, Republicans held the advantage. This advantage was particularly pronounced in Senate open seats, where Republicans got more than three times the amount Democrats did from PACs, and in the category of Senate incumbents, where Republicans outraised Democrats from PAC funds by better than 3 to 2. In contrast, the edge the Democratic candidates held in the two categories where they led was slight.

Conservatives Get More PAC Money Than Liberals

The total impact of PAC money is to favor conservatives (whether Republicans or Democrats) over liberals. This is especially true for ideological PACs. Labor PACs give heavily to moderates and liberals, but the proportion they provide of PAC contributions to candidates for federal office is diminishing: 24 percent of PAC money in 1982 and 1980, down from 29 percent in 1978, 36 percent in 1976, and 50 percent in 1974. In contrast, ideological (mainly conservative) PACs' share of the PAC contribution total has risen from 6 percent in 1974 to 13 percent in 1982, and the establishment PACs' share has risen from 43 percent to 63 percent over the same period.

There is no official way to ascertain how liberal a member of Congress is, and some are conservative on some issues (say, defense) and liberal on others (say, social policy). Everyone would agree, however, that members of Congress who receive a zero on the annual voting record compiled by the liberal organization Americans for Democratic Action (ADA) are far more conservative than those who receive 100 percent. Eighteen House members were given zeros by the ADA in 1980. The average amount received from PACs by the fifteen of these who ran for re-election that year was $64,134. Of the eleven rated 100 percent, ten ran for re-election. They received an average of $47,215, or $16,919 less than the conservatives.

Two of those who received zeros for their House votes in 1980 ran for the Senate that year against liberal incumbents. Conservative Steve Symms, with $638,000 from PACs, defeated liberal Frank Church in Idaho. Church gained only one-third of Symms's total from PACs, $210,000. In Indiana, Dan Quayle defeated liberal Birch Bayh with the help of $600,000 in PAC funds. Bayh, incumbent though he was, mustered only $446,000.

Other important liberal-versus-conservative match-ups in 1980 showed the same pattern. Challenger James Abdnor, who received a 1980 ADA rating of 11 in the House, defeated George McGovern (ADA rating of 56) with the help of a $679,000-to-$292,000 advantage in PAC funds. John Culver of Iowa, with an ADA rating of 78, was defeated by Charles Grassley, who received a rating of 17 for his votes as a member of the House of Representatives. Grassley was the highest recipient of PAC funds in 1980, receiving $722,000, compared with $329,000 for Culver.

The Role of Ideological PACs

The role of ideological PACs is often misperceived by the media, a fact illustrated by the treatment accorded to the New Right groups, especially the National Conservative Political Action Committee (NCPAC). In the 1980 elections, NCPAC worked effectively to defeat liberal candidates, which resulted in a great play-up of its power in the media. In 1982 NCPAC used crude techniques such as personal attacks on Senator Paul Sarbanes in Maryland, which backfired. Many voters took offense and rallied in behalf of Sarbanes, with their checkbooks and their ballots. As a result, NCPAC had less effect than expected. Hence, since 1982 its power has been played down in the media. Probably in the next election this or some other ideological PAC will surprise the media again—by doing more than is now expected.

The drastic swing in the perceived effectiveness of ideological PACs is well captured by a 1982 *Wall Street Journal* account: "Whatever happened to the New Right? On the morning after the 1980 elections, the political landscape was littered with the carcasses of defeated liberal Democrats. . . . This year, though, the story is vastly different."

NCPAC itself has reportedly conceded that it has been much less effective. The same rise and fall were reported for the religious groups politically active on the Right, particularly the Moral Majority. When all is said and done, the leaders of the New Right are said to be frustrated by the "sea change from 1980."

This does not alter the simple fact that NCPAC and other ideological PACs have an effect. Their exact magnitude changes over time and is difficult to assess with precision, given that they are only one player among several. But to say that the performance of a new fullback on a football team varies, and that others contribute to the outcome of the game, is not to belie that he does affect the outcome of the game.

Whereas most ideological PACs are simply PACs that promote an ideological perspective, there is one important exception: a group of PACs tied to people in the oil industry, more particularly to the new millions made since 1973. These PACs are ideological in the sense that their first priority is to promote a viewpoint, in this case highly conservative, opposing large government and advocating a *laissez-faire* economic perspective. Their support for measures that benefit their members financially, like decontrolling energy prices or ending the windfall-profits tax, is a secondary motivation for their efforts, although of course not incompatible with their first ideological priority.

The money from these PACs flows almost exclusively to GOP candidates. Those Democrats upon whom their manna falls are usually conservative Southerners, such as Representative Phil Gramm of Texas (who switched party allegiance after the 1982 election). The table below lists contributions by the four largest independent oil PACs. (It does not include contributions from PACs of various oil companies, or gifts by oilmen as individuals.)

Oil PAC Contributions to Federal Candidates: 1981–82

	To Democrats		To Republicans	
	Number of Candidates	Amount	Number of Candidates	Amount
Dallas Energy PAC	2	$ 7,000	79	$237,000
Louisiana Energy PAC	10	22,500	85	233,500
HouPAC	24	19,709	134	167,136
Intermountain PAC	5	4,700	65	111,250
TOTALS:	41	53,909 (6.7 percent)	363	748,886 (93.3 percent)

Source: Federal Election Commission

There are ideological PACs of all stripes, but the greater amount of money is raised by archconservative PACs and, as has already been documented, flows heavily to GOP and conservative challengers. Six conservative PACs raised more than 78 percent of the money raised by the top ten independent PACs in 1981–82. These six conservative PACs accounted for nearly half of all the money raised by nonconnected PACs in 1981–82. The net effect is to tilt the system further toward conservatives and the GOP.

PACs Outgun Political Parties

Political parties are weak, almost irrelevant paupers, outspent and outgunned by PACs. PACs' contributions outstripped by almost four times those of political parties to congressional campaigns in 1980. Even the small portion of contributions that parties provide—6.0 percent of all campaign funds in 1980, and 6.8 percent in 1982—comes to them in part from PACs. According to one source, Joseph E. Cantor of the Congressional Research Service, these figures underestimate the role of the parties. Since they are so far the only statistics available, however, they are commonly relied upon. No one doubts that PACs have both benefited from and helped to cause the decline of political parties. I will return to this issue later, in the context of a more general examination of the relationships between interest groups and political parties.

PACs Come between a Constituency and Its Representative

Several PACs, especially ideological PACs, "specialize" in pouring out-of-state money into local races. One state reports that 60 percent of the money spent on local elections is coming from out-of-state sources. Local party activists are frustrated by limits imposed on their local supporters, under the $1,000 rule, while the independent expenditures paid for by out-of-state money are not hindered by such limits in congressional elections. And large, nationally based PACs such as BankPAC and AMPAC can give $5,000 to the candidate of their choice. Out-of-state money supports a variety of causes, but some of the largest amounts flow from Southern and Southwestern oil PACs, all conservative, to oppose Northern liberals.

Besides the fact that the people of a district will end up with representation that is ideologically different from what they themselves would otherwise favor, a representative who is busy heeding out-of-state PACs' agenda (for instance, NCPAC's focus on cutting social spending and the balanced-budget amendment) will be less attuned to the local needs of the constituency, which are often primarily nonideological. Thus interest groups undermine the cornerstone of the U.S. representative system: *local* representation.

The Un-PACed Poor

Groups without PACs do not do well. Explains Representative William Coyne, Democrat from Pennsylvania: "In the business of congressional lobbying . . . some are more clearly equal than others. It is clear to any observer that the arguments of the auto dealers industry have been given greater weight by Congress than those of consumers."

Senator Daniel P. Moynihan said, referring to a standing-room-only attendance of lobbyists "working" for a new tax bill full of exemptions for their clients: "When the Administration proposed to abolish the only piece of social legislation that passed during the Carter Administration, the Child Welfare and Adoption Assistance Act of 1980, there may have been a dozen people here. Look who's there today. It's squalid." Senator Robert Dole put it best: "There aren't any Poor PACs or Food Stamp PACs or Nutrition PACs or Medicare PACs."

It is sometimes asked in jest, sometimes bitterly: "What's all the fuss about? For a while the liberal activists had the edge; now business has regained its edge. What's wrong with that?" Adds Lloyd N. Unsell, executive vice president of the Independent Petroleum Association of America: "In 1976, for example, George Meany's AFL-CIO political legions reportedly contributed $16 million to congressional candidates of primarily leftward persuasion. . . . I did not hear Common Cause or Ralph Nader condemn George Meany's political arrogance. . . . Only when the business-industrial community finally took a page from labor's book . . . did the PAC idea become a 'corrupting' influence."

Two wrongs don't make a right; both kinds of PACs plague the house of democracy. While somewhere someone may have stated that PACs are an affliction America owes to corporations only, this is certainly not my position, nor a logical one to hold. Whatever is PACed is at least to some extent bought. If the founding fathers had wanted American democracy to use dollar bills as ballots, they would have placed cash registers where ballot boxes now stand. All PACs, of all stripes, are incompatible with a democratic, representative, system.

IN TOTO: UNDERMINING
DEMOCRATIC REPRESENTATION

PACs work to gain "wholesale" advantages by influencing the outcomes of elections—"wholesale" because the advantages are likely to encompass the term of the elected official, as opposed to a "retail" deal, which would require obtaining the support of a member of Congress for one or a few bills or tax concessions at a time.

What is the *cumulative* effect of the "wholesale" approach? Again, are there not PACs for every interest, so that they balance out one another? The evidence suggests otherwise. Examined *in toto,* PACs favor the GOP, conservatives, and incumbent candidates, and as a result undermine the representative system. To say that citizens who favor candidates that the PACs favor would not mind is like saying that anyone who participates in a race does not wish it to be fairly refereed unless he or she is sure to win. The essence of a democratic system is acceptance of the outcomes of a fair "race."

Also, the supporters of the Republican and conservative candidates should recall the days when labor union PACs outnumbered and outspent corporate ones. In 1974 labor PACs outnumbered corporation PACs 201 to 89. Labor PACs contributed $6.3 million to congressional candidates in 1974, while corporations, health lobbies, and other establishment PACs contributed only $4.4 million. True, it is difficult to imagine that now, after the corporations have developed their political muscle, they will grow flabby again. But it is not safe to assume that you can keep a system permanently "bought" by always outbidding all others. Labor is already on a comeback trail. Thus, on grounds of both principle and expediency, an unPACed world is fairer, more democratic, and reliably representative.

Last but not least, the organization of PACs themselves is not exactly democratic or representative. There are very few studies of the inner working of PACs. However, from a few accounts in the press and interviews that I have conducted, the following picture emerges. *Only a minority of PACs poll their contributors as to who should receive the funds, or allow contributors to designate to whom the funds will go or to elect members of a committee to make these decisions.* Most PACs are run like corporate charity drives. There is considerable pressure to give; a handful of higher-ranking executives decide to whom to give; and most contributors are lucky if they get an annual report on what was done with their money.

The Wall Street Journal reports that "some middle and senior managers" at PACed corporations "are increasingly feeling pressured to cough up part of their paychecks." Managers are said to contribute to ensure that their careers will not suffer. At one company, Dart Industries, Inc., guidelines suggested what amounts to give, and if an executive failed to deliver his or her quota, he or she would get "a sell" directly from Mr. Dart. The law prohibits only "physical force, job discrimination, financial reprisals," actual or threatened, which at least technically leaves the door open to financial incentives such as raises and to unlimited psychological pressure.

A legal authority, William T. Mayton, raised the question whether voluntary contributions are at all possible where the fund-raiser and those who give are in a hierarchical relationship, as they are bound to be in a corporation. My twenty years of organizational studies lend support to the conclusion that hierarchy and truly free consent are difficult to reconcile.

Similarly, labor unions, whose members are but 20 percent of the labor force, are hardly representative of labor—or of their own members. Indeed, many times labor-union members do not follow their leaders' guide when *un* PACed, voting and contributing on their own. For example, most labor unions supported Carter in the 1980 election, and 94 percent of labor PACs' contributions went to Democrats, but 44 percent of those from union households voted for Reagan. They did not pay much more attention to their leaders in many other elections. That is, "voluntary" participation in labor PACs therefore channeled money to candidates that perhaps as many as half of the members did *not* wish to support, and away from those they wished to promote.

In short, most PACs are highly oligarchic. There is no effective way for the contributors to determine what is done with their funds, hardly a sound basis for a democratic society. The charge of oligarchy has often been leveled against political parties. But their caucuses, primaries, election of delegates, and conventions make them citadels of democracy compared with PACs.

More than democratic civility is at stake. If the feeling spreads among the public that the system is unrepresentative, because PACs tilt it away from those the electorate favors, a rise in extra-institutional political action, from demonstrations to rebellion, cannot be far behind. (Our historical experience, which I examine later, underscores this point; it is not an idle threat.) The same must be said about the tilt toward conservatives and incumbents, which makes the system respond only belatedly, if at all, to new social groups and issues and to technological change. (The opposite tilt would result if the system were bought by gung-ho social activists.) It is in the longer-run interests of all involved to preserve the integrity of the representative system.

CHAPTER THREE

RETAIL:
Buying Vote by Vote

When lawmakers are elected, and appointed to a committee or sub-committee, they often bring with them a set of unspoken obligations to the PACs who helped them get there. However, those who got in without acquiring sufficient or the "right" kind of obligations are not immune to the influence of PACs, either; nor are they inaccessible to new PACs. Congress is kept very attentive to PAC needs, according them exactly the kind of careful husbanding that the public interest deserves, and citizens at large are entitled to, between one election campaign and another.

PACs add to the web of obligations as soon as the election results are in, by helping elected officials pay off campaign debts. In 1982, for instance, more than a third of those elected to the House had campaign expenditures exceeding the funds they had raised before the election. Their debts ranged from $124.80 for Representative Toby Roth to $773,000 for Representative Tom Vandergriff. Most debts were between $10,000 and $100,000.

PACs are particularly keen to rush to help here, because they are betting on a sure thing (an elected candidate in contrast to an election outcome). Also, here PAC help is particularly obligating, for elected lawmakers find it very difficult to raise money from individual citizens shortly after their election.

PAC assistance never stops thereafter. Raising funds for campaigns is no longer an activity limited to election times. It goes on, especially in the House, practically year-round. Contributions are offered and accepted, solicited and anted up, when legislation is being drafted, considered in committee, voted on on the floor, or considered for repeal.

The notion that PACs get anything in return for their pains is sometimes challenged. Their corrupting influence is denied. I turn, therefore, to review the evidence that they are richly rewarded for their efforts, either from the public till or from the thwarting of the public will. In the process of analysis we shall also see exactly how they manage to swim so freely around the law that limits campaign contributions. This knowledge suggests where new barriers must be erected if the public realm is to be protected.

THE NATURE OF THE EVIDENCE

In reviewing the evidence, culled from a variety of sources, I follow procedures and logic like those used in presenting scientific data in other areas—say, in contending that cigarettes cause lung cancer. The first step is to show "association" (that is, a statistical correlation). For instance, data show that more cases of lung cancer develop among those who smoke than among those who do not. This association suggests a connection between the "inputs" (cigarettes) and the "outcomes" (lung cancer). I shall report data that show an association between sizable campaign contributions by private interests and legislation favorable to them.

But for those who are skeptical, a statistical association does not suffice; it could be coincidental, they argue. They ask to be shown the process or the "mechanism" by which an "input" causes an "outcome" —to stay with the analogy, the process by which smoking cigarettes causes lung cancer. This is a more demanding test, which, by the way, the data on the connection between cigarette-smoking and cancer have yet to withstand. Actually, both in science and in public-policy analysis, we are often in a situation akin to that of a police officer who finds next to a corpse a man with a smoking gun in his hand, but can find no one who saw the shooting. Circumstances make the man with the gun a highly plausible suspect; ballistics findings and gunpowder on his hands and clothes may further serve to convict him—but one can always argue that someone else might have been the killer.

To apply such logic to the issue under study here, we need to go beyond establishing statistical associations. This is not easy, because private interests are usually quite careful not to tie their campaign contributions (or fees) openly or directly to specific legislation. We can, though, get a reasonably good notion of the corrupting process, the ways in which money turns legislators, and thus the government. Evidence comes from several kinds of witnesses: people who got the money; people who gave the money; and people in positions to observe both, in the transaction. But let me take these one step at a time.

SOME STATISTICAL EVIDENCE

Item: Containing Health Costs versus the AMA

Hospital costs have been rising more rapidly than other expenses for years, and have been widely considered one of the four major "engines of inflation," right next to energy, housing, and food prices. Their rapid growth led the Carter administration to propose in 1979 a system aimed at slowing them down. Aside from stemming inflation, which was at the time the leading domestic problem, the proposal was estimated to be able to save consumers $40 billion over a five-year period. Yet in November of 1979, the House voted 234 to 166 against Carter's proposal, substituting for it the Gephardt Amendment, a voluntary cost-control plan backed by the AMA. The voluntary plan was widely regarded as likely to be ineffectual, if not useless.

Time called special-interest lobbying "the force that proved decisive" in blocking the Carter hospital cost-containment efforts. For their 1976 and 1978 campaigns, *those who voted for the AMA plan had received four times as much money from AMPAC and several state AMA PACs as those who voted against it.* Of the 234 members of the House who voted "aye," 202 had received contributions averaging $8,157, for a total of $1,647,897. In contrast, of the 166 who voted against the AMA plan, 122 had received contributions averaging only $2,287, while 44 of those voting in the negative had received nothing at all. Forty-eight of the top 50 recipients supported the plan of their generous supporters. The average AMA contribution to these 50 representatives for the period in question was $17,300.

An earlier attempt at hospital cost-containment legislation never got to the floor. It was defeated early in 1978 in the Health Subcommittee of the House Ways and Means Committee—whose members had received a total of more than $63,000 in the previous two elections.

In July of that same year, the legislation was voted down in the Interstate and Foreign Commerce Committee. The total of all contributions (in the 1976 election cycle and in the part of the 1978 election cycle prior to the vote) to those who sided with the AMA on this vote had been $85,150; those who opposed the AMA had received a total of $16,109 over the same period.

Proponents of PACs sometimes argue that PAC contributions are rewards for past votes rather than attempts to influence future votes. Thus, it is particularly illuminating to look at the votes of House freshmen, who have no previous voting record on which to base such "rewards." In the 1979 vote on the floor of the House regarding the AMA voluntary hospital cost-containment plan, 48 freshmen sided with the AMA; 37 of them had received contributions averaging $9,454 to their 1978 campaigns (before they had ever set foot in the House). Of the 25 freshmen who went against the AMA, a majority had received no money at all. The rest (12) had received contributions averaging $4,717, about one-half the amount given to freshmen who later supported the bill.

The question may be asked: why do PACs grant opposing members of Congress any contribution at all? The answer is that a member has the ability to do much more than vote "nay" on a final count. He or she can oppose a bill in earlier rounds, when it is being drafted, and seek to amend it in ways unfavorable to its proponents. Or the member can help the bill along all the way but vote against it on the last count, for the record to his constituency.

Representative John J. Rhodes, long the minority leader in the House, and highly respected on both sides of the aisle, described this last tactic in his book *The Futile System:*

> It is not uncommon . . . for a Member of Congress to vote according to public opinion in his district on the final passage of a bill even though he may have voted in a completely opposite direction in committee or during the critically important amendment process on the Floor. The Member knows that his vote on final passage is the one most likely to receive attention back home. His previous votes, often beyond public view, are likely to be unknown. But they may have been far more important than his vote on final passage.

It is not only a matter of yes or no votes. Most legislation, however clear the bill's purpose, requires clarification of numerous nuances in its wording. Decimal points, levels, percentages, effective dates, extents of coverage—all must be set at some point. Even the most fervent environmentalist must decide just what constitutes a "reasonable" level for a pollutant that is being regulated, how much time to allow for a change in technology, and so on. Little wonder lobbies find it wise to spread some of their particular kind of cheer to practically all takers. Very few members of Congress take none. Among those are William Proxmire and David Boren in the Senate, and Representatives Andrew Jacobs, Jr., and Jim Leach.

The following table, selected from the many available, may do more to give one a feel for what's going on. On the Gephardt Amendment, the AMA-backed substitute for the Carter hospital cost-containment plan, 48 of the top 50 House recipients of contributions from AMA PACs voted the way the money would have them vote; all the other "nay" votes came from those less well backed.

Top 50 House Recipients of Campaign Contributions from Political Action Committees of the American Medical Association During 1976 and 1978 Congressional Campaigns Who Voted on the Gephardt Amendment

(48 of 50 recipients voted in favor of Gephardt Amendment)

Representative	State/CD	Amount	Vote
1 Paul	Texas 22	$56,000	Y
2 Hall	Texas 1	35,000	Y
3 Gramm	Texas 6	30,000	Y
4 White	Texas 16	28,500	Y
5 Kelly	Florida 5	25,250	Y
6 Marlenee	Montana 2	22,900	Y
7 Livingston*	Louisiana 1	22,500	Y
8 Holt	Maryland 4	20,650	Y
9 Devine	Ohio 12	20,100	Y
10 Snyder	Kentucky 4	20,000	Y
11 Wyatt	Texas 14	20,000	Y
12 Bauman	Maryland 1	19,575	Y
13 Carter	Kentucky 5	17,500	Y
14 Clausen	California 2	17,385	Y
15 O'Brien	Illinois 17	17,250	Y
16 Spellman	Maryland 5	17,250	N
17 Myers	Indiana 7	17,000	Y
18 Ashbrook	Ohio 17	16,600	Y
19 Benjamin	Indiana 1	16,000	Y
20 Abdnor	S. Dakota 2	15,600	Y
21 Beard	Tennessee 6	15,083	Y

Representative	State/CD	Amount	Vote
22 Evans	Delaware AL	15,000	Y
23 Symms	Idaho 1	15,000	Y
24 Quayle	Indiana 4	15,000	Y
25 Grassley	Iowa 3	15,000	Y
26 Hopkins	Kentucky 6	15,000	Y
27 Leath	Texas 11	15,000	Y
28 Stenholm	Texas 17	15,000	Y
29 Trible	Virginia 1	15,000	Y
30 Wampler	Virginia 9	14,700	Y
31 Spence	S. Carolina 2	14,500	Y
32 Evans	Georgia 8	14,200	Y
33 Duncan	Tennessee 2	13,912	Y
34 Dornan	California 27	13,800	Y
35 Chappell	Florida 4	13,600	Y
36 Martin	N. Carolina 9	13,561	Y
37 Hubbard	Kentucky 1	13,550	N
38 Johnson	Colorado 4	13,500	Y
39 Corcoran	Illinois 15	13,500	Y
40 Stangeland*	Minnesota 7	13,500	Y
41 Volkmer	Missouri 9	13,100	Y
42 Huckaby	Louisiana 5	12,816	Y
43 Lent	New York 4	12,600	Y
44 Wydler	New York 5	12,600	Y
45 Coleman	Missouri 6	12,540	Y
46 Fuqua	Florida 2	12,400	Y
47 Stump	Arizona 3	12,230	Y
48 Gudger	N. Carolina 11	12,100	Y
49 Shelby	Alabama 7	12,000	Y
50 Pursell	Michigan 2	11,750	Y

KEY   *Includes any funds received during 1977 special elections   Y—voted for Gephardt Amendment   N—voted against Gephardt Amendment

Item: Curbing Real-Estate Fraud versus the Real-Estate Lobby

A 1979 housing bill contained a section that would have given the Department of Housing and Urban Development (HUD) the authority to crack down on, or at least put a crimp in, the shoddy practices by which land developers sold people inaccessible lots, or charged them outlandish fees for minimal or nonexistent services. The bill as drafted by the House Banking Committee would have allowed HUD to issue "cease and desist orders barring developers from the fraudulent sale or lease of property under interstate land sale laws."

Instead of enacting the section, the House, by a vote of 245 to 145, passed an amendment backed by the National Association of Realtors (NAR) that eliminated any enforcement powers the bill might have given HUD. The political-action committee of the NAR had awarded $1.1 million to congressional candidates in the 1978 election, and $670,000 in the previous election. Of the 245 voting in favor of the NAR amendment, 203 (83 percent) had received NAR contributions, averaging $3,665. Of the 145 voting against it, 74 had received nothing, and the other 71 had received substantially smaller donations than those in favor, an average of $1,440.

Item: Taxing Oil's Windfall Profits versus the Oil Lobby

When deregulation of U.S. oil prices in 1979 allowed American oil companies to charge whatever OPEC charged, oil-company profits suddenly climbed sharply. OPEC had increased its oil prices fourfold in 1973 and soon followed that jump with other steep increases. Nobody could claim that U.S. production costs had suddenly increased four times, then doubled again in a few years; the gain was basically fortuitous. Hence, Congress decided to impose a tax to collect some of this "profit."

The oil companies opposed the tax from the outset. When the measure came to the floor of the House, with a tax rate somewhat lower than had first been suggested, they went to work to cut it some more. They lobbied for an amendment that would end most of the tax in 1990, long before the scheduled date, and reduce its level until 1990 below that recommended to the House by its Ways and Means Committee.

The amendment passed 236 to 183. What role did large contributions play? Of the 58 representatives who had received more than $2,500 from oil PACs toward their election or re-election in 1978, 55 voted for the industry's measure. One, who had received $8,000, voted "present." Only 2 who had received more than $2,500 voted against this measure. In all, 196 (83 percent) of the 236 who voted in favor of the amendment had received the support of the oil-industry PACs, an average donation of $1,963. In contrast, only 71 (39 percent) of the 183 House members who opposed the measure had received oil-PAC money, and the average contribution to them was $690, about a third of that received by supporters.

Item: UAW Versus Auto Buyers

Business is not the only group that uses PAC money in the hope of winning special-interest legislation. The United Auto Workers donated $1.4 million to members of the House of Representatives in the 1980 and 1982 elections. In December 1982, it won a major legislative victory when the House, by a vote of 215 to 188, passed the "domestic content bill," which required that as much as 90 percent of all parts used in American cars be manufactured in America. Members voting in favor of the bill had received a total of $1,342,778, eighteen times the $72,175 received by those who opposed the measure. The correlation is in part due to the UAW's marked preference for Democrats, but even among Democrats, there was a strong correlation between the amount received and support of the bill. The 171 House Democrats who supported the UAW's position received an average of $7,709 each, six times the average of $1,244 received by House Democrats who voted "no" on this measure. The domestic content bill, which would have been highly inflationary if enacted, was not approved by the Senate.

The List Goes On

There are many additional instances of the same general nature. Briefly:

The dairy industry has been milking American taxpayers for years through price supports for its products. The cost to the public in one year, fiscal 1982—a year when food stamps and Medicaid were cut—was $2 billion. Even after giveaways to the poor, over 530 million pounds of cheese sits rotting in warehouses. After decades of leaving the dairy industry alone, the budget cutters tried to trim the dairy subsidy. But a vote in the House late in 1981 defeated a move by Representative Barney Frank, Democrat of Massachusetts, to cut $600 million over four years out of the $2-billion-a-year program. Those who voted with the industry on the Frank amendment received, from January 1981 through May 1982, an average of almost $1,600 from the principal dairy PACs, whereas those who opposed the industry on that amendment gained an average of $200.

In the second half of 1981, 216 representatives cosponsored a legislative veto of an FTC rule requiring used-car dealers to disclose known defects in cars to potential buyers. Of that number, 180 received a total of almost half a million dollars for the 1980 and 1982 election cycles from NADA, the National Automobile Dealers Association. Sixteen became cosponsors within ten days of receiving contributions. In 1982, the veto resolution passed easily in the House and Senate. Representative Toby Moffett put it bitterly: "This should be called the used Congress rule."

Of twelve representatives who, from the beginning of 1979 through June 1982, had received more than $3,000 from contractors involved in building the Clinch River Breeder Reactor, not one voted in July 1981 in favor of deleting funds for this much-criticized project, which has yet to be built, after a decade of planning and $1.15 billion in federal funds. The following table presents an overview.

Amount Contributed	Number of Members	Percentage Who Voted to Retain Funding for Clinch River
$3,000–$7,200	12	92
$1,500–$2,999	45	76
$ 50–$1,499	252	49
$ 0	120	29

Sometimes PACs win in a committee but lose in the full House. On August 17, 1982, the House Energy and Commerce Committee voted to weaken the auto-emissions standards set by the Clean Air Act Authorization in 1977 (which itself weakened the standards set by the original act). By a vote of twenty-six to sixteen, the committee supported a bill that would allow carbon-monoxide emissions to double, despite the fact that automakers had been meeting the current allowable level. The bill also opened loopholes in the enforcement of the act. The auto industry claimed the standards hurt an already depressed industry, even though foreign cars also had to meet the standards, so there was no competitive disadvantage. The PACs for the four major automakers (General Motors, Ford, Chrysler, and American Motors) and the NADA PAC donated more than $160,000 to thirty-five of the forty-two members of the committee between January 1979 and July 1982. Those who supported the weakening of clean-air standards received an average of $5,338, more than four times the average amount received by opponents, about $1,331. Fourteen members each received more than $5,000—only one voted against it; fourteen members received between $1,000 and $5,000—four out of that group voted no;

fourteen received $1,000 or less—eleven of these opposed the measure. All but one of the members who received more than $3,500 voted to loosen the standards, while all but one who received no PAC money voted against the auto industry.

The 1983 repeal of the withholding of tax on dividends and interest is a rather different kind of case. Here the main political pressure was generated by a direct appeal of the special interests to the grass roots; they mobilized people to write masses of protesting letters to Congress. However, campaign contributions also helped. Such contributions were received by more than 80 percent of the 334 members of Congress who cosponsored the repeal bills. The 231 House cosponsors got a total of $563,115; 41 Senators—$323,118.

Other statistical data, not listed here, are available on other votes, but the pattern seems evident. Data on the Senate are also available. For example, in the Senate in 1981, on four measures important to the nuclear industry, the top ten 1980 beneficiaries of PACs representing nuclear-power interests cast just one vote against the industry position, or less than 3 percent of their votes. In the Senate as a whole, in contrast, the number of votes that went against the industry was more than twelve times as high. The issues voted on included funding for the Export-Import Bank (which finances nuclear projects overseas) and the size of the appropriations for nuclear-power programs in the federal budget.

Statistical data for the Senate are more difficult to compute because we are dealing with a total of 33 persons up for reelection versus 435 in the House, because the Senate is much smaller than the House, and because only a third of the Senate is up in each election. This makes statistical analysis much less reliable, and individual idiosyncracies much more consequential.

The main point is that in 1983 there were more than thirty-three hundred PACs, aside from other organized lobbies, each pulling and tugging the system its own way. We shall see below that very little public policy was untouched by their influence.

Not all bills backed by PACs end up the way PACs wish. For example, an attempt to exempt doctors and some other health professionals from the jurisdiction of the FTC failed in the Senate in 1982 (though it passed the more permeable House), when intense publicity about the special status to be accorded doctors *et al.,* and about the PAC drive, to the tune of $3 million, proved too embarrassing.

In general, PACs tend to do poorly on environmental issues, such as the Clean Air Act and the Clean Water Act, because the issues have wide *and* active public support. (There are highly toxic dumps in most parts of the country, and people from a great variety of backgrounds and political persuasions find them quite disconcerting.) That is, PACs do not always carry the day, even when they extend themselves. There are, however, many instances—far more than those presented above— in which where the money went, there went the legislation. This is especially true for the many items coming up daily that are neither in the public eye nor reported in the press.

So far this is only what social scientists call a statistical correlation, not a proof of cause or effect. The arguments that members of Congress would have voted that way anyhow or that they got the money for other reasons, such as their general philosophy, which have been raised, I'll deal with shortly. However, no matter how these arguments are resolved, the statistical data show that money and lawmaking go together. Why and how remain to be seen.

PACKS OF PACS

Some people argue that no matter how much money a PAC raises, it can only direct $5,000 to a particular candidate for any given election. Often a representative needs at least $100,000, and sometimes much more, while the cost of many Senate races averages over a million. A lawmaker, this argument goes, would not "sell" his or her vote for such a paltry sum. As Mobil said of the $5,000 limit in an ad in defense of PACs ("the voice of real people"): "That's hardly enough in these days of costly campaigns to 'buy' 30 seconds on TV, let alone an election."

In support of the same argument, the vice president of public affairs for Avon Products, Robert R. McMillan, writes: "It is sheer nonsense to think that a $5,000 maximum contribution by a PAC could cause a member of Congress to vote against the interests of his or her constituents."

Strong words. One wonders: Even if the contribution was not known to the public? Even if he or she had a thousand "votes" to sell to various PACs per annum? One should also note that a PAC may give $5,000 for a primary, and another $5,000 for the election itself. More important: an interest group may be—and many are—

served by numerous PACs. This arrangement is legal, provided the various PACs are not staffed by the same persons, do not control one another through bylaws or other means, and do not make substantial exchanges of funds. However, there is nothing to prevent PACs that are distinct under the law from having the same philosophy, lobbying for the same interest, sharing information on candidates—and "rewarding" the same public representatives for the same private service.

The dairy industry provides a case in point. Dairy interests are promoted by the Associated Milk Producers, based in Texas, which sponsors CTAPE (Committee for Thorough Agricultural Political Education); Dairymen, Inc., based in Louisville, Kentucky, which sponsors SPACE (Special Political Agricultural Community Education); and the Mid-America Dairymen, which sponsors ADEPT (Agricultural and Dairy Educational Political Trust).

In addition, there are many other, smaller, dairy PACs, each supporting "friends" of the industry. All in all, there are twenty-one PACs representing the dairy industry, though some are state affiliates of larger PACs.

Between January 1975 and July 1978, six members of the House Agriculture Committee received $20,000 or more each from various PACs of dairy groups. Representative John Jenrette, Jr., received a hefty $59,900. Representative Jerry Huckaby got $42,000. Representative Richard Nolan of Minnesota received $37,225. Wisconsin's Alvin Baldus collected $34,400. Note that these figures are exclusive of contributions from individual dairymen, which are likely to have been made but are difficult to trace.

Oil outdid the dairy industry. One hundred eighty-three PACs formed by oil and gas interests pumped $3 million to federal candidates between January 1, 1981, and May 31, 1982, making them the largest single industry group. Some of the PACs included in this figure represent corporations with other interests besides energy, but all were significantly involved in oil and gas. The PAC of LTV Corporation, in the oilfield supply business, pumped out $173,055. Dallas Energy PAC, a "nonconnected" PAC supported primarily by executives of independent oil companies, gushed $136,000; Amoco, one of the nation's largest oil companies, $116,320; Mid-Continent Wildcatter's Association, $108,250; Tenneco, $102,450; and so on.

Not all the multi-PACs are concerned with economic matters.

Some go after foreign policy. During the 1981–82 election cycle, thirty-one Jewish PACs contributed to candidates supportive of Israel $1.67 million. The PACs are reported to work closely together to increase their clout, and benefit from the guidance of one lobby, the American Israel Public Affairs Committee.

Because of the multiple PACs, several members of both houses were able to collect amounts that make the legal limits of $5,000 almost irrelevant. In 1982, Senator Orrin Hatch of Utah received $77,615 from oil interests; Senator Richard Lugar of Indiana, $65,133; Senator Malcolm Wallop of Wyoming, $59,400; former Senator Harrison Schmitt of New Mexico, $52,750. The largest single oil and gas beneficiary was Senator Lloyd Bentsen of Texas, who tanked up on $83,408. Representative Phil Gramm of Texas led the House, with $66,750 from oil and gas interests.

In addition, groups of PACs are galvanized by specific issues. The four major automakers may not always agree with NADA, but they put up a united lobbying front when it comes to clean-air standards. A special-interest bankruptcy bill was promoted by PACs of the American Bankers Association, the National Consumer Finance Association, the Credit Union National Association, Household Finance Company, Beneficial Finance Company, and Sears Roebuck, among others.

None of these figures include contributions by individual members of the same organization which invites PAC money. For instance, former Representative Millicent Fenwick raised $13,650 from the top executives of a Wall Street investment firm, more than the maximum the firm's PAC could give.

Representative Martin Russo of Illinois was the author of a clause in Reagan's 1981 tax bill that would have saved commodity traders $400 million per year. He received thousands of dollars from various individual commodity sources in the first six months after his re-election in 1980, *during* consideration of the Reagan tax bill and the commodity traders' loophole. Nineteen women who listed their only occupation as homemaker each gave $500 on the same day, June 3, 1981; all but one had the same last names as those of commodity traders. This type of coordinated donation has much the same effect as the old "double-envelope" routine, used by corporations in the pre-PAC days: individual contributions from many corporate employees were delivered in one large envelope, with the company name prominently displayed. Technically, the corporation had not broken the law against corporate giving, but the connection between the corporation and the aggregate campaign gifts was established.

Some PACs, because of their greater resources, experience, or political connections, serve as pack leaders to smaller PACs. Explains PAC manager Stephen W. Thomas:

> If BIPAC [Business-Industry Political Action Committee] contributes to a candidate, its action may well trigger, or at least encourage, contributions to the same candidates from other business PACs. Similarly, a candidate who receives support from COPE [the AFL-CIO's PAC] is virtually assured to some level of funding from other labor PACs.

The Chamber of Commerce publishes a widely watched opportunity list, which calls attention to close races and identifies pro-business challengers who have a chance to unseat a less friendly incumbent. This listing can serve as a lightning rod to draw funds from all over the country to a floundering campaign.

The White House also steps in. Assistant to the President for Political Affairs Edward J. Rollins noted while speaking to the press that it would violate federal election law for groups that make independent expenditures, such as NCPAC, to "coordinate" their activities with Republican Party campaign committees or the White House. Then, without blinking an eye, he continued, "Very clearly we will be meeting with them regularly to tell them where we're heading and let them tell us what they're doing." In short, although there is a $5,000 limit on a PAC's contribution, that limit serves as a minor obstruction rather than a major obstacle to concentration of large funds.

■ We have seen that as the money goes, so goes the legislation. Or, as PAC advocates argue, the "right" kind of legislation "draws" money. In either case, laws and campaign contributions go tightly hand in hand. And the amounts involved are far from paltry. But what about the process? *How* does private money sway the vote of a member of Congress, affect the making of one law after another?

CHAPTER FOUR

LEGALIZED CORRUPTION

The evidence indicates that, all too often, where private monies flow, there go the laws of the land. This obvious corruption of democratic government—by the people, for the people—invites an obvious response: "There ought to be a law." The trouble is that there already is a law. To understand how it is regularly and easily circumvented is to understand how contemporary plutocrats impose their will on the public.

"THERE OUGHT TO BE A LAW"

Offering a member of Congress money for a vote on specific legislation or for any other specific action (such as sponsoring an amendment or intervening with a federal agency) constitutes an act of bribery. For an interest group to offer such a specific payment, or for a member of Congress to accept it, violates the Federal Criminal Code (Section 201 of Title 18): "Whoever, directly or indirectly, corruptly gives, offers or promises anything of value to any public official . . . with intent . . . to influence any official act," it states, is guilty of bribery or attempted bribery.

On the other side of the coin: "Whoever, being a public official . . . directly or indirectly, corruptly asks, demands, exacts, solicits, seeks, accepts, receives, or agrees to receive anything of value . . . in return for . . . being influenced in his performance of any official act" is guilty of accepting a bribe. In either case, the fine is $20,000 or three times the bribe, whichever is greater, and up to fifteen years in jail. In addition, those convicted can be barred from "holding any office of honor."

Even if such a payment is made in the form of a campaign contribution (that is, paid into a fund set aside for this purpose), rather than slipped into a lawmaker's pocket, it is still a bribe under existing law, because the statute specifies that one may not offer or promise to give anything "to any other person or entity" in return for a public official's favor. Likewise, no public official may agree "to receive anything of value for himself or for any other person or entity." At issue is the motive or interest: if the contribution is given as general support, fine; if it is given to gain a specific favor, a *quid pro quo,* it is tantamount to a bribe.

The public is thus confused by the existence of a strict, encompassing prohibition on payoffs and the correct perception, supported by abundant evidence, that members of Congress heed the special interests. Little wonder the public tends to assume that "politicians" accept money "under the table," Abscam style. But, to reiterate, such payments are not where the main problem lies. Lobbyists have found several channels through which large sums can be transferred to the campaign chest or personal use of a member of Congress, in exchange for which a member can deliver public goods to private hands, without violating the letter of the law. How is it done?

IMPLICIT SPECIFIC DEALS

Legalized corruption works routinely these days by deals, struck between a member of Congress and a representative of a private interest, that are *implicit,* rather than fully spelled out, but nevertheless *specific,* relating to clear outcomes. Deals can be fashioned implicitly because when a lobbyist representing a private interest approaches a member of Congress, the member knows quite clearly what general position the lobbyist seeks to advance. A lobbyist who represents, say, the National Education Association will be in favor of increasing or maintaining educational expenditures, and opposed to cutting them. If this is the month Congress is considering abolishing the Department of Education, and the member being visited is a member of a committee due to report to Congress on the merits of the department, and the

NEA has recently testified in favor of maintaining the department, it would require a very obtuse member of Congress not to understand what an NEA lobbyist was after.

Nor is there a legal prohibition on the lobbyist's explicitly arguing the case, say, for public support for education and for maintaining the Department of Education. *And* the lobbyist will violate no law if he or she promises to support the member of Congress with campaign contributions, and deposit them before or after the vote (typically both).

The only step that is prohibited, and which hardly ever needs to be negotiated, even when the lobbyist and the member of Congress meet alone behind closed doors, is explicitly, openly, and directly tying a contribution to a specific vote. Thus, a lobbyist could not legally say out loud, *"If* you vote in favor of bill X we shall pay $5,000 into your campaign chest and invite you to address our next convention in the Bahamas, all expenses paid, plus a $2,000 lecture fee." Sophisticated special-interest groups, such as the AMA, have separate funding and "briefing" divisions and send two representatives, one to spell out the case, the other to deliver the check, but it is neither illegal nor uncommon for the same person to do both.

The law, at least as ordinarily interpreted,* allows one to deal, arrange, imply, suggest, pay off—only not to spell it all out. Not much of a deterrent. Hence, what seems initially a door closed to legal deals, forcing lobbyists to make illegal bribes, is in effect but a small hindrance, almost a matter of formula or style. There are certain words one cannot—and need not—say; otherwise private interests and members of Congress are home free.

FROM THE HORSE'S MOUTH

Two sources of information on how it is done are the people who are involved in the deals: the lobbyists and the members of Congress who are being lobbied. Most of those still in business are unwilling to talk

---

*Common Cause, in an ad declaring war on PACs, called such transactions *"perfectly legal"*! This might be going a bit too far. It might be better to test in court the assumption that implied deals, carrying what Archibald Cox has called an "unspoken obligation," are not quite legal. It is, though, correct to say that the present interpretation of the law condones such deals.

for the record other than to defend their part in the dealing. But privately they admit, and not only to me, that implicit deals do indeed take place frequently, are even common, "routine," and that the cumulative result is a corrupt Congress, playing first to private interests and attending to the public as a secondary priority.

No Quid Pro Quo?

Some lobbyists and members of Congress are willing to speak for the record, with varying degrees of openness. They range from those who, while seeking to justify the system, in the process reveal some of what is going on, to those who openly call it the way it is.

Some defenders of the PACed system do not deny that private monies carry legislation, but insist that the votes of lawmakers are not bought, because there are no *explicit* deals. It is this subtle distinction that allows lobbyists to swear up and down they do not buy Congress (explicitly, that is), and, at the same time, *looking at the same situation,* allows former members of Congress, some scrupulous ones still in office, and some unabashed lobbyists to state that the fix is on (implicitly).

Representative Mike Synar, testifying before a congressional committee's task force on a bill he cosponsored to restrict interest groups' activity, sees specific deals struck, though only implicitly: "No one here today is suggesting that PAC money buys votes. But it would be naive in the extreme to ignore the 'quid pro quo' implicit in PAC contributions. That money is given . . . to influence the legislative process."

"The process," testified former Representative Bob Eckhardt, "has all of the advantages of bribery and none of its risks."

Representative William Brodhead, who decided not to stand for re-election, observes that there are ways to avoid the explicit offer of a bribe without losing the desired effect. He describes the process quite completely:

> The legalities are observed. You're talking about very subtle people on both sides. But when they couple an invitation to meet their PAC director with a pitch to vote for such and such a bill, well, then it's pretty clear. . . . When we're all through talking about the legislation, they'll say, "Could you give me the address of your campaign committee?"

Brodhead adds:

> These people who are contributing to these campaigns are not
> stupid. They're buying something. It used to be a group would just
> agree with your philosophical outlook and would be willing to
> make the campaign contribution on that basis. Now votes are given
> in exchange for campaign contributions. That's what's happening
> around here.

An unidentified "Washington representative" of a defense contractor put the onus on Congress when he explained that showing a
member the merits of a weapon for which he or she has to vote an
appropriation is not enough: "You still have to meet their expectations
with PAC contributions." Craig Palmer, a representative of the
American Dental Association, admits, "Obviously, we contribute to
members who support legislation we're interested in." Republican
conservative Minority Leader Robert Michel, commenting on farm
legislation, said, "The dairy industry spreads an awful lot of money
around, and that gets reflected in votes out here."

Talking about the decision by the home-builders' Build-PAC to
demand specific statements of interest and support from those it bank-
rolls, a Cincinnati home-builder, Jay Buchert, explains: "Before, builders viewed political contributions as investments that may or may not
pay off. . . . We don't have that luxury anymore. Now we have to
look at them as investments that *will* pay off."

NCPAC, which specializes in counter-efforts, was quite a bit more
explicit. Its letter to Representative Stephen Neal read in part: "If you
will make a public statement in support of the president's tax cut
package and state that you intend to vote for it, we will withdraw all
radio and newspaper ads planned in your district. In addition, we will
be glad to run radio and newspaper ads applauding you for your vote
to lower taxes."

Outspoken former Representative Millicent Fenwick testified: "In
my mind there is no question that there is a connection between these
contributions and votes. . . . Members have told me they received
such-and-such an amount of money from one of these groups and
could not vote with me."

Members of Congress are not at all reluctant to point to special
services when they write to ask for PAC funds. Representative Benja-

min A. Gilman of New York, in a form letter soliciting contributions from many business PACs, writes that he has "consistently voted for tax relief for you and small businesses." Representative Romano Mazzoli lists his efforts in reducing anti-trust restrictions on companies doing business overseas.

With so many implicit deals taking place daily, it is no wonder that once in a while a lobbyist will get carried away, forget the amenities, and spell it all out. Thus, Senator Charles McC. Mathias, Jr., of Maryland charged in 1979 that one PAC had threatened to withhold contributions from his re-election campaign if he voted against a bill its industry favored. Professor Larry J. Sabato, who reported the incident, writes that the PAC has been identified by sources other than the senator as that of the Bristol-Myers Company.

Senator Dick Clark reports the following conversation with an official of the Machinists and Aerospace Workers Union, who sought to change Clark's vote:

> He said to me, "Okay, if that's the case, we won't support you."
> I responded: "Look at my voting record as a whole. Don't make a decision like this based on a single vote." His reply was: "We don't give a damn about your overall voting record. We're interested in this bill—period."

Senator Howard M. Metzenbaum told me that a labor union that supplied him in his primary in 1982 would not even answer his calls to their PAC when he was raising money for his senatorial campaign, after he voted against one of their pet bills.

Writes Lester L. Cooper, Jr.: "The business PAC I managed . . . contributed to [Representatives] Bob Eckhardt, Bob Kastenmeier, Ed Markey and Andy Maguire in 1980—*because they had helped that company on a major issue.*" Clear enough, I believe.

Mark Green, president of the Democracy Project, collected evidence of *quid pro quos* like mushrooms after an ample rain. He reports:

> In the mid-1970s, a labor union that gave [Representative Leon] Panetta a $1,500 contribution asked for support of pending "cargo preference legislation." When Panetta asked about the substance of the bill, he was told, "I don't have to tell you anything substantively —we gave you money. We support the bill, and we expect you to."
> . . . Republican Representative Claudine Schneider of Rhode Island recently tried to persuade a Republican colleague to oppose more

funding for the Clinch River Breeder Reactor. He declined, explaining, "Yes, but Westinghouse is a big contributor of mine."
. . . Another Republican Representative, Jim Leach of Iowa, tells how he once suggested to an urban Democrat with no dairy constituency that it would be wisest for him to oppose a dairy price support measure, and was told, "Yeah, but their PAC gave me money. I have to support them." . . . A New York Democrat admitted that he voted for the Alaska Gas Pipeline, even though he opposed it on the merits, because "I didn't want the construction unions contributing to my opponent." . . . When Representative Dan Glickman of Kansas asked a colleague earlier this year to join him in opposing a measure that would forbid the F.T.C. regulating auto dealers, he was told, "I'm committed. I got a $10,000 check from the National Automobile Dealers Association. I can't change my vote now."

These incidents have been reported before. As far as can be determined, they did not lead to the filing of charges against the parties involved, *which goes to show how explicit implicit deals can be.*

Some see virtue in explicitness. Senator J. James Exon was the main sponsor of a bill dear to the heart of the National Office Machine Dealers Association. Their PAC contributed $5,000 to his campaign chest in 1982 even though he was not up for re-election and received only one other PACed gift in 1982. When told that the dealers openly linked their contribution to this legislative effort, he did not call in the Department of Justice, or return what seems like a bribe. He stated that this is "a more or less refreshing concession, and a measure of candor on their part."

Most deals, though, are not that open. Nor need they be.

ONE-STOP SHOPPING

If you believe that by now you have heard everything, hold on. For those who do not have a big lobbying staff, or do not know their way around Congress, or simply want to make their legislative shopping easier, Representative Tony Coelho is said to have set up a one-stop shop. He is running it not for his own enrichment, but to channel more PAC money to House Democrats, who feel that the Republicans are raking in the dough while they are left behind. Tony says about himself, "I'm a seller."

In the opinion of one Democratic Party leader, who refused to be quoted by name, but whose credibility I can vouch for, having known him for more than twenty years, Coelho sells legislation. An interested party can stop in his office and get help with drafting a bill, with finding a sponsor and cosponsor, representatives to usher it through committee and to vote for it on the floor. It saves a lot of running around, as long as you provide the necessary campaign contribution chips. The volume of business? The Democratic Congressional Campaign Committee, which Coelho chairs, raised $5.7 million in 1981–82, compared with $1.8 million in 1979–80 under a previous chair, and before the new services were reportedly offered.

However, it must be noted that Coelho's staff deny that their congressman is in the legislative business. They insist that they collect the money, and the legislative work is done elsewhere. Only on "very rare occasions" will Coelho or his staff help the contributors in drafting legislation, and so on. "With the media, these days, you got to be careful what you are saying" about the connection between raising funds and legislation.

A Coelho representative calls "completely accurate" a *Wall Street Journal* report stating that "potential contributors almost invariably want something from Congress. Both House members and top House aides say Mr. Coelho often asks individual lawmakers to listen to their requests and to help them if possible." This in turn is reported as putting "subtle pressure" on the lawmakers not to endanger the potential contribution.

The Congressional Quarterly reports:

> Among many Democrats, however, the more common concern is about possible pressure on members to make themselves inoffensive to business at the expense of their personal values. As one congressional aide told a reporter earlier this year, no one wants to be "fingered as the fink who cost the Democrats a contribution." Says another Democratic aide: "The problem is the extent to which . . . Tony is sort of arranging marriages."

The phrase "one-stop shop" may imply more than Coelho does, and may not capture quite aptly what he does mean. It is, though, clear that, instead of directly approaching a member of Congress and attempting to buy his or her support, one may turn to strategically placed members—chairmen of the parties' campaign committees, for instance—and solicit their middle-man help.

THE ULTIMATE CATCH

It is NOT *that a member of Congress who openly and explicitly accepts payment in exchange for passing a law will be brought up on charges, convicted, and sentenced.* The reader may well stop here and say: Wait a moment, what was that? Such, at least, was the response when the point arose in a lengthy discussion with one of the men in charge of investigating members of Congress. He is Craig C. Donsanto, director of the Election Crimes Branch, Public Integrity Section, of the Department of Justice. Mr. Donsanto, an energetic, witty, almost cheerful man, can cite the laws at issue quickly from memory, and has many years of experience in the area. He is careful not to express personal viewpoints or advance policy positions. He just explains the law to his visitor. The cumulative effect of what he recounts is nevertheless stunning.

The strongest barrier against convicting a corrupt member of Congress is a provision of the Constitution, often referred to as the "speech or debate" clause (Article 1, Section 6). The key phrase states that "for any Speech or Debate in either House, [members of Congress] shall not be questioned." The courts have broadly construed the section to prohibit questioning a member of Congress, or introducing any evidence concerning his or her vote, debate in Congress, or all "things generally done in a session" of Congress in relation to legislative business. The historical origin of the article is the British bill of rights. It was added when, in the seventeenth century, kings were arresting members of Parliament who voted in ways they disliked. The idea was to protect lawmakers from undue pressure, *not* to shield them from prosecution in bribery cases. However, several Supreme Court cases have been interpreted to cover such acts.

In *United States v. Johnson* (1966), the Court found that "a former member of the House of Representatives could not be prosecuted on a conspiracy charge where conviction on the charge required proof that the legitimately legislative act of making a speech before Congress was the result of bribery." In the case, Representative Thomas F. Johnson from Maryland was charged with accepting more than $20,000 in campaign contributions in exchange for helping to arrange a "review" of an indictment against two officers of a savings-and-loan company, and making a speech in behalf of savings-and-loan institutions on the floor, which he did. (On the other hand, in the case of *United States v. Brewster,* in 1972, a former senator was convicted for only taking a bribe without claim that he performed, in exchange, any legislative act.)

You can imagine how difficult it becomes to convict a member of Congress of bribery if evidence of how he acted in exchange for the favors he pocketed, how he consummated the crime, may not be introduced. This is not idle speculation. In 1976 a New Jersey Representative, Henry Helstoski, was indicted "on charges that he *solicited* and *accepted* bribes from Chilean and Argentinian aliens in return for introducing bills to block their deportation." Helstoski and his aides were charged with running the extortion scheme for more than seven years. The court threw out several counts of the indictment because they depended on testimony regarding his legislative actions.

When you talk to Craig Donsanto you can sense how little enthusiasm remains, after such experiences, at the Department of Justice for going after corrupt members of Congress. (In the Abscam cases, which required a highly contrived setup, no actual legislation was involved, and hence, with difficulties, convictions were obtained. But this feat is not easy to duplicate.)

The assistant director of the FBI's Criminal Investigative Division, Oliver B. Revell, states, "The Helstoski decision gave us considerable difficulties." He hurries to add that there is "no diminution in authority, capacity, or desire to act" if information comes to the FBI. In effect, he said, "several investigations against Congress members are in process although of course I am not at liberty to divulge them." We shall have to wait and see whether the courts will be less protective of members of Congress in the future.

Members of Congress acting individually, or Congress as a body, may waive their immunity, but unless the public outcry is stupendous, they are very unlikely to do so. Thus, members of Congress who slip from implicit to explicit trading of their offices need not worry; under most circumstances they can hide behind the Constitution. Just to give them a little extra protection, Congress wrote into the federal election laws that the statute of limitations for campaign finance violations is *three years.* Five years is customary in federal criminal violations.

JUSTIFYING PAC WAYS

"We Support Philosophy, Not Buy Candidates"

Some lobbyists argue, "We aren't buying votes," insisting that donations are "based on the basic philosophy of a member," as a spokeswoman for the AMA put it. The notion that PACs, especially PACs that seek to advance an economic interest—which means most PACs—favor a candidate merely because of his or her general philosophy is belied by the fact that these PACs expect *specific* favors, *aside* from philosophical agreement, in exchange for "contributions." That is, the evidence shows that these PACs do not mind at all if they can support a candidate with whom they are *also* philosophically in sync —as, for example, a business PAC supports a conservative candidate —especially if a candidate's philosophy will lead him or her to do the PAC's specific bidding. Nor do PACs object at all to *converting* a candidate to their philosophy in addition to gaining the specific items they desire. But, if push comes to shove, they will take their pound of public flesh, whatever the candidate's philosophy, as long as he or she delivers the specific goods.

The conversion of Thomas A. Luken illustrates that more than philosophy is required to be an economic PAC's darling. Luken was elected to Congress from Ohio in 1974, as a staunch liberal Democrat. He had been a campaign worker for John F. Kennedy; a civil-rights marcher in Selma, Alabama, in 1965; and a reform-minded councilman and mayor. Once elected to Congress, he turned conservative and pro-business. By the 1980 campaign he had become one of the favorites of pro-business PACs and received from them $174,778, 59 percent of his total campaign contributions.

But this obviously was not enough. Besides turning from pro-labor and liberal to pro-business and conservative, he also was in the forefront of the fight for an industry-backed amendment that would have seriously weakened the Clean Air Act. He voted for exempting doctors, dentists, and optometrists from FTC consumer-protection regulations, and against FTC regulation of used-car dealers. He voted against President Carter's hospital cost containment and with trial lawyers to defeat no-fault auto insurance. Among his key contributors were PACs of the AMA, GM, Dow Chemical, U.S. Steel, Peabody Coal, and Kennecott Corp.

While most PACs are sympathetic to groups philosophically opposed to big government, they typically want more "government" for *their* members. Senator Gary Hart reports:

> I hate to get on the plane for Denver. For three hours the lobbyists just line up in the aisle to get a word with me. Most of them are special pleaders for business, and they generally have two messages. The first is that there is too much government, too much taxation and spending—and that they want something specific from the federal government.

Nowhere is the philosophy-is-a-bonus position of these lobbies clearer than when it comes to writing specific concessions or privileges for their clients into the tax law. Typically, when the fine print of a tax law is written in the early hours of a new day, the Senate Finance Committee room is filled with scores of lobbyists, elbow to elbow, many of whom stay right through the whole process, which for a recent year (July 1–2, 1982) took seventeen hours. They do not stand there for amusement, or out of philosophical kinship.

When the 1982 tax law was being drafted, for instance, a General Electric representative argued for repeal of new leasing provisions, "after first taking maximum advantage" of them. GE acknowledged "that this would likely increase profits for its important equipment leasing subsidiary—while hurting many of the other firms," hardly a general pro-capitalism or pro-business position. GE was opposed, among others, by Senator David Durenberger of Minnesota, who is said to have "strong ties to his state's railroad industry and Republic Airlines, headquartered in his state," which were interested in preserving the rules.

When the leasing rules were tightened in the summer of 1982, Republican Senator Slade Gorton of Washington, the state where Boeing makes its home, sponsored a special six-month extension period for the old (looser) leasing regulations for some aircraft. The change would substantially benefit Boeing, which was about to sell a batch of planes to Eastern Airlines, although it would provide little or no benefit to other airplane manufacturers. It would also hurt Continental (which argued that there are too many empty seats as it is), and was opposed by American, which competes directly with Eastern in several markets.

Hidden in the 1982 tax bill was also a provision that would cost a few oil companies with Alaskan operations at least $389 million "extra" in taxes, because it would repeal a special tax break they enjoyed. With the help of Senator Max Baucus of Montana, it was promoted by other oil companies, which claimed that the special tax break allowed its beneficiaries to compete unfairly.

Occasionally the scramble to serve special interests leads to unintended results more suitable to a comedy of errors than to the nation's top legislative body. In the summer of 1982 Senator Thad Cochran introduced an amendment to the tax bill that would have kept open a loophole for the Masonite Corporation. The wording of the amendment inadvertently canceled a similar benefit for the Gulf Oil Corporation. In turn, Gulf Oil canceled a multibillion-dollar transaction (takeover of Cities Service Corporation), which was deemed unprofitable without the special break. So much for philosophy.

The willingness of many members of Congress to support a measure that has been PACed, even when it flies in the face of their general philosophy, stands out in a study conducted by Congress Watch, called the "Hypocrisy Poll." Selected for the study were nineteen senators and representatives well known for their *laissez-faire,* conservative, anti-government-spending position. As a group, these members of Congress received more than 80 percent of their PAC money from business and business-related PACs. But on the three particular votes covered in the study, concerning government intervention in the market place, they disregarded their free-market philosophy and opted for the specific governmental benefit sought by their PAC-backed interests.

The first vote concerned the government's requirement that the Alaska natural-gas pipeline be financed in part by consumers, rather than wholly by the private contractor that had agreed to build it; the second concerned government funding of the Clinch River Breeder Reactor, a project the free market had consistently refused to support; the third concerned the Export-Import Bank, which through subsidized loans is supposed to spur foreign trade, but actually is mainly a boon to a few large corporations. Nine of the nineteen members of Congress managed *one* "free-market" vote each. The remaining ten voted against the free-market position on all three votes.

PACs zero in, heavily, on committee chairmen, subcommittee chairmen, and congressional leaders. The House Health and Environment Subcommittee voted in 1982 to dilute the Clean Air Act significantly. The twelve members who voted for weakening the act got a total of $197,325 from the PACs of the seven major industries affected. Republican Senator Steve Symms of Idaho, who gained $97,500 from affected industries during his 1980 campaign, introduced several amendments favored by the industry. "It was clear he had no idea what was in those amendments," says one senator. Members of his committee even wondered, "Which campaign check had that amendment attached to it?"

Representative John Dingell, who is chairman of the House Energy and Commerce Committee, which has been called a "PAC heaven," and who sponsored the bill that would weaken the Clean Air Act, said about the bill's twelve supporters on the House Health and Environment Subcommittee: "The 'dirty dozen' have done very well raising funds for their campaigns." The twelve received an average of seven times more PAC money from industries that supported the bill than did those on the subcommittee who opposed the bill.

This preoccupation with committees, especially with certain committees, lends further support, if more is needed, to the suggestion that philosophical agreement is not the first thing PACs are after. Chairmen are often less ideologically pure than the rank-and-file. Foreign policy and law and order should be at least as relevant to ideology as economic issues. But what makes the difference is where the spoils are and where control of them rests—in select committees and with chairmen. PACs crowd where the payoffs lie.

"Just Buying Access"

Sometimes the rationalization given for cash on the barrelhead, instead of denying what is there for all to see, explains it as buying not a vote, but only the time, ear, attention of the lawmaker. Justin Dart, a California industrialist, puts it somewhat sarcastically: "With a little money, they hear you better." "If you make contributions, it gives you a better chance to get them to hear you and make your case," says Michael McLeod, a lobbyist for the Chicago Board of Trade.

Observes Representative W. Henson Moore, about your chances with a PAC versus without one: "If he [the member] knows you aren't politically active, he may be polite to you, but if you really want to see him perk up and be interested in what you say, let him know you represent a political action committee that is going to be active in the next election."

In response, as we have seen, there is reason to believe that in many instances giving (or withholding) money constitutes the direct exercise of power, not merely the opening of communication. Second, while it is possible that in some situations lobbyists just buy time to plead their case, even this is a factor in corruption, a step removed and only somewhat attenuated. Those with the bucks still gain a privilege other citizens have a hard time getting.

No member of Congress can hear out most, or even many, of those who want to express their views. On the contrary, as most members of Congress dash from vote to vote and from one committee meeting to another, very few can get to them, however good the cause. Hence, even if all that lobbyists get for their money is access, the ability to buy access still corrupts the system. And, to reiterate, they do get much more.

True, some other, "irrelevant," criteria will also gain one access: knowing the member's son or daughter, being a Nobel Prize–winner, and so on. But two wrongs do not make a right, and money is by far the most common way of deflecting the attention of members of Congress from listening to a cross section of their constituents.

"No Causal Link"

The question of time sequence is important in matters of cause and effect: causes are supposed to precede, not follow, effects. Representative Thomas Tauke, discussing the kind of statistical data introduced above, observes, "Studies of this kind always suggest that votes follow contributions. But usually, contributions follow votes." Writes Senator Steve Symms: "I must object to your implication that campaign contributions influenced my voting record on the Clean Air Act. Contributors to my 1980 campaign for the U.S. Senate had no idea what my committee assignments would be. My eventual appointment to the Environment and Public Works Committee, where I have become closely involved with revising the Clean Air Act, was unknown to me until January of 1981."

Several studies have applied high-powered math to votes and contributions and found little correlation. Others found that while a member of Congress's ideology and constituent needs were more powerful than money contributions, money made a difference. These various studies include a work by two economists, James B. Kau and Paul H. Rubin, published as a book: *Congressmen, Constituents, and*

Contributors; an unpublished Ph.D. thesis by Candice J. Nelson; and studies by political scientists John P. Frendreis and Richard W. Waterman, Diana Evans Yiannakis, and Kirk F. Brown, among others. Most of these studies used a methodology worked out for objects—not people. The logic is that if you, say, drop acid on a rock and it then disintegrates, the acid might be the causal force. However, if the rock disintegrates before the acid is dropped, the acid could hardly be the cause. Unlike rocks, however, people can *anticipate;* they can act now in anticipation of a payoff to follow. Hence what is later in the time sequence can still be a causal factor. Moreover, a given contribution —or vote—is *not* a discrete event but part of a sequence that has many steps. Votes are *followed* by contributions that *precede* other votes, which are followed by more contributions, *ad nauseam.*

Actually, in most of the cases reported above the contributions were made *prior* to the relevant votes. In another instance, a handwritten note delivered to several PACs by the chairman of the House Ways and Means Committee, Dan Rostenkowski, says that Representative Wyche Fowler "is a valuable member" of the tax-writing panel and, because he faces a tough re-election fight, could use "an additional contribution." This occurred *during* the consideration of the 1982 tax bill. PACs do it before, during, and after.

The question of timing is much less important than Tauke and Symms suggest. Knowing that contributions will follow is almost as good as having money in hand. No lobby would be so impractical as to welch on an implied promise and maintain hope of gaining attention to its interests next time around. And there is always another vote— which the contributions that came after this one will precede. At issue here are *continuing* relationships.

PACs' before-during-and-after greasing of legislation is illustrated by the following incident, which concerns a bill to limit competition in office machines that was opposed by both the Department of Justice and the FTC, and was openly promoted by the National Office Machine Dealers Association. Initially their PAC set out only "to support legislators who are sympathetic to our views." But it soon turned out that the PAC had an interest in only one bill—the one seeking to limit competition. The Dealers' PAC gave $5,000 to Representative James J. Florio just before he ushered the bill through a subcommittee he chairs, another $5,000 after it cleared. The PAC also gave him a $2,000 speaking fee. Another $5,000 was paid in several installments to Representative William Alexander during the months he served as the main House sponsor of the bill.

And PACs keep tabs. A congressional aide, a former student of mine, wrote to me:

> That corruption exists on Capitol Hill, probably does not come as much of a surprise to many Americans. Unfortunately, they are not aware of the extent of the problem which your article aptly describes. As a native of Philadelphia, I am well accustomed to corruption. . . . More recently however I have been exposed to the problem more directly. Lobbyists always come in and out of our office asking to speak to the different legislative assistants. Not too long ago I spoke with a lobbyist about a bill and told him he probably could be assured of my boss's vote. When my Member did not make it to Washington because of a cancelled flight, the lobbyist called me to ask why he had missed the vote. He added that he would have to explain my answer to a committee reviewing "PAC" requests.

Sometimes the benefit for the PAC is not immediately visible, but it is rarely much delayed. Explains Representative Henry B. Gonzalez: "PACs have donated campaign funds by the millions of dollars, and the full impact of it didn't show up right away. But it did show up —in tax bills. There is a direct relationship between those massive donations and their representatives' votes on tax legislation."

The high-powered mathematical studies, which find relatively few direct links between where the cash flows and the votes wash up, completely ignore a common Washington practice of log-rolling. Accordingly, a lobbyist representing several interests arranges for a contribution now and collects a favor at another time, on a seemingly unrelated issue, serving one client or another.

Lobbyist Boggs made large personal contributions to the re-election campaign of several congressmen involved in the Abscam scandal. Such contributions provided no immediate return, but they helped maintain Boggs's reputation among these and *other* members of Congress that he is a friend who can be called upon when others are likely to desert you. Put that into your computer.

Buying by the "Record"
Some lobbyists insist that they do not buy specific votes—because they take into account other votes cast by a member of Congress, his

or her record. An oil-company spokesman, Carl Meyerdirk, explains: "Certainly, we take a look at the voting records of people we support. I'm sure everyone who makes contributions to political campaigns does. But we certainly don't buy votes in Congress that way." (By "that way" he means explicitly, one at a time.)

Protesting a *Time* report, a PAC chairman writes: "As a matter of policy, Lockheed's PAC does not concern itself with single issues. Each of the five Senators shown on your chart is an advocate of a sound national defense. It is this record that has earned them the support of Lockheed employees."

The first issue is, *what record?* To the extent that the total performance of a member of Congress is fairly evaluated, we are moving in the direction of democratic representation, although even in this case the question remains what criterion of evaluation is used: total service to a special interest, or to the public? However, the record typically taken into account by lobbies is not "the record" but a few, select issues, often very few, only those of interest to the lobby's narrow band of special concerns.

The following example is typical of the Washington scene. In the summer of 1982 the eighteen trustees of the Realtors PAC met to review the recent records of sixty individuals who planned to run for Congress that November. They concluded that forty of these sixty candidates had been sufficiently "helpful" to the real-estate industry to deserve a contribution, typically $5,000. Thirteen, considered uncooperative, were given not a dime among them. Decisions on seven others were postponed until more information could be gathered.

Earlier in the year, 132 other candidates had been reviewed, of whom 97 were supported. Other such meetings are regularly scheduled, a fact not, of course, hidden from the politicians. To avoid any misunderstanding, the checks are delivered by a realtor personally to those RPAC favors.

In addition to cash, RPAC has made in-kind contributions. For instance, a friendly candidate got a phone bank to help his campaign. (Such donations in kind figure in the legal limit on contributions, but in certain instances they may be counted at a lower proportion—50 percent, or even 5 percent—of their original value.) Moreover, RPAC spent $100,000 in 1980, and $189,000 in 1982, in behalf of friends or against opposing candidates; these independent expenditures are not limited by law.

Far from providing general, nonspecific support to people who are for the most part in line with RPAC's philosophy—or who support its broader interest (say, in private enterprise)—RPAC requires a candidate being considered for support to complete a seven-page questionnaire to determine both details of philosophy *and* positions on many issues of specific interest to the PAC. In addition, the candidate's voting record is examined with a fine-tooth comb. Regular "report cards" are issued on how closely the candidate toes the RPAC line. "The realtors aren't satisfied just with a candidate's position; they want him to work for their goals with some enthusiasm." Local realtors are encouraged to interview candidates and send their conclusions to RPAC headquarters.

From a candidate, Thomas E. Cronin:

> Some PACs want you to fill out a questionnaire and sign a statement; others may do it orally. They want to know where you stand on pending legislation that affects them and what your views and political philosophy are. The statements are intended to assure themselves and their members that you are going to be with them on most issues considered crucial to them.

All this may sound like routine politics until one recalls that the decisions at stake are not for whom to vote, but to whom to pay. All these realtors have already cast their votes as citizens and, if they wish, can contribute money as individuals. Now they seek to make sure, by using their aggregated economic power, that the campaign chests of candidates who do their work "with some enthusiasm" will be well filled. This is not a democracy at work, but shades of plutocracy.

"Money Does Not Guarantee"

To state that aggregated, focused funds play a significant and rising role in the nation's capital is not to deny that other lobbying mechanisms are also at work, or to imply that the electorate at large has no influence. And interest groups use other means than cash. They provide members of Congress (or their staffs) with biased information, "socialize" (wine and dine and butter them up), promise jobs in their districts, hire them if they lose the election. But in the end, the only plausible reason lobbies add top dollars on top of all this is that money delivers lawmakers' support on specific acts, and if PACs were to rely on other means alone, the final outcome would not be satisfactory to them.

A *Wall Street Journal* series on lobbying described the role of campaign contributions compared with other factors in obtaining legislative results:

> Money, specifically campaign contributions, is the fuel that generates much of this lobbying prowess. "I won't even take a client now unless he's willing to set up a political-action committee and participate in the [campaign-donations] process," Robert McCandless, a lobbyist, says. Although Mr. Boggs [an influential lobbyist] and some others won't go that far publicly, a major asset clearly is their ability to funnel funds to politicians from clients and friends.

Not all members of Congress are involved. A few take no PAC money. Senator Lawton Chiles will accept contributions only from PACs affiliated with businesses in his home state, and only up to $100. He applies the same restrictions to individual contributions to his campaign. Representative Barber Conable, Jr., refuses PAC campaign contributions of more than $50. Representative Jack F. Kemp accepts PAC money only from groups which have no business before the committees on which he serves.

Some politicians get money from so many sides at once that they are hardly dependent on any one. For example, Dan Rostenkowski is in a pivotal position in so many ways that he may well not be beholden to any one interest. One fund-raising party alone raised over $160,000 for his 1982 campaign, despite the probability that he would run unopposed. However, most members of Congress are more likely to be in a position to serve only a few interests, especially those that are affected by their particular committee or subcommittee, so they are not so much in a position to take their money and run.

It may be asked: Are you saying our lawmakers have no views of their own to which they are committed, on which they are not for sale? They do, but usually concerning only a few issues, whereas they cast literally hundreds of votes each year. A member of Congress may feel strongly about abortion, the death penalty, and clean air, and vote his or her beliefs on these issues. But on many scores of other questions that are usually not matters of conviction—how much commodity traders are charged by the government for a regulatory service it provides them; an amendment to prohibit the executive branch from studying public utilities' prices; an import ban on Mexican grapes that compete with a California grape; a doubling of the funds being authorized to close out an old weapons project; or any of countless other matters to which public attention is limited but which are of great interest to a select few—on such questions most members of Congress are quite open to deals.

In short, when one considers the words of those who lobby and those who are being lobbied, speaking both privately and for the record, there can be little doubt about how those in office are reached. Routinely, private interests get members of Congress to heed them on specific votes, in exchange for campaign contributions (and fees), while observing the law technically.

At one point, as I worked on this book, it occurred to me that I should use various personal contacts I have developed over the years to find some lobbyists or PAC-men to tell me about incidents of *quid pro quo,* of some elected representative's having explicitly agreed to deliver a piece of legislation in return for a campaign contribution. I then realized that my time would be wasted. Even if I had the signed confessions of several scores of lobbyists or members of Congress, nothing of significance would be proved. There is no need to look for a smoking gun. Indeed, it would deflect attention from the main point. The point is that implicit *quid pro quos* work about as well as explicit ones. And few doubt that these are common.

THE EFFECTS

What are the cumulative effects of the "retail" efforts of the PACed interest groups? What do they add to the biases that the "wholesale" approach introduces into the election of representatives? The cumulative effects of the retail approach are mainly of two kinds: psychological, in the sense of affecting the "political culture" (the tone, quality, and ways of politics), and "real."

A Sordid Climate
A highly unwholesome political climate is fostered, one in which members of Congress, especially representatives, constantly need to get PACs to pay their debts from the last election and to gain their underwriting in preparation for the next one. Observes Elizabeth Drew: "The ability of even the best of the legislators to focus on broad questions . . . has been seriously impaired. The race for money on Capitol Hill has turned into what one House member has described as 'a fever.' " She goes on to cite a lobbyist: "I think we're reaching

the point where legislators make decisions only after thinking about what this means in terms of the money that will come to them or go to their opponents."

Conservative former Senator S. I. Hayakawa called PAC money "a huge, masked bribe." The National Asphalt Pavement Association decided, after six years of PACing, to get out of the business, because the climate fostered by PACs "threatens the very future of our government." Senator Thomas Eagleton has stated:

> The current system of financing congressional elections is a national scandal. . . . It virtually forces members of Congress to go around hat in hand, begging for money from Washington-based special interest, political-action committees whose sole purpose for existing is to seek a quid pro quo. We see the degrading spectacle of elected representatives completing detailed questionnaires on their positions on special interest issues, knowing that the monetary reward of PAC support depends on the correct answers.

When people smoke marijuana in the open you know that the laws not only are occasionally violated, but actually are failing. Hence the significance of the following observation as to how far the PACed atmosphere has been corrupted: " 'There has been too much discussion around here about how what we do in the House and on our committees is going to affect our ability to raise money,' said Rep. James M. Shannon (D-Mass.). 'I mean, people aren't embarrassed about saying this anymore.' "

You must be a "hero" not to take money. Senator Larry Pressler said that FBI officials complimented him for refusing a bribe. Pressler said an acquaintance had invited him to meet in a Washington home with a group of men representing Arab businessmen. The men asked Pressler if he could help the businessmen get into the United States, and Pressler mentioned use of a private bill. The men then mentioned their interest in donating money to his campaign. At that point, Pressler said, he stormed out of the meeting. "I turned down an illegal contribution," he added. "Where have we come to if that's considered heroic?" Sadly, I must report, heroes are rare in Congress, and those who are quick to tout themselves would be better off silent. I saw Pressler's Abscam tape in the FBI headquarters. He did not storm out of the meeting any more than you "storm" out of a dinner party after you have finished dessert and bidden farewell to your host.

Soliciting and Intimidating

If there is such a thing as gradations of depravity, actively soliciting sin is surely a cut below yielding to temptation. That is one reason the nation was shocked to learn that Nixon's aides were actively soliciting corporations to contribute to his re-election campaign in exchange for White House favors. In the PACed world of Washington, D.C., scores of lawmakers actively solicit PACs to contribute to their campaign chests, touting in the process what they have done for the special interests. More than five hundred such requests were received by one small trade-association PAC alone over a three-month period. An analysis of these letters by a hardened observer of the Washington scene, Albert R. Hunt of *The Wall Street Journal,* led him to the following note: "What emerges are some shameless campaign solicitations, underscoring the need of politicians of both parties to rely more and more on special-interest money. All this is legal, but it involves a lot of pandering, hyperbole and even outright misrepresentations." The manager of the PAC that provided the unsavory sample of letters added: "It's all kind of obscene."

When some reform-minded representatives introduced a bill, in 1983, that would have slowed down PACs, the Congressional Black Caucus PAC rushed out a solicitation letter. Its executive director, David Greene, asked the PAC directors for "a strong letter of support for the continued existence of PACs as we now know them"—and "a donation of $5000 as soon as possible."

Intimidation is another result of PAC power. Its most genteel form is discouraging unPACed people from running for office. This came up in conversation with Senator Ernest F. Hollings and Representative Berkley Bedell early in 1983, when Representative Albert Gore, Jr., was said to be planning to run for the Senate. There seemed to be no serious opponents on the horizon, I was told. Still, both legislators agreed, Gore needed to raise about $2 million to cover his campaign expenditures and "to scare off any potential challenger." Such efforts tend to keep those who are not well heeled—those who are not PACable or not well PACed, and those who are unwilling to wheel and deal with PACs—from running. In short, they keep out potential representatives of the more vulnerable members of society—or people of integrity.

Equally serious is the fear of PACs. I worked with Representative Les Aspin when I chaired a task force set up to explore social policy (part of the New Framework Group which Aspin and Daniel Yankelovich formed to promote new basic ideas on public affairs). I found him to be one of the brightest and most conscientious representatives I have had the privilege to know. One day I asked him why he did not speak up more often against special interests. He reflected for a moment and then repeated a refrain I have often heard in the halls of Congress: "The PACs have a long memory. The public does not."

PAC managers themselves point to their long memories. "We did nothing for Barry Goldwater" in 1980, said George Meade, vice president of government relations for the American Trucking Association, "because we had problems with him in committee. Lowell Weicker's asked us to fund raise, and we've given him an emphatic 'no.' "

The champion PAC-money raiser in 1980 was Charles Grassley, Republican of Iowa, who raised $722,000 from PACs in his effort to defeat the incumbent senator, John Culver. Grassley won. Liberals, faced with such force, explain that they must be cautious on issues that are heavily PACed the other way, speaking out *at most,* one liberal explained to me, on a single issue at a time.

But more than atmosphere or public climate is polluted by PACs. They have quite real consequences.

A LIST OF CONSEQUENCES

1) Numerous bills that the clear majority of the public favors are not passed. For instance, gun control.

2) Numerous bills not in the public interest are passed, such as continued large subsidies for dairy farmers. (The question of how one defines the public interest is discussed later.)

3) Bills are passed that have been modified or diluted in line with PAC preferences. (Susan J. and Martin Tolchin's new book, *Dismantling America,* provides ample examples of how bills are gutted when it comes to writing or implementing regulations, often in a collaboration between a special interest and a supportive White House.) Some have been repealed altogether. For example, in 1983 the banking lobby obtained the repeal of a requirement to withhold tax on dividends and interest.

4) When many PACed interest groups lock horns over the same bill, the government is often stalemated. Such a stalemate has been the

fate of bills seeking to regulate the flow of immigration to the United States for fifteen years, and was one reason many of Carter's legislative initiatives went exactly nowhere. Carter was reluctant to deal with a PACed Congress and did not know how. A recent case in point is the attempt by the Reagan administration to fashion a bill to deregulate natural gas. It ran into a "zoo" of interest groups, each with its own agenda, including producers of "old" gas and new gas; divergent pipeline interests; conflicting gas distributors; and divergent consumer groups (industries versus the Citizen/Labor Energy Coalition).

5) When the PACed interest groups engage in what the director of the Office of Management and Budget, David Stockman, aptly called a bidding war, the interest groups play off the two main political parties against each other, neutralizing them. And they force the President to keep upping the ante to get out of a PACed Congress what the White House needs, such as the President's 1981 economic-recovery bill. (See the next chapter.)

6) PACed interest groups' pushing and pulling prevents the formulation and implementation of a coherent public policy in a given area. (See the discussion of national security in Chapter 6.).

7) PACed interest groups exact a cumulative cost on public policy until the cost becomes prohibitive. (See the discussion of the tax code on pp. 85–88.)

8) PACs seem to add a tool for agents of foreign powers and alien economic interests to influence the United States Congress. According to the law, a foreign country, corporation, or agent cannot make campaign contributions. But law firms representing Japanese and Korean trade associations and corporations make sizable contributions to "relevant" members of Congress, although it is not possible to show that these gifts are billed to their clients.

These effects together contribute to what has been referred to as the "ungovernability" of the United States. But not enough blame has been accorded to interest groups in most discussions of the phenomenon. Although other factors also make governing exceedingly difficult, interest groups are a major cause.

CHAPTER FIVE

THE SCOPE OF CORRUPTION:
Perverting Economic Policy

AT THE MARGIN—OR THE CORE?

"OK," one may say, "there is evidence of political corruption, here and there. But how encompassing is the effect? Is it eating away at the margin, or has it wormed its way into the core?" Before I answer this question, some brief observations about the question itself. From an ethical viewpoint, selling one's public office is an immoral act, striking at the heart of what this country stands for, whether one is acting alone or along with a crowd. One transgression does not excuse others.

From a pragmatic viewpoint, condoning isolated incidents opens the door for them to multiply and break out, and to become the *accepted* way of doing business. Public outrage and vigorous condemnation are sources of the antibodies that keep the society's defenses up against such infestations. One should not take lightly even isolated incidents.

Unfortunately, however, isolated incidents are not the problem. Recently, political corruption has spread way beyond such low levels. Indeed, it is my thesis that its cumulative effects are undermining both the ability of the system to function effectively and our sense of its legitimacy—that the country is governed fairly. To undermine these is to strike at the core. It is more than unethical and potentially threatening; it undercuts the country here and now.

In examining the cumulative effects of interest groups, I combine the effects of newly PACed interest groups with the previous—and continuing—work of old-fashioned, PACless interest groups. The effects are so intertwined that it is pedantic and unnecessary to ask exactly where one stops and the other rings in.

I examine first a particularly telling recent incident, in what is called in business-school classes a "case study." What a case. Then I turn to the U.S. tax code, which many agree is so worn out by interest groups that we had best forget about mending it and get ourselves instead a whole new code ("flat," or based on consumption, or some other code). This leads me to examine the role of interest groups in dulling the tools of economic policy, including the most recent rage, "industrial policy." Last but not least, I look at the role of interest groups in causing inflation.

REAGAN'S 1981 SUCCESS: LEADERSHIP OR PAYOFFS?

The historic context is important: after four years of the Carter administration, widely perceived as ineffectual, the President personally inept and unable to get his legislation through Congress, Ronald Reagan was elected by a landslide. He sent Congress his economic plan, the centerpiece of which was a reduction of government expenditures and of taxes, in line with the conservative, anti-big-government social philosophy and the supply-side economic theory on which he rode into power. Soon Reagan's program ran into trouble in Congress, especially in the House. Indeed, on the eve of the final votes on his 1981 budget and tax bills, it was not clear whether he would carry the day. When he did prevail, winning his budget cuts on June 26 and approval of his tax package on July 29, his success was attributed largely to his great skill as a communicator, in addition to his personal touch in relating to individual members of Congress.

A typical comment of the day was that of William P. Bundy, who had served previously in Washington both as assistant secretary of Defense and as assistant secretary of State: "The president has shown both a capacity to speak persuasively to the American people and a skill and organization in dealing with Congress that have not been seen in Washington since at least the days of John Kennedy or the Lyndon Johnson of 1964–65."

As the two critical congressional votes neared, the President had appealed to the people to support his program, making two major TV speeches, each of which had resulted in an avalanche of mail, telegrams, and phone calls to members of Congress in support of the President. In the press, on radio and TV, in the halls of Congress, it became common to call Reagan the "Great Communicator" or the "Great Persuader." "By now," cracked *Washington Post* editorial writer Mark Shields, "Ronald Reagan has been called a brilliant communicator a couple of million times."

While Reagan's communication skills played a key role in his 1981 victory, another element of the process was all but disregarded at the time, in practically all accounts of the forces in play: *The President was forced to make very major concessions—valued at scores of billions of dollars —to select interest groups. In effect, he had to buy their support.* They in turn helped swing enough Democrats to give Reagan's program a majority in the House, where the GOP had only a minority. For instance, despite the President's adamant opposition to government handouts, he reversed his position on sugar price supports on June 25, just days before the vote on the budget, to help win the votes of representatives of sugar-growing districts, especially in Louisiana. The cost to the public: roughly $2 billion a year.

Other such payoffs helped keep all the Republicans in line, a rather rare thing in congressional votes. Midwestern farmers had for years been keen to change estate laws. (Many sons and daughters of small farmers are said to have to sell the farms after their parents die, to pay the tax bill that results from rising land values.) These farmers had been denied in previous years, but not when Reagan needed to keep Midwestern Republicans in line.

A special tax concession to independent oil companies was initiated by some Democrats in the hope of winning the support of a group of Southern and Southwestern representatives for the Democratic alternative to the President's bill. They offered to extend the $1,000 tax credit, due to expire, that offset the windfall-profits tax for "small" gas and oil royalty holders. The White House, however, outmaneuvered the Democrats—by granting the oil companies a better deal. Reagan surprised everyone by raising the credit to $2,500. "There are half a dozen bills in to make the $1,000 credit permanent," said oil-industry lobbyist Harold Scroggins, "but that $2,500 credit, that's one thing I had never heard before." In a similar way, "All Savers" certificates were introduced to please the savings-and-loan industry and legislators close to it.

In addition, an especially well-heeled donor to election campaigns was served. Elizabeth Drew reports that the chairman of Warner Communications, Steven Ross, with a $20-million income from stock options in 1981, promoted more favorable tax treatment of such options. Whereas the Carter White House had turned him down, regarding as an outright bribe his reported threat to cease raising funds if not satisfied, he got favorable tax treatment in 1981. He was a large individual contributor to Democrats in Congress in 1981.

Although the concessions to interest groups cited so far can be traced more or less directly to a deal to secure a congressional vote, others can only be surmised to have taken place from the results. Compare the initial tax bill President Reagan sent Congress with the one his "media blitz" is said to have secured. Initially, the President asked for only two items: a 10-percent cut in individual tax rates for three years, and a major acceleration in the schedule by which a business can write off from taxes any new equipment, machinery, or plants it acquires. That bill itself was hardly free from interest-group influence: its details had been worked out in close consultation with a coalition of business groups. The main "onslaught," however, was to come later.

Over the months between the launching of the drive for the bill (February 1981) and its passage (July 1981), Congress added—and the administration endorsed—scores of specific concessions to scores of special interests, some widely based, some limited, some extremely narrow. A concession estimated to be worth $27 billion through fiscal 1986 was made by changing the leasing regulations so that, through complicated arrangements, corporations that had more tax breaks than they could use could "sell" them to companies able to use them. A provision specially tailored for AT&T, allowing a retroactive reclassification of telecommunications equipment, was valued at a revenue loss of $8.1 billion. For the benefit of utilities, an exclusion was made allowing stock dividends to be reinvested in utilities tax-free, at a cost of $1.6 billion, and an exclusion for oil and gas interests cost $11.7 billion. Changes in estate and gift taxes, including the one already mentioned, amounted to an estimated $15.3 billion. The "All Savers" certificate, of value only to upper-income taxpayers, promoted by savings-and-loan associations and seen as a bailout for their industry, cost $3.3 billion in lost revenue. Quite a few other concessions were inserted, for a total cost estimated at more than $177 billion in fiscal

years 1981 through 1986. President Reagan gave no indication that he
would veto or actively oppose any of these. On the contrary, he and
his advisers signaled support, including the proposed exemptions in
their own revisions of the bill, realizing that securing these concessions
to interest groups was necessary for passage of the bill.

Soon after the enactment of the 1981 tax bill, the whole Reagan
economic program ran into economic and political troubles. Experts
and politicians alike, members of Congress and officials in the White
House sought to modify the program—because the resulting deficits
were too large. While the depth of the recession and the steep increase
in defense spending also contributed to this problem, clearly, if the tax
bill had not included the $177 billion granted to various special inter-
ests, the deficits would have been substantially smaller, and the President would have been better able to "stay the course," to continue to
try to implement his program. Indeed, his first major reversal of policy
and course, the 1982 tax *increase* of $99 billion, was substantially
smaller than the total of the concessions to interest groups, and clearly
would not have been needed if those concessions had not been made.

Quite a few Americans came to feel that the Reagan program was
unfair, and many doubted its effectiveness as an economic cure-all:
"voodoo economics" was an early label that stuck. These are criticisms
based on what one sees as just, or on experts' views of how the
economy functions. However, whatever one's persuasion, one can
hardly wish a program to stand or fall because a pack of interest groups
have sunk their teeth into it.

The fate of Reagan's economic centerpiece is but a case study. It
is hardly trivial in its own right, since it affects the economic well-
being of a nation, and to some measure that of the world, for at least
four years. However, its significance is still larger: it illustrates the
wider problem. The basic tools of the nation's economic policy, it is
widely agreed by experts, have ceased to work properly, because so
many interest groups have left deeper and deeper marks on them.

INTEREST GROUPS UNDERMINE THE TAX CODE

More Holes Than Code

The effects of interest groups are not always readily visible, because
extensive, deliberate efforts are made to conceal them. That is not
surprising, as typically the efforts of interest groups are dedicated to

satisfying the few at the expense of the many. But there is one area in which the cumulative effects of special interests are highly visible —the tax code. The Federal Tax Code runs to more than one thousand tightly packed pages. The *Dictionary of 1040 Deductions for 1982* lists over eighteen hundred exclusions, exemptions, deductions, and credits. As a result, an estimated *half* of all personal income escapes federal income taxation.

Practically all of the loopholes represent concessions made to one interest group or another. The tax breaks for various categories of individuals (from veterans to U.S. citizens working overseas) in tax year 1984 are estimated to amount to $203.5 billion; those for investors, business owners, and farmers, an additional $35.6 billion; and for corporations, a further $67.9 billion. All breaks total $327.5 billion. This is 299 percent higher than the 1974 total of $82.0 billion, an increase in tax breaks much faster than that in the Consumer Price Index or in federal budget receipts (estimated, for the same period, to be 114 percent and 151 percent respectively).

Some of the tax breaks, such as tax credits for the elderly, deductions of charitable contributions, and deductions of homeowners' mortgage interest, apply to large segments of the population. However, *even most of these go very disproportionately to those who are better off,* since tax deductions and exemptions are of no value to most of the poor, who have little or no income and hence pay no taxes anyhow, and of limited value to those with low incomes. For each new dollar in deductions, the median family saves about 25 cents in taxes; higher-income families save nearly twice that much, making these deductions of great value to the well off and the rich.

In this context, it is not surprising that one prank worked so well. A rumor was circulated in the Senate early in 1983 that the Reagan administration was planning to impose a tax on toys, but that a lobbyist for Neiman-Marcus had gotten high-priced items ($150 plus) exempted. Senator Howard Baker found it believable. Senator John East spoke up against it, in strong terms.

According to Treasury Department estimates, of $156.6 billion in revenue lost through thirty-three loopholes in the 1982 tax law, $52.3 billion helped taxpayers with adjusted gross incomes of $50,000 or more. In other words, 33.4 percent of the benefits went to the top 4.4 percent of taxpayers. The provision most slanted toward upper-income taxpayers was the exemption of interest on state and local bonds; 94.1 percent of the estimated revenue loss of $4.6 billion went to that upper 4.4 percent of taxpayers. The lower tax rate on capital gains, excluding home sales, another of the provisions that most favored the well off, also accounted for one of the largest revenue losses, $13.2 billion. Of that amount, 63.5 percent benefited upper-income taxpayers.

Corporate taxes have almost ceased to exist. From providing 32.1 percent of federal revenues in 1952, they have declined to 6.6 percent in 1983. And the amounts collected are offset by refunds. While theoretically a corporation may be taxed 46 percent on its income, very few paid nearly that much, even before their effective tax rate was further reduced, cut, and slashed in 1982. A study by the congressional Joint Committee on Taxation established that in 1981 twenty of the nation's large commercial banks paid in total only 2.7 percent tax on domestic income, or $53 *million* on $1.9 *billion* income. There are industries that did even better: instead of paying taxes, the paper-and-wood-products industry and railroads received substantial refunds. As former Representative Charles Vanik, who served as a ranking member of the House Ways and Means Committee, put it: "If any of them [corporations] are paying taxes, it will develop that they are paying only on a temporary basis—they get it back in refunds."

Tax subsidies for intangible drilling costs granted oil companies estimated benefits of $2.9 billion in fiscal 1982; "percentage depletion" saved "independent" oil companies another $2.3 billion. Hog farmers (and a few others) are allowed to treat income from their sales as capital gains, rather than ordinary income, at an estimated tax saving of $1.1 billion a year.

So far we have discussed tax loopholes that favor large groups of individuals or whole industries. Quite a few favor only very narrow-based special interests. The 1982 tax bill contained an exemption from certain record-keeping requirements in the leasing of equipment that made it easier for American Motors Corporation to get $100 million in tax breaks on equipment for an Ohio plant. It backdated a provision of the leasing rules that applied to paper plants, and thus saved Scott Paper Company several millions of dollars. It extended certain deductions for hotel firms, a provision favorable to Marriott Corporation projects that had fallen behind schedule. A twist in new rules concerning the tax treatment of acquisitions benefited the Beatrice Foods

Company. It granted other special concessions to certain athletic clubs and veterans' groups. In 1982 alone, members of Congress introduced some 1,846 bills seeking tax deductions, credits, or exclusions.

The Secondary Effects of Tax Privileges

Tax privileges to private interests cause more than loss of revenue, diminution of resources available to the public realm, and, as a result, pressure to raise tax rates for those who do pay to bring in the needed revenues. They also put pressure on the private sector to make decisions that are irrational.

For instance, several tax breaks (including cash accounting, modes of accounting certain capital expenditures, and special estate-tax rules) were designed specifically to benefit farmers. In concert with other breaks, they distort most farming decisions, attracting outside investors and speculators and squeezing out small- and medium-size farmers. For decades farms have been used by many as primarily a tax shelter. Also, tax breaks induce farmers to sell cattle not when it makes marketing sense, but at a time when the proceeds qualify as long-term capital gains. Because building "confinement facilities" (particularly suited for raising hogs) is especially tax-attractive, farmers raise more hogs and fewer other crops than they would otherwise. And so on.

Since these tax benefits gain little for small farmers, who have little profit to be taxed, small farmers are in effect disadvantaged. The tax privileges accorded to bigger farmers (and outside investors) are one reason the family farm is being pushed to oblivion.

In the sixties and seventies, residential housing attracted more and more investment capital, while factory plants and equipment were often under-maintained and suffered from under-investment. As a result, the United States' ability to compete overseas was undercut. A major factor was that home ownership had become a very attractive tax shelter as a result of a whole slew of tax privileges.

Similar far-reaching, deep, "distorting" effects (preventing rational economic decision-making) can be seen in all sectors of the economy. Policies often attributed to big government are, on closer examination, often the secondary effects of privileges granted to some interest group. And, within each group, proportionately more of these privileges go to the more affluent members.

A Code beyond Repair

Economists have estimated that if there were no exemptions the "flat" tax rate could be as low as 19 percent and still yield the same revenue. It is widely agreed that a lower tax rate would have enormous economic benefits, since high tax rates are discouraging people from working hard, saving, and investing. Lower rates would also free up money locked into tax-shelter investments that make little sense for economic reasons. And the ingenuity and resources often dedicated to tax avoidance would be used to spur the economy.

Equally troubling is the eroding sense of legitimation. A tax code, even more than other government actions, rests inherently on the willing compliance of the millions affected. Forcing payment from millions of unwilling people would turn a country into a police state, filled with tax inspectors, frequent foreclosures, and jails. Willing compliance by most citizens rests, in turn, on a sense that taxes are fairly imposed and not excessive. This sense of fairness has been eroding in the United States in recent years, as special interests have gained more and more favorable exemptions, unavailable to most taxpayers.

Tax compliance is a serious problem, according to IRS studies. The "tax gap," the amount lost through noncompliance with tax laws, *tripled* between 1973 and 1981. Berdg Kenadjian, head of the IRS task force studying the problem, found that the "underground economy" may have been growing faster than the GNP since 1972. Roscoe L. Egger, Jr., commissioner of Internal Revenue, estimated in 1983 that over $300 billion in income goes unreported, and about $87 billion per year in taxes goes unpaid. A survey conducted in Oregon, a state seldom cited for its disregard for law and order, found that one out of four citizens admitted to having actually cheated on taxes. Cheating is believed to be even higher on state than on federal taxes.

The point of all this is that although it is true that interest groups have been with us "always," that they are "part of the system," their recent cumulative effects have done more than bend the system or damage it here or there; *they have made effective tax policy nearly impossible.* For decades, the response to loopholes was tax reform. But for every loophole closed (rather few) or narrowed (a few more), numerous new ones opened. As we have seen, the cost of loopholes is rising faster than budget receipts or inflation, making the code ever more leaky and unfair.

Since 1981 there has been a growing consensus that the U.S. tax code is beyond repair. Instead of vainly attempting to fix it, we should scrap it, and a new tax code, free from loopholes, such as a flat tax or a tax on consumption, should be instituted. However, the same interest groups that have riddled the tax code with overlapping holes, until it looks like an overused rifle target, those that have prevented effective tax reforms, have so far successfully blocked all attempts even to give serious consideration to shifting to a different tax system. To the extent that it is considered, the first item on the agenda should be a very strict review of all demands for exemptions in the new code. Those are already rising, just-in-case.

FROM CREDIT TO INDUSTRIAL POLICY

Credit Allocation

Similar damages caused by interest groups are evident in other main tools of economic policy, although the cumulative damage is not so visible elsewhere as in the tax code. One major tool of economic policy is the distribution of credit. Credit provides much of the capital necessary for industry, commerce, new technology, education, hospitals, housing, and numerous other activities. A significant portion of American public opinion and many economists hold that public allocation of credit is anathema to a free market, a highly damaging form of government intervention. Credit should be granted by lenders to borrowers according to economic logic, no other. Allocation of credit by national policy is considered to be an alien thing, done in Europe and Japan but inherently "un-American."

As a matter of fact, though, while in the United States there is no one central bank that allocates credit according to a national plan, credit is allocated daily in the public realm by scores of government agencies and congressional committees, each close to one or more interest groups. The total amount of credit thus allocated amounted to $73 billion in 1980, a sharp rise from the 1965–69 average of about $14 billion.

Credit is usually allocated not by providing it to some groups while denying it altogether to others, but by providing it to interest groups at more favorable terms, which are unavailable to other businesses, industries, and individuals. While typical small businesses in 1980 had to pay 18 percent or more for loans, when available, and large corporations had to pay the 15-percent prevailing prime rate, students were granted loans interest-free until graduation, then at 5- or 9-percent interest, depending on the program. Large-scale exporters could arrange credit on favorable terms through the Export-Import Bank; and sugar growers, shipbuilders, and many others could get loans guaranteed or subsidized in various ways through government programs.

It is not that the various recipients of special treatment are not "worthy" by one criterion or another. The problem is that the allocations are made not in line with a national set of priorities, or a national economic conception or policy, but in line with the relative clout of the private interests involved.

The Fate of TAA

In other areas of economic activity, interest-group pressure did not blunt major tools of economic policy, but shattered them, rendering them unusable. The history of Trade Adjustment Assistance (TAA) illustrates well how interest groups first weaken, then undermine, and finally in effect destroy a tool of economic policy. TAA was created in 1962 to help workers displaced by imports to readjust, thereby reducing humanitarian and political objections to unlimited imports and facilitating the adjustment of the American economy to shifting international market conditions. Assistance was to be in the form of benefits, supplementary to regular unemployment benefits, paid those who lost their jobs because of increased imports. In addition, workers displaced by imports were to be retrained for other jobs, in nonaffected industries. According to Brookings Institution scholar Charles S. Frank, the idea of Trade Adjustment Assistance is based on the premise that tariff reductions "presumed to be of net benefit to the nation as a whole should not impose disproportionate costs on certain segments of the population."

Initial qualifications in the program limited the number of participants. Those seeking aid had to prove that foreign competition related to a specific government trade concession was a major factor in their unemployment. Between 1962 and 1974, only thirty-five thousand workers qualified under this standard, at a small cost to the government. The qualifications were liberalized (partly in response to pressures from organized labor) in the 1974 Trade Act, which also authorized the President to cut tariffs up to 60 percent.

Under the 1974 provisions, workers had to demonstrate only that imports were "a substantial cause," rather than a major factor, in their loss of jobs. "Substantial cause" itself was defined in such a way that increased imports need not be the only or even the major cause for an affected industry's problems. Particularly detrimental was the elimination of the requirement that job losses be tied to specific trade concessions made by the government. This widened the scope of the program considerably, undermining its original function of cushioning workers against job losses caused by government actions.

In TAA's first year under the new standard, the program received a much higher volume of applications than previously, covering 347,727 workers. The number of participants doubled. The amount paid in cash benefits alone rose from $9 million in 1973 to $69.9 million in 1976, to $259 million in 1979. The recession of 1980 pushed the cost of the program up to $1.5 billion.

As the payments rose, others sought to be included in the program, and "copies" were enacted by Congress in other areas. The Redwood Parks Act of 1978, for example, "provided handsome cash, education and medical benefits to loggers who lost their jobs," benefits so generous, reported *The Washington Post,* that "loggers with seniority have been vying to be fired in order to enroll in the program."

Furthermore, by 1980 most of the aid was going not to workers in industries that were being reduced by imports, but to workers who were merely on temporary layoffs. A study by the General Accounting Office found that almost three-fourths of those who received TAA benefits went back to work at their old jobs. Thus the program served for the most part only to subsidize a higher level of unemployment benefits for some workers than for others. Very few took advantage of possible retraining benefits: only 3 percent of those qualified ever enrolled, and only 1.2 percent completed the training.

In fact, the effect of the program, as it was reshaped under special-interest pressure, produced the opposite result of what was originally intended. When a recruiter from General Dynamics tried to convince laid-off Youngstown, Ohio, steelworkers to move to a plant in the Northeast, they were reluctant to do so. They were receiving substantial benefits under TAA, while at the same time hoping that their plant would reopen. Thus, a program supposed to encourage adjustment of the labor force had actually reduced workers' mobility.

EDA Follows

The fate of the EDA has been quite similar. The mission of the Economic Development Administration was to help areas under significant economic distress by funding public-works programs, technical-assistance grants, business loans, and loan guarantees. The "distress" could be a result of economic misfortunes, such as a decline in an area's major industry, or of floods or other natural disasters that have had a disruptive effect on a region's economy. In 1965, when the program was started, 12 percent of Americans lived in areas that qualified. However, areas were rarely decertified even when conditions improved, and members of Congress pushed to have their districts included so that lucrative public-works projects could be directed to their areas. By 1979, most of the nation's population (84.5 percent) lived in areas deemed eligible for EDA programs.

At one point the Carter administration tried to reduce the areas qualified for EDA assistance so that only 61.9 percent of the population would remain eligible, but the effort failed in Congress. In 1982 the EDA sought to decertify a number of areas, including Beverly Hills, California, in an attempt to cope with the Reagan administration's budget cuts. But Congress blocked the move for review and decertification. As of March 1983, about 85 percent of the nation still qualifies. The end result has been to destroy the possibility of targeting EDA funds to areas in serious need of economic rehabilitation or redevelopment. A useful economic lever was bent until it became one more barrel of pork.

And—Industrial Policy

I have chosen to focus here on taxes and credit, but the same effects could be shown in other areas, from public training of workers (CETA) to export assistance (DISC), from deregulation (trucking) to farm subsidies. American economic policy has been permeated by interest groups to the point of being rendered ineffectual and alienating. There is, though, one area that deserves special attention, because there are some who believe that in it lies our economic salvation, and yet we cannot draw upon it—you guessed it—because of powerful interest groups. I refer to industrial policy.

The advocates of industrial policy include many of the most popular thinkers with whom the Democratic Party consults, such as

Robert Reich, Lester Thurow, and Felix Rohatyn, and several of its presidential candidates. Conservative Republican Senator William Roth, Jr., of Delaware favors a Cabinet-level Trade Department to formulate an industrial policy. Some business leaders, from Lee Iacocca (Chrysler) to Irving Shapiro (DuPont) also support a national industrial policy. There are different versions of industrial policy, but the essence of the idea is that the government ought to help American industries to compete more effectively overseas and to adjust more rapidly to changes in technology. The main way this is to be achieved is by helping high-tech industries, especially computers, robots, and bio-tech, develop. The government would also help to scale down and reconstruct the old basic industries of autos and steel, if not close them out, while "retraining" and transferring the workers to new jobs. Japan, West Germany, the United Kingdom, and France are cited as nations with successful industrial policies. One main reason opponents give for the impossibility of even considering using this economic policy in the United States, and one main reason proponents worry, is our vulnerable political system.

In March 1983, economist George Eads, former member of the White House Council of Economic Advisers, testified before a subcommittee of the House Banking Committee. At issue was the idea of creating a modern version of the Reconstruction Finance Corporation, a bank many consider a vital tool of industrial policy. Eads stated that although he agreed that market forces are not perfect, and that government action is needed to correct them, he still opposed the bank. He feared it would turn into a political football, with members of Congress and interest groups demanding aid for their constituents and disregarding that the goal of distributing aid should be to make the economy more competitive, productive, export-rich, technically innovative. Other experts who have examined the issue tend to concur.

In effect, very little is untouched by interest groups, even factors that have only an indirect effect on the economy, one step removed. Interest groups got Congress to prohibit any study that could "relate to" or "lead to" the possibility of changing the way federal power authorities, such as the Tennessee Valley Authority (TVA), charge for the power they provide; to prevent any modification or reform of the National Laboratories (such as Brookhaven and Los Alamos); and to authorize the inclusion of high-sugar cereals in the $1-billion nutrition program for poor women and children. American millers, bakers, and school-lunch administrators have lobbied Congress to reduce the 4 million tons of wheat the United States keeps for international famine relief. The National Association of Broadcasters has opposed Radio Marti, a government-sponsored radio station to beam U.S. messages to Cuba, out of fear that Castro will retaliate by jamming American commercial broadcasting. If you close your eyes and throw a dart at a map of U.S. economic activities, it will land on one distorted by the government, which in turn is driven by special interests.

INTEREST GROUPS AND INFLATION

There are varying economic theories as to what causes inflation, the nightmare of the U.S. economy in the seventies. Fear of runaway inflation pushed the country into "sado-masochistic recessions" (Walter Heller's term) four times between 1970 and 1982. One school of economists attributes inflation to excessive "printing of money" (more technically put, to excessive growth in money supply); another school, to high deficits; still another, to low productivity.

These economic theories are challenged by what, lacking a better term, I'll call socioeconomic theories. Several social scientists have pointed to the inherent vulnerability of the democratic form of government to inflation. Politicians, they argue, find it easier to yield to public demands for more government services than to reject them. And once inflation is launched, democratically elected representatives find it difficult to administer the painful medicine required to curb long-term inflation.

As I see it, while there is a fair measure of truth in these twin observations, blaming "the public" is far from wholly justified, since there was a public in periods during which inflation was much lower, for example, in the early sixties. And a public exists in democratic countries such as Switzerland, where inflation used to be quite low. Inflation gets out of hand because countries have become, not more democratic, but less. It rose following the explosion of interest groups —and the decline of countervailing forces—which left the lobbies in a position to pressure the polity to yield to their endless demands.

One proponent of this view is Nobel Prize–winning economist George Stigler, who suggests that "every industry or occupation that has enough political power to utilize the state will seek to control entry" into its field. Examples include not just doctors and airline companies, lawyers and truckers, but numerous other licensed businesses and occupations, from beauticians to dry cleaners, from broadcasters to funeral directors. All use their ability in effect to limit competition, thereby driving up prices.

Political scientist James Q. Wilson refutes Stigler, by pointing to occasions on which the government acted to increase competition—for example, by taking steps toward the partial deregulation of airlines and of the import of oil. However, these examples might be seen as exceptions to the rule—most occupations and businesses stay licensed *and* regulated—and as instances in which the "monopoly" costs were so high and visible that making some concessions to the public's demands for reform took precedence.

How the few hold up the nation of many—and thereby cause inflation—has been illustrated by Barry P. Bosworth, former director of the Council on Wage and Price Stability. After pointing out that an agricultural acreage set-aside (paying farmers not to plant) and trade restrictions for shoes and steel are inflationary, he elaborates how they work:

> Sugar, which is still an issue now, is my favorite example. The last time I counted, we had roughly 13,000 sugar producers, and there are 220 million sugar consumers. The issue is really over whether or not we ought to double the price of sugar. If you want a domestic sugar industry, we double the world market price. You say the outcome of that is pretty obvious: there are 220 million people on one side, 13,000 on the other.
>
> But it doesn't work that way. The 13,000 sugar producers are going to vote for or against a President or a Congressman or a Senator solely on the basis of how they vote on sugar. They could care less about SALT talks or the Panama Canal. On the other side, you have 220 million sugar consumers who will never know what hit them. They won't understand why prices went up, and even if they do, they don't care when it comes to the vote.

Bosworth then adds that a similar development took place in Congress. Senator Russell B. Long from Louisiana was interested in sugar, and much legislation had to go through his Finance Committee. So was former Senator Frank Church from Idaho, then chairman of the Foreign Relations Committee. "Things get tangled up. The President has to work with these people. But they say, 'You can't talk to me about four or five issues and knife me in the back on this other one.' "

Almost everybody is so familiar with farm subsidies that we tend to lose sight of their magnitude and significance. They have been in place for fifty years, and have grown greatly in recent years. In fiscal 1982 they amounted to $11.9 billion, and they were expected to rise to $15 billion in fiscal 1983. Aside from the direct cost to the taxpayers, the program keeps U.S. farm prices above world market prices.

There are numerous other ways, not reflected in these statements, by which interest groups make people pay more than a free market would require. Take one: a regulation promoted and protected by the milk lobby that imposes a prohibitive surcharge on reconstituted milk (made from milk powder), which is cheaper than fresh milk. According to 1980 estimates, using reconstituted milk could save consumers $399 million a year and reduce the government's annual stockpiling costs by another $230 million.

Labor unions use their organizational and bargaining power, including their ability to strike, not merely in the market place. They also use it in the political arena to lobby for such items as the Davis-Bacon Act, which inflates wage rates in the construction industry.

In 1980, while I was working as a senior adviser in the White House, inflation was running wild, at more than 13 percent a year, threatening the economy, social stability, and President Carter's re-election prospects. Among the forces fueling inflation were explosive commodity prices. Gold was selling at $850 and silver at $35 an ounce. Copper prices were hitting new highs. Aside from driving up the prices of all products that include these commodities, their very high prices fed inflationary psychology and became a symbol of runaway inflation. Among the measures I advocated at the time was the sale of silver from U.S. strategic stockpiles, controlled by the General Services Administration. The United States had stocked more silver than was indicated by any reasonable assessment of possible need.

I was told flat out that members of the congressional committees that oversee GSA are beholden to mining interests and would block any such move. Indeed, soon thereafter a bill was introduced to make the government *buy* more silver. One of the representatives sponsoring it was George Hansen of Idaho. His relations to silver interests have been recited already.

Big government may well be inflationary, but what inflates government is not merely the rise of social programs (the cause most likely to be cited by conservatives) or defense spending (liberals' favorite target), but also the use of public funds to pay for special favors to private interests. For example, from the area of water projects, courtesy of a report cited by William Ashworth:

> U.S. Steel's pushing winter navigation improvements on the St. Lawrence Seaway; E. I. Du Pont's seeking harbor improvements for its new plant in Gulfport, Mississippi; Westvaco Paper Company's supporting Gathright Dam in Virginia as a means of flushing their manufacturing wastes downstream into the Atlantic Ocean; "two oil rig manufacturing companies who want a quicker route to the Gulf of Mexico" planning the destruction of three bayous in Louisiana. . . . All these projects, of course, would be accomplished by federal agencies using federal funds for the primary benefit of a few monied private interests.

A major engine of American inflation is health costs, which for years have been rising more rapidly than other costs, thus exacerbating inflation in general. Hospital costs per patient day rose on the average about 16 percent a year through the seventies, while the Consumer Price Index rose on the average about 8 percent a year. Several factors propel health-cost inflation, top among them interest groups. One of the best accounts of interest groups' power is contained in a new study of American medicine by Paul Starr, a Harvard sociologist. He found that in earlier decades the AMA sought to keep doctors scarce and salaries high by lobbying for low enrollments in medical school and against federal aid to medical students. (At one point the AMA was indicted of violating the Sherman Antitrust Act by fighting the rise of more economical group-practices.) In recent years, the AMA has opposed most schemes that would have reduced health costs through the use of public-health nurses, prenatal care, and a score of other cost-control measures. In 1983, lobbyists for the hospital industry fought to continue to maintain a provision of the Medicare legislation which required the government to *secure* profit-making hospitals a return on equity that in 1982 averaged 19 percent of their investment. (It was above 15 percent in mid-1980 and almost 23 percent in late 1981.)

If such interest-group capacity to semi-administer prices were limited to a few items, it would not be of great consequence, but numerous items in the economy are managed to one extent or another. Labor costs amount to roughly two-thirds of all production costs, and are often set by multi-year contracts, negotiated by labor unions.

Utilities, from local telephone service to subways to electricity, are in effect regulated monopolies, affected by power politics, not governed by the market.

Free competition may be vital for a vigorous economy, but interest groups often pay lip service to it while limiting imports from overseas (beef, sugar, textiles, shoes, steel). Nor do they necessarily welcome domestic competition. A case in point is the soft-drink industry lobby, which pushed an exclusive distribution-franchise bill through Congress in 1980. This allows distributors to negotiate exclusive territorial contracts with individual soft-drink manufacturers—what amounts to a legalized monopoly. (*The New York Times* referred to it simply: "The soft drink deal was long ago bought and paid for with campaign contributions," as if each household was notified, with each purchase of a Coke, Pepsi, or Seven-Up, about how the legislation was PACed.) Soon the beer distributors lobbied for the same setup.

All these mechanisms directly inflate prices. In addition, they *indirectly* push up labor costs (by jacking up cost-of-living allowances) and government expenditures that are indexed to inflation, including very large military and civilian pensions and Social Security payments.

Economist William S. Peirce of Case Western Reserve University has discussed the "public choice" school, which has an increasing following in political science and in economics. This school, which studies the conditions under which individuals unite to form publicly active groups, suggests that taxpayers, welfare recipients, consumers, etc., are rarely able to form such groups. They are too numerous, their relationships too amorphous, and above all their incentive *per item* is too small. Just a few pennies more on a pound of sugar does not give rise to a consumer lobby. On the other hand, the producers and labor groups are smaller and more homogeneous, have a high stake, and hence can be mobilized more easily.

What Peirce and other followers of this approach overlook is that the masses of unorganized individuals resort to the public realm to protect them from interest groups' exploitation precisely because they cannot match interest groups' power in the market place, item by item, group by group. And they rely on public authority to preserve the conditions of competition, to cut down those that undermine it. Hence *economic* damage is inflicted (never mind the subversion of democracy) when interest groups capture the public realm.

Economist Mancur Olson, in his 1982 book, *The Rise and Decline of Nations,* draws a similar picture. He finds that interest groups, in mature industrial societies like ours, seek to control wages, fix prices, and protect their members from competition by limiting free trade. They also work to slow down the introduction of new technology, to hamper the flow of resources, and to win subsidies. As their political clout grows, overall economic efficiency diminishes, and economic growth slows. Finally, the interest groups focus on increasing their share of the take, not the total of what is to be had; they seek reallocation rather than growth.

Olson provides data to show that in countries where interest groups are stronger, such as the United States, economic growth is slower than in countries where they are weaker, such as Japan. And he shows that within the United States, regions where interest groups are stronger, such as New York City and the Northeast, do less well economically than those where they are weaker, such as the Southwest.

Olson finds interest groups at the root of a phenomenon that has puzzled economists: the combination of high inflation and high unemployment, stagflation. Presumably, if unemployment is high, workers will agree to work at lower wages; hence labor costs, and with them prices, will fall. However, Olson finds that pressure from interest groups prevents the sides from reaching "mutually advantageous bargains," as labor unions pressure their members not to lower their wages, and industries seek to protect their share of the market by forcing competition out (for instance, by limiting imports), rather than by lowering prices.

IN SUMMARY

There is room to debate *how much* control interest groups have over the market place and the tools of national economic policy-making, and which interest groups are most to blame. Some observers point to labor unions, social groups, and environmentalists; others to corporations, banks, and farmers; still others to long lists of small groups that hold society up for ransom, from fourteen thousand sugar farmers to a bunch of independent oil corporations, quick on the PAC trigger.

In toto, though, there can be little doubt that interest groups are a major cause of inflation and poor economic performance, and that they distort the nation's economic tools, from the way taxes are raised to the way credit is used, prices are set, and international trade is conducted. It is difficult to see how economic policy can be effectively fashioned and implemented until interest groups' power is curtailed. Meanwhile, more than the economy is undercut. The difficulties in forming a viable and fair economic policy are a major source of resentment, of alienation. This, in turn, undermines the work ethic, fouls the investment climate, and heightens distrust in the democratic form of government.

CHAPTER SIX

NATIONAL SECURITY:
Mangled by Interest Groups

SIX AREAS OF CORRUPTION

If there is an area in which one would expect the interest groups to restrain themselves, it is that of national security. Conversely, if this sector of public policy-making is found to be permeated by interest groups, one can hardly expect any other area to be immune. The evidence indicates that national security is mangled by special interests. These include major defense contractors (or industries with defense interests, such as aerospace), service associations (some of which mix retired service personnel with those on active duty, and with representatives of defense industries), thousands of smaller businesses and subcontractors, trade associations, labor unions, numerous local constituencies (in the areas in which defense generates jobs), and the armed services themselves, when they act as lobbies.

These various groups do not all pull together, working in cahoots with one another. There is no single, unified military-industrial complex which has captured the nation's public decision-making. Nor is private gain the only source of corrupting influence. Yet together, evidence shows, those interest groups have penetrated national-security decision-making to the point where independent or professional decision-making geared to national-security goals cannot prevail.

The undue role of private interests is evident in six major areas:

- A strong bias in favor of procurement of weapons, which contributes to a tendency to neglect the development of a security strategy and hinders efforts to ensure that the balance of various kinds of armed forces (infantry versus naval, for instance) will reflect a national strategy.
- The purchase of inferior weapons (weapons that fail to meet specifications, while superior ones are available), as well as the continued production of obsolete weapons.
- A bias in favor of costly ("big-ticket") items and complex technology over simpler, less costly items.
- A tendency to favor buying new items rather than properly maintaining those the military has already bought.
- A strong inclination to favor hardware over personnel, particularly dangerous in that it favors nuclear forces over conventional forces.
- An inflation of the total defense budget until it undercuts the economy, the social order, and its own effectiveness—and hence national security.

All these matters are surrounded by considerable controversy. For example, for each weapon a group of experts finds below specifications, there is a person or group who will champion it. Those who call for less reliance on technology are confronted by those who find high technology most effective, and so on. It is not my purpose to settle these arguments, but to show that they take place in a forum so invaded by special interests that it is difficult, if not impossible, to explore the issues and reach decisions on their merits.

Although the impact of special interests is quite evident, we shall see that the specific profile of private power is different in national security from that in other areas. True, PACs have been set up by defense industries just as by others, and are as busy in defense as elsewhere. However, because the older, pre-PAC forms of lobbying are particularly powerful in this area, PACs are an addition to the unwholesome brew, not the main ingredient. U.S. security has been hostage to special interests long before the age of PACs, and PACs largely serve to cement existing favored positions, forge additional links between defense manufacturers and members of Congress, and increase the awesome power of big defense corporations over smaller ones.

INTRODUCING THE MAIN INTERESTS

Before I report on the effects of special interests on the various facets of our defense, let me line them up, for brief inspection.

The *defense industry* is a rather concentrated business. While there are twenty-five thousand prime defense contractors, only thirty-three of these account for over half of the prime contracts. The largest defense contractors include General Dynamics ($3.5 billion from the Department of Defense [DOD] in 1980); McDonnell Douglas ($3.25 billion); Hughes Aircraft ($1.8 billion); Grumman ($1.3 billion); and Northrop ($1.2 billion).

The largest PACs in the defense area have been set up by the largest DOD contract recipients, and by some runners-up. Together, the PACs of the ten largest contractors shelled out more than $1.5 million to federal candidates in the 1982 election. These include the PACs of United Technologies, which gave $211,025; Lockheed, $183,330; General Dynamics, $176,990; Rockwell International, $175,233; General Electric, $149,125; McDonnell Douglas, $136,675; Hughes Aircraft, $136,265; Boeing, $128,400; Martin Marietta, $131,500; and Raytheon, $115,479.

True to form, defense PACs concentrated their dollars where they would count most. For instance, in 1982 McDonnell Douglas and Lockheed PACs favored with their dollar endorsement thirty-six of the thirty-nine members of the House Armed Services Committee who were running for re-election, and all fourteen of the members of the Subcommittee on Procurement. PACs of Rockwell International, Raytheon, and Hughes Aircraft contributed handsomely to all ten of the members of the House Subcommittee on Defense Appropriations. The chairmen of the appropriate committees, Representative J. P. Addabbo (House Armed Services Committee) and Senator John Tower (Senate Armed Services Committee), did particularly well. These two names will come up again.

Typically, the argument is made that all defense PACs buy is access, not favor, as if special access were not a favor and as if that were all they paid for. Representative Norman D. Dicks of the House Subcommittee on Defense Appropriations claims: "You know who shows up at your fund-raiser. If people are helping you, you're certainly not going to turn them down if they want to come in and see you."

But others are either more blunt—or more carefree. "We actively support the candidacy of members who would further the interests of the McDonnell Douglas Corporation," said Thomas Gunn, head of McDonnell's Washington office.

Sometimes, it is reported, the White House gets involved. Professor William H. Lewis, director of George Washington University's Security Policy Studies program, was helping to set up the office of Under Secretary of State for Security Assistance during the transition from the Carter to the Reagan administration. He recalls receiving numerous phone calls from defense industry representatives concerned about their overseas programs. One was from a consultant to Northrop Industries, whose head, Thomas V. Jones, supported Reagan during the election. The consultant intoned: "The [new] President wants you to support the Northrop F-X." Lewis asked for written confirmation, which was not forthcoming. He further checked with the National Security Council staff. He was given the green light long before the new administration had a chance to review its defense policy and budget, let alone such important questions as which combat aircraft would be appropriate for sale to less-developed nations.

The *labor* defense parade is led by the International Association of Machinists and Aerospace Workers and the United Auto Workers. In other areas they may confront management or support liberal politicians. Here they tend to lobby closely with defense contractors. "We catch them [members of Congress] in crossfire," the head of an aircraft manufacturing corporation told me.

As might be expected, Gerry Whipple, representing the UAW in six Western states, is gung-ho on the B-1 and opposed to converting swords to plowshares.

> California has been built on food, defence and oil: you can't expect us to convert into industries for garbage disposal or cheap houses. There are some super-liberal congressmen with their heads in the clouds who dream of building houses instead of bombers: but workers can't have pride in making low-cost housing, when the low-income families just use them for putting garbage in the hall.

Because the amounts involved are staggering, because this is the only sector in which all the funds are public in source and hence subject to political decisions, and because all fifty states and most congressional districts are cut in in a big way—DOD money has been subject to logrolling and pork-barreling by members of Congress prodded by local interests since long before interest groups became PACed. The irrational way military bases are kept open to satisfy local political pressures is well known; it mirrors the considerations by which post offices used to be kept open.

A typical item in *The Wall Street Journal:*

Perhaps the most common congressionally imposed cost in the defense budget is the expense of operating bases that the generals no longer want but that senators and representatives won't allow to close. One example: Congress has explicitly barred the military from moving a maintenance unit from New Cumberland, Pa., to Corpus Christi, Texas. Pentagon officials believe the change would save millions, but Pennsylvania's representatives don't want to see the jobs move out.

This 1983 report continues:

Last year, as every year, Congress saddled the Pentagon with a long list of unrequested things to buy or build, plus others to avoid: The Army must buy milk and U.S. mined coal but mustn't recycle certain types of aluminum; an armory must be rebuilt in Buffalo, and a new parking apron built at a Michigan air base.

Senator J. Bennett Johnston, Jr., from Louisiana got the Senate Appropriations Committee in 1982 to split the army's purchasing of Multiple Launch Rocket Systems between the company the army wanted as sole supplier and companies in his district. The army estimated the additional cost at $93 to $105 million. Representative J. P. Addabbo demanded that the navy buy radar from a contractor near his district, Sperry Corporation. Waste: over $2 billion. Scores of other such incidents are on file and others can be traced practically daily.

Congressional Quarterly succeeded in quantifying some of the known items. It estimated that the House Armed Services Committee padded the 1983 defense budget by some $296 million—69 percent of which ended up in the districts represented by members of that committee.

When L. Mendel Rivers was chairman of the House Armed Services Committee, his district in Charleston, South Carolina, got itself a naval station, a shipyard, an air base, an army depot, a missile plant, and a mine-warfare center. Sixty percent of the industry in the district was reported to have become defense-based. A sign at a roadway in the district used to read, simply: "Rivers delivers." When Representative Carl Vinson became chairman of the same committee, he got so many defense projects for his Georgia district that an air-force general told him one day: "Sir, if you try to put one more base in Georgia, you will sink your state."

Although there are long lists of what has been pork-barreled each year, most items are not traceable, because

> In most instances, Congress's clubby rules make it difficult to pin down the individuals responsible. Deals are made in private; defense items are traded for favors elsewhere in the legislative agenda; and members push projects as favors for others, obscuring the true origins of an idea.

As a result, *"Congress votes itself [and the nation] regional or local defense programs instead of a national defense structure,"* stated Senator Barry Goldwater. When the cry in Congress was for lower defense spending in 1983, Senator John G. Tower asked his colleagues if any one of them was willing to accept a cut in defense spending in his own state. Senator Tower found very few takers. (Senator David H. Pryor of Arkansas would have done without nerve-gas production in his state.) More typical are coordinated drives by corporations, labor unions, and local community leaders in favor of their localities' share of the spoils. Thus, even Senator Alan Cranston from California, who has made peace his main presidential campaign issue, has been fighting for the B-1 bomber. The prime beneficiary of the $4-billion down payment involved, and the scores of billions to follow, is Rockwell International, headquartered in California. Lockheed got Atlanta's liberal Mayor Andrew Young to travel to Washington, D.C., to argue for the C-5B, production of which would bring eighty-five hundred new jobs to Georgia. These two will stand for hundreds of such accounts that can be listed.

When the President needs votes in Congress, defense expenditures are typically used as rewards. A recent example: "To win the votes of Long Island Congressmen last August [1982] for Reagan's tax increase, the White House promised to buy 20 more A-10s." The A-10 is built on Long Island.

Service associations are of and by civilians, but they act to promote the cause of one armed service or another. These include the Association of the U.S. Army, the Navy League, and the Air Force Association. Their membership runs into the hundred thousands of individuals. In the Army and Air Force associations, a high proportion are on active duty with their respective services. The service associations have corporate members, and these corporations pick up a sizable proportion of the associations' costs, including those of their annual dinners, "seminars," conventions, and so on. But a discussion of service associations' close links to defense industries will have to await an exploration of the details of lobbying.

And there are *trade associations,* groups of defense manufacturers such as the Aerospace Industries Association, the American Ordnance Association, and the National Security Industrial Association, among others.

The *armed services themselves* act as lobbies. Up to a point, their promotion of competing views of the nature of the Soviet danger, the kind of defenses the United States requires, and so on, is part of a wholesome and very American pluralistic way of deliberation and decision-making. But, we shall see, the armed services go much further, to absurd lengths, to advance *their own services,* adding to the cacophony of voices that render defense decision-making more a brawl of special interests than an orderly, rational process.

PROCUREMENT "DRIVES" OUT STRATEGY

In a world free of special interests, defense experts and duly appointed defense authorities might draft a defense strategy, within guidelines laid down by the President and the National Security Council. This strategy might then be reviewed by the White House and the appropriate congressional committees, leading to requests for modification, clarification, and adaptation. After several reiterations of this process, a thoroughly worked-out strategy would result. It, in turn, would serve as the basis for guiding the armed services as to which mix of personnel they were to recruit and train, and which weapon systems to develop and purchase.

Such a strategy would reflect the nation's position, as articulated by duly vested authorities, on such questions as: Would the United States initiate a nuclear war even if attacked only by conventional forces? Should the United States be able to fight on several fronts simultaneously if attacked only on one front by the U.S.S.R. (and thus able to choose the theater most propitious for our counterattack)?

Should the United States intervene in Third World countries in order to prevent Soviet takeover, even if indirect?

Once answers are formulated in that hypothetical world free of interest groups, "suitable" forces would then be tailored to the strategy. For instance, if we are not to be the first to start a nuclear war, and our most likely opponent, the U.S.S.R., has a large conventional force, we would need to be able to match that force (if not in numbers, then by a higher quality of personnel and of conventional weapons). If we plan a major Third World role, we might need sizable forward bases around the world and forces able to fight guerrillas, which would not be a high priority if we focus our efforts on countervailing the U.S.S.R. in Europe.

This is not, however, the way it is done. As incredible as it might seem, the fact is that the United States does not have an overall, worked-out military strategy. Louis J. Walinsky observed recently in the prestigious journal *Foreign Affairs* that "this country and its NATO allies have until now, incredibly, lacked a meaningful and coherent strategy of defense against the Soviet Union." Moreover, "military spending proposals have not clearly been related to specific threats to our national security or to a coherent defense strategy." He proceeds to cite a long list of defense experts who make the same point.

A position paper issued in 1983 by a Democratic think tank returns to a common criticism: "The United States lacks a coherent strategy for its military forces." It goes on to acknowledge that this "failing" of the Reagan administration is "not entirely its exclusive property."

In March 1983, six former members of various cabinets, of both parties, wrote jointly to President Reagan's National Security Adviser, William P. Clark, that they find U.S. defense outlays not linked to a strategy.

The record of the last decade suggests that to a large extent *procurement "drives" strategy, rather than serving it.* The Department of Defense repeatedly bought weapons systems because each was justified as a valuable technology, with little concern for an overall strategy and a mix of forces and weapons tailored to it. Interest groups are not the only reason the United States is weapons-happy and strategy-shy, but other factors need not concern us here; the role of interest groups is a sufficient threat in its own right. And they help push U.S. defense efforts away from strategic coherence.

Bill Keller, of the *Congressional Quarterly,* writes in an article entitled "In a Bull Market for Arms, Weapons Industry Lobbyists Push Products, Not Policy": "The arms lobby tends to avoid policy debates —such as the desirable size of defense spending overall or strategic arms limitations—but concentrates instead on marketing its own products."

A congressional expert on the research-and-development process attests: "Most of the defense programs are technology-driven rather than threat-driven." He adds: "It's more a matter of coming up with a new way of doing something and then working it in and adapting it to your warfare ideas."

Richard Sellers is a credible observer. He is the director of the Washington office of the American Security Council, a leading lobby for bigger defense budgets, with some twelve hundred corporate members. Not pacifistic or anti-industry, he says about the contractors: "They're so attuned to next week's allocation of government money they're not looking to the long-range national security interests of the country."

An extensive study of the influence of eight major aerospace firms' lobbying and campaign giving was sponsored by the Council on Economic Priorities, a liberal not-for-profit research group. Gordon Adams, the group's director of research on government relations, commented, "It is this network that makes it almost impossible to have a debate about alternative weapons systems, defense strategy or defense priorities."

Just as the tax code has special interests written into it—to the point where an overall tax concept is no longer visible—so our defense posture reflects the outcome of contractors' lobbying, service rivalry, and pork-barreling over C-5, B-1, F-18 production, rather than reasoned analysis of a no-first-strike posture, or a hardened second-strike one, or any other coherent posture.

It might be said that little harm is inflicted thus, that it does not much matter whether a weapons system is built by Boeing in Washington or Lockheed in California or McDonnell Douglas in Missouri. Indeed, there is a certain virtue in distributing weapons purchasing so as to keep in business several major corporations that specialize in defense. However, one should not disregard the fact that not all corporations and districts are equally adept at producing whatever weapons system is being lobbied and pork-barreled at the time, and that the nation would benefit from having a weapons provider selected by merit, not political clout.

The pressures by special interests exacerbate an American tendency to avoid strategy, a tendency that has other sources. Strategies are inherently difficult to formulate. After all, we deal with hypothetical futures, under circumstances no one has ever faced, which are quite difficult to conceptualize. And we have a deeply ingrained national tendency, deeply rooted in our pragmatic, empiricist tradition, to concern ourselves with details and not with the whole picture. However, interest groups feed into, and on, these ingrained tendencies.

BUYING INFERIOR AND OBSOLETE WEAPONS

Beyond the combination of a pro-procurement bias and neglect of strategy, interest-group pressures frequently result in the purchase of inappropriate weapons. That is, setting aside the question of how many and what general kind of weapons the U.S. defense requires, the decisions to buy *specific* weapons systems—a highly technical matter —are made under the undue pressure of special interests.

Senator William Proxmire of Wisconsin has pointed out that "the heaviest lobbying pressure—and the most potent with Congress—is to hold on to old weapons, keep old assembly lines rolling." Congress "primarily keeps things alive that ought to die" and increases production runs, according to Jacques S. Gansler, former deputy assistant Defense secretary for materials acquisition. " 'Canceling an established program is extraordinarily difficult,' said William A. Long, the Deputy Under Secretary of Defense for acquisition policy, adding that each weapon developed a constituency in Congress, in its armed service, and in industry." Reports *The Wall Street Journal:* "History shows that once big weapons programs get rolling—generating jobs and business contracts—they are politically almost impossible to stop."

A few examples will serve to illustrate the role of pork-barreling and of defense contractors in the procurement of inferior weapons and in the continued production of obsolete weapons. A light attack aircraft used by both the navy and the air force, the A-7, saw extensive action in Vietnam. By the late seventies, however, it was considered so badly out of date that a Pentagon official described it as a "flying dump truck." The Pentagon stopped requesting money for the plane years ago, but year after year funds were appropriated by Congress.

"It's [Senator] John Tower's project," explained an air-force officer, referring to the fact that General Dynamics builds the A-7 in Tower's home state of Texas. Despite the fact that the A-7 is "so out of date a lot just go into storage," Tower convinced the National Guard Association to "take his side and lobby for it."

It is often noted that defense contractors are successful in keeping an obsolete weapons system alive, and getting more orders for it than seems rational. To repeat: once a weapons system has emerged from the research-and-development system to a prototype stage, it has often acquired a "constituency" in industry and Congress which makes it very difficult to kill. Typically, *Forbes,* in an article concerned strictly with finding profitable stocks for its readers, recommends Rockwell, the producer of the B-1 bomber, with the following logic:

> The B-1 program has been a political football for many years, but the critical first-production unit was funded in the fiscal 1982 budget. Congressional appropriations on the fiscal 1983 budget should lock the B-1 program in place. Opposition is likely to become less effective thereafter. This is true for two reasons: the program's momentum and the broadening base of political support as the prospects of jobs in Ohio, California, Texas, New York, Oklahoma, and Washington become more tangible.

Services acting as lobbies and service-related lobbies come a close second to contractors in lobbying for weapons systems suitable to their continued existence, rather than merely to national needs. There are many reports about interservice rivalries that result in highly irrational decision-making.

I gained a sense of the intensity of these rivalries through a trivial incident. During an off-the-record national-security seminar in Washington, D.C., a civilian suggested that the command of the rapid-deployment force be changed. He asked about a particular theater command post: "Must the post have an *army* man?" (Missions and posts were tightly divided among the services at a famous post–World War II meeting at Key West. Since then the division is usually fiercely upheld, even when technology and circumstances require adjustments.) A Pentagon man shouted from the back of the room: "Does the Pope have to be Catholic?"

The services are repeatedly reported to act as if each of them is the only one entrusted with most if not all facets of U.S. military security. They fight one another with stories leaked to the press, self-serving information provided to the White House—and lobbying in Congress. At the least, their rivalry has resulted in enormous waste and overstocking of weapons. Harvard political scientist and hawk Samuel P. Huntington points out that conflicting services have continually developed similar weapons for the same mission. For instance, the army developed an intercontinental missile, Jupiter; the air force—Thor. Other examples include the army's Nike versus the navy's Talos; the army's Missile Master air defense control system versus the air force's SAGE.

It is reported that in Vietnam the impact of interservice rivalry was anything but trivial, costing many lives. The army could not provide close air cover, because it is not allowed to have "fixed-wing" aircraft that weigh more than 5,000 pounds—this military capability being reserved to the air force. To avoid an army incursion into air-force turf, an army field commander needing backup had to alert his HQ and so forth up the army chain of command; in turn, the message was relayed back down the air-force chain of command, until it reached the airplane circling above the field commander's head. To prevent direct communication, army and air force stuck to different frequencies. The resulting delays are reported to have caused numerous casualties.

For the same basic reasons, the army relied on helicopters, which it was permitted to buy because they do not have fixed wings, but lost many men because helicopters were more vulnerable to enemy fire than fighters. Even official estimates put the loss at forty-nine hundred helicopters. (There is no similar estimate of the number of lives lost when helicopters were shot down, or of the resulting defeats in various battles.) The lobbying pressures thus go beyond buying the wrong weapons; in combat, our soldiers are stuck with them, and our ability to win is undercut.

HIGH ON TECH, BUT
LOW ON PEOPLE AND MAINTENANCE

The connection between lobbying and procurement is easy to see. But many of the effects of defense lobbying are much more subtle and indirect, and noticeable more in accumulation than individually. Nor, I am the first to acknowledge, can these links readily be indicated. The evidence is largely circumstantial; a major national study of the problem is very much needed. But bear with me as I first detail what many observers consider irrational decision-making before I point to those who seem to profit from it.

The U.S. military is often reported to accord much higher priority to buying complex technology than to buying simpler items; to buying new weapons of any kind than to maintaining old ones; and to investing in weapons than to investing in personnel. These tendencies were flagged in a study by Ret. Captain George W. S. Kuhn for the archconservative Heritage Foundation. They were pointed out by the congressional Military Reform Caucus, an ideologically mixed group including liberal Senator Gary Hart; conservative Senator Sam Nunn; Representative Jack Edwards, Republican from Alabama; and other members of Congress specializing in military oversight. The same tendencies were reported by the General Accounting Office, the auditing agency of considerable independence and expert standing that was established by Congress. They were indicated, albeit more indirectly, by several in-house Pentagon studies and by outside observers, including James Fallows in his book *National Defense*. This is not a consensus of all interested in the process. The Pentagon and the defense contractors, as well as several independent experts, do not agree.

Since these various criticisms of U.S. defense have been made frequently—and responded to—I will just review them quickly. To reiterate: my task is not to establish whether or not the criticisms are correct, but to point out that the issues cannot be explored in a professional, independent, even sensible manner because of intense pressures by special interests.

How Much High Tech?

The military preoccupation with high tech is often discussed in terms of "quality versus quantity" of whatever the armed services are buying, be it anti-tank weapons or aircraft carriers. A bias is reported in favor of buying fewer items in order to be able to afford much more costly items which have more advanced capabilities. Critics point out that after a point, quantity makes up for quality, that it is more effective to have thousands of simple anti-tank weapons than a few score of very complex and "able" ones. They further maintain that high-tech items often malfunction, and that they require sophisticated soldiers, whereas many soldiers the United States is saddled with in the volunteer army are barely literate. Also, many of the professionals needed to maintain the equipment are hired away from the armed services by the private sector. (The military did better on both counts during the 1981–82 recession, but this advantage is expected to diminish quickly once better economic conditions prevail.)

The General Accounting Office concluded that military planners are mesmerized by high technology. Choice examples: The F-15 fighter plane is so dependent on sophisticated electronics that battlefield repairs require diagnostic computers, and these computers have numerous reliability problems of their own. To perform at all they must be kept air-conditioned. Electronic parts integral to the army's Cobra attack helicopter cause its anti-tank missile-firing system to fail on the average of once every hundred hours. The navy's MK86 weapons control system, at the heart of all the newest combat ships, has more than forty thousand parts and, during a period studied in 1979, was usable only 60 percent of the time.

A similar argument was made by John M. Collins, a retired army paratroop colonel and author of a major defense study, *U.S.-Soviet Military Balance.* He writes about the "seductiveness of high technology" that has led the United States to buy a wire-guided anti-tank weapon that works well only in open territory. It requires a soldier to stay in position until its slowly unwinding wire unfolds. And the ammunition costs so much that most U.S. teams would go into combat without ever having fired a live shot.

Pentagon analyst Franklin Spinney concluded his 1980 study of weapons systems with the statement: "Our strategy of pursuing ever increasing technical complexity and sophistication has made high-technology solutions and combat readiness mutually exclusive." This is reflected in a 90-percent *decrease* in tank production and a 95-percent drop in fighter-plane construction over thirty years (1950–80), which highlight the extremes of sacrificing quantity for hoped-for quality.

A panel of National Guard officers, in a report entitled *VISTA 1999,* points out that "the procurement of expensive, complex equipment to the exclusion of most other equipment has created a fundamental contradiction between what we have and what we need." The report laments the trend of buying the most complex weaponry available and argues, for example, in favor of developing an inexpensive tactical fighter to replace the A-10. (A-10s cost $10 to $12 million each; design studies indicate that a tactical plane of the kind needed would cost less than $3 million.)

The report states: "The national defense would be better served by providing the National Guard with lower cost weapons with proven 'here and now' effectiveness coupled with higher reliability, reduced maintenance problems, and procuring them in sufficient numbers to provide multiple battlefield coverage."

Captain Kuhn points out that the Department of Defense "has long committed most of its development resources and analysis to achieving the most complex battle tasks through technology. Tactics have been driven by technology and—to borrow a basketball analogy—hinge on low percentage mid- and full-court shots at the expense of less difficult and more effective lay-ups and twelve-footers." The results? Weapons with "markedly lower kill-rates in actual combat."

Sometimes high technology can produce a fair-size chuckle in what is otherwise a rather grim business. I owe to Curt Suplee the following account of a study of the DIVAD anti-aircraft cannon by Gregg Easterbrook:

> We're about to pay $5 billion for this mega-tech wingding festooned with multiple radars, laser range finders, infrared sights, firing computers and more computers to back up *those* computers. But, Easterbrook reports, the thing can't hit a maneuvering aircraft, won't work at night or in the rain, sends out a radar signal so strong that the enemy can pinpoint its position and aims less effectively than the human eye. And at a demonstration for top doggies last February, they switched on the electronic brain and "the gun immediately swung at full speed away from the target and toward the reviewing stand. . . . Brass flashed as the officers dove for cover. Then the gun slammed to a stop, but only because an interlock had been installed the night before to prevent it from pointing directly at the stands.

Not everyone agrees that the U.S. defense officials are obsessed with costly high tech. An air-force representative pointed out that while some high-technology systems have been poorly designed, "it is a myth that high technology is inherently less reliable." Others explain that high-technology items can do more. For instance, the navy's controversial F-18 Hornet doubles as both an interceptor and a strike-fighter, reducing the number of planes needed on a carrier. The success of American equipment adapted by the Israelis in the 1982 confrontation with Syrian forces armed with Soviet weapons (especially F-16 and F-15 fighters versus MIGs, and M-

60A1 tanks versus Soviet T-72 tanks) is often mentioned as favoring the high-technology items under the toughest of tests: actual battle conditions.

It should be noted that those who question the preoccupation with high technology do not call for an army of foot soldiers, equipped with hand-operated anti-tank weapons and shoulder-carried anti-aircraft weapons, *but for a change in the mix.* They do not call for a low-tech system but for a more balanced high-tech/low-tech mix of items.

I do not claim to be able to judge which technological mix is the right one for the defense of the United States, although I must admit that the argument for a somewhat "lower" mix seems plausible. My main point is that the question cannot be explored on its merits in the context of interest groups fighting by and large for high tech, using not only technical data and briefs but all the instruments of lobbying as well, PACing included. Before I spell out this unfortunate parallelism between the directions in which interest groups push and weapons technology is bending, I will point to some other irrationalities that have been reported in our defense posture.

Procurement Versus Personnel and Maintenance

During much of the seventies, the U.S. defense budget was being cut down on resources committed to people—salaries, training exercises, and maintenance of equipment it already has—to buy more and more hardware. The Reagan administration defense plans for the next years clearly accentuate these tendencies.

In 1982 the U.S. Army decided deliberately to stunt the growth of troops over the next five years to free funds for its biggest weapons-buying drive since World War II. The result is to be a force much smaller than the 870,000 called for by DOD plans. Critics have pointed out that the army is trying to introduce simultaneously fourteen major weapons, which it will find difficult to absorb appropriately. The same holds for the defense budget in general, as highlighted in the following chart. The proportion of the defense budget dedicated to personnel is projected to drop sharply over the future years, while that of procurement is expected to rise sharply. This is a pivotal fact to keep in mind for the discussion to follow on which parts of the defense budget are more profitable to outside interests.

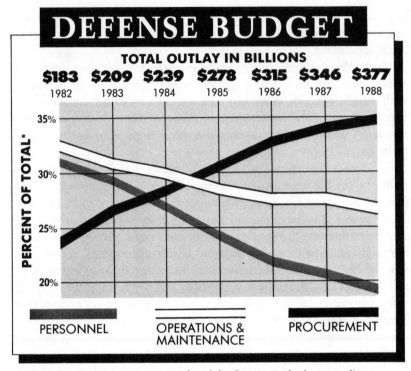

DEFENSE BUDGET

TOTAL OUTLAY IN BILLIONS

$183	$209	$239	$278	$315	$346	$377
1982	1983	1984	1985	1986	1987	1988

PERSONNEL   OPERATIONS & MAINTENANCE   PROCUREMENT

*Remaining percentage goes to research and development and other expenditures.

Captain Kuhn points out that the U.S. Army plans *(Army 90)* call for no increase in the number of divisions, a small increase in the size of each division (from seventeen or eighteen thousand men to twenty thousand or so), but much increase in the number of heavy artillery pieces per unit. Also, the use of a new tank is planned that will require twice the present daily fuel supplies. These changes, together with others that also favor hardware over people, will make the army, Kuhn argues, less maneuverable and more vulnerable to logistics snafus.

The Military Reform Caucus called for dedicating more resources "to attract and promote people who have the character, skill, and initiative to succeed in combat." This is compatible with the notion that it is impossible to match, gun by gun, tank by tank, the U.S.S.R.'s huge conventional capabilities in areas close to *its* borders, and that the United States will instead have to show more initiative, flexibility, and mobility, to use the advantage of the more individualistic entrepreneurial Americans versus the rigid, bureaucratic Russians. But to do this would require a greater investment in people.

In 1975, the U.S. Navy was ordered to send ships to the Gulf of Thailand when the *Mayaguez* was seized by Cambodian forces. But because of unmet maintenance needs, reports Representative Les Aspin, not a single ship could do so at full speed. Many air-force fighters were not "mission capable," and ground forces were short of spare parts, conventional ammunition, and training funds. The Carter administration began and the Reagan administration has accelerated efforts to correct these tendencies toward what General E. C. Meyer called a "hollow army." But two years into the Reagan administration, the old pressures for buying "big-ticket" weapons at the cost of maintenance reasserted themselves. One major reason is that corporations and services originally vastly underestimate the costs of a weapons system, and once it is being built, it must be paid for; the place to go for the additional funds, within a given budget, is the other items on that budget: maintenance and personnel.

Maintenance costs rise sharply with the complexity of the weapons system, yet the Department of Defense plans to increase complexity while reducing the funds available for maintenance. This is not entirely the result of outside pressure. In part it reflects a budgetary trap, sprung by the services. They secure funds for hardware now, on the assumption that such decisions are more difficult to reverse later, and that once the weapons systems are purchased, they will "justify" large maintenance expenditures. There is also a theory that maintenance can be simplified—for example, by replacing faulty parts rather than fixing them. But, we shall see, private interests accentuate this bias toward neglect of maintenance.

A misunderstanding to be avoided: suggesting that *proportionately* more and more funds are dedicated to weapons and fewer to personnel and maintenance is not to imply that the latter are not doing better under the accelerated defense buildup. So many new billions are being pumped into the Pentagon that even relatively neglected areas gain. Relatively speaking, however, personnel and maintenance are left behind the favored technology.

UNHAPPY COINCIDENCE DEPARTMENT

Decisions on which weapons system the Pentagon is to purchase, we have already seen, are not guided by a carefully worked out strategy, but are often compelled by technology. Most interest groups favor hardware, and, among the hardware items, high tech. The services, and the service associations that back them up, find status in commanding "the state of the art" and sophisticated gear, their motivation not much different from that of someone who buys a high-horsepower sports car loaded with extras—for simple urban transportation. Members of Congress can bring jobs to their districts if new money is spent on weapons production, but not if it is spent on increasing the number of soldiers, sailors, and aviators in the ranks. Corporations, especially the larger and more powerful ones, are driven by the profit motive to concentrate on high-tech and "big-ticket" items and largely to avoid "personnel," with maintenance ranking in between. *There is at least a close coincidence between where profit and other motivation for special interests push, and the directions our defense efforts are bent.*

This unhappy parallel is easiest to see between the interests of industries, labor unions, and congressional districts, and the push away from expenditures on personnel. Most of the personnel money goes simply to pay salaries and fringe benefits to the millions who staff the armed services. These include not merely the foot soldiers, but also the numerous (more highly salaried) professionals, from computer programmers to physicians, and of course the brass.

Next, there are items of service to the personnel, such as uniforms, boots, and parachutes. However, as a frustrated defense contractor explained to me, "These are not line items," and so "you can't get hold of them." On prodding, he explained that lobbying with Congress, which you have to do to get a share of whatever is being dished out, only works if the money has been set aside for the specific purpose. What you are peddling must be a separate item in the budget; if it is merely included in a larger category, Congress cannot directly channel money to you; the decision is left to the DOD staff, which is much less corruptible.

Many weapons systems used not to be mandated as "items," until Congress separated them out during the sixties. This was done partly because each one costs so much that it deserves separate legislative

review, but also because items can be pork-barreled more readily and
—more recently—PACed.

Reporting about a 1983 congressional proposal to cut out some
high-cost items such as an aircraft carrier and some F-18 fighter bombers, *The Wall Street Journal* adds that "Weinberger and defense contractors vow to resist strongly" such budget reallocation, as if the U.S.
secretary of defense—appointed by an elected president and accountable to Congress—and a bunch of corporations with obvious private
interests in the matter had about the same patriotic standing in strongly
resisting the Congress of the United States.

The profit preference for big-ticket items and high tech over the
"common-ticket" items, lower tech, and maintenance is less sharply
defined. "Money can be made in all of them and lobbying takes place
in all of them," explained the Washington vice president of an aircraft
manufacturer. Four points, though, stand out.

First, whoever captures research-and-development orders often
gains a disproportionate share of the rest of the defense budget. And
R & D is closely tied to high tech, and often, although much less
exclusively, to big-ticket items. To see this point it is useful to focus
on three large chunks of the defense budget: R & D, procurement, and
operations and maintenance (in fiscal 1983, $24, $90, and $70 billion,
respectively). While R & D is the smallest of the three and procurement the largest, R & D "drives" procurement. That is, often the
corporation that wins a major R & D contract also gains the orders
once the fighter, missile, or whatever it developed goes into production.

But that is not all. Within operations and maintenance, much of
the maintenance money goes to whoever has built the hardware in the
first place, because the same firms tend to manufacture (themselves or
via subcontractors) the spare parts. Hence, once a corporation wins the
R & D head, it typically carries away the production body and the
maintenance tail as well. And there is no other equally effective way
to participate in the multibillion-defense-dollar hunt.

Second, profits tend to be higher on items of which one can be
the sole provider—few of which are "common-ticket" items. If a
corporation can develop (via R & D) a new technology (say, a new
fighter for the navy), it can capture a "market share" and get itself a
cash machine that will generate regular orders for years. Jacques

Gansler found a "very large increase in program concentration that has taken place over the last few years." ("Program" here means construction of a weapons system.) The consequence, that very often "a contractor is either a winner or completely out of competition," results in what Gansler identifies as a severe form of oligopoly.

A 1961–62 Senate investigation established a pattern that has changed since only in details, not in essence. An investigative subcommittee chaired by John McClellan found that once a weapons-system producer had been selected, DOD tended to stay with it, however unreasonable the costs and profits. For instance, it was established that bills submitted by Douglas Aircraft that showed a profit of only 7.6 percent actually reflected a profit of 44.3 percent, or $45.5 million on less than $103 million. (Profits were parlayed upward by collecting mark-ups from DOD for the costs incurred—and profits obtained—by suppliers, subcontractors, and sub-subcontractors.)

In 1983 the Pentagon became unhappy with the work of Avco on the new M1 Abrams battle tank; it sought to break Avco's monopoly position, and get a second supplier for the M1 engine. Avco responded by trying to improve its work and by lobbying in Congress against allowing any competitive group to work on the tank. The House Armed Services Committee voted to *prohibit* the Pentagon from seeking a second source. While the Senate sought to encourage the army to seek a second source, the House prohibition prevailed in the end.

As these lines go to press, 60 percent or more of DOD contracts are awarded without competition (only one source is solicited in 40 percent of the contracts; another 20 percent follow noncompetitive negotiation). Also, DOD often provides part or all of the R & D funds, so the risks are relatively small compared with such an endeavor in the civilian market.

Although a corporation often does not make much money out of the R & D phase, it will tend to rake it in from the production runs to follow, and it will do even better if every few years it can add some marginal improvements, which are relatively inexpensive but render the previous runs obsolete. A Pentagon official suggests that the move from the A-7 Alpha to the A-7 Bravo and through the A-7 Echo are cases in point.

Third, if a corporation is the only producer of the particular weapons system, close cost accounting is very difficult. "We rape them [DOD accountants] each time," confides an aircraft producer.

Now contrast this high-tech work with the mass production of standard, common-ticket, low-tech items, such as bullets for the M-16 or regular hand grenades. Many other companies can bid against you. You may even face competition from overseas—and from the army's own foundries. (This can happen in high tech, too, but is less likely.) And cost accounting is much closer. True, if a corporation can produce large quantities of such an item, the *volume* of profit (as measured in dollars) might be large even when the profit margins (as measured by percentages) are small. (Colt Industries is said to be making "good money" on standard items.) However, in the high-tech business a corporation can have it both ways: have a relatively exclusive product with both a high rate of return "percentage-wise" and a large volume of dollars because the costs of such items run into billions.

Last but not least, there is the extra lobbying and PACing that big corporations, the majority in high-tech and big-ticket businesses, can more readily afford, which further helps to beat out smaller manufacturers, who are more likely to be in the production of lower-tech and common-ticket items—or may also be the less profitable subcontractors of the big ones. PACing is not at the root of the advantage of big corporations; it just further magnifies it.

Such advantage in the civilian market is commonplace. Banks will loan large corporations money at lower rates; cities will ply them with tax concessions, often not available to small businesses; and so on. However, in defense work big corporations command extra benefits.

First, they get breaks from DOD that they typically do not pass on to their thousands of subcontractors and that are not available to most small businesses. Jacques Gansler, who studied the defense industry extensively, has reported that in more than 85 percent of the instances in which the prime contractor had an advantageous cost-plus-fee contract with DOD, the prime contractor got the subcontractors to accept a less desirable fixed-price arrangement. The advantage is very hefty, since the risk of not recovering one's costs is largely eliminated for the "prime," but not for the "sub." If costs rise higher, the prime contractor gains further—in that the higher the costs, the higher the prime's fee (fees are typically calculated as a percentage of costs). However, under the same condition the subcontractor loses more, because his total take is fixed, and overruns are common. Also, reports Gansler, "primes" often have a clause in their contracts with the government to protect them against extraordinary inflation, but they do not provide such a clause to their "subs." And the DOD regulations are so numerous that small businesses have a hard time maintaining the necessary staff to comply.

A study by the Small Business Administration found that the Pentagon often edges out small businesses in the production of spare parts, granting the prime contractor of the weapons system at issue a virtual monopoly. One reason, congressional critics of DOD say, is "the cozy relationship that frequently binds manufacturers to military officials."

In addition, big corporations can lobby in ways that small businesses cannot. They can afford their own full-time lobbyists; an average Washington office runs to fifty people, although not all are lobbyists. And they have their own PACs. (An unpublished study by Gary J. Andres shows that the larger a corporation and the larger the share of the market it has succeeded in gaining, the more likely it is to have a PAC.) To supplement their own PACs, corporations participate in trade-association PACs and wield disproportionate influence in the lobbying conducted by service associations.

This influence is facilitated by a considerable degree of interlocking leadership. Many of the presidents of the Air Force Association have been from industry, for example. Peter J. Schenck, who was president from 1957 to 1959 and has been a director since 1955, was an executive of a succession of defense-related companies, including General Electric, Raytheon, and Mitre Corp. From 1954 to 1970, former Secretary of the Navy Dan Kimball was on the national advisory council of the Navy League; he was president of Aerojet General Corporation. Admiral Robert B. Carney was a director of the Navy League from 1957 to 1960 and has served on the advisory council since 1960; from 1956 to 1966 he was chairman of the board of directors of Bath Iron Works. And so it goes.

An aircraft manufacturer mused: "You cannot buy the guy [a Pentagon official] a $20 dinner, but you can buy a 'table' for $1,000 at a service-association dinner and request that he be seated next to you. Then you get his ear for 4–5 hours. And you can fly him to a resort where the association meets, ostensibly for him to brief you, 'to get information,' but in effect so you can lobby him." Corporate membership dues for some of the trade associations are considerable. In the early seventies, fifty-nine corporations each paid dues of $75,000 a year to one industry association, a feat most small businesses would find difficult to match.

The Pentagon's own auditors reported in 1983 that defense-industry executives serve on the Defense Science Board in violation of the laws prohibiting conflict-of-interest. The Board advises the Pentagon what future weapons to buy. The industry executives vote here on matters that directly benefit their corporations.

Most small businesses find it very difficult if not impossible to match such lobbying and contributing; and the few that have PACs of their own have puny ones. There are, of course, exceptions to any rule. One small defense contractor from Florida is reported to have parlayed a $500,000 defense contract into a $20-million one, because he knew whom "to pay and [where to] play." But political clout runs largely the other way. Reports one lobbyist retained by a smaller business: "Each time, I pointed out that small companies did not seem to be getting much chance to prove their ability, but this got me nowhere. Repeated intercession by some powerful member of the Armed Services Committee in either the House or the Senate was required to get a Pentagon contract for a small industrialist in his constituency, so strong is the grip Big Business has on the Pentagon."

In short, private interests, especially profit-makers, especially large corporations, have a vested interest in promoting hardware, costly big-ticket items, and, above all, high tech. They have next to no interest in personnel. This also happens to be the direction in which our whole defense effort is tilting. One would have greater confidence in decisions to play up high tech and neglect the troops and lower-tech items, if these decisions could be made in an environment free—or freer, at any rate—from pressure by parties with other interests than national security.

A PREDISPOSITION TO NUCLEAR WAR

The pressure in favor of weapons, especially high-tech and big-ticket items, and away from standard items and above all "personnel," tends to favor nuclear strike forces (many of the weapons are in effect delivery systems such as missiles, submarines, bombers) and to neglect conventional forces, both foot soldiers and professionals. *Interest groups thus lower the threshold at which the nuclear option would be considered in case of a major confrontation.*

In a typical decision, the House Armed Services Committee decided, in May 1983, to freeze the size of army, navy, air force, and marines at existing sizes, instead of adding the 37,300 troops the President had requested, "rather than eliminate expensive superweapons."

The shortage of conventional forces and the excessive reliance on nuclear ones was highlighted in a study conducted over eighteen months by twenty-seven highly regarded U.S. and West European defense specialists. Their findings are included in the 1983 Report of the European Security Study, and were fully endorsed by the Reagan administration.

A report prepared for the "expert group" on improvements in NATO's conventional defenses stated in 1982: "The 'conventional option,' defined as the capability to guarantee halting and repelling *conventional* Soviet aggression, has repeatedly been discussed in NATO. At the NATO summit in Lisbon in 1952, a proposal for the conventional defense of Europe was made. . . . None of the governments represented there, then and now, have seen themselves being in a position to gain the domestic support to pay the financial and political costs for such a force structure." When President Reagan sought to send some 5,000 U.S. troops to Central America for maneuvers and show of force, in the summer of 1983, the Pentagon—also recently committed to maintaining some small forces in Lebanon and Chad on top of the "regular" commitments in places such as South Korea and Germany—found its conventional forces stretched too thin. It requested a delay of the maneuvers. In 1983, the shortage of ammunition in U.S. warships was still such that ships coming off station overseas had to transfer some weapons to those going on station, according to Pentagon spokesman Henry E. Catto, Jr.

Assuming that a conventional force fully able to stop the U.S.S.R. is not available, what about relying first on conventional forces, to delay the nuclear flashpoint? The continued relative neglect of conventional forces has made conventional defense less likely to last even a few days, or hours. "The risk now exists that the imbalance in conventional forces would require the *early first* use of nuclear weapons to compensate for the deficiencies in conventional forces," concludes the NATO report.

This last bias is so ominous that it deserves closer attention. The U.S.S.R. and its allies have a definite advantage in conventional forces, although if one takes into account the United States and its allies, and the higher quality of the forces of the West, the Soviet edge is not so large as it is sometimes made out to be. The more the West builds up its conventional forces, the more it will be able to contain direct Soviet challenges—and certainly indirect ones via proxies—without resorting to nuclear weapons and raising the risk of an all-out nuclear war.

This is not a wholly speculative point. Twice, when the United States found the going rough in rather limited local Third World confrontations of conventional forces, the call to "nuke them" has arisen, even though the provocation was much smaller than that of a direct Soviet attack with conventional forces. When American military forces failed to free the hostages in Iran, there appeared on car bumpers across the United States the slogan "Nuke the Ayatollah" or "Nuke Iran." And when U.S. conventional forces were losing the war in Vietnam, some military experts advocated the use of tactical nuclear weapons. In short, as long as the superpowers resist nuclear disarmament, he who seeks to avoid, or at least delay, nuclear war must favor building up conventional forces relative to nuclear ones. This is the opposite of what the United States has tended to do, and among the reasons are that interest groups push for items associated with nuclear war and that corporations find little profit in conventional forces.

THE BALANCE BETWEEN NATIONAL DEFENSE AND THE PRIVATE ECONOMY

Finally, there is a cumulative effect of the various pressures by private interests that is resulting in a distortion, not within the U.S. defense posture but between it and other national needs. The issue is sometimes put in terms of "guns versus butter": the more resources defense absorbs, the fewer are left for the private economy. However, in recent years the competition for resources has been at least as keen *within* the federal budget. Here it has been more a question of guns versus food stamps. The Reagan administration has tried to cut social programs while increasing defense expenditures, whereas many a liberal would prefer to slow down the increase in defense spending and dedicate more resources to social programs.

If it were not for special interests, the issue would have been largely a matter of value judgment: how much one cares about the poor, sick, disabled, social justice, and social order, versus how much one fears a Soviet attack. There obviously is no "scientifically correct" number of billions of dollars for either defense *or* social programs. Figures such as "at least 7-percent growth in defense expenditure per year after inflation" tend to acquire a life of their own, as if 7 percent were enough, 5 percent too little, 9 percent too much by some demonstrable test. It is merely a question of what one believes; no one knows. Take the high mark. For a person who believes that the U.S.S.R. is preparing a nuclear strike as well as a series of conventional attacks, that it is an evil empire set on a "Pearl Harbor," no level of defense spending is "enough." Civil defense can be purchased at untold billions, along with space weapons, chemical-biological weapons, and so on. On the other hand, buying more MXs, B-1s, and so on is utterly ridiculous if one subscribes to the oft-repeated dictum of the peace movement that the United States and the U.S.S.R. each already possess enough power to blow the world to smithereens, or, as it is sometimes put, to kill every man, woman, and child several times over.

A political system can work out such value differences, although not necessarily easily. One can always be charged either with recklessly undermining U.S. defenses (if one opposes buying more weapons), or with recklessly risking nuclear war (if one opposes arms reduction). But such working out becomes exhaustingly difficult if it is attempted in the context of PACed interest groups and lobbies that represent arms manufacturers, trade associations, labor unions, in addition to "normal" pork-barreling and interservice rivalries, seeking more profits, jobs, and glory, all quite irrelevant to finding the "proper" level and kind of defense for the nation's security. As Senator Dale Bumpers, Democrat of Arkansas, says, "You can't have a sensible debate about how much is enough for defense when those PACs are contributing so much. The decisions aren't based on what the likely mission of the Pentagon is going to be." Under such multiple pressures, *the tendency is to work out the differences by upping the total,* adding on at least some of what each proponent promotes in the name of national defense. The result is a very great strain on the national economy, social order, and security, and on world peace.

President Eisenhower wrote some choice lines on the subject: "I patiently explain over and over again that American strength is a combination of its economic, moral and military force. If we demand too much in taxes in order to build planes and ships, we will tend to dry up the accumulations of capital that are necessary to provide jobs."

To reiterate, the situation is not all—or even mainly—the work of PACs. It is common knowledge that the various armed services act as unabashed interest groups. They lobby Congress for "their" weapons systems, often in coalition with some defense contractors, labor unions, and local leaders, as well as the service associations. True, the rivalry is not a complete detriment. The opposite system—a unified system with one central command—would invite the danger of locking into one wrong strategy or technology; our "wasteful" multi-service approach provides the United States with a margin of safety. However, practically every observer of our defense forces agrees that the United States has carried a good thing much too far. Nowhere is this more evident than at the top.

The Joint Chiefs of Staff, the highest military authority, is composed of representatives of the various armed services who continue to head their own services. They act as lobbyists for their services, not as people whose duty it is to serve the unified armed forces. Their strong tendency is to scratch one another's backs: I'll agree to support buying what your service wants if you endorse my buy-list, explained General David C. Jones, upon retiring from his job as chairman of the Joint Chiefs of Staff in 1982, to a private national-security seminar in Washington, D.C. The staff that backs up the Joint Chiefs of Staff is also service-bound. (If they become too JCS-oriented, they tend to be sidetracked when they return, as they must, to their services.) And data on weapons performance are service data. *It is hard to imagine a system better designed not to make wholes out of parts, and not to countervail strong tendencies to add on rather than coordinate and allocate.*

True, none of these distortions reflects only the pressure of special interests, PACed or otherwise. For instance, American fascination with technology, even gadgets, is not limited to the military. The private sector, too, tends to worry first about its hardware (machines) and only secondarily about its labor force. And our preoccupation with details versus the strategic whole has deep cultural and psychic roots, which are evident in our defense posture. But it is clear that the special interests exacerbate these tendencies, and that as a result, the Department of Defense and Congress find it difficult, if not impossible, to correct for them. Politicians are egged on to yield to their innate weaknesses, including the dangerous temptation to rely on nuclear weapons for our defense where conventional forces would serve. A stronger indictment of the influence of interest groups, PACed and otherwise, in public policy is difficult to conceive.

PART II

PRIVATE POWER VERSUS AMERICAN DEMOCRACY: The Lessons of History

CHAPTER SEVEN

THE OTHER SEPARATION OF POWERS

What is that bulwark of American democracy that evidence shows is being severely undercut? Why is it so pivotal? After all, other elements of the American democracy, from the secret ballot to freedom of the press, are basically intact. What is that *other* separation of powers that democracy requires, above and beyond the very familiar one? What lessons arise from our historical experience to guide our future?

THE PUBLIC/PRIVATE SEPARATION OF POWER

A democracy cannot be sustained unless the separation of public power from private power is maintained. Individuals, groups, and organizations that amass power in the private realm—economic, social, even moral— must not be allowed to control decisions made in the public realm, which is the province of the government, of duly elected representatives and those appointed by them. This prohibition holds for powerful individuals (the "super-rich"), corporations, labor unions, associations of many kinds (from the Mafia to the Chamber of Commerce), and wielders of religious or secular moral power (from the Catholic Church to Ralph Nader). It is not that those who command private power are not to be consulted, or not to "have an input." But lawmakers, the President, and judges must be free from *control* by private power; that is, their ability to render autonomous decisions must not be undercut by outside forces. When private power commands the means necessary for an official to be elected or re-elected, or to be effective in office, as we have seen is the case in the age of PACed interest groups, the loss of public autonomy cannot be far behind. Soon elected officials become obligated and, in varying measures, controlled by those to whom they are indebted.

In recent years much has been made of one side of the problem: the danger of those with public power, especially in the federal government, intervening, regulating—controlling—the private sector. The private sector, it has been repeated countless times, must be allowed to follow its own logic and rules. Accordingly, much has been made of the need to reduce the role of government, to contain the public realm.

At issue here is the other side of this essential separation of powers, of which we often lose sight amid preoccupations with big government and private-sector vulnerability: the dangers to democracy that result from the penetration of the public realm *by* private interests. The question has been raised as to whether there is such a thing as a distinct, separate public realm, or whether it is merely the meeting ground of various private forces. It suffices to say here that indeed there is a set of persons and institutions and, above all, loyalties and ethical obligations that are properly designated as "public." These involve matters affecting the whole, as distinct from the parts; the community, as distinct from the individual members; the shared past—and future— as distinct from the immediate desires of individuals or interest groups. How such public interests are identified is a subject to which I return below. But, for present discussion, there is little question, to anyone familiar with U.S. history, that Americans have traditionally had no difficulty in recognizing a public realm, or defending it from those who sought to capture it for their private uses.

For the public sector to discharge its duties and fulfill its responsibilities, it, too, must remain autonomous, free from outside subjugation and allowed to follow its inner rules and logic. Lawmakers must be able to follow the mandate given them by the electorate—undistorted by the policies of corporate board rooms, labor-union hiring halls, or the officers of the Moral Majority. Heads of federal agencies, those who administer public programs or implement laws, must heed the President and be accountable to Congress, not to private powers. Judges must be free to follow the law's tradition, and its evolution.

If not, government of, by, and for the people will become government by and for special interests. Not only do special interests make the government unrepresentative; they also make it impossible for the government to serve common, shared goals (such as national security), advance public interests (such as economic growth with little inflation or unemployment), and work out—as a fair arbitrator—compromises among private parties. Above all, the government will respond to the needs of the privileged few (those who command private power, the plutocrats), ignoring the many. Such unrepresentativeness and neglect of the nation's needs will lead, sooner or later, to demands that the government be *made* to work for the people, especially in a society in which the population is educated and informed and the means of communication and organization—of political action—are available.

If demands to enhance representativeness are not heeded, the populace will withdraw into bitter alienation, if not rebellion—as Americans did when British rule was unresponsive. Faced with the prospect of such uprisings, the power wielders are compelled to choose either to restore to the public realm a greater measure of citizen participation and equality of access and service, or to try to maintain their privileged status and power by brute force. In short, the preservation of democracy requires broad-based, open participation in the public realm, that is, *a measure of equality in the public realm that is not available to members of the society in the private realm.* This condition in effect defines democratic citizenship. It stands in direct contrast to extensions of private privilege to encompass public power. These extensions violate the implied social contract, which makes a people "accept" a considerable measure of social and economic inequality in exchange for participation as equals in the public domain.

The virtues of the constitutionally mandated separation of powers (*within* the public realm, among the three branches of government), is part of the litany of the virtues of American government. The "other" separation of powers—the protection of the public realm from private power—has been rather neglected in recent years. In the following discussion I'll show how the rise of democracy is associated historically with the rise of the separation of the public from the private realm, and how the tendencies of private concentrations of power to recapture the public realm cannot be overcome once and for all; they tend to recur—and must be countered again and again. At the beginning of this century, in the Progressive Era, we dedicated more than a decade and a half to such a drive; we are overdue now for a second Progressive Era, to restore the autonomy of the public realm, freeing it from concentration of private power. Though history may not repeat itself, and prior reforms cannot be exactly replayed, solutions to the problems that plague us now in this area are suggested by some eye-opening precedents.

OUT OF FEUDALISM: DEMOCRATIC CITIZENSHIP

The Unlocking of Statuses

The analysis of the central role of the separation of public from private power draws on the work of T. H. Marshall, a social scientist little known by the larger community but widely recognized within the social-science community. His study of the historical growth of democratic citizenship is as significant for modern democracy as Adam Smith's theory about the free market place is for the philosophy of *laissez-faire* economy.

Marshall's starting point is the European feudal society, in which no rule applied universally, equally to all. Individuals as a class had no inherent rights other than those the church claimed for them as God's children. In a typical feudal society, individuals were located within a hierarchy. They were either super-lords, sub-lords, or vassals of varying degree down the hierarchy to serfs. A lower-ranking person's actions were largely determined by his lord—or his lord's lord—drawing on what was traditional or embedded in local custom. Lords framed contracts specifying duties and rewards, which their subordinates could not refuse. There was, by and large, no alternative way to make a living. If life grew unbearable, a serf might flee to the feudal estate next door, but this was no more tolerated than similar escapes by black slaves in the American South before the Civil War. That is, *there was in general no separation of the private and public realms or powers;* one was either a lord—hence dominant in most matters—or a subject, across the board.

A villager could not leave his lord's land without the lord's consent, could not own land or any other personal property. A villager could not marry another lord's tenant. The lord could change arbitrarily the services and rents due him. A village could not bring a civil suit against the lord. In other words, a low-ranking person was powerless in all his life's positions or statuses: economic, social, political, and legal.

Marshall calls this phenomenon "status fusion" because a person's position in any one of life's hierarchies was "meshed" with similar statuses in the other hierarchies. If one was subjugated economically, one was sure to be equally subjugated in most if not all others. I'll call it *interlocked statuses* to emphasize the parallel to another fusion: the interlocking of directorates, which are nothing but high-level statuses fused together because they are held and controlled by one and the same set of persons.

Marshall found a gradual evolution over centuries from feudal, authoritarian regimes to the social foundations of modern democratic government. The means was *the separation of statuses,* which, in turn, made the separation of public and private realms possible. (Without this separation of statuses, the question of whether the private or the public realm is in control does not even arise.) With this evolution, one's position on one of life's ladders—say, economic—no longer dictated one's social, political, and spiritual standing. Instead of people's being inferior *or* superior in most if not all areas of life, they became equal first in one, then in another, while remaining unequal in still others. *Marshall's main historical finding is that this progress was not only slow, but also uneven.* People were not simultaneously granted the same rights and the same measure of equal status in matters political, economic, social, and spiritual. Marshall has traced the gains people made during this gradual process by dividing them into three historical phases: legal, political, and socioeconomic.* (Legal and political are public realms; social and economic are private.)

In analyzing British history, Marshall found that legal equality arose first, political equality later, and progress toward socioeconomic equality still later and more slowly. In other words, *constitutional democracy preceded social democracy.*

Legal rights, equality before the law, and due process had much

---

*Marshall uses different terms. He calls them "civil," "political," and "social." My "translation" aims to bring his terms closer to terms used elsewhere and throughout this volume.

Since my main concern here is with the separation of the public realm from the private one, differences between various kinds of private power—economic versus social, for instance—are not explored unless directly relevant to the point at hand. But this should not be taken to suggest that those who amass one kind of private power —say, economic—necessarily command a parallel amount of another—say, social.

progressed in England by the seventeenth century. One of the major breakthroughs came with the introduction of the legal notion that a person had the right to sell his labor to anyone, not just the lord of the village the person lived or was born in. Whatever significance this change had later for a modern economy, allowing free mobility of labor, the initial effect was one of enhanced legal rights, granting everyone the same right previously reserved for lords, to relocate freely.

In the next phase, the right to participate in political life, to vote and run for office, became more widely shared, more nearly an equal right. Prior to 1832, the right to vote in England was based on land ownership, which in itself was hereditary. The great Reform Act of 1832 extended the right to vote to "leaseholders and occupying tenants of sufficient economic substance," but this still included only about one-fifth of the adult male population. As Marshall puts it, the right to vote was still "the privilege of a limited economic class." But that class was extended by each of the successive Reform Acts, until finally the Act of 1918 shifted the basis of the right to participate in public life "from economic substance to personal status."

The point is that the tight link between socioeconomic and political status (like legal status previously) was severed: one no longer depended on the other. Whatever one's (private) socioeconomic position, one had, if not always in practice, at least an accepted claim to the same legal-political (public) rights. *Democratic citizenship,* in the sense of equal status in controlling and participating in the public realm, was thus created by the breaking of the feudal status lock, by status separation. Or, to put it differently, social and economic privilege no longer bought, or secured, or was considered a justified basis for superior public status.

Marshall thought that the next phase in continued progress was obvious: the next step in the historical march toward equality was going to take place within the socioeconomic area. Among the steps taken in this direction in England were the introduction of a *progressive* income tax designed to take more from those with a higher income and thus reduce the inequality of income; introduction of a tax on estates aimed at reducing the inequality resulting from the amassing of property and its accumulation over the generations, thus increasing the equality of wealth; and the introduction of various welfare programs, which amount to "transfer payments"—moving resources from those better off to those less well off, another step toward socioeconomic equality.

In recent years, it has turned out that the cumulative effect of all these and other such drives to reduce socioeconomic inequality has been rather limited. In the United Kingdom, for example, income distribution was not made significantly more equal. Attempts to push in this direction stifled, or were perceived to stifle, the economy and led to a conservative backlash and a demand for reduction of the pressure for socioeconomic equality, in the form of Thatcherism in Britain and the Reagan policies in the United States. This oft-discussed conservative backlash is not my concern here. My subject is the attempts by private groups to reverse the status separation, to make socioeconomic status and power again *the* basis of status in all realms, including political and legal, undermining the separation of public from private power, on which democracy hinges.

Significantly, the generations during which modern representative democracy has thrived, we shall see shortly, are those in which the interlocking of statuses was broken, in which a considerable measure of equality in public life was introduced while a considerable degree of inequality in the socioeconomic (private) realm persisted. In feudal society, Marshall emphasizes, there was "no principle of the equality of *citizens* to set against the principle of the inequality of *classes.*" Or, as sociologist S. M. Lipset puts it, "Modern industrial democratic society is historically unique in seeking to sustain a system of contradictory values." It is this essential separation that is now being endangered.

The Democratic Balancing Act

Social scientists, like Marshall, used to see history as a story of unfolding progress. People and institutions were expected not merely to change, but to improve. From the Dark Ages, in stages to be sure, rose democracy. Our age is sadder and may be wiser. We are no longer quite sure that history necessarily marches, as a good trooper, regularly in the right direction. On the contrary, it is my thesis that, in order to sustain the foundation of a free society, there needs to be a constant balancing act. There are always forces that push the public realm to penetrate the private sector, tending to tyranny, *and* there are forces that seek to allow private groups to dominate the public sector, leading, depending on the nature of these private elites, to a theocracy, an aristocracy, or a plutocracy. One may argue comparative evil, but all constitute a loss of balance. Historically, as I will discuss later, democracy is sustained as long as the excessive rise of either private or public power can be followed by a correcting force that restores the separation of these two powers, preventing one from dominating the other.

The following brief historical excursions illustrate both how the separation of the public and private realms was achieved early in the history of the United States as a democratic nation, and how that separation has since been challenged—and reclaimed. These illustrations will help our understanding of the new challenge we face now from private power.

I use the term "brief excursions" advisedly. The reader is familiar with the background, and all I seek is to point to some known vistas to give concreteness and substance to what might otherwise be rather abstract generalizations.

CHAPTER EIGHT

FROM PLUTOCRACY:
The Rise of American Democracy

The separation of the public and private realms essential for democracy was gradually gained in Colonial and especially in post-Revolutionary America. Progress took place on three levels still pertinent today: the right to vote (to determine who will command public power), the right to run for election (the avenue into public power positions), and the separation of public and private elites (determining whether those elected are drawn largely from the same circles that dominate the private sector). In recounting our history, I present no new historical findings; on the contrary, some rather familiar historical facts indicate the lessons the story of our origins provides for our future.

FIRST TIER: VOTING RIGHTS

Several early American colonies were more business enterprises than states or political entities. Here the "owners" of the companies were those who had the principal say in their management. After these companies ceased to exist and the colonies became political institutions, similar notions continued to prevail. As historian Kirk Porter puts it: "The underlying idea was that a man's property entitled him to vote —not his character, his nationality, beliefs, or residence, but his property." The ease with which this assumption was made was increased by the practice in England of restricting the right to vote to freeholders who owned land worth at least 40 shillings' rent a year, a standard that had been continuously in effect since 1430.

As the colonies grew and developed, the property standard remained in place, although varying rationales were offered for its existence. One was the argument that those who own the land should be the ones to rule it. Another was that those with land are the pillars of society and the state. As historian Chilton Williamson explains it, propertied persons have "a common interest in and a permanent attachment to society and the state."

Both arguments were woven together in a statement by the Maryland Upper House around the time of the Revolution: "The freeholders are the strength of this province not the freemen. It is their persons, purses and stocks [which] must bear the burden of government, and not the freemen who can easily abandon us."

Another argument often cited was that working people, because of their poverty and dependence, were "as vulnerable . . . to the blandishments and threats of their employers as were tenants to those of their landlords."

Immediately before the Revolution, more than half of the colonies still maintained an "uncompromising landed-property qualification." New Hampshire required property worth £50. Rhode Island required property worth £40 or with a rental value of 40 shillings a year. In some Southern colonies where land was cheap, the standard was expressed in acres, as in Georgia and North Carolina, which each required 50 acres. Especially in the Northeast, various provisions were enacted to enfranchise the wealthiest and most important of the urban merchants and businessmen.

Besides economic bases for public rights, there were also social ones. Rhode Island allowed the eldest son of a freeholder to vote. Southern colonies denied the vote to free blacks regardless of property holdings (as did Northern states later, when the number of free blacks became significant). In some colonies, Catholics and Jews were specifically barred from voting. The common thread of these provisions, writes Williamson, was that only "desirable elements of the population" could vote.

A common justification, to the extent that one was felt necessary, was that "free, white, twenty-one, native-born Protestant males who were the owners of property" were best suited to look after the "stability of the commonwealth." Thus, participation in the governance of the American colonies was differentiated on a socioeconomic basis; those with more power in the private realm had more public say. *That is, government was plutocratic.*

While clearly plutocratic, the American colonial governments were more democratic than that of England. A much higher proportion of the colonial population actually owned land, and it was much easier to gain land or property—that is, for a freeman to become a freeholder.

Two factors served to change the plutocratic rule. One was the surge of democratic thought that preceded the Revolution. Originally developed in the confrontation with English rule, the arguments for democratic principles that the plutocrats marshaled to argue for freedom for the colonies were turned inward on the plutocrats themselves. The second factor was the evolution of more industrial, urban centers, especially in the Northeast. From Boston to Philadelphia to Charleston, a class of shoemakers, smiths, and tradesmen saw themselves as responsible parties and were increasingly incensed that because they lacked land, they were denied a say in the country's public life. At the same time, settlers in the rural western regions were also agitating for more equitable representation.

For both philosophical consistency and political expediency, to win the support of the freemen in the battle for "freedom from the tyrants," compromises were made whereby anyone who paid taxes could vote. Depending on the level of taxation required, these amounted either to a less restrictive but still plutocratic system, or to *de facto* universal manhood suffrage, since in some colonies nearly everyone was taxed to some extent. The requirement sometimes could be fulfilled merely by paying a poll tax the day of the election. By the time of the Revolution, all the colonies continued to have property or taxation requirements, but the general tendency was toward easing these rules and allowing more and more of the population to vote.

Vermont was incorporated as a state in 1791 with universal manhood suffrage to those of "quiet and peaceable behavior," thus becoming the first state specifically to base the right to vote on status as a resident rather than on ownership of property or payment of taxes. Maryland, after bitter political in-fighting, allowed all free white adult males to vote in 1802. Maine was incorporated as a state with universal manhood suffrage in 1819. However, some states, such as Virginia and

Rhode Island, retained restrictive property requirements well into the nineteenth century.

New states on the western frontier were particularly democratic. Between 1815 and 1820, Indiana, Illinois, and Missouri were incorporated as states with universal manhood suffrage. The rigors of pioneer life agitated against class divisions.

Although a few states kept either a property standard or a tax requirement on the books well into the twentieth century, by about 1860 all states had universal suffrage for adult white males, either in law or in practice. To be sure, many battles to enfranchise Indians, women, immigrants, and blacks were yet to be fought, but the presumption that citizenship implied the right to vote had been established, and it was on this principle that those further battles would be based. The movement toward one-person–one-vote enfranchisement serves as an easy, albeit far from complete, measurement of the separation of the public and private realms. The closer we are to full enforcement of one vote for every person, the closer we are to status separation, because no matter whether one has much, some, little, or no socioeconomic (i.e., private) power, one still commands equal sway in public life.

The separation of the political (public) power of a voter from the socioeconomic (private) power of a member of society, and the increasing accessibility of that political power to all citizens, regardless of socioeconomic differences, is directly relevant to our current PAC problem. The PACs are based on the aggregation of individual contributions from members of a specific interest group (corporate, labor union, or whatever), often, we shall see, directly backed up by funds from corporate or other organizational treasuries. Individuals' ability to contribute, in turn, is directly determined by their income and wealth, their economic status. Thus, for commodity speculators, realtors, and bankers to contribute regularly—and increasingly—to be sure their votes will count is much less a sacrifice than for blue-collar workers, the unemployed, people on welfare, senior citizens, or others who are economically vulnerable. Essentially, the more an individual's ability to contribute political money to a group counts (and that group's ability to aggregate funds expands), the less an unsupplemented vote matters—the greater the violation of the separation of private and public status. As a result, the less well off are disenfranchised, partly or completely.

SECOND TIER: RUNNING FOR OFFICE

The separation of political from socioeconomic power has been examined so far from the viewpoint of the diminishing effectiveness of the voter. But there are other ways that private power can grab the public reins. One is to restrict who can run for election. During the Colonial Era in North Carolina, one needed at least twice as many acres to be eligible to hold office as one needed to vote. In New Hampshire one had to own real estate worth £300, six times the £50's worth voters needed. South Carolina's ratio was a richer 10 to 1. New Jersey also set a higher criterion for candidates than for voters: they must own £500 pounds in land and personal property, or 1,000 acres, ten times the level required of voters.

A rich person can represent the needs and views of a less well off person, but there is some question whether most persons of a radically different economic and social background from their constituency's can be as "sensitive" as those elected from the ranks. At issue is not one or a few representatives, but the complete exclusion of persons of lower status from serving as representatives. Moreover, a symbolic rejection of the "worth" of lower-class persons takes place in a government that excludes them systematically from elected office. For similar reasons, the issue of how many Hispanics, blacks, and women are in the U.S. Congress is pertinent, although there are of course no longer any legal limitations on their serving.

THIRD TIER: SEPARATION OF ELITES

Nowhere was the initial fusion of public and private power, and their gradual separation, more evident than in the elite positions themselves. Social scientists use the term "elite" to refer to those at the top of a hierarchy, whether in business, politics, or some other category. It is a neutral term without the implication either of choice people of high quality (elites may be inept, but still reign), or of malign intent (as in the Left's attack on "the power elite").

The main relevant question, both for the historical and the contemporary situation, is whether the elite of one sector—for instance, economic—are also the top power wielders in another sector, if not in all. If these elites largely overlap, we have an *interlocking elite*. This means that despite separation of the rights to vote and to run for office from wealth, race, or religion, or other sources of private socioeconomic power, people at the top in the private realm somehow succeed in staffing or controlling the top public positions. Under such circumstances the separation of public and private powers is rather limited.

During the Colonial Era, despite significant differences among the colonies and changes over time, elites were interlocked to a rather high degree. Nor would one claim that this was an era of model democracy. The plutocrats who often dominated the colonies' public life were a fairly small part of the community. Wealth was highly concentrated. By about 1700, according to records of the northern Chesapeake region, only 1.5 percent of freemen left estates valued at the time of their death at £1,000 or more; and 2.2 percent, estates of between £500 and £1,000. Three-fourths left estates valued at £100 or less. The last group largely worked their own land and were typically unable to accumulate wealth and, even after they gained the right to vote and participated in local affairs, had little say on colony-wide public life. This country was then largely the land of the great planters in the South, the large landholders and principal proprietors in the middle colonies, and a small group of merchants, lawyers, and professionals in New England. These elites had, according to several historical studies, one shared attribute: they were, with the exception of prominent religious figures, the men of greatest wealth in each colony. It was from their ranks that the King or governor or proprietor appointed judges, provincial secretaries, members of the governing council, and treasurers, and they tended to dominate the popularly elected branch in the assembly (the "lower" house).

Virginia provides a vivid illustration. Over an eighty-five-year period, nine landed-family names account for nearly a third of the ninety-one members appointed to the council (upper house); fourteen family names for almost another third. Thus, twenty-three families accounted for over 60 percent of the council from 1680 to the Revolution.

Since sons of aristocrats married daughters of aristocrats, these family names often represented large interrelated families. Lucy Higginson was the direct ancestor of seven councilors and of the wives of eight more—so that fully "one sixth of all Virginia councilors after 1680 could refer to the good lady as 'Grandmother Lucy.' "

The council became, according to one historical study, "a body of uncles, cousins, and brothers-in-law, who, when they put up a united front, were often able to guide their relatives and supporters in the lower house, checkmate the governor at any hostile move, and run the colony generally in the interests of their own extremely privileged class."

The situation was similar in the other Southern colonies, including Maryland. In Pennsylvania, wealthy Quaker merchants and large landholders dominated political life. New Jersey, though it has a complex history, was run mainly as a proprietorship, and its council members were almost completely allied with the principal proprietors. In New York, under a nearly feudal system of land grants, "manor lords" controlled the administration of justice, the election of representatives, and the collection of taxes. Their inordinate power led to the Great Rebellion of 1766, "a symptom of the widespread discontent among the lower and middle classes." New England had a great variety of governmental arrangements, but the same almost complete dominance of each colony by a very limited wealthy class.

The *possibility,* no matter how remote, that someone without noble ancestors may become part of the power elite figured in the wide acceptance of the overlapping of the public and private elites. As historian Arthur Schlesinger, Sr., puts it: "The American aristocracy, however undemocratic once it took form, was undeniably democratic in its method of forming."

By the time of the Revolution, the colonies had had firmly entrenched plutocratic governments for as long as a century and a half, despite ever-increasing equality of suffrage.

At the beginning of the nineteenth century, historian Leonard Richards states, the same top men "dominated *all* affairs—not only political affairs, but economic, social, and moral affairs as well." And historian Richard P. McCormick found that "those who were recognized at the time as 'the gentry' wielded decisive influence." Nor were those in power reluctant to use it to perpetuate their hold. Aaron Burr worked with wealthy Democratic partisans and helped to set up an anti-Federalist bank to loan money to Democrats in New York City, enabling them to buy land and thus to qualify for the vote. The new voters created in this way became, according to George Thayer's history of American election practices, *Who Shakes the Money Tree?,* "a formidable force on behalf of Burr's candidacy for President in 1800." (The Jefferson-Burr election was so close that it had to be decided in the House of Representatives.) Manasseh Cutler secured aid for a land promotion scheme in 1786 by sharing profits with influential members of Congress.

The separation of elites increased gradually. After the Revolution the country was in the sway of a "psychological democracy," excited by democratic ideals, and the ever-expanding suffrage led both to the perception of a much greater measure of democracy than actually existed, and to a growing demand for it. Jefferson, the ardent democratic theorist and champion of universal suffrage, was elected president in 1800, although at the time only two states chose presidential electors by popular election. During Jefferson's presidency, such actions as the Louisiana Purchase enhanced the role of the federal government, which was less tied to private interests than were the various state governments, a point of great significance for ages to come.

Steady progress was made in the years that followed. More offices were filled by election, rather than by appointment. By the time of Andrew Jackson's election in 1828, only two states did not popularly elect their presidential electors. Flourishing newspapers, their cost reduced in many cases to a penny, increased the common man's ability to follow politics. Jackson's election was the first "modern" election in that mass appeals were made to the voters rather than merely to parties and the political apparatus of the various states. Jackson himself, though rich and conservative, rose from humble beginnings. Still, the nomination process was outside the control of the common man, and the policies of the various factions also owed little to popular input.

In short, the interlocking of elites eased somewhat but did not cease. Richard Hofstadter points out, for instance, that "even in those states and territories where suffrage was broadly exercised, men who owned and speculated in land and had money in the bank were often accepted as natural leaders, and political offices fell to them." The industrialization of America that followed provided plutocracy with a whole new power base: nationwide "great combinations," corporations, holding companies, labor unions, and other large-scale organizations that reflected economic and social interests.

CHAPTER NINE

SECURING DEMOCRACY:
The First Progressive Era

THE POLITICAL EFFECTS
OF THE INDUSTRIAL REVOLUTION

Once the separation of the private and public powers is advanced, once the foundations of democracy are introduced, they tend not to stay put. It is not accidental but in the nature of things for the separation to be threatened, for forces to arise that seek to re-fuse positions of private and public power. The rise of these forces, in turn, calls for renewed efforts to sustain the separation of powers ("reforms"), to maintain the democratic foundations. The Progressive Era, early in the present century, illustrates this dynamic and provides the most relevant historical "model" of both the nature of our current difficulty and how it might be overcome.

Without adding to the very extensive body of historical work on this era, or entering questions of historical interpretation *per se,* as important as those might be, we can use examples from a much-studied era of American history to highlight some lessons concerning plutocratic dangers and democratic responses.

At the onset of this era, we find the United States has become, after more than two generations of hard work, investment, and entrepreneurship, the most successful modern industrial economic power in the world. Industrialization is in full swing. Despite the ups and downs of the business cycle, periods of boom and bust, the long-run trend is up. The gross national product is three times as great as it was in the 1870s. Steel, coal, electricity, oil production have reached unprecedented highs. Huge amounts of new wealth have been generated in the construction of railroads, the extraction of oil, and the forging of the empires of capital required to finance large-scale operations.

The Industrial Revolution was carried forward by, and created, new American business plutocrats. They amassed wealth *per se* and, at the same time, used it as a source of public power. They also used wealth to dominate the working of the private sector. Jay Gould, Andrew Carnegie, the Rockefellers, Harrimans, Morgans, and others accumulated fortunes of a magnitude previously unknown. They used their large concentration of private power to direct public policy to reflect their interests in local, state, and federal governments. And they used it to undermine free competition within the private sector, at times by illicit means, just as they were not above using illicit means to gain control of the public realm.

When abuses of the public realm and monopolistic practices in the private one became more prevalent, and were highlighted by muckraking publications and public investigations, reform movements followed. A leading one was the Progressive movement. The abuses the Progressives rallied against were rooted in deep changes that took place as the economy was transformed from the preindustrial, colonial one to the industrial, post–Civil War one. In colonial days, small farmers with a little land were fairly self-sufficient. They grew or made much of what they used and would try to sell tobacco or some other cash crop for the money they needed for tools and other items. In contrast, by the late nineteenth century farmers had become dependent on large farm-machinery corporations. Combinations and concentration led to the domination of a given market by one or two companies. "Trusts," the general name for monopolistic corporations or combinations of corporations, were also formed in oil, sugar, whiskey, and beef, to name only a few. They constricted competition and controlled prices. The Sugar Trust, for example, controlled about 98 percent of sugar refining in the United States. Furthermore, the farmers became dependent on the railroads, which were in effect local monopolies, controlling transport of crops to markets and crop storage in trading centers.

Industrial workers toiled long hours in unsafe and unhealthy conditions, as did coal miners. These people could read daily about the exploits of the super-rich. People felt abused, and powerless to affect

the course of events. In the words of eminent historian Richard Hofstadter, the increasing degree of corporate monopoly "became the
object of a widespread hostility which stemmed from the feeling that
business was becoming a closed system of authoritative action."

The state and federal governments were dwarfed by the nationwide accumulation of wealth and private power in the late nineteenth
century. Hofstadter summarizes the situation as follows:

> In the earlier nineteenth century these governments . . . had been
> small entities in a world of small entities. Into the midst of this
> system of diffused power and unorganized strength the great corpo-
> rations and investment houses had now thrust themselves, gigantic
> units commanding vast resources and quite capable of buying up
> political support on a wholesale basis . . . *a private power far greater
> than the public power of the state.*

A single railroad headquartered in Boston, for example, employed
three times as many persons as the Massachusetts state government and
took in more than five times as much revenue.

In 1912, concentration in the financial sector led to an investigation
by the House Banking Committee. It concluded that 341 directorships
in 112 major corporations, with aggregate resources of $22 billion,
were held by those tied to the interests of J. P. Morgan's financial
empire. America faced the spector of "a single network of interests
commanding more than three times the assessed value of all the real
and personal property in New England . . . or more than all the
property in the twenty-two states west of the Mississippi." Morgan
commanded so much wealth that, during a financial crisis in 1895,
President Cleveland turned to him for a loan of $65 million in gold
for the U.S. Treasury. The new plutocrats were the economic giants
of the day. The Progressive movement took them on at all levels of
government—city, state, and federal. The details of the struggle are
instructive.

REFORM DRIVES

In the Cities

In 1900 many cities were subject to plutocratic domination. In San
Francisco, a progressive coalition finally broke the rule of Abe Ruef,
a lawyer who collected large "retainers" in exchange for arranging city
contracts and special treatment.

In Toledo, Sam "Golden Rule" Jones made sweeping away corruption his cause. He antagonized the political machine and business interests alike by refusing to participate in the usual patronage and favoritism in the granting of contracts. It was control over such economic benefits that gave political machines their strength and durability—and that bound them closely to dominant local economic interests.

In Cleveland, Tom L. Johnson put competent people in charge of the water works, regardless of political affiliation. When the railroads would not respond to the city government demands, he set out to develop a competing system, and raised the tax valuation of the railways. Lincoln Steffens, who exposed urban corruption in a series of articles, many of which were collected in a book, *The Shame of the Cities,* declared Cleveland under Johnson to be the best-governed city in America. Reform movements occurred in many other cities with varying degrees of success and duration.

In the States

On the state level, plutocratic penetration equaled that of the cities, and faced similar reformist movements, as of the turn of the century. An outstanding example of Progressivism was Robert M. La Follette of Wisconsin. He decried machine control of public life, and business control of the political machine, and fostered a vision of more public control of government. He and his followers obtained a direct primary system (replacing selection of candidates by party bosses), curbs on campaign expenditures and on lobbying, and a corrupt practices act to eliminate the trading of money for votes. They mobilized widespread public support for their crusade against the excessive use of money in the political process.

In California, Governor Hiram Johnson led the Progressives in a fight against the domination of state politics by the Southern Pacific Railroad, utilities, citrus growers, among others. They found that bribery of state and local officials was almost the rule rather than the exception. The Progressives took on the entire political system: the corrupt political machines of both parties, first in the major cities, then on the state level. They succeeded in introducing the "initiative," which allowed the people to propose legislation of their own (such as California's Proposition 13), and the referendum, which allowed the people to register their opinion on legislation passed by the legislature or on other matters.

Reform administrations made progress in a dozen other states between 1901 and 1910, adopting the initiative and the referendum, and fighting for more direct participation by the public in the nomination process, which at that time was largely a function of the party bosses and machines, and for direct election of senators, who were then selected by state legislatures.

On the National Level

The overall success of city and state Progressive efforts was impressive, but uneven and often subject to reversal. For example, once in office La Follette used the machine to sustain his power. Some reform laws that were passed proved to be quite effective; others were poorly enforced or were toothless to begin with. State governments could not stem the tide of business concentration, both because they had been "outdistanced" by the new giant nationwide corporations and because such entities were constitutionally beyond their reach. *Increasingly, the task of countervailing the "trusts" fell to the federal government.* Thus, as a long coal strike drew on and on and the coal-mine operators, whose corporations were controlled by J. P. Morgan, remained intransigent, smaller businessmen appealed to President Theodore Roosevelt: "Is J. Pierpont Morgan greater than the people? Is he mightier than the government? . . . Morgan has placed a ban upon us which means universal ruin, destitution, riot and bloodshed. . . . We appeal from the king of the trusts to the President of the people."

Roosevelt's intervention ended up settling the strike through arbitration. With that event, and the initiation of litigation against business monopolies under the newly passed Sherman Antitrust Act, Roosevelt became known as the "Trustbuster." In political cartoons, he was pictured as bigger and more powerful than the special interests, whereas until then he, and McKinley before him, had been pictured as compliant little boys subservient to the grotesquely obese figures of the Trusts. And the President had come to represent the "unorganized" against the consequences of larger economic concentration.

That a Progressive president, free from entanglements with private interests, reached office only by accident, through the assassination of President McKinley, rather than by election, underscores the extent to which economic power had come to dominate the political process. As extreme examples, include the poor people who were paid in cash for their votes, the dead who rose to vote, and employers who threatened to fire their employees unless they voted "correctly."

Equally detrimental was the control of the nomination process by political machines. This ensured a series of presidents, both Republican and Democratic, who protected business interests through high tariffs and military protection of brutal strike-breaking, and by ignoring the increasing concentration of business. Benjamin Harrison, elected president in 1888, complained about the "strings" attached to his election victory: "When I came into power I found that the party managers had taken it all to themselves. I could not name my own cabinet. They had sold out every place to pay the election expenses."

Throughout the Progressive period, the Senate acted as the champion of wealth and industry, regardless of the administration or the party in power. Until 1913, most senators were elected by state legislatures with no popular input, and, Hofstadter notes, candidates needed the backing of the railroads or utilities to be selected by the party machines.

In a study of lobbies, William Ashworth explains how state legislatures, which appointed most senators at the time, in effect represented industries: "Ohio sent oilmen; Nevada sent silver mine owners; Maine, Michigan, and Oregon sent lumber barons; New York sent bankers. It was in a very real sense the ultimate pork barrel, a legislature of lobbyists." There were numerous allegations of bought senatorships. Senators were often plied with favorable loans and sales of stock at below market rates. Immune to public anger, they consistently prevented tariff reform, election reform, railroad regulation, and changes in the monetary system opposed by business.

According to Ashworth, "Early lobbyists' techniques were often coarse, running heavily to such gambits as cash bribes, florid dinner parties, and the procurement of willing women. . . . This activity reached a zenith toward the end of the nineteenth century in the Senate, which by the last two decades of that century was openly in the hands of special interests." The *Congressional Quarterly* puts it starkly: "Bribery of members of Congress was a well documented practice in the 19th and early 20th centuries."

The Senate was frequently referred to as the "Millionaires Club," a term that captures the public's resentment of the Senate's allegiance to narrow economic interests. While the Senate occasionally responded to public outcries against the trusts, it was only with token legislation. For instance, the Sherman Antitrust Act was passed in 1890, but it "made no attempt to define the offenses it penalized, and created no machinery for enforcing its provisions." It was "flung out to appease the restive masses," but was vague and virtually ignored by Presidents Harrison, Cleveland, and McKinley before Roosevelt breathed new life into the bill.

Public resentment continued to build. One historian reports that "antirailroad sentiment was diffused throughout the population, from poor farmers to San Francisco merchants and industrialists." Richard Hofstadter phrases it most bluntly: "Still more widely felt was a fear founded in political realities—the fear that the great business combinations, being the only centers of wealth and power, would be able to lord it over all other interests and thus to put an end to traditional American democracy."

As a result of this wave of anger, the Democratic Party came under the control of the Populists and William Jennings Bryan, but business interests maintained control of the Republican Party. Mark Hanna, the boss of the Republican Party, was considered by many to be "the spokesman of big business in politics," to personify "the liaison between big business and the government," according to Mark Sullivan in his widely acclaimed history, *Our Times*. Hanna backed McKinley and managed the flow of money from the trusts to his candidate. He capitalized on industrialists' fear of Bryan's populist "hordes" to collect substantial assessments, even by Watergate standards: $400,000 from the meat-packing trust and $250,000 from Standard Oil alone, for instance. Business tycoons such as railroad magnate J. J. Hill bought control of newspapers to keep them on the right side, and railroads offered special rates for people to travel to hear McKinley speak. Industrialists threatened their workers: "Men, vote as you please, but if Bryan is elected . . . the whistle will not blow Wednesday morning." McKinley won easily. Weeks after he took office, the Dingley Tariff Act, which increased protective tariffs to the highest levels in U.S. history—an average of 57 percent—was passed with virtually no discussion, despite its complexity. The bill, which ran to hundreds of pages of rate schedules, covered many if not most imported products.

The public's outrage continued to grow, and it was in this climate that Roosevelt was suddenly and unexpectedly thrust into the presidency by McKinley's assassination in 1901. Roosevelt was young and something of a political maverick. His brashness and originality had enabled him to move up the ladder without incurring too many debts, aided by his fame as a hero of the Spanish-American War of 1898. It was his appeal to reform-minded Western Republicans that won him a place on McKinley's ticket.

Roosevelt was concerned about the power of the trusts. About six months into his presidency he brought litigation under the Sherman Antitrust Act against J. P. Morgan's Northern Securities Company. Roosevelt had to wait two years to obtain a decisive Supreme Court ruling on the Northern Securities case. In the meantime he moved slowly, reassuring the business community that he was not opposed to business corporations *per se,* only those that were so large a power concentration as to jeopardize the public interest.

After successfully prosecuting the Northern Securities railroad monopoly, Roosevelt initiated litigation against the meat packers' trust. He also initiated and gained Congress's approval of a prohibition on corporate contributions to candidates for federal office—despite the fact that he himself had benefited from such contributions to his campaign. This generated one of those lines that can serve as an epitaph of the era: "We bought the son of a bitch, and he didn't stay bought," were the words of a Carnegie associate.

In support of his move, Roosevelt himself composed some lines, for his 1905 Annual Message to Congress, that speak as directly to today as to yesterday: "The fortunes amassed through corporate organization are now so large, and vest such power in those that wield them, as to make it a matter of necessity to give to the sovereign— that is, to the Government, which represents the people as a whole— some effective power of supervision over their corporate use." For the words "corporate organization" can be read all large-scale organizational interests, not merely those of business.

Roosevelt also proposed a Bureau of Corporations to investigate interstate commerce, to uncover unfair practices and restraint of trade. Despite much congressional opposition to the measure, it quickly passed. Rockefeller's Standard Oil Trust had been in the news at that time; it was reported to be getting unfair railroad freight rebates, exactly the type of practice the Bureau of Corporations was supposed to uncover. Therefore, the news that Rockefeller was trying to block this legislation (by wiring congressmen to oppose it, for instance) gained much public attention.

Roosevelt used separate legislation to end the practice of railroad freight rebates, a move that is particularly illustrative of his first term. By demanding and receiving large rebates on its own freight, the Standard Oil Trust was able to operate more cheaply than any competition and to force many competitors either out of business or into its trust. Through the prohibition of the practice, Roosevelt sought to ensure fair competition without trying to regulate what the result of that competition would be. Roosevelt's initiatives "encouraged everyone to feel," as Hofstadter writes, "that the country was governed from Washington and not from Wall Street."

In 1904, Roosevelt easily won election in his own right, soon becoming more oriented toward social democracy. Rather than merely seeking to curb the largest industrial combinations, he now proceeded on the notion that government, acting as the people's trust, must see that private wealth and power, "in addition to being used in the interest of the individual or individuals possessing it, is also used for and not against the interests of the people as a whole." With the Hepburn Act, the Interstate Commerce Commission was given the power to set railroad freight rates at socially desirable levels, a long way beyond prohibiting rebates and monopolistic practices.

Roosevelt also sought to use the power of the federal government to protect citizens and regulate economic activity. He fought for (but lost in Congress) a minimum-wage law for railroad workers and an eight-hour workday. He succeeded in obtaining pure-food-and-drug legislation.

After a less Progressive interlude, the presidency of William Howard Taft, Woodrow Wilson became the Democratic candidate in 1912, advocating many Progressive ideas. Once elected, he moved from constitutional democracy toward social democracy, in stages not too dissimilar to those of Roosevelt. Wilson's principal early achievements were a substantial downward revision in the tariffs imposed on almost everything, and the creation of the Federal Reserve System to decrease the power of the "money trusts" of J. P. Morgan and other financiers. Major new antitrust legislation was conceived as a means of "rolling back," reducing business to smaller, more competitive units, although this was later de-emphasized in favor of a Federal Trade Commission that would investigate and oversee business, for the same basic purpose.

Wilson's bill to remove protective tariffs, "everything that bears even the semblance of privilege or of any kind of artificial advantage," was sidetracked in the Senate. He pointed to the effects of the special-interest lobbyists who "were swarming" over the body of the Senate. He was greatly troubled "that the people at large should have no lobby and be voiceless in these matters, while great bodies of astute men seek to create an artificial opinion and to overcome the interests of the public for their private profit." When a congressional investigation revealed massive lobbying, and established that some senators had stocks in the industries they were trying to protect from Wilson's tariff reductions, the Senate was forced to go along with the President, and the Underwood Tariff Act was passed.

Following revelations by *The Chicago Tribune* that the 1910 Illinois senatorial election had been the effect of an outright wholesale bribery of the state legislature, the resistance to direct election of senators collapsed. A constitutional amendment was ratified in May 1913, according to which senators were to be elected by the states' electorates, not their legislatures.

Wilson also wanted to make the government solely responsible for issuing currency and regulating the money supply. He calmed the fears of the bankers by having regional central banks under private control, but regulated by a federal agency, the Federal Reserve Board. This move ended the near monopoly on credit that had been held by New York bankers. Thus, by 1917 there was progress on many fronts, although how much is both difficult to measure and subject to disagreement.

An Aside on Down-Sizing

Over and above seeking to free the government from the grasp of private power, as exercised by the old plutocrats and the new industrial ones, especially "trusts," La Follette and other "local" Progressives saw the need to use government to protect the citizens from the effects of high concentration of economic power within the private sector. If competition and the free market were to work, undue concentration of private power had to be prohibited (something even Adam Smith believed the government should do).

The limitation sought on the concentration of private power is of considerable importance and is often confused with other kinds of

government regulation. It needs to be highlighted, both for its historical significance and for its contemporary implications. When there are
large concentrations of private power (personal or corporate or in
other organizations, such as labor unions), it often is not sufficient to
reduce their penetration into the public realm. Preservation of *both*
democracy and the free market requires *down-sizing*, reducing the large
power concentrations, which entails going beyond "cleaning up" the
public realm on the national and local levels. For instance, when oil
monopolies bribe senators, it is often not enough to outlaw bribes. The
monopolies will continue to dominate the private sector and soon will
find other ways to use their disproportionate private power to penetrate the public life.

The issue is very much with us today, in the age of multinational
corporations, "international" labor unions, and what some see as new
concentrations of corporate wealth and power following the merger
mania of the early eighties. It seems inherent in regimes with plutocratic tendencies. Harvard political scientist Carl J. Friedrich wrote
about the Venetian plutocracy (eleventh and twelfth centuries): "Not
the rule of wealth, but rather the use (or abuse) of governmental
powers motivated by the desire to retain a monopoly on the acquisition
of wealth, was the distinguishing feature." Venice's traders, he continues, felt the need to seize "the control of public affairs in order to
protect their interests and forestall the rise of competitors."

After further illustrating his point with the history of the German
cities (the Hanseatic League) and early English history, Friedrich ex-
presses its relevance for modern times:

> It is an ever recurring phenomenon of constitutional history that
> democracy turns into an oligarchic plutocracy. There can be little
> doubt that at least in Athens the rise of the oligarchs was due to the
> hatred of the rich for the democracy, which was constantly threaten-
> ing to deprive them of their wealth.

And the need to stem plutocratic tendencies is very much present
in American history. "Woodrow Wilson," Friedrich writes, "maintained at one time that the united capitalists and industrialists are the
masters of the American state." At other times, however, Wilson was
less pessimistic, and was actively cutting back their power.

Reducing domineering concentrations (whether or not they are
monopolies in strict legal terms) of private power to nonthreatening

size, so that their public influence will be lowered and market domination will be avoided, was—and is—often attacked by the champions of large concentrations of private power. They present it as an attempt to dominate the private sector by government intervention, a call that rallies all private interests against the down-sizing. But down-sizing does *not* affect most private interests; on the contrary, it is as essential for the working of the private realm as it is for the public one.

It cannot be denied that reforms, once they get started in the direction of down-sizing, often tend to keep going—attempting to promote equality within the socioeconomic realm, as Marshall expected. The Progressives, for instance, sought not only to break the influence of railroads on governments, and reduce their monopoly, but also to guarantee fair and efficient operation and to limit profit to "reasonable" levels. Soon the Progressives also looked to government to prevent the exploitation of workers, especially women and children, and to protect consumers from unsafe products. The government, as viewed by the more radical Progressives, should check the power of private business, all business—not just monopolies and their kind. State governments could and did pass many such laws, banning child labor, regulating the meat-packing industry, reducing the legal length of workdays, and bringing other reforms.

However, the fact that in this and in other historical situations, reforms aimed at maintaining the separation of public from private power, and down-sizing "great combinations," evolved into drives to promote socioeconomic equality by the use of public power, does not prove that such a connection is inevitable, or that "down-sizing" is not needed, even if one does not favor equality. Constitutional democracy and social democracy are not inevitably linked, even though promoting one tends to whet the appetite for the other.

Essentially, in seeking to reverse the undue intrusion of private power into public policy, the Progressive movement as a whole sought to work in two spheres. One was regulation of the private realm (though the extent of the public realm's role was a matter of dispute among Progressives). The second was political reform ensuring that the government would be more responsive to the will of the people, and less so to that of private interests.

In the latter endeavor they were quite successful. The secret ballot, direct primaries, referendum and recall, campaign finance reform—all measures that would have been thought laughable by the political machines in 1888—were enacted by 1914. Further, following the passage of the 17th Amendment in 1913, "Senators had to go directly to the people for their nomination, not to the railroads and utilities as before." Since then, no plutocrat has again been able to exercise the amount of political control that men like J. P. Morgan, John D. Rockefeller, Andrew Carnegie, and Jay Gould did toward the end of the nineteenth century. Though political machines were far from dead and new ones continued to appear, Progressive principles had gained such widespread acceptance that the government grew, to put it simply, more democratic.

Historians have argued that the Progressives fought the machines and the plutocracy to make government more efficient, professional; that they were striving more for a meritocracy than for greater democracy. Also brought to bear in this argument is the Progressives' sociological base, largely "old middle class" professionals who sought to mediate between the new industrial magnates and the new working class. All this may be true. But even if their method of reform was paired with professional intentions, the result was a less interest-group-dominated, less corrupt, more autonomous public life, and hence a more democratic one.

In other words, constitutional democracy, benefiting both from greater separation of public and private power and from the downsizing of high concentrations of private power, fared better than did progress toward social democracy, the equalization of the private realm by public power. Indeed, sociologist William Schneider attributes the much greater success of the Progressives, as compared with the Populists, to their concentration on "common" (cross-class) "public interest" and "public good" issues, versus divisive socioeconomic issues.

An overview of the Progressive movement shows a return to a higher degree of autonomy in public life. This was achieved both by reversing plutocratic incursions and by finding new ways to involve the public at large in politics. Through this process, the movement attacked what it considered excessive concentrations of private power, with some Progressives moving beyond these political reforms into social reforms.

Finally, the Progressive endeavors show, despite their incomplete success and what some consider mistaken steps, that plutocratic tendencies can be curbed and democracy shored up, and illustrate some of the ways this can be achieved.

CHAPTER TEN

DEMOCRACY AS AN INTER-CLASS DEAL

The brief historical excursions behind us suggest that the separation of private from public power is essential for democratic government. Without this separation, either private interests will capture the public realm, or public power may come to dominate the private realm.

Additionally, the struggle to preserve the democratic bulwark is not won once and for all but must be continually sustained, as Teddy Roosevelt found, and Woodrow Wilson after him, and as the generations that followed—up to today—have also discovered. The reason is that the success of a democratic system rests on a delicate balancing principle.

The concentration of private power, which results from the working of the economy (for instance, the accumulation of more wealth by some groups than by others), and the rise of self-awareness among these groups, must not be "leveled" or wiped out by public power. Otherwise, a totalitarian society will result, defined precisely by the domination of the public realm over society and by the liquidation of private powers.

Conversely, private powers constantly seek to expand their sway by penetrating the public realm, trying to make it work for their narrow purposes. Hence its autonomy must be shielded. The result of these opposing forces is a constant series of shifts in the balance of power between the sides. This by itself is not troubling but, on the contrary, an essential part of the dynamic, as long as neither side tilts the system too far in one direction.

Whereas in the 1970s conservative thinking, whose greatest fear is the penetration of the private realm by public power, captured much of the American public, in previous periods of American history, such as the Jeffersonian, Jacksonian, and Progressive eras, the opposite danger loomed larger. Actually, both are always potentially present.

The evidence accumulated in Part I concerning the role of PACs and, more generally, of interest groups suggests that now the supporters of democracy must concentrate attention on the danger of private invasion of the public realm. This realization brings up the questions: What inducements do the wielders of private power require to agree to limit their power, and to consent to a much larger degree of equality in the public realm than in the private realm? What will make them restrain themselves—or agree to be constrained—from shaping the public realm in their private image? The answer is to be found both in the realm of ideals and in expediency.

THE ROLE OF DEMOCRATIC IDEALS

Social science teaches us that people often do not coldbloodedly calculate how best to serve their self-interest or other materialistic needs. They are moved by sentiments (such as loyalty to their nation or community) and ideals. Throughout history people have sacrificed their lives for causes they believed in. They have contributed funds, energies, and time to organizations and social movements that advance causes they hold dear, not for their own sake but for the sake of others, society, and democracy.

Americans *believe* in the Constitution and the American democracy, albeit in varying degrees. Among these believers are the power wielders—and the people they care about, their friends and families. Virtue is on the side of democracy and the separation of powers.

The spread of the democratic ideal, on the eve of the Revolution, played a major role in the gradual transformation from a rather plutocratic society toward a democratic one. In the feudal age, the interlocking of statuses was justified by prevailing religious dogma and widely accepted as legitimate, but with the advent of modern democracy, private penetration of the public realm was increasingly considered inappropriate behavior. Muckrakers gained wide attention to their charges that the Senate had turned into a Millionaires Club, that Rockefeller was wiring instructions to members of Congress, that "trusts" (monopolies) were buying political influence, that machine bosses controlled town halls—because their audience, the citizenry, viewed such conduct as objectionable.

Americans were from the outset more democratic, and more chary of private power, than members of most nations, and they grew more so over the generations. It is revealing that Europeans kept asking American visitors a decade ago what all the fuss was about Watergate, and more recently about Abscam. Americans' sensibility in these matters fosters self-limitation among the powerful and serves as a basis for action against them when they do not curb themselves. It provides a shield for American democracy, one forged out of commitments to values.

EXPEDIENCY COMPELS

Expediency propelled private power holders in the same direction as did democratic ideals. If one uses the feudal era in Europe as a starting point, one can see political history ever since as the rise of one social group after another, each gaining some measure of power. There were groups of merchants and craftsmen through medieval times, but industrialization brought to the fore first the bourgeoisie (industrialists, financiers) as a major class, and later the working classes. Each clamored for more equality, a larger share of whatever society allots—wealth, prestige, political power—for its heretofore underprivileged members. That is, for more equality in the public *and* private realms.

To Confront or to Adapt?

What followed has often been correctly depicted as a kind of comparative experiment in ways to deal with rising expectations and demands, and with *new* private powers. In France the monarchy and its allies within the aristocracy opposed any significant accommodation to the demands of the rising bourgeoisie. The regime was overthrown and the king and aristocracy were stripped of both their public *and* their private privileges, if they survived the transition at all. The Russian tsar and aristocracy, also unable to adapt, fell to a similar fate in 1917.

On the other hand, in the United Kingdom, before the French Revolution and especially after it, significant accommodations were made; new classes were absorbed by the regime, which in the process was gradually and for the most part peacefully modified, rather than destroyed. The feat was accomplished twice: the society governed by a monarchy and a landed aristocracy absorbed the bourgeoisie, and the resultant capitalist democracy absorbed the rising labor classes, avoiding radicalization but giving rise to welfare capitalism.

Similarly, in the United States, whatever "aristocratic" tendencies there were in the colonial days were overcome by the widening governmental participation of the new capitalist groups, followed in turn by at least a partial incorporation of the labor classes.* At the outset of the Progressive Era, socialists, anarchists, and Populists had a significant and growing appeal. However, considerable accommodation and reform kept the labor movement even less radicalized (that is, revolutionary) in America than in the United Kingdom—and in both countries, labor was much less radicalized than in such Catholic-dominated countries as Spain, Italy, and France. Further, the United States, spurred by riots, later accommodated the blacks, and youth riots in the sixties were followed by a lowering of the voting age from twenty-one to eighteen in 1971.

The Lesson

The most important point, commonly overlooked, in the often told political history recited above is that in the absorbing process, the opening of society to newly active classes, *equality is enhanced much more in the public than in the social or, especially, economic realm.* It is as if the rising, potentially rebellious classes were offered a deal by the

---

*A social-science aside is necessary here. The term "class" is usually used to describe a group of people of similar economic background: workers, farmers, business people. There are groups in society, such as blacks and youth, who share an interest and who have become, to one degree or another, politically aware and active. Since the basis of their shared interest is not mainly economic, but a characteristic such as race or age, they are often referred to as "social groups," rather than classes, although they behave like classes in the sense of being aware of shared interests and acting in unison. To avoid the cumbersome phrase "classes and other social groups," I use "classes" to refer to all such groups, without presuming that their interests are necessarily, merely, or largely economic (although they all have such an interest), and without implying that the United States has a clear or rigid class structure.

privileged, dominant ones: Give up on your attempt to change the society totally—especially to win encompassing reallocations of wealth and private power—and we will give you *much* public equality and *some* measure of social progress and economic benefits, though certainly not socioeconomic *equality*.

Following Marshall's sequence, examine the absorption of blacks. Although blacks gained the legal right to vote after the Civil War, the effective right to vote, especially in the South, was earned by a long struggle, which culminated in the 1965 Voting Rights Act. Since then, thousands of blacks have gained elective office, even in the South. Legal desegregation was also largely achieved in the 1960s. However, much social segregation remains in housing, in schools, and even on the job and in higher education. Economic differences between whites and blacks have been reduced, but whereas in the public realm the equality of one-person-one-vote is approximated, and the right to run for office is widely exercised, in 1980 the median income of black families was 58 percent of that of white families—only a slight improvement from the 1950 figure of 54 percent.

Similarly, members of all classes are free to vote and run for office, but differences in income and wealth have been only slightly reduced. In 1981, the lowest fifth of American families received 5.0 percent of all income, while the highest received 41.9 percent. The middle three-fifths received 11.3 percent, 17.4 percent, and 24.4 percent respectively. Thirty years ago, the lowest fifth received 4.5 percent, while the highest received 42.7 percent; the middle three-fifths got 12.0 percent, 17.4 percent, and 23.4 percent respectively. Despite the controversy among specialists over how to measure economic differences, the conclusion stands: differences have been reduced but are still considerable.

Exaggeration of the differences between the realms should be avoided. Despite one-person-one-vote rule in the public realm, economic wealth and social power have continued to carry weight in the public realm, at the height of the Progressive reforms and ever since. For instance, wealthy people can draw on their own millions for their presidential campaigns, as Nelson Rockefeller and John F. Kennedy did, a resource obviously not available to a blue-collar candidate. Also, inequality in the socioeconomic realm *has* decreased to some extent. *Even taking this into account, however, there is little doubt that equality in the public realm is significantly higher than socioeconomic equality.*

Tug-of-War

Here one can see a sociological source for the tug-of-war between the private and the public realms. The rising classes, especially to the extent that they have given up "direct action" in the private realm (strikes, sit-ins, demonstrations), seek greater socioeconomic equality by exercising public power, as evident in the classes that supported the New Frontier and the Great Society, the great expansion of government-propelled programs and regulation of the private sector in the Kennedy and Johnson eras.

At the same time, the more established socioeconomic classes seek to preserve their privileges within the private realm by limiting public penetration of that realm. This is the social basis of the opposition to big government, social programs, and regulation.

Each set of classes pulls the system in its own direction, with first one, then the other gaining a bit. But in the process *both* sides refrain from abusing democracy because both sides have a stake in sustaining the implied deal. *Both* gain from it the advantage of working out differences peacefully, via the representative system rather than in the streets, while each harbors the not-so-secret hope that it will gain— if not now, then after the next election—some advantage by using the public realm.

The deal tends to come apart when one camp succeeds in gaining a strong upper hand in both the public and the private realms. The Great Society is seen by conservatives as a socioeconomic reform, driven by public power, that went too far in affirmative action, business regulation, public expenditures, and other programs. In the Reagan Administration, as the liberals see it, the pendulum effect is much in evidence, as those who have high socioeconomic power make increasing attempts to use it in the public realm to make the political (and legal) systems work better for them than for the rest of society. It is inevitable that those who benefit from or ideologically favor a social democracy now feel attacked, while those opposed to it feel they have not gone far enough in rolling it back.

Whoever is right, one thing is clear: just as extensive public control of the private realm would be totalitarian, and would violate the implicit inter-class deal on which democracy rests, so—now—the opposite danger looms: ever-larger inequality in the public realm, because of PACed penetrations by private powers, would tend to interlock statuses and spur a move toward plutocracy; this would violate the deal that is one of the sociological bases of democracy.

In a society in which many people are educated, publicly aware, and active, and in which the means of communication and organization are readily available, even though hardly freely, *a successful drive to interlock statuses is an open invitation to rebellion.* If, on top of socioeconomic inequities, large segments of the public are in effect excluded from equal participation in the public arena, the conditions will be ripe for massive alienation, which, history teaches us, may express itself in large-scale withdrawal and social disturbances, and, at the extreme, may lead to a revolution. This point has been made about uprisings as disparate as the American Revolution and the Watts riots.

Such a rebellion may well not take a political form, at least for quite a while. The large proportion of Americans who feel alienated (60 percent by 1980)—and who have felt that way for years—may initially take to expressing their antiestablishment feelings in more personal ways, from cheating on taxes to allowing the work ethic to weaken, from being more rowdy to erupting in more ghetto riots (as in Miami). Needless to say, such a massive withdrawal exacts huge economic, social, and human costs that no plutocrat can welcome. Beyond these expressions, when large segments of society feel that they are ever more excluded, and that the government is not responsive to them but is in the hands of special interests, they constitute a sociological powder keg. They become a mass waiting to be ignited at a point and by a leadership that are not specifically predictable, but likely to blow up in one form or another.

The costs of massive withdrawal and the threat of rebellion are the expedient reason that those who command a great deal of private power are wise to follow what their ideals prescribe: to allow participation by all in the public realm, and to make necessary socioeconomic reallocations and other accommodations. This is the opposite of what has been happening since the PACs took off.

Just as the privileged groups give up something to avoid mass rebellion and violence in a constitutional democracy, so do the disadvantaged sacrifice. They consent, in effect, to refrain from pushing for social democracy with all the means available to them, in order to preserve the constitutional system. It is a "deal" precisely because both sides give up something and both get something in return—as long as both sides hold up their ends of the bargain.

PART III

THE CASE FOR INTEREST GROUPS AND A REBUTTAL: What's Wrong With Interest-Group Politics?

CHAPTER ELEVEN

THE CASE FOR THE INTEREST GROUPS

INTEREST GROUPS
AS REPRESENTATIVE DEMOCRACY

Beyond PACs: The Interest Groups

PACs are all the rage these days. "The PAC-men: Turning Cash into Votes," warns a recent cover story in *Time*. Books are written about them. Legislation is drafted to stop them. Although we have seen there is ample reason to worry about this "additional" tool, PACs are only the most recent popular means of private power's invasion of public life.

There is, however, also a danger in preoccupying ourselves exclusively with this most recent manifestation of corruption: if we succeed in cutting off the Hydra head—by outlawing all PACs, for instance —another head will grow in its place. The deeper, underlying question must be asked: can the intrusion of private power—rather than merely this or that manifestation—be blocked? And before this question is broached, we must face up to the challenging argument that it *ought not be curbed.* We must respond to the viewpoint that interest groups, PACed or otherwise, are an inevitable and, on balance, beneficial part of the democratic process.

Political Scientists' Conventional Wisdom

"What do you think of interest groups?" I asked a class of advanced students at The George Washington University, seven blocks from the White House and a few subway stops from Congress. The class voted twenty-one to four that interest groups were, "on the whole," beneficial. One student abstained; three considered them, "all said and done," detrimental to American democracy. When the class broke up, one of the students mumbled that he was sick and tired of having to go through it all one more time; he had already taken his fill of political-science classes and had heard it all: "interest groups are good for you."

The students had learned their lessons well. They had acquired what at least in some circles passes as the "conventional wisdom" of the discipline they were studying, political science. Sciences tend to develop communities of assumptions, conceptions of the way the world is composed, how it functions and changes, that are shared by the community of the members of the particular branch of science. Thomas Kuhn, a leading authority on the subject, refers to these as "paradigms." They organize one's thinking, he explains, to provide a context for numerous bits of information; they bring order to seas of detail.

When a science encounters isolated facts that contradict its prevailing paradigm, its conventional wisdom, the scientists will not rush to throw out the paradigm, but will question and requestion the new facts. This is quite sensible; after all, the weight of the evidence is behind the paradigm. If the incompatible facts persist, they are labeled "stubborn facts," a term that reflects the intellectual disharmony and discomfort they cause. Often they are simply left to coexist with the old conception.

Only if such facts accumulate, and often only after a new and more fitting paradigm is evolved, is a discipline ready for what Kuhn calls a "paradigm shift"—a major change of perspective, outlook, world view. (When, in some fields, the old conceptions finally break down before a new one is evolved, intellectual disarray results.)

A political-science paradigm of democratic government views interest groups as an integral and beneficial component of democratic government (or a "pluralistic system"). For decades, this political-science viewpoint has been advanced, in opposition to the prevailing public view. Political scientist Harmon Zeigler describes the public view, under the heading "Traditional distrust and organized groups": "From the beginnings of the American republic, the assumption has been made that pressure groups, irrespective of their goals, are evil because they conflict with the fundamental attributes of democracy."

Zeigler then cites a whole series of publications over the years that define interest groups as a threat to democracy. He contrasts this public anti-interest-group view with a sophisticated political-science view. According to the latter, "the criticism exemplified in the writings cited above is based upon a concept of democracy which is both inadequate and naive." The naïve concept, Zeigler explains, is that of electoral democracy, the view that government should represent the public will and that the public will is expressed through the electoral process. Accordingly, concessions to special interests are viewed by the public as subverting the public will, as undemocratic.

Similarly, political scientists Norman J. Ornstein and Shirley Elder observe, "The American press has historically emphasized lobbying scandals and the insidious influence of groups over politicians." There follows a reference to James Madison's view that interest groups "were *inherently* bad." This tradition is contrasted with the political-science paradigm, evolved out of the work of Arthur F. Bentley (especially *The Process of Government*) and David B. Truman *(The Governmental Process)* and also advanced by Lester Milbrath *(The Washington Lobbyists)* and other political scientists. (I'll turn later to conflicting political-science perspectives.) The political-science paradigm, Ornstein and Elder report, "tends to portray groups in a rather favorable light."

V. O. Key, Jr., one of the most revered political scientists, writes: "The view that pressure groups are pathological growths in the body politic is likewise more picturesque than accurate. It is a safer assumption that the group system developed to fill gaps in the political system." A report of the Committee on American Legislatures of the American Political Science Association, the official organization of American political science, concludes that "lobbying is not a sinister practice but constitutes a legitimate and indispensable part of the legislative process."

"Most persons, without being very precise about the meaning of the term, already seem to know that lobbying is 'dirty,' " writes Lester Milbrath in an often cited study of lobbyists. Milbrath finds, "It is curious that lobbying, which is protected by the constitutional right to petition, should be so thoroughly distrusted by the press and the public." He blames largely the press for this misappreciation of the lobbyists: "The press plays up the unsavory and sensational aspects of lobbying, printing very few stories about the ordinary, honest lobbyist and his workaday activities—presumably because they would not 'sell.' "

In contrast, Milbrath finds that there is very little that is dirty in "new" lobbying; "old" lobbying entailed money "under the table" and entertainment, but such measures are no longer condoned or useful and are practiced by few. "There are a few corrupt individuals in lobbying. . . . The whole process, as a whole, however, is remarkably clean." Milbrath may somewhat underestimate the dirt still present, but his main point is well taken: illicit influence-buying is not the problem. As we see below, he finds lobbyists not just clean but valuable and irreplaceable.

The *International Encyclopedia of Social Science,* published in 1968, carries an article on "interest groups" by Henry W. Ehrmann. He focuses on the "functions" of interest groups, rather than on their dysfunctions. He observes that "the liberal and radical traditions in both Great Britain and the United States were . . . unsympathetic to 'special interests.' " In contrast, he notes, political science has established that interest groups are "indispensable for the functioning of a modern democracy," although they must be limited to using legitimate means.

A thorough reading of the writings cited so far would uncover qualifications and concessions to the critical view of interest groups, but some political scientists have risen to high eloquence in defense of lobbyists and interest groups. Writes Ohio State University political scientist Aage R. Clausen:

> The latest word is that the legislator, at the national if not at the state and local level, is not the helpless and corrupt tool of the all-powerful interest groups that he was once made out to be. It has nearly gotten to the point where the poor lobbyist representing the group interests has become a pitiable figure, beseeching the congressman's ear, plying him with favors without the slightest guarantee of any return, while running the risk of being scolded and scorned like a common cur!

Nor is the positive view of interest groups limited to political scientists. An anthropologist who lived among and reported upon the "tribes on the Hill," J. McIver Weatherford, denounces those who believe that lobbyists have evil influence on the Hill as closed-minded, biased people, akin to those who believe in black magic. Indeed, he writes, "lobbyists play this role of scapegoat for everything that cannot be explained otherwise." He goes on to argue that lobbies serve as errand boys for power centers in Congress, that instances of unethical conduct are rare, and that evidence shows they are "integral" to the representative system.

An extensive defense of PACs is the work of political scientist Herbert E. Alexander. His *The Case for PACs* was issued and publicized by the Public Affairs Council, an organization of business executives that organized a campaign in behalf of PACs.

Although all this has passed as a piece of conventional wisdom among political scientists for decades, there were and are important political scientists much more critical of interest groups. I think, for instance, of E. E. Schattschneider, especially his study *Politics, Pressures and the Tariff*, published in 1935. Theodore Lowi roundly attacked interest groups in his book *The End of Liberalism* (1969). Mancur Olson's recent work, which I have already discussed, sees in interest groups the source of economic decay. Robert Dahl, in much of his work and especially in his 1982 book, *Dilemmas of Pluralist Democracy*, is particularly cognizant of the dangers, not just the virtues, of interest groups. So far, however, the criticism has not been enough to topple the paradigm.

Political-science colleagues of mine who have read drafts of these pages have protested: Not all political scientists take this position. Granted. And many of those who do also recognize that interest groups can pose dangers. True. And you should not generalize about political scientists. Fine. But among the other comments of several of the same political scientists were: "There is no evidence of cause and effect between campaign contributions and congressional votes in behalf of special interests," and "All the talk about Congress being bought is vastly exaggerated." One cannot escape the conclusion that at least a rather significant, quite likely still dominant, group of political scientists tends to hold that, when all is said and done, interest groups are more beneficial than harmful. Their detailed arguments follow.

THE "FUNCTIONS" OF INTEREST GROUPS

Political scientists use the term "functional" to indicate the contribution of an individual part to a larger whole. For example, one may talk about the "functions" of the carburetor for the working of a gasoline-driven auto, or of the family for society. Specifically, political scientists have often identified the following "functions" of interest groups in a democratic government:

Interest groups provide a mechanism for political representation above and beyond the electoral process.

Elections are infrequent and each voter has but one vote to cast. There is a large volume of decisions made in the public realm, in between elections. Many voters' interests and concerns are deeply affected by these decisions, and hence citizens seek to have their views represented more frequently and on more issues than the electoral process can accommodate. Interest groups provide for such representation. In that sense, the more voluminous and encompassing the public business, the greater the "need" for interest groups.

Karl W. Deutsch, Harvard professor of government and former president of the American Political Science Association, while recognizing some of the dangers of interest groups, explains the deficiencies of the electoral process and the ways interest groups help: "Voting conveys no precise information as to which problems and issues are most important to which groups of voters, what their priorities are, and just what each group wants done. High on power but low on information, voting by itself is a blunt instrument indeed."

How is the gap closed? By other modes of participation that convey more specific information as to who wants what. "Activists" and "active groups" are the main modes listed. And "interest groups articulate the interests of their members. They put into words . . . vaguely felt needs, fears, and expectations." Other modes, such as congressional hearings in which citizens can attest to their needs and views, are informational but "lack the power to compel responsiveness."

Political scientists Thomas A. Reilly and Michael W. Sigall first signal their membership in the pro–interest-group school: "Lobbying is an activity recognized as a normal part of the political system." The function emphasized: representation. "It is one of the means by which political leaders learn about the demands of various sectors." Lobbying is not merely informational (otherwise public-opinion polls would serve) but it can back information with power. Lobbying activities "channel support"—or "threats of sanctions"—to public officials.

Milbrath examined the various services lobbyists perform. He finds some of them more valuable than others, but one tops them all: "There is no substitute for one service—the clash of viewpoints. The creative function this serves in alerting decision-makers to all possible alternatives outweighs all the waste and frustration involved in lobbying. Officials . . . could never find a substitute for the essential representational function that the spokesmen for organized interests provide."

Milbrath concludes his book by stating that lobbyists help the political system's stability and lead to wiser and more intelligent decisions than would be made without them. His very last words: "If we had no lobby groups and lobbyists we would probably have to invent them to improve the functioning of the system."

Administrative syndicalism.

Interest groups are said to supplement the electoral process not merely by providing a channel of representation through which the various segments of the public can make their views known to the legislature between elections; they also enable the public to deal directly with the executive branch. The electoral model assumes that public policy is either formulated by the President and scrutinized by Congress before it is implemented by the executive agencies, or formulated by Congress via laws the President approves and implemented by the agencies. In either case, government agencies are supposed to be mere handmaidens that carry out the public will as expressed through the proper institutions, functioning properly. Under this mode it is inappropriate for the public to influence *directly* decisions of the executive agencies because influencing them would deflect the agencies from responding to the *appropriate, legitimate* authorities. Indeed, such an influence is considered a major form of corruption, a violation of proper public administration that civil-service reforms try frequently to stamp out.

In contrast, what might be called a pro-interest-group theory of administrative syndicalism argues that in the modern state executive agencies daily make a very large number of decisions, which neither Congress nor the President can possibly oversee. These decisions affect every aspect of the economy, personal life, and society. The only practical way to make them in a responsive manner, taking into account the public feeling on the specifics involved, is to consult, involve, and "participate" the public in these decisions—in between elections. To some extent, this is achieved by the various citizens' advisory groups attached to most agencies and by lobbyists in Congress. But the main avenue is for agencies to contact interest groups, since it is not possible to consult millions of citizens. And, often the interested groups are most actively concerned, it is said, and hence they ought to be involved.

As a matter of fact, it is pointed out, executive agencies and subagencies are deeply tied in with various interest groups: the Department of Agriculture with the Farm Bureau and other farm lobbies; Department of Labor with labor unions; Treasury with banking; Commerce with business; Small Business Administration with small business; and so on. Similarly, before the Department of Education was created it was part of HEW, but a commissioner of Education was not as a rule appointed without consulting the teachers' lobbies; a surgeon general without the AMA; and so on.

The total picture that emerges is of a government in which the various segments of the public, through their interest groups, find direct representation via an agency or a subagency. V. O. Key, Jr., explains:

> The doctrine recurs that the role of administrative agencies should be to function as advocates within the government of the interests within society with which they are concerned: the Department of Commerce should look out for business; Agriculture, for the farmer; the Bureau of Wildlife Management, for the sportsmen. Adherence to this doctrine by public officials, as often occurs, paves the way for harmonious relations between organized groups and their opposite numbers within administration.

This administrative syndicalism does not replace the electoral process and legislature, as it does in fascist-syndicalist theory; but it is said to supplement it and significantly enhance its effectiveness.

Interest groups provide a bridge between the administrative and legislative branches of government.

This bridge is said to be especially needed when the executive and the legislative check and balance each other so thoroughly that they find it difficult to work in tandem. Some observers have pointed to the resulting "stalemate" of government (a viewpoint popular during the Carter administration). Others have expressed fear that an "imperial" presidency would result from the search for extra-constitutional ways to make Congress collaborate with the executive, since constitutional means seem not to suffice (one interpretation of the abuse of presidential powers by Richard Nixon and others).

Interest groups are said to alleviate the excessive separation of the legislative and executive branches by approaching both with the same advocacy, the more readily because they are not confined by the same institutionalized strictures that limit the maneuverability of the legislative bodies and the federal agencies.

The term *iron triangle* is used to describe this three-way relationship. Reference is to the strong links forged among a specific interest group, an agency or subagency (that is, a unit of the executive branch), and the "relevant" congressional committee(s) or subcommittee(s).

Although not all, or even most, of those who describe these relationships write about them with enthusiastic approval, it is widely suggested that these iron triangles help significantly in making a fragmented government pull together and work. Political scientist Gordon Adams, who studied iron triangles in the defense area and is on the whole quite critical of their grip, reports: "Washington office staffers [of lobbies] can become so central to the flow of information that they become the medium for communications between the other two sides of the 'iron triangle.' "

A Pentagon source cited by *Business Week* explains the freedom of lobbyists from the kind of strictures that limit government officials: "The best thing about corporate lobbyists is that they pass on to us a lot of stuff that they've learned on Capitol Hill. It's usually the quickest way for us to find out what's happening up there." Usually Pentagon officials cannot hang around members of Congress or their staffers, wine and dine them, to collect information of interest to themselves (although "liaison" people do some of that); lobbyists can and do.

Interest groups are avenues to mediation.

Mediating structures stand between the state and the individual, protecting the individual from undue control, if not subjugation, by the state. Political scientists Dell G. Hitchner and William H. Harbold explain: "Most important, perhaps, as government extends its regulatory activity, raises its levels of taxing and spending, and penetrates ever more deeply into the realm of private interests, the group may feel obliged to organize in order to defend its position."

Frequently, virtues associated with voluntary associations are also attributed to interest groups, most recently even to PACs. Thus, political scientist Herbert Alexander states, "PACs and the interest groups they represent serve as a safeguard against undue influence by the government or by the media." And "PACs increase participation in the political process."

Interest groups contribute to political socialization and political culture.

This virtue interest groups are said to acquire by keeping their members informed, politically aware, and active, and by providing them with the opportunity to learn and exercise political skills. The interest groups' efforts help ensure that these skills are not monopolized by a limited social stratum but are widely spread through society. PACs claim that they "encourage participation by their membership as part of their civic responsibility." Henry W. Ehrmann suggests that "the socialization of the citizen by interest groups often proves more effective and lasting" than that of political parties.

Sources of information.

The Committee on American Legislatures of the American Political Science Association put it quite clearly and strongly: "Pressure groups frequently constitute invaluable sources of information in making public policy."

TWO UNDERLYING ASSUMPTIONS

Democracy Builds on Groups, Not Individuals

One core assumption that underlies all these specific "functions" interest groups are said to fulfill is that the political process of a pluralistic democracy is—and ought to be—based to a large extent on group processes, not individual action. This contrasts with the notion that what makes democracy work is individuals casting votes they personally choose to cast, the dominant public view.

More about these social groups and their significance shortly. Suffice it to note here that political scientists view these groups not merely as socially significant but also as the political building blocks. V. O. Key, Jr., one of the most influential political scientists, writes about the "representative function of private groups": "Obviously, organized groups, for good or ill, perform a function of representation in the political system. The characterization of the lobby as the 'third house' puts the point vividly if somewhat exuberantly." Key goes on to explain that elected lawmakers may do well in representing local, geographically defined interests, but when it comes to representing interests that cut across localities—national ones—lobbyists are needed.

Legislators could speak authoritatively for the more or less homogeneous interests of their districts in a less complex society. . . . The growth of the number of specialized interests in society and the increasing complexity of legislative questions created tasks beyond ready performance by spokesmen for geographical areas. No legislator could regularly be relied upon to look out for interests that spread across many districts. Organized groups supplement the system of geographical representation.

As Key sees it, interest groups are particularly needed in a *modern* political system.

The general theme will be argued that pressure groups collectively may be regarded as a functioning element of the political order.

Interest groups have existed since the founding of the Republic, yet the great proliferation of organized groups came in the twentieth century. The evolution of our complex array of private organizations has been a secondary consequence of changes in the social order that created political needs met only inadequately by the older political institutions and procedures.

Why? Because, explains Key, modernity entails specialization, which in turn requires coordination among the new cleavages. The old political system cannot reflect these. And hence: "The new types of interests needed new mechanisms to formulate and state their needs— instruments better suited to the purpose than the older type of geographical representation of interests."

Interest Group "Consensus"

A second underlying assumption of the pro-interest-group conventional wisdom is that if all the interest groups, or at least the main ones, are involved in the formation of public policy, a "consensual" policy can be evolved. This is expected because these interest groups represent the major segments of the society, their needs and values, as well as their power. Thus, in the formulation of economic policy, if big business, small business, labor, farmers, and consumer representatives are involved, the resulting policy will be sanctioned by consensus. Or, in religious matters, at least the three main groups, Protestants, Catholics, and Jews, are to be consulted. It is not suggested that such a system provides a precise, all-encompassing, or egalitarian representation of the various segments of the public, but—it is argued—neither does the electoral process. Moreover, interest groups do not replace the electoral process, but merely supplement it by providing more chances of representation.

IN SUMMARY

An item of political-science conventional wisdom is that interest groups are a necessary and—on balance—benign part of democratic government. Certainly not all political scientists agree. Several major figures have questioned this consensus, and even its supporters have qualified it. (David Truman, for instance, wrote about the need for "the rules of the game.") Still, it provides an elaborate explanation of how interest groups—PACs included—"function" to supplement and sustain democracy. Basically, the pro-interest-group contingent would argue that interest groups provide a basis for participation in the political process, and hence government. As I see it, this theory, at best, projects on our times ideas that may have held under earlier conditions. It also disregards important differences between interest groups, and, above all, ignores the need to balance the pluralism of interest-group politics with a fair measure of national unity.

CHAPTER TWELVE

A LOSS
OF BALANCE

THE CASE AGAINST INTEREST GROUPS: OUTLINED

Political scientists are correct that the electoral view of democracy is simplistic and partial. There is much more to democracy than occasionally casting a ballot. And the ballot does *not* suffice to "make" politicians carry out the will of the majority—or else be replaced with a more attentive crew if they fail to heed the voting public. Much "representation" does take place between elections, and via mechanisms other than the ballot box. And elections themselves are hardly free of *group* influence.

The public, though, as I shall argue in detail, is correct in sensing that the recognition that groups do participate in democratic government, and do so via mechanisms other than elections, does *not* justify an acceptance of interest groups as a benign element of democratic politics. Part of the resolution of this paradox (see Chapter 13) lies in the distinction between group politics and the invasion of the public realm by special interests. In turning now both to critically assess the pro-interest-group "conventional wisdom" and to advance my own position against interest groups, I will require three steps:

1. An *analytic* clarification of the differences between simple pluralism (sometimes referred to as interest-group politics) and pluralism within unity (in which interest groups are constrained by the bonds of the national community).

2. A *historical* perspective, which suggests that the balance between pluralism and unity has tilted dangerously toward pluralism and away from unity.

3. A *differentiation* to show that not all groups at issue are interest groups; that many of the functions said to be served by interest groups are actually rendered by other, more benign groups. This point I will treat in Chapter 13.

PLURALISM WITHIN UNITY

My main case against interest-groups politics rests on a concept of democracy that I refer to, lacking a shorter or better term, as pluralism within unity. That is, within a viable democracy the pluralism caused by divergent constituencies must be balanced by the community itself.

One core assumption here is that there are, in society—as political scientists have suggested—a diversity of needs, values, and interests, and that in a democracy these must be represented. The needs must be communicated to the policy-makers, who should respond to them in the political process. If these needs are being suppressed or ignored, the government is not democratic.

It is also valid to assume that the interests represented are often of individuals aggregated into groups. The government is, as a rule, not responsive to an individual. While exceptional individuals, from Billy Graham to Ralph Nader, influence it for good or evil, they are the exception and not the rule. Even in the electoral process, it is aggregation that makes the difference, not each single vote. And the individual votes cast often reflect group pressures and education.

Most important, in the nonelectoral political processes individual voters have much less consequence than aggregated ones. For instance, compare one visit to a member of Congress by a representative of a group, with separate visits by individuals within that Congress member's constituency. Group representation, it should be further noted, is not a simple compendium of the preferences of the individual members. It reflects the results of group processes such as compromise and consensus-building in some cases, and oligarchic controls by the officers of the group in other instances. In short, pluralism of groups is the common basis of our politics, not of individuals. So far I am in agreement with the pro-interest-group theory.

Apart from the needs of the individual, the needs of the community shared by the various groups must be served. Otherwise, "common goods"—defense, for example—will not be adequately served as the groups struggle for their share of whatever the community produces and allocates. Also, limits to inter-group conflict must be introduced and enforced, if the groups are to work out their differences in a civil manner and arrive at reasonable compromise.

It has been said that in the U.S. Senate the members, the individual senators, vie with one another over legislation they favor but at all times take into consideration "the club," their need to continue to work with one another the next day. The same holds—or should hold —for the nation as a whole. After all, management and labor, blacks and whites, men and women, North and South, will still be members of the same nation—and function in the same economy—tomorrow; they will certainly need one another as much as the senators will.

In this light, the fact that we need a cumbersome concept, pluralism within unity, becomes understandable. One part captures the multi-group pull, the plurality, and the other part the need for community, for unity. Together they call attention to the need for balance within a society.

It might seem self-evident that a society needs to balance centrifugal forces of special interests with some community-sustaining centripetal ones. It is not. On the contrary, in recent years an ideology has been newly expounded and promoted (although its roots are in the eighteenth century) that would transfer from the market place into politics the idea that each individual or group may follow its own interests, and that an invisible hand will so arrange the aggregation of all these individuals and groups as to provide the most for all. It is either denied that the community has needs of its own or asserted that the community is served in this way. No special efforts to sustain unity are deemed necessary. Libertarians, *laissez-faire* conservatives, and those whom elsewhere I called New Whigs all share in this view. Their concern is protecting the plurality, protecting the constituting elements —not protecting the unity, or the "commons" from the elements.

There is a fair measure of cross-fertilization between these ideologies and the pro-interest-group theory. First, extreme advocates of both, we shall see, deny the very existence of a public interest and view politics as merely an arena in which private interest groups interact. The social world is depicted as a free play of interest groups, which limit one another in a kind of free market of politics.

Adds Henry S. Kariel, in the *International Encyclopedia of the Social Sciences:* "A considerable part of American academic research continues to follow the lines first suggested by Arthur F. Bentley's *Process of Government* (1908) . . . that government is but a responsive instrument for keeping stable the natural equilibrium of competing interests, and . . . that public policy is most usefully understood as the product of the free play of group pressures."

Kariel then points out, "So thoroughly has the group basis of politics been accepted that scholars could characterize the goals of Populism, Progressivism, and the early New Deal as irrational whenever these goals were [not] reducible to the special interests of the groups that advanced them."

Grant McConnell writes about "the conviction that these associations balance and counterbalance each other, with automatic benefit to society." He further notes that "government, especially the national government, parties, and 'politics' in general, have been deplored as threats to liberty."

The government, writes William E. Connolly, is viewed either as an "arena" or as an "umpire." It is either a setting or it is a neutral referee, not a realm, with its own missions, proper power, and legitimacy (other than that limited legitimation which is entailed, maybe, in the role of a referee). "Perhaps there was no such thing as 'the public interest,' or if there was, perhaps it was unknowable," writes McConnell of the skepticism of the 1960s. He adds that although these ideas were "always" in the background of the American mind, they were propelled forward by the publication of Arthur Bentley's book in 1908. From it, "a later generation" extracted the idea that the active participants in politics are private groups, sometimes cooperating, sometimes clashing, which make "the whole of politics a giant parallelogram of forces." Public interest and values were considered meaningless. More on this later.

The intellectual most often credited with having invented the invisible-hand perspective would be quick to disown it. Adam Smith, in his book *The Wealth of Nations,* argued that while each enterprise should pursue its own interest, and this in turn would lead to the greatest combined wealth, the government was needed to set shared rules within which this competition could take place. He argued for the government to establish and enforce the rules of the economic game, including protection of the market place from the development

of monopolies. In his companion book, *The Theory of Moral Sentiments,*
he went further and argued for the need for people to be committed
to one another as persons, not as means, based on the "fellow feeling"
we have for one another. "We have," Smith argues, "the strongest
disposition to sympathize with the benevolent affections. . . . We enter
into the satisfaction both of the person who feels them, and of the
person who is the object of them." For Smith, this empathic ability
forms the basis of human happiness and virtue. Thus, Adam Smith did
not favor a free-for-all; certainly not in the political, social, and ethical
realms.

Indeed, all the major social philosophers, such as Locke, Hobbes,
and Rousseau, different though they are, have recognized the need for
a community, as well as the contesting individuals and groups. Indeed,
if Hobbes and Rousseau erred, it was more in the opposite direction.
They were so concerned with the consequences of lack of unity that
they tended unduly to promote the concern with community, undermining the pluralistic element of the needed balance.

The fathers of modern social science recognized the same basic fact.
Take Émile Durkheim. He observed, in discussing business contracts,
that they rest on precontractual relations. They build on the assumption that most partners most of the time will be trustworthy and
"decent" with one another; that they will not exploit inevitable
changes in the situation to break contracts, or seek to exact the last
possible ounce of flesh in each transaction; that they will honor the
underlying relationship. Parties to contracts must realize that in the
longer run they need each other, and so ought to let the other "get
away" with some gains—to be willing to entertain some losses—in
order to sustain and nourish the relationship. Explicit constraints
spelled out in the contract help to clarify relations, but once they are
activated, once enforcement is sought in court, the underlying relationship is gravely undermined.

Viewed in this context, the pro-interest-group conventional wisdom underplays the unity issue, when it does not disregard it altogether. That is, if interest groups are accepted and legitimated—
without an explicit limit to their power, and without provisions for
effective countervailing forces—they are likely to carry their divisive
pluralism to an extreme, at which point the centrifugal forces will tear
apart the polity and the community.

Unrestrained, interest groups will tend to hinder the development

of a nationwide consensus and of shared policies. And they will promote policies that neglect needs that are not the interest of any one
group, as well as the common goods. They will escalate inter-group
conflict until the system is unable to function effectively and becomes
frustrating and alienating, if not violent. This seems to be the direction
in which the United States has been moving, as suggested in my
discussion of national security, economic policy, and other areas of
public policy.

Because the need to balance plurality with unity is central to my
whole thesis, I will dwell on it a bit longer. The sociological principle
involved is illustrated in the relations among ethnic groups and races,
another area of inter-group relations. Those who favor pluralism call,
correctly, for recognition of racial and ethnic differences, allowing
them expression in educational institutions, in hiring and promotion
at work, and in political representation. They further point out, in
sharp contrast to the melting-pot notion of stewing all groups into one
American gruel, that we are all richer—culturally, socially, personally
—when we allow the large variety of American ethnic and racial
groups to maintain their separate identities and subcultures.

So far, so good. However, all this assumes that the ethnic/racial
groups see themselves and conduct themselves as *subcultures,* as *sub-
groups* of the larger American community, that they see themselves first
as American and second as members of this or that group, not the other
way around. Otherwise society will lack the bases for conflict resolution, consensus-building, and service to shared goals. Hence, when
some black groups called for a separate *nation*—the code word for an
all-encompassing group, not a subgroup within a larger union—the
call was viewed as a threat to American society, quite different from
the call to allow blacks the same share and place within the American
community that other groups have attained. Similarly, bilingual education is properly viewed as quite suitable when it seeks to maintain
subcultural identity and knowledge, but not when it seeks to maintain
primary loyalty to the group—to the exclusion and rejection of the
encompassing community. Bilingualism, yes; ethnic supremacy or bi-
nationalism, no.

The same holds for interest groups. Recognizing them as part of
pluralistic America does not in itself define their limits and constitute
recognition of the need to preserve the unity, the community, within
which they can be "pluralistic."

IN HISTORICAL PERSPECTIVE

The balance between the two forces, the one that needs to be contained and the one that must be upheld, changes according to prevailing historical circumstances. Thus, if one lives, writes, or is politically active in an authoritarian or totalitarian country, in which unity is highly promoted and pluralism suppressed, one ought to favor more openness, more representation of interests, more pluralism. At the same time, if one sees that unity is neglected—institutions meant to work out effective national policies, and consensus of support for them, are stalemated or captured by interest groups, and citizens are growing cynical—it is time to weigh in on the side of unity.

In both situations, though, the full picture does not change: a well-functioning polity requires a balance of the two forces. True, the precise point of perfect balance may escape definition, nor is it necessary for the system to be in perfect balance. But when the polity tilts heavily in one direction, it needs to be pulled in the opposite one.

If one views it from this historical perspective, it is illuminating to note that the political-science conventional wisdom regarding the "functions" of interest groups was formulated and gained popularity largely in earlier generations. Bentley's main work, *The Process of Government,* was published in 1908. Although initially it had little impact, it fed into the conventional wisdom in later decades. David Truman's influential *The Governmental Process* saw the light in 1951; V. O. Key's book, extensively cited above, was first published in 1942. In short, it was before 1960 that the pro-interest-group conventional wisdom evolved. As is often the case in such matters, once it was ensconced, many political scientists continued to elaborate and draw on it even though it had fallen out of step with the changing balance of forces (just as some political scientists, we saw, never subscribed to the prevailing view).

INTEREST GROUPS RISE, UNITY DECLINES
(1960 TO 1980)

The evidence presented next suggests that in the 1950s interest groups were weaker on the national level, and the forces for unity were more pronounced than they are now; this relationship is now reversed.

In the last two decades the level of integration of the American national political system and the effectiveness of its institutions have diminished. In the same period, the power of interest groups—of all kinds—has grown. The net result is a system much less able to contain them and to "digest" their inputs.

Political scientist Everett Ladd concluded, after referring to the rise of thousands of new lobbies: "The U.S. might have adjusted satisfactorily to the new factionalism if it were not for the enfeeblement of the institutions to which a democracy looks for help in adjudicating group claims and fitting them into coherent national policy."

As a result the current application of the pro-interest-group theory is more damaging than when it first gained popularity. This approach to democratic theory always neglected the unity element, but the bias was much less problematic when this element was relatively strong.

Base Line: 1960

To suggest that the level of unity within the United States declined from 1960 to 1980 is not to imply that it was particularly high in 1960 or earlier. Indeed, it was not nearly so high as, say, that of the United Kingdom and other well-integrated nations, for many historical, structural, and social reasons, which persisted after 1960. Because they are so thoroughly familiar, I will only list them quickly, as background factors.

American society in 1960 was highly heterogeneous in its racial, cultural, and demographic composition compared with Britain, West Germany, France, Italy, and many other Western nation-states. It was larger than most, and stretched out over more territory, including parts separated by thousands of miles of sea (Hawaii) and another country (Alaska). The United States had no national police force. The content of education, and thus the values that were transmitted to the new generation, were almost exclusively subject to local decision-making, not shaped by a unified national curriculum as, say, in Israel or France.

At the same time, the federal structure of the U.S. government (compared with the unitary structure of, say, Britain) allowed the political institutions to function relatively effectively without a high level of unity. Its responsiveness to rising social demands seems to have enhanced the effectiveness of the political institutions up to 1960. There was a relatively high sense of effectiveness and legitimacy within the electorate during the fifties.

Declining Unity: 1960 to 1980

The developments that together resulted in a lower level of national unity and political effectiveness are well known. They are not reported here as new research findings, new insights, or a conceptual breakthrough. On the contrary, these often reported observations are listed together merely so that the conclusion to which they jointly point will come into focus.

DECLINE OF SHARED POLITICAL BELIEFS. Sociologists have pointed to the difficulty the heterogeneous American people has in forming a set of positive shared beliefs. Americans have found it easier to share opposition to an alien set of values, those of communism. In 1960 the American majority was still united by a strong shared world view that saw expanding communism as a sinister worldwide force and the United States as the leading world power entrusted with the duty to curb it. Containing the Soviet "empire" provided a world view defining "them" as evil and hostile and "us" as carriers of light. It offered a rationale for specific foreign policy acts, such as U.S. support of anti-communist regimes in Greece and Turkey in 1946–47, and the CIA role in overthrowing Mossadegh in Iran in 1953. And the Soviet threat was used to justify a host of domestic activities, such as increased national expenditures for research and development, science education, foreign-language training, space efforts, etc.

This "anti" consensus was much weaker by 1980. Division within the communist camp (especially between the U.S.S.R. and China) and within the West (especially between the United States and De Gaulle's France); the deliberate psychic disarmament of the United States, beginning with President Kennedy's Strategy for Peace (1963) and expanded by President Nixon's opening to China; the various détentes; and the dissension about the war in Vietnam, all resulted in a diminished ideological consensus and commitment.

THE RISE OF ALIENATION. Since 1966 pollsters have regularly published data on the trust Americans put in various institutions. In 1966, 43 percent said they had "a great deal of confidence" in the major institutions of American society, but by 1980 only 22 percent said they felt that way. (Data represent the average confidence in nine major institutions.) The political institutions particularly lost trust; the ratings of confidence in Congress and the executive branch were a low 10 and 14 percent respectively in 1978.

Everett Ladd called attention to the difference between a sense of loyalty to America and commitment to its basic political system, and a sense of its performance and competence. Whereas the public, data show, has lost little of the former, it has lost much of the latter.

Another set of data is striking because although it covers rather different matters, and the statements people were asked to agree or disagree with express strong disaffection, it closely parallels the trust-in-institution data. As often as these data have been cited, it still seems telling to recall that the proportion of Americans who agree with the statement that in the United States "the rich get richer and the poor get poorer" had increased from 45 percent in 1966 to 78 percent in 1980. Similarly, the proportion who feel that "what you think doesn't count much anymore" increased from 37 percent to 64 percent over the same time period. An index of disaffection, combining data on six such statements, shows a steady increase, from a minority (29 percent) in 1966 to a hefty majority (60 percent) in 1980.

DECLINE OF VOTER PARTICIPATION. The proportion of the voting-age population not voting for any candidate in presidential elections has steadily increased over the last two decades. In 1960, 37.2 percent didn't vote; in 1980, 46.8 percent didn't vote. Both Carter and Reagan were elected by segments of the electorate much smaller than the nonvoting "party": Carter by 27.2 percent versus 45.7 percent nonvoting, Reagan by 27.0 percent versus 46.8 percent.

True, not all the decline is based on a diminished sense of civic competence and the value of political participation. It also reflects, for instance, a lowering of the voting age from twenty-one to eighteen in 1971, and lower registration among younger voters, who are more geographically mobile than older voters. Nevertheless, it is widely agreed that a significant part of the growing voter apathy is due to a rising disaffection from the national polity.

ECONOMIC TRENDS. A rapidly expanding pie is commonly viewed as more conducive to conflict resolution within a community than one that is growing slowly or not at all. The annual growth in real gross national product (after "deducting" inflation) averaged 3.9 percent from 1960 to 1970. It slowed to an average 3.5 percent from 1970 to 1979. In 1980 the GNP decreased by 0.2 percent.

Even these unhappy statistics are misleadingly optimistic. They disregard the fact that there were not only more Americans than before (because of population growth), but that a much higher proportion than before were working outside the household and hence required tools, equipment, capital. Consequently, while the total GNP continued to grow a bit, GNP *per employed worker* increased only 1.9 percent per year from 1963 to 1973 and, according to estimates, a meager 0.1 percent per year from 1973 to 1979. The result is fewer resources to be allotted, and increasing strains among competing demands.

The 1973–80 period saw different parts of the United States affected in radically different ways by the sharp increase in energy prices. Such states as Texas, Louisiana, Alaska, and Montana, rich in energy—"the American OPEC"—experienced very large increases in state revenues, income to their industries, and jobs. Others—especially in the Northeast and the Midwest—experienced very sharp increases in costs. New England, for example, depends on oil to supply 85 percent of its energy needs, compared with 45 percent for the rest of the country. The price increases after 1973 pushed energy costs in Northeastern metropolitan areas to a level 97 percent higher than that in the rest of the country. The net result of such differences was greater strain on national unity.

INSTITUTIONAL CHANGES. Congressional "reforms" and the increase in congressional staff had a double effect particularly relevant to the issue at hand. They weakened the national political system *per se,* and they increased the power of the interest groups. The main relevant congressional reforms are those that resulted in more fragmentation and less ability to act in unison: the weakening of the seniority system in selecting committee chairmen, and the proliferation of subcommittees, which created numerous autonomous power centers.

One Washington observer, summarizing the effects of "democratization" in the House, states that it has reduced the power of the committee chairmen, who used to exercise more control than they do now over their committees, and that the House Rules Committee no longer exercises independent authority over which bills are open to floor debate. She continues:

> The committees tend to be self-selecting. . . . In large part, members go on committees because they favor the things that those committees can do. . . . Once they get on the committees, they pursue legislation to further the interests that they went on the committees to further. Interest groups suggest legislation . . . and hearings are held, and then, the case for the legislation having been made, like as not there is a bill.

The personal staffs of House and Senate members and the staffs of congressional committees grew from 5,100 in 1960 to 14,600 in 1980. With members of Congress overworked and staff members often the ones preparing draft bills and recommendations for votes, interest groups have found they can now "work" the large staff directly without necessarily dealing with any elected official.

THE OTHER SIDE OF THE LEDGER. In the face of the rise in centrifugal forces, there seems to have been no major new development to help sustain national bonds or the effectiveness of political institutions in the same years. The rise of television, "the electronic village," provided a shared national stage, but little of what played on it was supportive to national unity. The great expansion of social programs and transfer payments may be seen as an accommodation of the polity to social pressures, resulting in some reduction in poverty and in the economic distance between whites and blacks, and between men and women (although certainly not all, possibly not even most, of the change is due to public policy). However, the net effect these changes have on national unity is hardly self-evident. The social groups involved seem far from satisfied with the pace and scope of the resulting reallocations, although the fact that their protests have become less violent, more muted, may suggest a measure of success within the political system. (Others may argue that these groups despaired and withdrew into less political forms of expressing alienation.) And other groups, those that favor the *status quo ante,* have grown resentful over the reallocations and withdrawn support from the system.

In short, with several forces working to weaken the national unity and relatively few working to sustain it, the conclusion that it diminished seems safe to make.

The Rise in Interest Groups

While the system weakened, the number, scope, and power of interest groups rose.

POLITICAL MOBILIZATION OF PREVIOUSLY INACTIVE GROUPS. Histories of democracies have often been told in terms of expanding voting rights, introducing into the polity groups that previously did not have access to the system, such as slaves, women, and men without property. At the beginning of the era under review, universal suffrage already existed, but it was only during this period, especially following

the 1965 Voting Rights Act, that black Americans in the South—
especially in the rural parts—gained an effective vote. This was followed by a very substantial increase in black participation as voters and
as elected officials. Youth voting rights were extended when the voting
age was lowered to eighteen in 1971.

Of even greater sociological significance was the fact that large
social groups, previously basically inactive politically, were mobilized
and became politically aware and active, including various racial minority groups, women, people concerned about the environment, and
welfare clients, for instance. Later, especially after 1974, there was a
sudden and considerable growth in corporate interest groups and an
increase in trade and industrial groups.

One keen Washington observer, Meg Greenfield, wrote: "I can't
remember a time in Washington when interest-group issues and politics so dominated events. And every day the units of protest and
concern seem to be subdividing into even smaller and more specialized
groupings."

And then came the PACs, adding a major tool to private interests.
I have already discussed their rise and effects, in Part I. Whatever one
may say about their ethical status, they clearly increased divisiveness,
not unity, in matters economic and ideological.

THE WEAKENING OF THE POLITICAL PARTIES. In the period under
study, by a wide variety of measures, the political parties' appeal, role,
and influence have diminished. Three political scientists, Norman H.
Nie, Sidney Verba, and John R. Petrocik, report: "Citizen affiliation
with the major political parties has been looked at from a number of
perspectives: party as a psychological identification, as a guide to
electoral choice and candidate evaluation, and as an object of affection.
In each case, the data confirm a decline." Citizens' identification with
the political parties declined. While the proportion of people who
identified with one of the major parties fell only 3 percentage points
between 1939 and about 1964, it declined 10 percentage points between
1964 and 1974.

Richard G. Niemi and Herbert F. Weisberg, reviewing the situation in 1976, report: "More and more people call themselves indepen-
dents rather than Republicans or Democrats. . . . Cynicism about
politics, especially party politics, has been on the rise. . . . Many read
in these trends 'the end of parties,' at least as we know them. Instead

of realigning, the present party system is said to be 'dealigning.' " They go on to suggest that they do not expect parties to disappear, which hardly anyone expects. In a volume they edited, they provide reports on party decline. One, "The Onward March of Party Decomposition" by Walter Dean Burnham, is followed by "The Erosion of Party Fidelity" by Philip E. Converse. Other writers have stressed the rise of the media candidates, especially since John F. Kennedy, whom they see as appealing directly to the masses, rather than being either selected by party bosses or dependent on party machines that would get out the vote and, in turn, have to be rewarded with patronage.

Finally, changes in Congress are faulted. Members of Congress have felt freer to deal with special-interest groups and were under less countervailing pressure from the multi-constituency, broad-based, and wide-scope groups that the parties represent. Everett Ladd, reviewing the situation, summarized it: "As the parties . . . withered, candidates for Congress and other elective offices were left to operate as independent entrepreneurs."

Most recently a revisionism of sorts set in. Political scientists now often argue that the parties' decline has been overstated. For instance, many of the voters turned independent have been found to actually harbor fairly consistent commitment to one party or another. Also, part of what has been depicted as party-decline is now described as party-change. For example, the greater reliance on the media. All said and done, as David Adamany points out in a comprehensive essay, the parties both changed *and* weakened. The parties' "principal competitors," he writes, are—the PACs.

IN SUMMARY

A widely held pro-interest-group theory argues that interest groups are an inevitable, integral part of the democratic process and, on balance, basically benign, chiefly because interest groups are viewed as a major avenue of representation to supplement the electoral process, viewed as requiring much augmentation.

My critical response, so far, has embraced an analytic view, regarding the polity as a balance between centrifugal and centripetal forces, rather than a boundless competition. In this context, the interest groups add too much power to destabilizing forces—not to community-building ones. Seen historically, they have grown in power while the union has deteriorated, which has further exacerbated the threat interest groups always pose. What remains to be seen is that the groups that provide a beneficial base for politics are not interest groups at all.

CHAPTER THIRTEEN

SPECIAL
INTERESTS
ARE NOT
CONSTITUENCIES

SOCIAL GROUPS, YES; SPECIAL INTERESTS, NO

Political scientists correctly perceive that the major foundation of
politics is groups, not individuals. The image of millions of individuals
casting ballots in the seclusion of the ballot booth, and these ballots
directing their representatives in how to run the nation—until the next
election—is a false one. Most individuals make up their minds before
they enter the voting booth, under the influence of groups and associations they belong to, from labor unions to churches to families and
neighborhoods. And the extensive political give and take that goes on
during the years between elections is not dominated by letters written
by individuals to their members of Congress (an activity that is itself
often group-spawned), but by group representation that affects both
the legislature and the executive—and even appeals to courts.

Although political scientists made a major contribution in recognizing the role of groups, it is, from the viewpoint of the issue at hand,
a dangerous overgeneralization to treat all groups as if they were
basically the same. This will become clear as I turn now to show that
groups are systematically and in important ways different in their
political roles: certain types are beneficial to the representative democracy; others are certainly not.

Many political scientists treat social and interest groups inter-
changeably, as if they were one and the same thing. The reason this

tendency is troubling in the present context is that it makes interest groups seem much more omnipresent than they are (though they are quite widespread enough). Also, we shall see, interest groups are credited with contributions to society that are actually rendered by social groups.

Interest groups represent interests present within the society vis-à-vis the political realm. To put it differently, interest groups have a social base (shoemakers, homeowners) that has an interest (limit imports, reduce taxes, etc.) that can be advanced—or set back—by the government. Interest groups are largely a one-way bridge leading from the private to the public realm. (Some traffic flows the other way, as when an interest group informs its members on what is going on in the capital. However, when this flow becomes significant, we are no longer dealing with an interest group but, more likely, a publication, such as the *National Journal,* or an educational association, such as the Foreign Policy Association.)

By definition, and by common English usage of the term, groups that are mainly private, without a bridge to the public realm (say, a chess club), *or* mainly public, without a base in society (for example, a faction within the legislature), are not interest groups. A chess club may, under some highly unusual circumstances, act as an interest group —if it were, for instance, to fight a local ordinance against games. But typically its members' actions are internal to the group, aimed at one another and not at affecting the government. Similarly, a group that is part of the government may occasionally act like an interest group, as when legislators seek to increase their salaries. Most often, though, the government represents the mechanism on which interest groups seek to have an impact, rather than acting as an interest group itself.

By this definition of interest groups, which closely follows the work of many others, *many social groups do not qualify as interest groups.* Neighborhood or block associations, religious congregations, social clubs, numerous voluntary associations (such as the YMCA and the Red Cross), and college communities are basically social groups or associations—intrinsic to the social realm, but lacking a significant political presence.

In contrast to this clear separation of interest groups from social groups, political scientist Gabriel Almond provides a fourfold typology of what he calls interest groups. One type is "non-associational interest groups," which includes "kinship and lineage groups, ethnic,

regional, religious, status and class groups." This leaves very few
groups not defined as interest groups and blurs, if it doesn't obliterate,
the distinction between social and interest groups.

An earlier definition by a political scientist, Earl Latham, likewise
confounds interest groups with groups whose purpose and sphere of
activity are social, cultural, and economic: "They are structures of
power because they concentrate human wit, energy, and muscle for the
achievement of given purposes." True, any such group, by virtue of
its social cohesion and organization, or its basis of similar, compatible,
or shared interests, is *potentially* an interest group, and it might occasionally act like one. But typically social groups are neither politically
involved nor active. As long as this distinction is observed, several of
the virtues frequently attributed to interest groups are actually to be
credited to this much larger universe of social groups, associations, and
organizations.

A major case in point is the body of social-science data indicating
that most people consult their kin, friends, neighbors, fellow community members, and voluntary associations when they decide for whom
to vote; this demonstrates the significance of social groups, not interest
groups, for the electoral process. When politicians employ charismatic
appeals or demagoguery, individuals are often able to resist the psychic
pressures generated by these appeals to their emotions, because of bonds
to other people they feel close to—people who either are not exposed
simultaneously to the same appeal or are not as susceptible to it. Men,
both historically and in recent years, have been more susceptible to
saber-rattling; women, more dedicated to peace. (Reference is to statistical averages, not innate traits.) Saber-rattling, then, is countervailed
by a "cooling-off" mechanism built into the family—of course a
private, not a public, group. Other psychic support mechanisms that
allow people to withstand pressure by the state are embedded in other
social groups, from neighborhoods to church-based associations. True,
some of these same groups may sometimes act as interest groups, but
this is not necessary for their role as a source of interpersonal anchor-
ing.

Similarly, social groups are quite adequate to protect individuals
from "mass" demagogic appeal. This statement is supported by studies
showing that people absorb messages communicated via radio and TV
in line with what their social groups approve; they also tend to read
newspapers that their group favors, and interpret the news in line with

their social group's precepts and values. In short, *social* groups provide much of the desired "mediating" structure.

"BAD" VERSUS "GOOD" INTEREST GROUPS

The Need for Distinctions (Sub-Aggregation)

Just as not all groups are interest groups, so there are important differences among interest groups, differences from the viewpoint of their contribution—or harm—to a democratic society. To lump them all together is as inappropriate as using the term "drugs" to refer to antibiotics and narcotics, without making any distinction.

Typically, references to interest groups include groups one senses intuitively are quite different. Political scientist Dayton David McKean, for instance, lists side by side the League of Women Voters and the American Cranberry Growers' Association. V. O. Key, Jr., refers in the same breath to the American Peace Society and the National Association of Manufacturers. Political scientist James Q. Wilson lists next to each other the National Council of the Churches of Christ—an organization of various Protestant and Orthodox denominations, with more than 40 million members, that supported civil-rights legislation, opposed American involvement in Vietnam, and favored recognition of the People's Republic of China long before this was popular—and the Foreign Oil Policy Committee, which lobbied vigorously to restrict oil imports to the United States. The motivating forces behind this committee were coal-mine owners who wanted to restrict the competition their product faced in the market place. The report of the Committee on American Legislatures, having just concluded that pressure groups are "legitimate" and "invaluable," adds, "However, some pressure groups, acting as organized minorities, attempt to thwart the public will and act generally in a manner detrimental to the general welfare."

For reasons that will become evident immediately, I find it useful to distinguish among three types: one I shall call special-interest groups (SIGs for short); another, constituency-representing organizations (CROs for short); and, finally, public-interest groups (PIGs). Since the main new distinction I introduce here is between SIGs and CROs, and since most interest groups are either SIGs or CROs, I will focus on this pair before turning to the PIGs.

Special Interest Groups
versus Constituency Organizations

Special-interest groups are organizations whose social base is relatively narrow, whose political representation is limited in scope—often to pecuniary interests—and whose beneficiaries are almost exclusively the groups' members. This is quite precisely what the term *special interest* suggests, in opposition to general interest, which implies a broader-based, more inclusive representation. The sugar lobbies usually —though not always—act as SIGs. Representing some fourteen thousand cane and beet farmers, they are preoccupied almost exclusively with promoting limitations on the importation of sugar and sustaining indirect subsidies for sugar farmers, so they can in effect sell their sugar to the government at above free-market prices.

Constituency-representing organizations are organizations whose social base is relatively broad, whose scope of political representation is wide, often encompassing both nonpecuniary interests (such as social status, values one holds, and symbolic issues) and pecuniary ones, and that seek to balance service to their members with a measure of concern for the community of which they are a part. The Urban League, the AFL-CIO, the Business Roundtable often—but certainly not always —act as CROs.

The three attributes used to differentiate SIGs and CROs are to be viewed as dimensions of a continuum, not as dichotomous variables. Thus, an interest group's social base may be very small (a few hundred tugboat pilots), merely small (fourteen thousand sugar farmers), relatively large (1.6 million teachers who are members of the NEA), or quite large (14 million members of the AFL-CIO). Similarly, it may represent chiefly a narrow interest, quite a few interests, or a wide gamut. And, the interest of the group may be represented in a raw form, or leavened with varying degrees of concern for the community, not as a public-relations posture, but as a genuine concern. Many religious groups that are politically active, for instance, combine both perspectives. The term SIGs refers to one extreme of this threefold continuum; CROs to the other pole.

The inevitable question arises, since three attributes are used to define SIGs and CROs—*size* of social base, *scope* of interests represented, and *strength* of the balancing commitment to the commonweal —what if a group scores high on some of the attributes but low on the others? Other types of interest groups result, which I will not discuss here, either because they have been discussed elsewhere at length (single-issue groups, for instance) or because they are categories populated by very few cases (such as groups that are broad-based, narrowly pecuniary in scope, but high in commitment to the commonweal). My main focus is on the two types that are either high or low on all three dimensions and that are quite common, SIGs and CROs.

Public-Interest Groups

Public-interest groups are organizations whose political positions concern the community at large, or primarily nonmembers, and whose focus is as a rule on nonpecuniary interests. The size of their social base tends to vary and hence cannot be used as a defining characteristic. Concern with the community is their most outstanding quality. Common Cause, Americans for Democratic Action, and Young Americans for Freedom often act as public-interest groups.

Most, if not all, interest groups—not merely public-interest groups —claim they serve the community or the public interest. The social scientist, it has frequently been noted, is hard put to tell what "the" public interest is. It is easier to determine whether or not those who benefit by the groups' actions are first and foremost the groups' members. At issue are not the futuristic, hypothetical, potential payoffs that interest groups are fond of promising to all, but those that line pockets here and now, or securely in the near future.

An Analytic Distinction

It is important to take into account at all times that the distinctions among the three types of interest groups are analytic, in the sense that any concrete group may display all three kinds of behavior over time, or even at one point in time. For example, when a longshoremen's union refuses to load goods to be shipped to Poland, in protest of the imposition of martial law in that country in late 1981, the union is acting as a public-interest group, although as a rule it acts as a special-interest group.* When foundations fight for tax exemption, special postal rates, and tax deductibility of contributions to themselves, they act as SIGs, not PIGs, though usually their main concern is the public.

---

*A case might be made that it is a CRO. To determine whether it is a CRO or a SIG would require a study of its conduct.

It also follows that a group that has acted for a given period largely as one type may over the years grow to resemble another type. For instance, a group initially concerned with public service may become more and more preoccupied with the privileges of its members.

In the following discussion I shall use the designation of SIG, CRO, or PIG as a shorthand, to suggest a group that acts *mainly*, in a given period, as the type indicated. No group ever "is" a CRO, SIG, or PIG; a concrete group at most approximates one analytic type more than the others. The discussion focuses on CROs and SIGs, because PIGs have received a relatively large amount of attention in recent research and theoretical deliberation, whereas the difference between SIGs and CROs is very often overlooked.

Two of my colleagues, who read a draft of this book before it was published, commented that the distinction I make among the three types of groups is "normative." Simply put, I like PIGs and CROs better than SIGs. There is a measure of truth in this comment. However, the basis of my preference is not a personal inclination, but the observation that SIGs are harmful to democracy, CROs and PIGs much less so—indeed, often supportive.

THE EFFECT ON PLURALISM WITHIN UNITY

It is my thesis that most statements made about "interest groups" both by the public and by political scientists apply much more forcefully to one type than to others. I start with the pivotal question: are interest groups "good" or "bad" for democracy? As I see it, the positive contributions often attributed to interest groups are frequently made by constituency-representing organizations, but not by special-interest groups. Public-interest groups have a unique and, on balance, positive role of their own.

SIGs Overload More Than CROs

All other things being equal, it is much easier to work out a policy with a handful of political groups than with hundreds—if not thousands—of groups. An early estimate of the number of lobbies put it, for 1950, at 150 national labor groups, 150 national agricultural organizations, and over 3,000 national business groups. Many of these are still active; in addition, more than 3,300 PACs have been formed. Thus, a new consensus for major items of an economic policy can be worked out relatively readily by dealing with CROs such as the Business Roundtable (representing some 192 of the largest U.S. corporations, which produce about half of the GNP), the Chamber of Commerce (representing some 200,000 companies and 1,400 trade associations), the AFL-CIO, and key farmer and consumer groups. The same political processes tend to become overloaded when they need to deal with the lobbies of many scores of corporations, trade associations, and splinter labor unions, plus the lobbies of each main farm product— from milk to peanuts, and numerous others. Indeed, one of the "functions" of CROs is to "digest" within them scores of potential SIGs and work out shared positions among them.

This is first of all a matter of sheer size. Since SIGs are by definition narrow in base, they represent only fragments of society, not large segments. Second, SIGs are, also by definition, more self-interested and less involved in the commonweal. This, in turn, will tend to make it harder to formulate a shared policy based on them.

John Gardner, the founder of Common Cause, has argued that the effect of SIGs is to immobilize government:

> Imagine a checker player confronted by a bystander who puts a thumb on one checker and says "Go ahead and play, just don't touch this one," and then another bystander puts a thumb on another checker with the same warning, and then another bystander and another. The owners of the thumbs—the interest groups—don't want to make the game unwinnable. They just don't want you to touch their particular checker.

David Riesman has provided a similar view of the American political system as one in which scores of "veto groups" each have enough power to block a step forward but not to provide support for positive action, so that a stalemate results. More recently, Suzanne Berger has pointed to interest groups as the source of "major new problems of 'ungovernability,' inflation, and economic stagnation." The fate of the immigration, welfare, and health-care reforms, stuck in Congress for years on end, are cases in point. Other laws may finally be hatched, but only after unduly long incubation periods. Overload does not necessarily block every bill, but it does exact a high cost from many.

SIGs Are More Determined Than CROs

SIGs can commit all their resources to the promotion of a single interest, whereas CROs must distribute theirs among a wide array of issues they, by definition, must represent. Hence one would expect the average SIG to be more determined and potentially detrimental than the average CRO if one compares their effects on a single item of public policy.

The stakes, even on a single issue, can be high indeed. For example, a change in public policy on oil pricing (decontrol) will generate an estimated $832 billion of extra revenue for the oil companies between 1980 and 1990. This means that dedicating even so much as a billion dollars to lobbying on this matter, an absurdly high figure, would pose no economic difficulty for the oil lobbies.

To move from theory to fact: Twenty-six PACs representing companies and trade associations related to the oil industry gave $1.1 million to congressional campaigns in 1977–78. When the new Congress convened, it voted not only to end most of the windfall-profits tax by 1990, a step widely favored, but also to lower the taxation rate previously recommended by the House Ways and Means Committee. The total savings to the industry was estimated to be $8.8 billion. A SIG can afford to commit large amounts to advance one issue or point.

CROs Satisfy More Than SIGs

To the extent that CROs influence the formation of a public policy, the policy will respond to several, if not all, the basic needs of those persons they represent. In contrast, because SIGs deal chiefly with one facet (or a few facets) of a person's needs, a policy that is shaped by SIGs is unlikely to respond to their members' other needs. For example, the National Parking Association may succeed in curtailing the scope of mass-transportation projects or delaying the implementation of air-quality standards for cities. This success may in turn improve its members' profits, but it would leave all their other needs—including transportation and environmental needs—without representation, at least via this interest group.

Both Are Inflationary, but SIGs More

Both CROs and SIGs can contribute to inflation, a point emphasized by neoconservatives. Writing about the "revolution of entitlements," Daniel Bell, like Milton Friedman before him, has called attention to the effects of shifting allocative decisions from the market to the polity. The market, these writers argue, exercises self-discipline, since the sum of its resources available at any one time is fixed. An increase in the allotment to one group—say, workers—must be accommodated by a decrease to another—shareholders. However, no such automatic adjustments are built into the polity: one can always allot more by printing more money. The more groups push for more, the higher the inflation.

Although neoconservative writers refer to interest groups in general, the examples they cite are the new politically aware and active constituencies and their organizations, those representing groups such as blacks, Hispanics, and women. Obviously, organizations representing the interests of other constituencies, such as small business, have the same basic effect. And SIGs are more demanding of pecuniary payoff than CROs, both because SIGs respond less to symbolic payoffs (which are not inflationary) and because they have less commonweal involvement.

Labor unions, under President Carter's voluntary wage guidelines and the "National Accord," showed a measure of commitment to the commonweal, reflected in their acceptance of wage increases below the rate of inflation. The AFL-CIO agreed to support President Carter's 1980 guideline of 7.5-percent to 9.5-percent wage increases, despite inflation of 11.3 percent in 1979 and 13.5 percent through 1980. Wages of all union workers actually rose less than inflation: 9.0 percent in 1979 and 10.9 percent in 1980. In contrast, SIGs showed less restraint during the same period. The hospital lobby, for example, fought the voluntary guidelines. Hospital room charges rose 11.4 percent in 1979 and 13.1 percent in 1980.

The Functions Revisited

Political scientists credit interest groups with five contributions to the democratic process. How do SIGs and CROs differ from this viewpoint? For reasons already indicated, it seems that whereas it is true that both SIGs and CROs may *supplement* the electoral process, SIGs, because of their large number and low commitment to the commonweal, go beyond supplementing it to overloading it. And the more restrained interest groups, the CROs, with a much wider base, are a much more appropriate source of additional representation between elections.

Although both SIGs and CROs may serve as *bridges* between the socioeconomic and the political realms, CROs tend to provide bridges that, taken together, carry most segments of society. In contrast, SIGs bring in only small fragments at a time, and satisfy at best only one facet, the pecuniary one.

The same holds for the *links* that interest groups provide between the executive and the legislative branches. Both SIGs and CROs fulfill this function, but the resulting policies are quite different, in terms of the scope and breadth of the public needs reflected.

The *mediating* function is more a task for social groups than for either type of interest group. Indeed, mediation is traditionally credited to the family, local communities, and voluntary associations acting as social groups, not as interest groups. It is these social groups that sustain individual personalities against undue influence by the state and rally to their help—by contributing funds for legal action, for instance—when the state seeks to oppress them. True, some PIGs, such as the American Civil Liberties Union, may be said to play a role here when they defend the Constitution, or individual and civil rights. Mediation, however, does not usually take the course of legal action; its power is within the social fabric that countervails the state and consists not so much of political representation as of a limitation on the effect of the psychic and economic pressures the government's agents can generate.

As for the *socialization* function, both kinds of interest group discharge it, although CROs seem to be more often membership organizations, and SIGs merely lobbies. Lobbies provide relatively few socialization opportunities, because there are no occasions for members to meet, exchange views, get to know one another, and so on. Typically, you pay dues to "your" PAC, and maybe get an annual report on what it did for you, but there is no more of a relationship. Moreover, one cannot help wondering whether socialization into political action by groups with a low commitment to the commonweal is as functional for the society as that by groups with a higher commonweal involvement.

As to the suggestion that interest groups are "invaluable" sources of *information,* as I see it that information tends to be highly tainted, a problem faced by both CROs and SIGs.

In short, having drawn a conceptual distinction among different types of groups, I suggest that, for several reasons, the positive contributions often attributed to interest groups in general come either largely from those functioning for the most part as constituency-representing organizations, or from social groups, but not from special-interest groups.

CHAPTER FOURTEEN

THE
PUBLIC
INTEREST

CAN ONE DEFINE "THE PUBLIC INTEREST"?

The argument has been made many times that the public interest cannot be defined and that PIGs are no different from any other interest group. David Truman, one of the originators of the pro-interest-group position, writes about some who "assume explicitly or implicitly that there is an interest of the nation as a whole, universally and invariably held and standing apart from and superior to those of the various groups included within it." Truman believes that "such an assertion flies in the face of all that we know of the behavior of men in a complex society."

Truman goes on to explain that assertions of "national" or "public" interest "do not describe any actual or possible political situation within a complex modern nation" and that in developing a group theory of politics we do not need these concepts.

Political scientist Karl W. Deutsch takes a similar position. To wit:

> According to some classic theories, deliberation should be carried out by wise men impartially pondering the common good, that is, the collection of objective interests or expectable rewards, direct and indirect, which all participants have in common. No selfish thoughts or special interests are supposed to distract them. In practice, however, few politicians are that wise, or unselfish, or free from links to special interests. Indeed, if they were any or all of these, they would not be representative of most of the people they are supposed to represent.

Murray L. Weidenbaum, an economist by training who has served in the government, argues that since "it is no simple task to identify *the* public interest in any specific issue of public policy . . . good policy consists of properly balancing and reconciling a variety of worthy interests." He defines neither worthy interests nor proper balance, a point I return to below.

All interest groups, it is said, seek to cloak their self-serving goals with public-interest garb. Sociologist Irving Louis Horowitz observes: "We have now reached the point at which nearly every special interest promotes itself as operating in the name of the general interest." Business administration professor David Vogel adds: "While denying that there actually existed such a notion as the 'public interest,' pluralist theory would appear to have little difficulty appreciating that various groups and individuals might seek to cloak themselves in its mantle."

Joseph Cantor ties the PACs in:

> PAC supporters object to the frequent pejorative connotation of the term "special interest" and the juxtaposition of it with another value-laden term, "public interest." They hold the view that all factions which advocate specific government policy objectives are, in fact, special interests, and that no one group has any more claim to the role of defender of the public interest than any other group.

The *denial of the public interest* is itself, whether intended or unwitting, an ideological argument against the public realm and in favor of private power. We have traced in some detail, in the previous discussion of Marshall's seminal study and the lessons of U.S. history, especially in the Progressive Era, the importance of safeguarding the public realm from private invasion. Nor is it particularly difficult to define the public interest: acts or policies are in the public interest when they either serve all the members of a community or advance shared goals, such as defense.

One may disagree on which policies do have such an effect. For example, some may see greater public interest in manufacturing more nuclear arms, others in unilateral disarmament. But this does not mean that the concept of public interest is useless. There are *clearly* policies that do not serve the public; policies that, for instance, may enable profiteers to earn vast sums to build weapons that do not work. As long as policies that serve the public can be differentiated from those that do not, the public interest is a viable concept. And the arguments among those policies that serve the public can then be settled by agreed-upon procedures. A look at public-interest groups will further illustrate the viability of the concept.

WHAT IS A PUBLIC-INTEREST GROUP?

We saw that the defining characteristic of public-interest groups is that they seek to serve the commonweal rather than their members. Some PIGs promote shared rules and procedures; they are system PIGs, if you will. For example, the League of Women Voters seeks to secure voters' rights and participation not for its members, but for the public at large; most of its members, it is safe to assume, would vote anyhow. Other groups promote a shared good they believe the public requires: from stronger defense or peace, to protecting the environment, to morals. One may call those public-cause PIGs.

Archibald Cox is quite correct when he emphasizes that "the public interest is not to be confused with interests of 'the government' or with 'the State,' as in an all-powerful Marxist State. The total public good in a free society is neither more nor less than the aggregate and fairly distributed welfare of *all* its individual members."

Of course, when the community benefits—say, if peace were to reign—the members of a public-interest group would also benefit, but this is a by-product of peace for all, not a special service for the members of this group. If a group does seek peace *for its members*— if, for instance, a street gang lobbies the police to arrange a truce with its rivals—we are not dealing with a public-interest group. And, to reiterate, a specific group may act as a PIG under some circumstances and not under others. To take one example, Public Citizen, the umbrella organization for Ralph Nader's citizen groups, opposed a bill that would have required filing reports with the government on grassroots lobbying efforts. The bill, supported by Common Cause, was intended to shed more light on lobbying by all organizations, a position Public Citizen usually supports.

The criterion we apply is that of actual service, not rhetoric or public posture. And from that viewpoint PIGs differ from SIGs and CROs. E. E. Schattschneider has pointed out that "special-interest groups often tend to rationalize their special interests as public interests." He asks whether the two kinds of groups can be distinguished, and he answers in the affirmative. He relies both on the "who benefits" criterion and on how membership is selected. As to the first point, he compares the National Association of Manufacturers with the American League to Abolish Capital Punishment, and remarks that while the former seeks to enrich its members, the members of the latter "obviously do not expect to be hanged"; nor are the members of the National Child Labor Committee "children in need of legislative protection." As to membership criteria, PIGs are open, and anybody can join; SIGs tend to limit their member-beneficiaries.

Similarly, political scientist Andrew S. McFarland defines a "public interest lobby" as "one that seeks to represent general interests or those of the whole public." He warns, though, that not all the groups that are called PIGs, or call themselves such, necessarily represent the public interest.

Fair enough. Whether a *specific* group is largely a PIG or not is an empirical question, not answered by what it proclaims to seek, but by what it does. Thus, on the basis of its stated goals the Sierra Club, a leading environmentalist group, is clearly a public-interest group. On the other hand, if it really does dedicate itself, as William Tucker argues in his book *Progress and Privilege,* to gaining privileges for its upper-middle-class members—say, untrammeled mountains to ski on —it clearly is a SIG. It may entail some effort to find out what a specific group actually is, but the distinction between public- and special-interest group is clear.

PIGs are to be found all over the ideological spectrum, not necessarily or even commonly on the Left or liberal or progressive. Among those who argue otherwise is Murray L. Weidenbaum, who writes that most PIGs are anti-business. Andrew McFarland notes: "Conservatives criticize public interest groups for masking liberal ideology in a public interest disguise." As I see it, groups that seek to uphold the society's traditional moral code (such as the Moral Majority), to keep up its defenses (Committee on the Present Danger), or to defeat the Equal Rights Amendment (Phyllis Schlafly's Eagle Forum) are all conservative or right-wing PIGs.

My view might be said to fly in the face of a survey by Robert Lichter and Stanley Rothman which shows that most leaders of PIGs are liberals: 96 percent voted for McGovern in 1972; 93 percent for

Carter, etc. However, this finding is strictly the result of the criteria for inclusion in what the authors called "the public interest movement." As I see it, there is no *one* public-interest movement; and while there is some bunching of liberal groups, there is another cluster of conservative and right-wing public-interest groups. Nor do these groups, of either camp, work closely together on many issues.

THE BALANCING ROLE OF PIGs

If one sees the political system as resting on a balance between unity-enhancing forces and centrifugal forces of special interests, system PIGs add to the forces that sustain the community. Whether their leaders and ideologues aspire to eliminate all interest groups or merely to curb them matters little from this viewpoint; public-interest groups are so weak compared with the two other main types of interest groups that at best they serve as a limited corrective. There is no realistic danger, at least in contemporary America, that they will undermine the foundations of pluralism. Various Nader groups may annoy the corporate, trade, and labor interest groups, but are no match for these groups' PACed power. Indeed, PACs have grown in number, scope, and power in the years since Nader became prominent. Common Cause may slow down the various other interest groups and force them to restrict somewhat the means they resort to, but there are no indications that Common Cause has put them out of business.

Explains *U.S. News and World Report:* "Many analysts assert that the reformers are letting conservative political action committees run circles around them with efficient, costly lobbying financed by computerized mass-mail fund drives. 'Nader and Common Cause come in and preach the morality of their position,' observes Panetta, 'while everyone else is practicing these sophisticated techniques.' "

The Panetta cited is Representative Leon Panetta, a California Democrat—friend, not foe, of PIGs.

HOW TO CONTAIN INTEREST GROUPS

If the power of interest groups of all kinds is deemed excessive, or if one main type is viewed as much more damaging to the democratic process than the others, there are at least three systematic solutions. One is to "level" the interest groups, sharply reducing their power. Another is to rely on the groups to contain one another. The last is to support a system that will limit the means that interest groups use, without seeking to eliminate them. If one uses football as an analogy, the first approach is to try to prohibit the game on the grounds that it is too violent a sport. The second—to expect players to refrain from pulling face masks and avoid other such abusive behavior out of fear that the other side will resort to the same abuses, a kind of mutual-deterrence approach. The third method is to establish rules and post referees to limit the scope of the confrontations.

Leveling

The leveling solution is very rarely broached even by strong advocates of political reforms. One almost never hears a case being made that we should abolish interest groups and make the electoral process the mainstay of representation and consensus-building, and public interest—as expressed by the public at large—the only guide of elected representatives. Much more typical is the call for "sunshine." Since special interests thrive when they can function covertly, out of public sight, Common Cause has supported legislation requiring that bill-writing and -rewriting sessions of congressional committees be open to the public. This, of course, assumes the continued existence of interest groups. Common Cause wants to force them out of the closet, not out of business.

Others, from James Madison on, have criticized the "leveling" approach as naïve if not dangerous. Naïve, they believe, because "the latent causes of faction," Madison's term for interest groups, are "sown in the nature of man" and hence are inevitable, impossible to eliminate. Dangerous, because attempts to curb interest groups may threaten constitutional guarantees such as freedom of speech, of assembly, and above all, of petition. James Q. Wilson made this point: "Interest group activity is a form of political speech protected by the First Amendment to the Constitution: it cannot lawfully be abolished or even much curtailed."

The elimination of all interest groups would also undermine pluralism, which—like unity—*is* an essential element of a free, democratic society. At the same time, sharply limiting special-interest groups, while tolerating, or maybe even encouraging, constituency-representing organizations (and public-interest groups), is compatible with a pluralistic yet unity-preserving democracy.

Self-Containment

Turning to the second approach, what about the notion that interest groups can contain one another, either through a system of checks and balances or by the mere existence of a multitude of interests pulling the polity and policies in divergent directions? James Madison implies this approach in Federalist Paper 51:

> It is of great importance in a republic not only to guard the society against the oppression of its rulers, but to guard one part of the society against the injustice of the other part.... Whilst all authority in [the federal republic of the United States] will be derived from and dependent on the society, the society itself will be broken into so many parts, interests and classes of citizens, that the rights of individuals, or of the minority, will be in little danger from interested combinations of the majority.

V. O. Key, Jr., writes, on the topic "balancing of interest": "In situation after situation legislators and administrators are confronted by groups pushing in opposite directions, a state of affairs which permits government to balance one off against the other and to arrive more easily at a solution thought to represent the general interest."

This theory applied to the world of interest groups is reflected in Milbrath's suggestion that they are largely self-neutralizing: he has discussed the issue under the heading "the balance of power in lobbying," which is an important clue. The balance-of-power theory in international relations refers to the notion that international stability, order, and peace are based on nations' balancing one another, rather than being restrained by a worldwide or regional system or community.

Milbrath elaborates: "An important factor attenuating the impact of lobbying on governmental decisions is the fact that nearly every vigorous push in one direction stimulates an opponent or coalition of opponents to push in the opposite direction." Milbrath believes that "this natural self-balancing factor comes into play so often that it almost amounts to a law. The great numbers of lobbyists in Washington may actually be a blessing instead of a threat to the governmental system. When groups push on both sides of an issue, officials can more freely exercise their judgment than when the groups push on only one side."

Milbrath himself mentions one main criticism of this view: that weak, unorganized groups, such as consumer groups, lose out. He counters this by saying that consumers have a chance to express themselves through "constituent pressures and the vote." But since other groups do, too, one in effect, by giving these other groups a second channel not available (or less available) to consumers, does render the system more subject to the power of producers' interests. One also moves power, as we have seen, from greater reliance on the relatively egalitarian electoral politics to an arena in which economic power and organizational power are much more important.

And self-containment (interest groups limiting one another without outside, "system" forces) cannot work when a SIG has a decisive role in a narrow field and faces no other interest groups, either because other interested parties are not organized, or because the SIG effect is concealed.

Some political scientists developed the idea that what is at issue here is a great difference in the size of the stakes for SIGs and the public. If sugar lobbies increase the price of sugar by a few pennies, for instance, this will enrich their members handsomely without outraging the public. A few cents extra per pound of sugar will not impoverish even the less privileged, and the public will hardly be motivated to counteract.

Although such situations abound, the stakes of the public-at-large are often *much* higher, and SIGs are not stopped. Nursing homes offer a prime example. Patients in nursing homes are no match for the owners. They are often quite old and/or disabled. Many have diminished mental capacities and are dependent on one or more drugs, including tranquilizers, some of which are administered by the owners to ease the "management" of the homes. Because patients often suffer severe trauma if they have to move to another home, it is difficult for them to pressure owners by threatening to take their business elsewhere. Many who have relatives in nursing homes ignore them, let alone act in their behalf. Quite a few patients have no kin at all. And nursing homes in New York (where many are located) pay fees to state legislators who can be legally retained as lawyers for the homes. Such a power imbalance can only result in gross and continued abuse of patients.

Also, the reach of interest groups, especially when they affect legislation on a "retail" basis, is often covert. The public does not know, as a rule, what lobbyists say or do. Each year thousands of laws are passed or modified, regulations changed, and budgets adopted.

While the media may call attention to a few at a time, many scores of others go unreported. By the time the public finds out that a subsidy has been rigged, a regulation weakened, and so on, years may have passed, and the action is often very difficult to reverse.

In areas in which several interest groups do clash, they frequently twist public policy by tilting it in a direction they all share. This phenomenon was observed in a 1930 study of pressure groups and tariffs by E. E. Schattschneider. He found the field dominated by domestic producers seeking different—but all increased—duties on imports. Consumers who would have benefited from lower duties were unrepresented. And, as reported in Chapter 6, most, if not all, the military lobbies favor procurement over expenditures on personnel, as much as they may fight among themselves about *which* piece of hardware the United States ought to buy.

Outside Forces

The notion of *self*-containment conflicts sharply with the social-science conclusion that contests must be contained from the outside by processes that do not rely solely on the contesting parties. Moral commitment (to playing by the rules, for instance), loyalties (such as to the shared community), and shared institutions (like the Constitution) are among the most-often-listed foundations of the unity within which wholesome diversity is possible.

When the capsule is well protected, we have competition, which is bounded conflict. Without the capsule, we have unlimited conflict, catch as catch can, which is ruinous, certainly for the polity and society, some say even in the economy. (Hence the concern about price wars in which corporations sell below cost to win a market share and undermine one another. Look at the U.S. airlines since deregulation.)

Aside from institutional factors, there are others, which are rooted in personality. My own work has provided additional evidence for the view that human nature is not merely calculative, utilitarian, or rationalist, but a combination of such elements with ethical commitments and loyalties. A comparative study of four attempts to build unity among nations illustrated the significance of the presence versus the absence of the community-capsule. I have already referred to Adam Smith's cogent observations on this matter.

If one agrees that self-containment is not to be relied upon and sees a need to contain interest groups without abolishing them, one is ready to consider the third approach, external limitations, and ask how this might be achieved. It would be best if one could enhance the forces that sustain the community and make it less vulnerable to interest-group pressures—forces that include a change of attitude (or heart) from excessive me-ism to greater civic commitments and revitalization of institutions (see Chapter 18). Since these forces are, by and large, not subject to deliberate change or public policy (although we all *can* contribute to their evolution), one's attention turns to specific reforms (Chapters 16–17). But, first, to the principles that must guide such an effort.

PART IV

TOWARD A NEW PROGRESSIVE ERA: Essential Changes

CHAPTER FIFTEEN

ARE
REFORMS
CONSTITUTIONAL?

The country is overdue for another Progressive Era, an age in which encompassing and thorough reforms will reverse plutocratic tendencies, curb interest groups, and overcome PACs. Easier said than done. Many of the reforms that spring to mind may do more harm than good by violating our constitutional freedoms. Prohibit lobbying? Where is the line that separates lobbying from the right of people to petition their government? Limit political advertising, the costliest item of campaign budgets? You just curbed the freedom of speech. This is not a matter of idle speculation: the Supreme Court struck down several reforms Congress enacted in 1974. It is therefore necessary for me to spell out the principles that provide the framework for specific reform measures I favor, and to show that such measures are not incompatible with our constitutional freedoms.

THE ONE-PERSON-ONE-VOTE IDEAL

Before one can suggest how to deal with PACs and lobbies, one must firmly address the underlying question: *can and should private power, specifically as it is embodied in economic power, be kept out of politics?* The main source of economic power was once personal wealth, accumulation of property. Today it is often organizational wealth, amassed by corporations and labor unions—above and beyond the old-style wealth amassed by individuals (the super-rich). However, the question applies to both old and new forms of concentration: are millionaires or organizations that command economic power (in corporate assets or individual coffers, or by the aggregate power of the organizations' members) entitled to more say in the public realm than other citizens, not so endowed or organized?

I address this question first on the level of ideals (what I judge the best of all worlds to be like) and then in the context of a practical world. Ideally, in a constitutional democracy, concentration of private power would *not* yield public power. The two would be separated, as embodied in the ideal of one-person-one-vote.

The essence of power is *inequality*. If one person has power over another, the second person has none over the first, at least in the matter at hand. In contrast, a one-person-one-vote world, if fully implemented, entails equality and is hence, by definition, a world free of power relations, because if everyone has the same say, then no one has any power. In such a world, all citizens would have the same leverage over the direction of public life, whatever differences of power might exist among them in the private realm. This is clearly an idealistic abstraction, but it serves as a useful measuring rod to assess whether a particular condition is moving toward or away from the ideal state, even if such a state cannot be fully reached.

To suggest that because a person is wealthy or a member of a select organization, he or she is entitled to a better bargain in the market place of political give and take, in appealing to voters, and in gaining the ears of elected officials is in effect to favor a property-weighted suffrage. This is clearly a plutocratic tendency. *How* plutocratic versus democratic a political system based on such a principle is depends on just how heavily wealth weighs in.

To illustrate the point, assume one had to buy the right to vote by paying X dollars at the ballot place before one was issued a ballot to mark. The higher the charge, the less democratic and the more plutocratic the system. While a charge of a dollar per voter might not keep many people away, $100 would, and a $1,000 charge would render the system highly plutocratic, in effect largely the property of the well off.

Grossly unequal access to the means necessary to reach, inform, persuade, organize, and mobilize voters has a similar effect, albeit one step removed. The use of television (and radio) is the single most costly item in today's election campaigns, closely followed by public-opinion polls.

Those with more money can buy more media time, and more data relevant to knowing how to sway voters. While media money and voter-analysis money do not directly buy elections, when one candidate has significantly more of these than another, he has essentially bought himself a significant edge.

Much of the U.S. legal tradition is dedicated to ensuring that the right of access to the market place of ideas will not be limited. Fair enough. The rich should not be kept out any more than the poor. *However,* one must also concern oneself with the danger that some participants will be so advantaged that others will not be able to participate on anywhere near fair footing. The fact that occasionally the advantage wealth buys can be offset (for example, if the disadvantaged candidate is supported by numerous volunteers) does not render money unimportant, any more than the advantage of having a gun becomes unimportant because unarmed persons occasionally overwhelm armed ones.

In contrast, imagine a system in which the cost of campaigning is kept low by shortening the campaign period (by mutual agreement among the political parties). Imagine, too, public financing of all general elections and an effectively enforced prohibition of private campaign expenditures, direct and indirect ("independent"), for or against a candidate. In such a world the democratic principle implied in the concept of one-person-one-vote—equality of public "power" —would be *approximated* and the effect of private concentration of economic power on public life significantly curbed. (The majority of PACs, it will be recalled, are pecuniary.) True, other private-power differences would still remain, and these are even more difficult to keep at bay than economic power; e.g., some candidates may simply attract more volunteers than others. But such assets do not provide nearly so great an advantage across the board as wealth, whether personal or organizational. To reiterate, volunteers cannot be shipped across the country in quick, costless transactions. Nor can they be converted from one use to another—for example, from public-opinion analysis to TV ads. They cannot be stored, made to grow while idle, and so on. Political money can easily accomplish all the above and then some. This is not to argue that one ought not to keep out of politics other concentrations of private power. But the aggregation of money, we saw, is clearly the most important one.

The situation is analogous to the ideal of general and complete disarmament (GCD). Even if achieved, it would still leave people with pitchforks, kitchen knives, and monkey wrenches, which some can wield more forcefully than others. Nevertheless, it would afford an immeasurably safer, more peaceful world.

In the world of practical realities, neither GCD nor complete separation of private economic power from public power is possible. However, this does *not* mean that therefore anything goes, that "more" makes no difference. This is what arms control and arms reduction— and various limitations on campaign spending—are all about.

What, then, are the most damaging plutocratic inroads? Where can the fair and effective ways of curbing private power be found? Although there may be as much disagreement about these as about which arms should be cut first—intermediate range missiles, nuclear submarines, or killer-satellites—one should not lose sight, in the debate about specifics, of the main point: *less* private money in politics is *more* democratic, at least as long as one accepts the one-person–one-vote ideal.

THE DEMOCRACY-TO-PLUTOCRACY LADDER

We have observed various ways in which private money finds its way into public life. From an idealistic viewpoint they all may "dirty" politics, yet some are much more corrupting than others.

Small Individual Contributions

Least damaging to the separation of public and private power are individual contributions, especially when they are small in size. A great virtue of numerous, small individual contributions (if private money is to play a role at all) is that they are not tied to a controlling command. That is why some members of Congress of high integrity, such as Barber Conable, Jr., will accept no contribution larger than $50. Not only can most people participate, but elected candidates will not be obligated to any one person or organization.

Large Individual Contributions

Large individual contributions are more damaging to democracy than small ones, because each single contribution is more obligating and fewer, more select people can participate. Recently it has been argued that the current limit of $1,000 (per election per candidate, for those not publicly financed) should be increased. As I see it, $1,000 is already excessive. A poor person would be unable to buy such a political chip, while a rich person would hardly be put out. (In 1981 a person was defined as poor if he or she was a member of a family of *four* whose income was $9,287 or less.) Actually, quite a few people who are not poor but whose incomes are low—say, $10,000 to $20,000 per family—would find a $1,000 contribution quite painful. In short, the larger the amounts of money individuals are allowed to use politically, the more we move away from the democratic ideal.

Corporate and Union Funds

In sharpest violation of democratic principles is the commitment of *organizational* funds to political use, which allows a unit that is not a citizen at all, that does not have the right to vote—and whose members, staff, stockholders, managers, whatever, already command such a right—to affect the outcome of elections. The violation is even worse if the unit—a corporation, bank, labor union—is wealthy, and so can readily commit large amounts. The prohibition on corporate campaign contributions is longstanding. Congress passed a law in 1907 making it a crime for a corporation to contribute directly to candidates for national office. The law withstood several challenges in courts. In one test of its constitutionality, the courts found it appropriate for Congress to limit the "corrupting" influence on elections of the "concerted use of money" by corporations. (The case referred to is *United States v. United States Brewers Association.*) The law has been part of the legal tradition of the country since the Progressive Era.

The underlying point is, as law professor William T. Mayton explains, that the corporation is a "unique business entity created and licensed by the state. It is imbued by the state with certain privileges," of which limited liability for the stockholders is the most important. "Such advantages make it ideally suited to accumulate capital—and power. Therefore, at the turn of the century, Congress, believing that measures were necessary to protect the state from its offspring," passed the law. Corporations have since grown in size and power. No wonder Congress continued the prohibition on corporate campaign contributions when it reviewed the campaign finance laws on several occasions during the 1970s.

While I emphasize the long tradition of outlawing corporate contributions to candidates for federal office, it should be noted that

American law is pieced together, rarely cut out of one cloth. In *First National Bank of Boston v. Bellotti,* the court implied that a corporation is like an individual, its free speech protected by the Constitution. The court therefore allowed a corporation to use its funds in a local political action (taking and promoting a position in a local referendum). This decision does not directly violate the notion that corporations should not contribute to candidates for *federal* office, nor does it concern campaign financing. Nevertheless, it leaves the door open to those who wish to give corporations free-speech rights. As I see it, despite that decision, in view of the potential size and impact of corporate contributions (consider Watergate), corporate (and union) funds are best kept out of politics. Their members are free to express themselves as individuals or as members of voluntary groups. Indeed, it might be said that if sizable individual contributions are the bombshells of private money, direct commitments of organizational funds are the nuclear weapons. They had better be kept under control.

PACs as an Organizational Piggyback

Most PACs serve as a new way of channeling into political action large amounts of funds aggregated by organizations. And most PACs use the infrastructure and resources of the organizations on which they piggyback their structure to build up political power. The significance of this point is often overlooked when it is suggested that PACs are nothing but democratic committees, collecting funds their members cough up voluntarily, to support a candidate of their choice. "PACs are truly the voice of the people—people who band together to make their electoral choices more emphatic by pooling their funds in support of one or more candidates," claims a Mobil ad.

Actually, contributions made to a PAC are made within a hierarchy in which, typically, senior executives solicit funds from junior ones, over whose salaries and promotion they pass judgment. There have been several reports about pressures to contribute; the deeper question is whether voluntary participation is ever possible within such hierarchical relations. And far from contributing to *their* candidate, most of those who give to such PACs are giving blind. The PAC directors decide who gains support, and—if they wish to—they inform the contributors who got what, after the fact. Often contributors are not even informed, let alone consulted.

Above all, most groups of citizens, trying to match a business or labor PAC, would have to work many a year before they might possibly command the ready-made political infrastructure and resources that corporations and unions provide to "their" PACs.

Let us say that you believe that bicycle riders' interests are being overlooked, and that behind this neglect are the auto-manufacturing corporations and the United Auto Workers. You set out to organize a PAC for bicycle riders. To begin with, you will spend a lot of time, energy, and money just to generate a list of potential members. The auto PAC will get its list ready-made from corporate or union computers. You must raise money to mail to those bicycle riders an appeal for funds and information about your activities. The auto PAC, meanwhile, will get a free mailing from its corporate or union parent. You will have to form an organizational hierarchy of local chapters, regional officers, and national coordinators. The auto PAC will get its organization ready-made from the corporations and labor unions. And so on.

In short, economic PACs use organizations' *existing* infrastructure and resources, including very considerable funds (not charged to the PACs), established communications, and authority channels. Under the provisions of the 1971 Federal Election Campaign Act (FECA) and subsequent amendments, corporations and unions are entitled to spend money from their treasuries to establish and administer PACs, to cover the costs of fund-raising and of partisan communications to stockholders and members, without having those expenditures charged against PAC collections. They amount to very hefty subsidies to PACs, in hard cash and in kind.

H. Richard Mayberry, Jr., a Washington lawyer who represents PACs before the Federal Election Commission, explains:

> All costs associated with the formation, administration and solicitation of voluntary contributions for a PAC may be directly paid from the corporate treasury and are not reportable to the Federal Election Commission (FEC). These so-called "soft dollars" provide a tremendous advantage for political participation by business. Other political committees and parties must pay all overhead costs from the monies they can raise from individuals and other groups.

How costly this is one can glean from the fact that when there is no such ready-made, paid-for infrastructure to build on, PACs must spend a high proportion of their funds to lay the foundations. Because PACs are not required to report the amounts spent by parent organizations on their operations, it is impossible to determine directly the extent of such benefits to corporate and labor PACs. One can see, however, that in the 1982 elections, corporate PACs contributed 62 percent of the money they raised directly to candidates, labor PACs 56 percent, but independent PACs—those with no sponsoring organization on which to piggyback—only 17 percent. These apparently were forced to spend much more of the funds they raised on raising funds.

If one combines the PACs' contributions to federal candidates with contributions to political parties *and* independent expenditures, the total still amounts to only 25 percent of what independent PACs raised, versus 65 percent for corporate PACs and 61 percent for labor. Most of the remaining 75 percent was dedicated to the costs of solicitation, operation, and other expenses. (The way the records are kept, it is not possible to establish whether some of these funds were simply "banked" for future use, but these are believed to be small amounts if so.) As these data highlight, the fact that people who feel strongly about an issue can set up a PAC, even when they have no organization on which to piggyback, does not belie the great advantage that organized economic interests have when they wade in. And, one ought to recall, most PACs do piggyback.

Finally, there seems lately to be a recurrence of *de facto* PACs, which circumvent both the letter and the spirit of the law. This practice, which outraged the public during the Watergate hearings, is sometimes referred to as "bundling." It requires an organizer to collect checks from individuals, made out to a single candidate (PACs must distribute their money among five or more candidates), and hand them to the candidate in the name of a business or some other interest group. The practice circumvents the disclosure laws (no record is filed) and limits on contributions (a PAC may not give more than $5,000 to a single candidate).

The Council for a Livable World "transmits" contributions to peace candidates, in 1982 a total of $533,899. I asked its president, Jerome Grossman, if "transmit" means that you collect individual checks, made out to a candidate, and give them to him. "That's right," he confirmed.

I pointed out ". . . this is what some people call *bundling.*"

He responded: "Yes; it allows us to exceed the limit of $5,000 . . . we give to some as much as $70,000."

Groups that bundle, such as the Council for a Livable World, may feel that they are on the side of the angels, because they promote peace or some other form of public interest. But such practices open the door to undisclosed PACing, in an environment in which such activity might well be much less voluntary than it is in the Council for a Livable World—say, in a workplace.

Boeing Company set up a "civic pledge program," according to which executives of the corporation, who volunteered to support a given candidate, could write checks *directly* payable to the candidate. All Boeing was to do was to collect the checks and turn them over as a bundle to the candidate. However, an examination of the list of donors reveals an oddity; look, for instance, at the list of donors to the Committee to Re-Elect Bill Fuller:

S. M. Lindgren; K. J. Luplow; Donald L. Martin;
Henry S. McMurray; Roy H. Okada; Robert E. Perdue;
Bertan J. Roundy; Herman Schaeffer.

The list is clearly a segment of the alphabet. It is extremely unlikely that executives whose names begin with L to S favor Fuller, while those with A to L or S to Z favor other candidates. The much more likely explanation is that *Boeing* chose whom to support and then asked segments of an executive list to write checks.

PACing and bundling are not so detrimental to the democratic process as straight organizational political contributions, because the need to raise the money from individuals limits the amount (a large corporation could easily commit more than almost any bunch of fat cats, billionaires excluded), and has a touch of democracy, because individuals may ask about the use of the funds (a problem a corporation is much less likely to face, and to which, when challenged, it may choose not to respond).

The following chart summarizes the various types of campaign structure in the order of their degree of democratic versus plutocratic quality:

THE DEMOCRATIC TO PLUTOCRATIC CONTINUUM.
1. *Democratic Ideal.* One-person-one-vote. Public financing. No private funding.
2. *Small individual political contributions.*
3. *Large individual political contributions.*
4. *Aggregation of individual political contributions by organized interests.* PACs and bundling.

    5. *Direct organizational political contributions.*
    6. *High Plutocracy.* Property-weighted suffrage. High
        charge per vote. Unlimited use of personal, aggregate,
        and organizational funds.

Two items do not find a convenient place in this ladder. One is large commitments of funds by individuals to their *own* campaigns. On the one hand, these somewhat resemble large contributions to the campaigns of others, in the sense that they constitute the introduction of concentrated private power into public life; on the other hand, we shall see, the Supreme Court views them quite differently. The sums involved, it should be noted, are considerable. For instance, Lewis Lehrman used at least $8 million of his own money in his 1982 senatorial bid in New York. One reason the Libertarians put up multimillionaire David Koch for the vice-presidential spot on their ticket is that being on the ticket automatically exempted him from any limits on his contributions to their campaign. He had promised to contribute $500,000 if nominated; in fact he gave $2.1 million. It is interesting to contemplate what difference a Rockefeller vice-presidency would make, under the present rules for financing campaigns. Those who feel less concerned about these monies, because they tend to go to conservative candidates, might wish to take into account that liberal millionaires, such as Stewart Mott, also throw their wealth around. Jane Fonda contributed or loaned $551,485 to the campaign of her husband, radical Tom Hayden. These contributions hence belong on the ladder between items 2 and 3, though, from my viewpoint, they are quite close to 3.

    "Independent expenditures" by PACs, working for or against a candidate but not coordinated with him or her, are basically PAC contributions, period. They are "worse" only in the sense that they are unlimited in the amount allowed, whereas PACs' contributions to acknowledged candidates are limited. Hence, pencil them in between 4 and 5.

IS IT CONSTITUTIONAL? "MONEY IS SPEECH!"

Has not the Supreme Court already ruled that "money is speech," that a person has a constitutional right to use his or her resources to advocate his or her personal beliefs in public, and hence that the use of a person's economic resources for electioneering is not to be curbed?

Yes, the Supreme Court decision in *Buckley v. Valeo,* in 1976, is often simply referred to as having ruled that "money is speech." *Actually, the Supreme Court ruled that contributions to candidates may be curbed* to eliminate the "reality or appearance" of undue influence. The court clearly distinguished between a person's using resources for his or her own political expression, which the court ruled may not be limited, and contributing money to someone else's efforts, which is not similarly sanctioned and so may be limited.

In an often cited passage, the court states that "a restriction on the amount of money a person or group can spend on political communication during a campaign necessarily reduces the quantity of expression." The amount of money spent, then, *seems* to be equated with the extent of freedom of expression. The court goes on to explain: "This is because virtually every means of communicating ideas in today's mass society requires the expenditure of money. The distribution of the humblest handbill or leaflet entails printing, paper, and circulation costs. Speeches and rallies generally necessitate hiring a hall" and so on. It *does* read like "money equals speech" and therefore should *not* be curbed.

But soon the court states: "By contrast with a limitation upon expenditures for political expression, a limitation upon the amount that any one person or group may contribute to a candidate or political committee entails only a marginal restriction upon the contributor's ability to engage in free communication." Hence, while the court allowed people to spend as much as they wish on communicating their *own* views, it let stand limits on the amounts a person may contribute to magnifying the voice of *others.* (The limit stands at $1,000.) And the court let stand the ban on the use of organizational funds, the most venal form of the political use of private power.

The main opening left for the new plutocracy lies elsewhere. The Supreme Court decided to allow unlimited "independent expenditures," those not explicitly coordinated with candidates they promote. This decision is troublesome because these so-called independent expenditures make a mockery of the other limitations on campaign expenditures. Any person or interest group can easily circumvent all the other limits set on campaign spending by spending unlimited amounts against the candidates' opponents—or in the candidate's behalf—as long as no explicit coordination takes place. Since it is very easy to determine which positions a candidate promotes, all an "independent" supporter must do is open the morning paper, or the campaign fliers, and pour money in support of positions reported in these readily available sources. One can only hope that the court will eventually reverse this ruling. *Time,* not exactly a reformers' mouthpiece, wrote of it: "Considering the history of politicians and politics in the U.S., the ruling seems extremely naive—leaving a mile-wide loophole for the return of the 'fat cat' to the campaign scene."

Meanwhile, given that it has been established that limiting political contributions *is* constitutional, the question is: which specific limitations are most effective (in terms of curbing the intrusion of private power into public life) and appropriate (in terms of our constitutional freedoms)?

CHAPTER SIXTEEN

WHAT IS TO BE DONE?

REFORMS: THE VIRTUE OF A PACKAGE

No Cure-All But . . .

Before a specific agenda for reform can be outlined, two points must be clarified. It is part of our political tradition that oversell and hype accompany most corrective measures promoted in public life. This or that bill will turn back "the tidal wave of crime." (Have you ever seen a tidal wave being turned back?) This or that social program will "eliminate poverty." (Have you ever seen a social problem eliminated?) In the same vein, in recent years reforms to clean up public life have been overpromoted.

One must accept, first, that there is no way to overcome political corruption once and for all. Its deepest source lies in a built-in tension between the private and the public realms. The two realms are, and *ought to be,* in a constant tug-of-war; as each tries to penetrate the other, they also check and balance each other. Democracy thrives as long as neither side wins. Violation of individual freedoms and the economy occurs when the public realm unduly intervenes in the private realm; political corruption occurs when private powers invade the public realm. It follows that when the forces pulling one way are prevailing, we need to weigh in on the other side, to restore the balance—not to "solve the problem, once and for all." There are no cure-alls.

To say that there is no *solution* to the problem is not to suggest

233

that significant progress cannot be made in restoring the public realm to its proper, autonomous status. There is disagreement on exactly how much was achieved in Jacksonian times, and in the Progressive Era, but few doubt that significant progress was made. No sensible person would have sought in, say, 1917, to restore the public life of, say, 1900, just because in 1917 it was, while definitely "cleaner," still far from "clean." State legislatures are now much less corrupt than they were in the early 1950s. Most telling, the federal civil service has been raised to a high level of integrity, although there are individual exceptions and some units that are far from adequate, such as the GSA. In short, reforms "pay" even if they do not rid society of corruption once and for all.

Much has been made in recent years of the fact that some reforms have "backfired." Curbs on individual contributions introduced in 1974 are said to have driven large amounts of political money into PACs, the present curse. Reforms the labor unions favored, in the hope of protecting their political involvement, resulted in a vast increase in the involvement of corporations, and opened the floodgates to PACs. The unions wanted to remove restrictions preventing recipients of government contracts from engaging in political action, the reason being that they held numerous government contracts to train workers and did not want to give them up. They did not realize that in winning their cause, they would be opening the doors for corporations that receive government contracts.

The term "ironic reforms" is used, time and again, to imply that reforms boomerang, and hence should not be attempted. Opponents of reform also blame human nature. Irving Kristol's statement is often cited in this context: Self-interest is not a problem but a condition. James Madison's words on the inevitability of "factions" also are regularly run up.

As I see it, reforms require the same "R & D" process used in developing technology. You start with an idea, and revise it. You build a model, test it, and modify it. You run a "pilot" batch, try it, and modify the product some more. The same needs to be done with items and programs of public policy. We need to try various approaches to improve our campaign finance laws, and must be prepared to have to make further adjustments, expect some missteps. But there is no reason to despair; corruption may be part of "human nature," but so is the nobler call to enhance integrity. And just as some institutional setups exacerbate our worst proclivities, others do curb them and reinforce our better side. Last but not least, many reforms that failed when we tried to fix the system one element at a time may work when they are introduced as part of a new system.

The Need for a Reform Package

Citizens who have been initiated into these matters may soon find themselves bewildered by the numerous suggestions current for specific reforms, suggestions are often promoted individually. Representative Joseph G. Minish proposed in the 96th Congress to reduce the contribution a multicandidate PAC can make to $1,000, instead of the currently allowable $5,000. Martin Franks, chief staffer of the Democratic Congressional Campaign Committee, suggested that the ceiling on individual contributions to candidates be raised from the currently allowable $1,000. A bill raising the limits on individual contributions to political parties was introduced by Representative William E. Frenzel, a Republican.

Most such suggestions, even if adopted, are likely to have only limited consequence. There is now a flood of private funds gushing into politics, running over and around whatever protective dikes still stand. To throw a truckful of sandbags here or there is a sign of good will or naïveté (if not theater-of-the-absurd), but is not the way to cope with a raging flood. *To curb political corruption, much more encompassing and substantial measures are needed; above all, they need to be introduced in combination, as a package.*

Although the following measures are of necessity explored one at a time, to allow for proper discussion, the *combined* introduction of as many as possible is essential for success. Otherwise they may well only deflect the flood briefly, until it pushes through some new way.

To have a fair chance to achieve significant reform the new Progressive package should include (a) the public financing of congressional elections; (b) measures to curb the flow of private money into politics; (c) steps to reduce the costs of running for office; and (d) acts that will promote the "visibility" of the political process. Furthermore, much more effective enforcement must be provided for all the rules, old and new. As the merits, and problems, of these building-stones are explored, the ways in which they support one another—the inter-reform linkages—will be indicated. Together these changes may well make for a reformed system; singly they are likely to fail.

PUBLIC FINANCING OF CONGRESSIONAL ELECTIONS

Full Rather Than Partial, but—Voluntary

The best way to reduce substantially the power of private money over public office is to cover the costs of campaigning from public sources. Such a plan already exists for presidential elections. It should be extended to encompass congressional elections. Participation should be *voluntary:* candidates who wish to participate would have to refrain from receiving private funds, but those who believe they would do better otherwise are free to do so. To encourage participation, however, private funds should be limited as much as possible.

Practically all other advocates of public financing of congressional campaigns call for *partial* public funding, on the grounds that full funding would be too costly and that there is "value" in small individual contributions. As I see it, costs can be reduced to a very considerable extent by some measures I discuss below. And, as I have already explained, small individual contributions may be the least problematic, but they nevertheless open a door best kept shut. People *can* participate in politics in numerous other ways; private money need not enter. Indeed, sending a check is probably the least meaningful, least involving mode of participation.

Like others, at this stage I recommend limiting public funding to general elections, not primaries. Let's first gain experience in introducing the system to general elections, and then extend it to cover also the costs of running in primaries. The main difficulties are with setting the qualifications for eligibility for public funding low enough but not too low. This task is difficult enough for general elections; it is an almost insurmountable problem for primaries, in which sometimes scores of people might initially seek to participate. If public funds were available at this level, the number of candidates would be very likely to grow considerably and debase the whole system. On the other hand, if private money is purged from general elections, it might well turn to seek to corrupt the primaries. Hence, once new qualifying procedures are developed and tested, public funding may well have to be extended to primaries.

Experience with Presidential Campaigns

We have acquired some experience with public financing of election campaigns, albeit not for Congress but for president. In general elections, the presidential candidates of the major parties are fully funded by the public, although acceptance of public financing is not mandatory. Once a candidate decides to sign up for public funds, he or she must refuse all other contributions, either from individuals or PACs. Each of the major candidates received $29.4 million in public funds in the 1980 general election. The amount is set by law as the equivalent of $20 million 1974 dollars, indexed to the CPI. Minor party candidates can obtain funds on the basis of how they fared in the last election. New-party or independent candidates can also qualify.

We have also learned that voluntary participation works. John Connally chose not to accept public matching funds for presidential primaries, both because he assumed he could raise more from private sources (limited for those who draw from the public fund), and because he wanted to make a symbolic gesture against those who rely on the government. President Reagan accepted public financing (he did not, however, check off a dollar on his return to help fund it). A system the major candidates participate in though they are free to opt out is clearly a workable one.

The experience with the presidential system further highlights the close link among the various reform measures: the more limitations there are on the political use of private funds, the more candidates will choose, voluntarily, to receive public financing. Put the other way around, the more one loosens the regulations on the amounts individuals and PACs can contribute, the more Connallys there will be. This is one reason for my recommendation, spelled out below, for setting the ceiling on private contributions as low as is compatible with the Constitution.

Aside from being workable, public financing seems to alleviate interest-group pressure. Public financing of presidential elections was first enacted in 1971 and then greatly strengthened after the Watergate revelations.

Fred Wertheimer, the president of Common Cause, testified:

> This system has worked—presidential candidates are no longer dependent on a relatively few "fat cat," large contributors and well-funded special interest groups for their campaign funds. The general election campaigns of the nominees of the two major parties in 1976 and 1980 were financed by federal funds—the aggregation of millions of one-dollar contributions from the voluntary income tax check-off.

Jimmy Carter, the first president elected under the new system, noted that public financing gave him "a unique freedom to make my decisions as President based upon my current analysis of what's best for you and me and this country." This is not to suggest that special-interest groups or constituency-representing organizations had no influence in the Carter era; it is enough to recall the role of the National Education Association in promoting a Department of Education to realize that interest groups did not roll over and play dead. But his administration seems to have been less corrupted by special-interest groups than the preceding administrations—in part, of course, because it did little in the first place.

Who Will Qualify?

If public financing of election campaigns is now to be extended to cover congressional elections, the question remains: who will qualify for it? If the requirements are too tight, the system will favor incumbents. If the requirements are too loose, many people who seek free publicity or who merely gamble on being elected will draw on the public funds. This would not only drive up the costs, but would soon debase the system.

Currently, public financing of presidential primaries uses the capacity to raise funds as a qualification. A candidate has to qualify by raising $100,000. This amount must be in individual contributions; it is exclusive of PAC contributions. The amount must include at least $5,000 each in at least twenty different states, and only the first $250 of each individual contribution is counted for this purpose. The candidates must abide by state-by-state spending limits on their primary campaigns, as well as a national primary-campaign spending limit, which in 1980 was $14.7 million.

Some states, notably Michigan and New Jersey, also have acquired some experience with public financing of races for governor, although there have been criticisms. When the availability of public financing encouraged twenty candidates to enter the New Jersey gubernatorial primaries in 1981, people complained that the system had encouraged several marginal candidates to run. On the other hand, no one was heard to complain that the voters did not have a choice, a reason frequently cited for the decline in voter participation in presidential races.

To reduce the role of private money in public life further (although it is marginal here) and to symbolize the taboo on it, the money-raising qualification for presidential candidates should be dropped. It should be replaced by the requirement that a candidate obtain the pledge of at least twenty thousand citizens in each of at least twenty-six states that if the election were held on the day of the pledge, the pledging citizen would vote for that candidate. (A more sophisticated requirement would be to change the number of pledges required according to the size of the voting-age population of a state. This number is currently used in an index for providing matching funds for presidential primaries.) If that proved either too difficult or too easy, the number of pledges required could be adjusted appropriately. A similar procedure might be tested in congressional general elections, requiring that a candidate who has not been nominated in a primary—for instance, a person running as an independent—collect a given number of pledges from a number of communities or subdivisions within the congressional district. Until a variety of methods is tried, it might well be impossible to tell whether a given qualifying procedure is too loose or too tight.

Pros and Cons

Opponents argue that public financing of congressional elections would protect incumbents, who would have less trouble qualifying than challengers; would be costly and unworkable; would put members of Congress in the position of writing rules that would affect their opponents' campaigns; and would undermine the political freedom of individuals and of PACs, which are depicted by opponents of public financing as part and parcel of American voluntarism and grassroots participation in politics.

At the same time it can be argued that, in fact, public financing would be a boon to challengers because it promises all who can mount serious campaigns that they will be provided with funds equivalent to those set aside for incumbents. The objection that Congress should not write the rules governing members' opponents' campaigns disregards the fact that Congress writes the rules anyhow; it prohibited corporate contributions, set the limits on individual contributions, and so on. And to the extent that campaign rules are deemed unfair or unconstitutional, they can be challenged in the courts.

Far from being excluded from participation, individuals not only could continue to express their political inclinations freely under a system of public financing, but would be better able to do so, on a more equal footing, to the extent that private contributions are diminished. All that citizens would lose in the process is their ability to purchase a disproportionate influence, measured by the size of their pocketbooks rather than by political viewpoint and dedication.

As to the argument that paying for all congressional elections would be costly, Gregg Ward, himself a PAC-man representing the Sheet Metal and Air Conditioning Contractors' National Association, and not a fan of public financing, provided an answer that I find difficult to improve upon. The total amount spent on congressional campaigns in 1982 was $344 million. Considering that in 1981 Americans spent $820 million on lipstick and $588 million on deodorant, such costs aren't excessive, says Ward. I agree; we certainly can afford to pay for cleaner politics. Moreover, the *direct economic* benefits to the public of cleaner politics, aside from the value of a more democratic government, are so immense that a more advantageous investment is difficult to imagine. There are numerous individual bills, from diluting the windfall-profits tax to jacking up the price of sugar and milk, that if defeated would return to the public many scores of dollars for each $1.30 (give or take a quarter) that public financing costs per head. (This figure is based on the costs of the 1982 election divided by the number of Americans.)

There is a fine way to recover a good deal of the cost of public financing of congressional elections: remove the tax credit now granted for contributions to PACs! The tax credit costs the U.S. Treasury about $117.6 million in fiscal year 1982. (Actually, as Representatives Matthew F. McHugh and Barber B. Conable, Jr., have suggested, it should be repealed anyhow.)

I call for the public to provide full coverage of campaign costs, costs we shall shortly see might be much reduced. Others have called for partial coverage—for instance, for public funds to "match" private donations and for both to be used in combination to cover campaign costs. This is less preferable: in effect, it keeps a role for income-weighted suffrage in the system, and it also complicates the system to a considerable extent.

Douglass Caddy includes in his book *How They Rig Our Elections* a list of reasons various people object to public financing (of any kind). First on his list:

"**1.** *So radical an idea [as public financing] should be subject to careful scrutiny before adoption.*" Although I do not see the idea as all that radical, I surely do not object to careful scrutiny, unless it is advocated to delay action. Let us scrutinize the objections—and act on them.

"**2.** *The belief that public financing will purify the electoral process in a way that no other reforms will is naïve and untrue.*" A high-class red herring. I do not know anyone who claims the result will be purification, only that public financing will help substantially.

"**3.** *Public financing is contrary to our tradition of private financing, a tradition which both weeds out unviable candidates and underpins the voluntaristic nature of our political system.*" First, public financing is *now* part of our tradition. Second, a candidate unable to pour in money, or to raise it, is not necessarily otherwise incompetent or "unviable." Last but not least, there are many other, less corrupting, ways to volunteer.

"**4.** *Public financing will repose power over campaigns in the bureaucrats, not the people.*" Congress sets the rules and a bipartisan commission (FEC) and its tiny staff oversee their enforcement. The same procedure is used for setting and supervising the rules for private financing. Unless one favors a completely unregulated flow of private money into politics, this is not a point against *public* financing. To reiterate: one may be against big government and still, like Adam Smith, recognize the need for a government to ensure fair competition, competition by some agreed-upon rules.

"**5.** *Public financing is yet another example of the subsidy philosophy.*" So is paying legislators. Not *all* "subsidies" are bad. See point 4 for amplification.

"**6.** *Public financing proposals prohibiting or unreasonably limiting private contributions may violate First Amendment guarantees of free speech.*" The Supreme Court has decided otherwise, ruling that the public financing of political campaigns does not abridge freedom of speech but, rather, furthers First Amendment values by using public funds "to facilitate and enlarge public discussion and participation."

"**7.** *Whether or not Americans support public financing is open to question.*" Fair enough, but wait until they learn more about PACs!

"**8.** *Public financing will unfairly work to the advantage of incumbents.*" If this is found true, more funds should be given to challengers (for instance, to match franking privileges members of Congress have), or spending by incumbents should be further restricted, especially during election months.

"9. *The problem of frivolous candidates.*" This problem requires serious attention. There is no sure-fire solution. A workable approach is likely to emerge following experimentation with various qualifying procedures.

The Proper Use of Campaign Funds

Experience suggests that public financing of elections must be linked with the introduction of some regulations concerning the proper use of campaign funds. Otherwise its own integrity might soon come into question. Candidates should be required to return public funds if they decide to quit the race after they receive them, and to turn over any surplus left after election day. Surplus funds raised for an election from private sources (as long as this is allowed) should be either returned proportionately to the donors or, better, turned over to a U.S. Treasury public-election fund, to help finance future elections. The same holds for interest earned while such funds are "parked." At the end of 1981, the collective surplus of House incumbents was in excess of $23.5 million.

Only expenditures directly tied to elections should qualify as proper uses of public funds or of private contributions—only costs for travel to and from the district in which the campaign is waged (not travel to resorts or trotting around the world); for campaign staff (excluding spouses and next of kin); and for fixtures needed directly for campaigning (such as phone banks, but not personal items).

The need for such restrictions may be obvious enough, but apparently it is not obvious at all to members of Congress. On the contrary, many use campaign surpluses as if they were personal petty-cash funds, except that the amounts are far from petty. The 1980 surplus of Senator Daniel Inouye, for instance, was a non-negligible $281,511. An exhaustive study by three investigative reporters, Bill Hogan, Diane Kiesel, and Alan Green, shows that members of Congress used surplus funds for every conceivable item, from frequent dining in Washington, D.C., restaurants to country-club dues, from safaris to gifts for their wives and children. Indeed, many simply used them to cover their credit-card bills, without itemizing.

Representative John J. Rhodes used $11,272 in surplus campaign funds to pay for two oil portraits of himself. Representative Robert E. Badham used $1,369 to buy his wife dresses. Representative Gene Taylor leased a campaign car from his own dealership—even after it had ceased operation; in effect, he transferred $4,885 from his campaign chest to his pocket. Senator Harrison Williams, run out of the Senate for his involvement in Abscam, took with him $65,781. When my children tell me that their friends working in ice-cream shops dip into the cash registers, and I state that this should not be done, I have great difficulties when my sons point out that our public servants do the same.

How venal Congress can get is illustrated by the fact that when it finally got around to limiting the personal use of funds contributed for campaign purposes, it exempted all members of Congress as of the time the bill was enacted, on January 8, 1980.

There is more to this than meets the eye. If one has the patience to delve into at least some of the details involved, one can gain an insight into—an eyeful of—how Congress works. On the face of it, the rules of the House and Senate ethics committees prohibit the conversion of surplus campaign funds to personal use. Law or no law, it is not to be done, according to standards Congress set for its members. House Rule 43, clause 6, prohibits the use of campaign funds for any purposes but reimbursement of bona-fide campaign expenses. Senate Rule XXXVIII, paragraph 1, rules that these funds may be applied beyond campaign expenditures to defray costs members have incurred in carrying out their official duties. However, personal expenses are explicitly prohibited from being charged as office expenses.

Nonetheless, when those rules are violated, the ethics committees are very reluctant to act. Both committees see themselves mainly as *advising* the members on what ethical conduct is—not as investigative, policing, or enforcement agencies. Indeed, while there have been numerous reports of the conversion of campaign funds to personal use, very few members have been reprimanded. It took fifteen alleged violations of the House rules by former Representative Charles H. Wilson, discovered over a seven-year period, for the House Ethics Committee to hold hearings. The committee upheld eight counts, and, upon its recommendation, the House censured Wilson in 1980. And when the House reprimanded three members as a result of the Korean influence-peddling investigation, "the debate on the reprimands left observers wondering if the House really took the issue very seriously," according to *Congressional Quarterly*.

The Senate Ethics Committee has issued some 370 "interpretive rulings," which "clarify" the code when senators request such clarification in anticipation of questionable transactions. But these rulings are used as easily to whitewash unethical conduct as to protect the code. A committee wanted to provide Senator Paula Hawkins with a $5,000 lecture fee. But since this exceeds the Senate-set limits, the senator obtained a ruling from the Ethics Committee that she could be accompanied by her husband, who would also speak some, and get the $3,000 in excess of the $2,000 she is authorized to receive by the rules.

The wife of Representative Norman Lent was hired as director of government relations of Nynex, a telephone company. She actively worked on behalf of bills of interest to it and, of course, was paid by Nynex. The question was if it is appropriate for Representative Lent, under the circumstances, to continue to vote, in committee, on legislation of interest to Nynex. He asked the House Committee on Standards of Official Conduct. The Committee told Lent that it was up to him. He interpreted that to mean it was proper for him to vote as if he had no personal stake in the matter.

Why, then, would members of Congress pass a law that, unlike in-house rules, has much more bite? (The law prohibits conversion of "surplus" campaign funds to personal use.) *Because although the members exempted themselves from the law, it did cover their opponents.* It was written so as not to apply to those who were members of Congress when the law was passed.

The electorate should demand that the law prohibiting the conversion of "surplus" campaign funds to personal use be the same for all, members of Congress and challengers. And the short (three-year) statute of limitations Congress set for its members concerning criminal violation of campaign finance laws should be extended to the five years customary in federal criminal-law enforcement. Penalties for violation of these regulations should be the same as for cheating on income tax. Unfortunately, the record clearly shows that all these regulations are quite necessary.

CURBING PRIVATE MONEY IN POLITICS

Anti-Plutocratic Measures

Ideally, the introduction of public financing of congressional elections should be accompanied by a ban on all private contributions.* As I see it, this would not violate constitutional freedoms. Although a person has the right to promote his or her "speech," there is no such right to promote by financial means (as distinct from advocating, say, by spelling out the merits of someone else's ideas) another person's speech to the detriment of still others who have fewer or no resources.

Such a ban would be further justified if there were another source of funds, the public source. Under these circumstances, everyone's "speech" would be ensured, on a more or less equal footing.

An opportunity should be created for the Supreme Court to review its 1976 ruling, so that limitations could be reinstated on "fat cats" using their own funds and on independent expenditures. In that ruling, the Supreme Court abolished the $50,000 limit on the amount a candidate or candidate's family could give to his or her own campaign, and the $1,000 limit on independent expenditures made in behalf of or against a candidate.

It is not difficult to provide the Supreme Court with an opportunity to review these issues in light of new arguments and recent experience. (Even though the court is obviously reluctant to reconsider matters, it has reversed itself on other issues.) Alternatively, Congress might pass laws that were similar to those struck down but were presumed to be less objectionable to the court.

In addition, it would be best to prohibit PACs from drawing on the ready-made infrastructure of existing organizations, on the ground that this practice is but a concealed form of organizational contribution. (At least, PACs should not be allowed to draw on the treasuries of corporations and unions for their expenses.) However, should it be maintained that because PACs have some affinity with "real" citizen groups they cannot be banned without endangering the freedoms

---

*If this were achieved, public financing of course would cease to be voluntary. The balance of the discussion, though, assumes that the ideal condition cannot be attained and hence focuses on a voluntary public-financing system.

guaranteed by the Constitution, their role should be limited as much as possible.

One way to weaken PACs was suggested by former Senator S. I. Hayakawa. He urged that donors to PACs be able to designate the candidate to whom their money is to go. This would largely curtail the power of PAC managers and blunt the power of concentrated funds.

Another method was suggested in a bill introduced in 1977 by Representative James A. S. Leach. It would prohibit all contributions by PACs and limit the contributions a member of Congress may accept to those from party committees and from individuals residing in a candidate's own district—this last provision serving to prevent outside interests from coming between a candidate and the people he or she is to represent. Leach's bill would limit individual contributions to $500. I would make it $50. (Most individual contributions are actually smaller as it is.)

So-called independent expenditures should be disallowed, or at least limited. At first blush it might seem that such a step would be particularly threatening to constitutional freedoms: how can one stop a group of citizens from advocating a viewpoint or a political position without undercutting democracy? But expenditures of that kind were never limited. The limits on independent expenditures—before the Supreme Court struck them down in 1976—applied only to expenditures *directly* related to a "clearly identified" candidate. That is, they did *not* curb the right, for instance, of a group of conservatives to promote their ideas, political positions, or even conservative candidates in general. Only those expenditures that directly helped specific candidates, or directly undermined specific opponents, were curbed.

The reason the court gave for removing this limit was that, because these funds are not given directly to candidates but are spent in their behalf, they are less obligating. But, as Justice White pointed out, there is little difference in obligation incurred between "coordinated" expenditures and independent ones. Besides, enforcing the no-coordination rules is nearly impossible. Hence, limits should be reapplied. Also, in the case of presidential elections, independent expenditures in support of candidates who voluntarily sign up for public funding are limited to $1,000; the limit survived a challenge when the Supreme Court divided, four against four, on this issue. Presumably, if congressional elections are publicly financed the same limit would hold.

A rather different approach is to discourage independent expenditures by providing, from public funds, matching dollars to any candidate "targeted" by these expenditures, or by buying response time from TV and radio stations, and ad space in publications, equal to that purchased by independent PACs. This could prove quite costly, at least until those who promote independent expenditures are deterred, but it has the virtue of not opening the door to a constitutional challenge, which banning such expenditures is sure to face.

Limiting the Total Candidates Can Accept

Because limits on the contributions that individuals may make can be readily circumvented (for instance, John Doe can make contributions via his spouse, children, and kin), and because limits on group donations can be nullified (by setting up multiple PAC fronts), as long as private contributions are allowed it is necessary, as a second line of defense, to limit the total amount of private funds an individual candidate can *accept*.

We have seen already that although the Supreme Court ruled that Congress may not limit the expenditures of candidates in general, it upheld such limits as a condition for voluntarily requested public funding. Because few presidential candidates can afford to forgo public financing of their campaigns, this condition has in effect limited the acceptance of private contributions. The idea should now be extended to congressional elections. Following another approval, the Obey-Railsback bill would limit the total that candidates could accept from PACs to $70,000. This bill passed the House in 1979 by a vote of 217 to 198, but died in the Senate.

A different and more complex approach is taken in a bill introduced by two Democratic (David R. Obey and Dan Glickman) and two Republican (Jim Leach and Benjamin Gilman) members of the House in 1983. This bill contains a voluntary plan for *partial* public financing of congressional elections, combined with ceilings on the amounts of PAC contributions and on campaign spending: contributions of $100 or less from individuals would be matched by public funds, provided that the candidate agreed to limit total spending to $200,000, and the total of PAC contributions to $90,000; participants and their families must also agree to limit use of their own funds to an additional $20,000. By leaving participation in the system voluntary, this bill manages not to run afoul of *Buckley v. Valeo*.

To protect candidates who sign up for the suggested plan from others, who choose not to participate in this mixed public-private plan because they expect greater amounts of private money than they could draw under the plan, participating candidates faced with nonparticipating opponents would have the limits on private contributions lifted *and* would receive *double* public matching funds. These provisions seek to encourage candidates to join the plan. Under them, "the candidate who chooses not to abide by the limits pays a very high price," explains Representative Obey.

Political scientist Michael Malbin argues that setting limits on the total amount of PAC funds a candidate can accept would only shift PAC money elsewhere. Malbin's point is well taken, but it need not lead one to abandon limiting PACs. Instead, one should make the curbs more encompassing and tie them to other reform measures which would make PAC money less alluring—especially measures that would reduce campaign costs.

REDUCE THE COSTS OF CAMPAIGNING

If the costs of campaigning were to be lowered substantially, the role of private money would be smaller and the burden of public financing of campaigns less taxing. Indeed, while the costs of sustaining democracy are not large compared to most other major items in the federal budget, they would run into hundreds of millions of dollars if congressional campaigns were covered and their costs were left uncurbed. The magnitude of the costs is already used by opponents of public financing as an argument against this reform measure. And the higher the campaign costs, the greater the pressure on members of Congress to turn to PACs and the fat cats. For both reasons, therefore, lowering the costs supports public funding and reduces the temptations of political corruption. There are two main ways to achieve this result—each with its own difficulties, each with a measure of success when used elsewhere.

Limit the Period of Campaigning
Limiting the duration of election campaigns is desirable even if one is not concerned with the effects of having to raise large amounts of money on the integrity of public life. More and more representatives of the public spend more and more of their time, and energies, on

campaigning. Campaigns start earlier, last longer, demand more. (Democratic candidates for the 1984 presidential election officially started to run in February 1983, more than a year before the first delegates were to be chosen, and a year and a half before the Democratic convention. Jimmy Carter spent 1974 and 1975 on the road, running.) Not only are such lengthy campaigns costly, but they also extend the period in which grandstanding and partisan and electioneering considerations pre-empt whatever commitment to the public interest preceded them.

A limit might take the form of prohibiting the expenditure of campaign funds, private or public, until sixty days before a primary and five months before a general election. This approach has been recommended previously. For instance, limiting the selection of delegates to the Democratic Party convention, by primaries or otherwise, to a period of three to five months was suggested both by the Winograd Commission, set up by the Democratic Party after the 1976 election to study the effects of party reforms, and by the Hunt Commission, established after the 1980 election for the same purpose. Former President Gerald R. Ford favors prohibiting campaign contributions before January of an election year, to "compress" the campaign period.

Also, the major parties should agree to hold their nominating conventions not more than three months before the elections. Radio and TV stations could be prohibited from carrying political ads by, or on behalf of, candidates for national office in other periods. (Because they use public airwaves, they are subject to regulation anyhow.) Newspapers might be asked to refuse out-of-season political ads voluntarily. Even better, the major political parties might voluntarily agree to such a ban.

Britain is considered the mother of democratic government and still a model democracy in many ways, whatever its economic and social woes. In 1983 it managed a national election campaign that lasted, from start to finish, three weeks. A candidate for Parliament is limited to "a precisely calculated amount of spending . . . $6,633.72. There is no question of bending the rules; an election agent, or campaign manager, who exceeded the limit last time was fined about $1,000, dismissed from his job, and barred from participation in politics, even from voting, for five years." This may be too much virtue —or corset—for Americans. (And the British have to deal with fewer people, in smaller territories.) But if Britain can do it in less than a month and with a pittance, we should be able to cap both the period and the expenditures, even if at substantially higher levels. Existing party rules on when primaries may be conducted are a small step in the right direction.

To reduce the advantage incumbents may achieve by generating news during campaigns, opponents should be entitled to equal time during the short campaign period. Also, limits introduced in 1973 on the right of members of Congress to mail free material to their constituents ("franking privileges") just before the elections should be extended to the whole campaign period. Limiting PACs, which on average favor incumbents, would further reduce the incumbents' advantage. There is no way to eliminate completely the advantages of incumbency, but, then, it also has its own disadvantages (most acts that please some constituents distress others; there is, too, generally some resentment toward those in office).

Some Free Media

TV and radio stations should be asked to set aside, as a public service, a limited amount of free time for candidates. The notion that these stations "owe" something to the public, in exchange for their use of public airwaves, is already well established. For instance, they are already required to carry a certain amount of public-affairs broadcasting. Free airtime would ensure some access to all candidates and reduce the power of additional time, time bought with private funds. Great Britain, France, West Germany, and Sweden provide some free airtime to candidates.

A different approach—suggested by the Democracy Project, run by Mark Green—calls for providing each candidate with some media time paid for from public funds. Green calculated that this could be done with an appropriation of $21 million, "a dime per citizen." Another version calls for the public to purchase for each candidate some media coupons, which candidates could cash in at stations of their choice, with the public being billed according to local costs.

In any event, a well-heeled candidate should not be able to drown out an opponent by buying large amounts of media time. Each candidate should have some free time, or time provided by the public. Aside from giving all candidates some access to the important electronic equivalent of the town meeting, such a provision would reduce the need to raise private funds and the temptations that go with it.

MEASURES TO BRING POLITICS
MORE INTO PUBLIC VIEW

The Role of Visibility

The more venal the special interest, the narrower the base, the more outrageous the violation of the public trust and interest, the more nefarious the means by which influence is acquired—the greater the desire to hide the process. Indeed, the quest for concealment is a major sign distinguishing special-interest groups (SIGs) from constituency-representing organizations (CROs). Lobbyists, as agents for SIGs, would prefer it not to be known that they drafted a bill, provided a member of Congress with tainted information, linked contributions to illicit favors, or even were seen with certain members of Congress. As one of Washington's top defense lobbyists told *Business Week,* "Visibility is the last thing I need."

In contrast, individuals working for CROs are anxious to show their constituencies that they are active on their behalf, and one of *their* major tools is quite akin to electioneering—openly mobilizing their constituencies.

True, sometimes constituency representatives act like special-interest lobbyists, and some lobbyists behave like constituency representatives. For example, in 1983 the banking lobby "went public" and succeeded in mobilizing large segments of the populace to their side. But most of the time used-car dealers, independent oil drillers, and Teamsters would rather have their way on the quiet side.

It follows that steps that enhance the visibility of the legislative process (sometimes referred to as "sunshine") tend to diminish the power of special-interest groups, without undercutting the legitimate representative process or hindering constituency-representing organizations. These measures also encourage groups to act less like SIGs and more like CROs, which, we have seen, benefits the democratic process.

"Sunshine" Requirements

Unfortunately, there is no simple set of measures that, if enacted, would secure visibility. The desire to conceal acts of political corruption finds many a way, and the steps to counteract it often have but limited effects—and exact some costs of their own. For example, in the Sunshine Act of 1976 Congress ruled that all meetings of government agencies that are run by a commission must be open to the public unless they fall under one of ten statutory exemptions—if, for instance, national security is at stake. Another "sunshine" reform stripped the chairmen of congressional committees of their power to close their committee meetings at will: now a majority vote of the committee is required. As a result, most "mark-up" sessions, in which bills are amended and approved for floor action, are now open to the public. True, these measures do not prevent private interests from trying to influence those who attend the meetings, and opening the meeting tends to make reaching consensus more difficult. Still, having open meetings is a step that, if added to others, helps move the political system away from corruption, by making it more difficult for lawmakers to advocate openly the case for special interests in these meetings.

New Curbs on Lobbying

Laws requiring lobbyists to register and to disclose some information about their activities have been on the books since the 1930s. Current law requires reports that include the lobbyist's name, employer, specific areas of interest, and quarterly receipts and expenditures, including entertainment devoted exclusively to lobbying.

Few were satisfied with the federal curbs on lobbying as they were when the Supreme Court in 1954 *(United States v. Harriss)* in effect rewrote the law, interpreting it in an extremely narrow sense. The law requires registration and reporting only of organizations or individuals whose "principal purpose" is to influence Congress. The court ruled that only *direct* contact with members of Congress constitutes lobbying under the act. Many Washington-based organizations, such as the Washington offices of major corporations, law firms, and even some individuals who dedicate a good part of their time to lobbying, say that their principal purpose is not lobbying but, rather, "dissemination of information" to members of Congress and to clients. In this way, they avoid having to register. In 1983, AT&T launched a massive drive to affect legislation concerning its reorganization. The *Wall Street Journal* reported that "AT&T sends a horde of lobbyists to fight a phone-bill proposal." None of them is registered as a lobbyist.

Since the early 1950s, numerous attempts have been made in

Congress to find a more appropriate definition of lobbyists or lobbying organizations. The problem the various draft bills grapple with is how to separate a professional lobbyist from a citizen exercising his or her constitutional rights of assembly, free speech, and petition.

While much ink has been shed on the subject, what it all comes down to is an effort to separate those who lobby professionally, for pay, and for a substantial amount of their working time, from citizens representing fellow citizens as needs and occasions arise.

Since no new legislation has been acceptable to both the House and the Senate since *United States v. Harriss,* a new Progressive drive will have either to promote one of the various previously suggested reforms, or to evolve a new, more acceptable version. As I see it, for starters, a lobbyist might be defined as a person who spends more than 20 percent of his or her working time in efforts to influence Congress; an organization would be defined as a lobby if it spends more than $10,000 a year on trying to sway Congress.

Disclosure Is Effective

Disclosure laws have been one of the more successful parts of campaign finance reforms to date. In fact, most of the data presented in this book would not have been available without disclosures required under the 1971 and 1974 campaign finance laws. Disclosure discourages candidates from growing highly dependent on any one source of funds (such as oil interests), or from drawing from sources that are politically embarrassing (such as individuals associated with organized crime), thus making it in a candidate's self-interest to acquire funds from a wide array of sources and from those that give no major offense to his or her constituency.

The disclosure laws at first generated complaints about the excessive record-keeping they required. But this need has been reduced by amendments passed in 1976 and 1979—and simply by the growing familiarity of candidates with the necessary procedures.

At the same time, certain things that are not now disclosed should be, especially the amounts spent by parent organizations on their PACs' infrastructure (if this practice is not abolished altogether). And the public facilities of the FEC should be expanded, to make it easier for the public and the press to use the data filed.

Another way to enhance disclosure, which deserves much more attention than it has so far received, is the use of stockholder resolutions. In 1983 the American Jewish Congress (AJC) asked twenty-three major U.S. corporations to disclose publicly how much they spent on lobbying Congress to approve an arms package including AWACs for Saudi Arabia. This action was sought by AJC members who were stockholders and hence could introduce shareholder resolutions directing disclosure by the corporate management. Nine of the corporations agreed to disclose voluntarily; the others included the resolution in their proxy material with the recommendation that it be rejected. (The Securities and Exchange Commission revised in 1983 Rule 14a-8, which defines the conditions under which stockholders can insert proposals in proxy statements. This made such action more difficult but certainly not impossible.) If more groups would fight for such disclosure, lobbying by corporations would surely become more circumspect.

Many other measures to enhance visibility have been suggested. Some would require cable-TV systems to set aside a channel to broadcast congressional proceedings and committee hearings. When this is done (by C-SPAN, for instance), however, very few citizens watch. More effective would be to require that all votes in Congress be on the record (forbidding non-roll-call votes, which are now used to conceal votes for special interests). This will hardly slow down the work of Congress, since votes can be cast, and lists printed out, even by a modest computer.

My purpose is not to list all the suggestions that have been made, but to illustrate the main ways the legislative process can be opened up to public scrutiny. Enhancing visibility is an important supplement to other Progressive measures, because it goes beyond curbing money to limiting the shady side of private power of all kinds. Lobbies are hampered by enhanced visibility; the democratic mobilization of citizens to participation in public life is best advanced in broad daylight.

CHAPTER SEVENTEEN

MORE BITE:
Beyond "Routine" Reforms

Too often, those not experienced in the ways of Washington, D.C., think that once a new law is enacted they can turn their attention elsewhere. The sad fact is that almost no laws take hold automatically. Indeed, many require considerable effort before they are made into regulations or applied in programs. Above all, those who care about their issues must concern themselves with enforcement. Quite a few laws are passed seeking to reform our political system in responce to public criticism, only to be left largely unenforced in accommodation to the lobbies and the politicians.

MORE ENFORCEMENT

In 1907 Congress enacted a ban on corporate contributions, but this law was often ignored with impunity. The same holds for the Federal Corrupt Practices Act of 1925. Not a single candidate was ever prosecuted under it, though "it was widely known that most candidates spent above the limits set in the act and did not report the full extent of their spending." A report by the American Enterprise Institute notes that in more than thirty years there were only six criminal prosecutions under the 1946 lobbying law, five of them unsuccessful.

A study by Common Cause of those who represent energy interests in Washington, D.C., found that only one group in ten is registered as a lobbying group; that more than half of the representatives are not registered as lobbyists, including many of those regularly reported in the press as lobbying; and that only a tiny fraction of the funds spent are reported as lobbying expenditures. Many if not all of these evasions of the requirements of the 1946 lobby-disclosure law can be undertaken with impunity, because the court interprets the law so narrowly.

The 1946 act is deprived of much of whatever limited power it has by the lack of a staff to enforce it or investigate violations of the act. The Department of Justice has not been of much help either. Senator Bill Bradley provided the following revealing details:

> A check of the records shows that after the general election of 1972, approximately 7,000 complaints lodged with the Secretary of the Senate and Clerk of the House were deemed strong enough to refer to the Department of Justice. Yet not one case was ever litigated. . . . Between 1971 and 1974 the Comptroller General sent the Department of Justice over 100 cases of serious violations of the law, yet only a few of those referrals were ever prosecuted.

Congress's own ethics committees are not to be relied upon. With rare exceptions, they move with deliberate lack of speed. Standards are set only when public outcry is at high pitch, and as soon as it wanes, as it is bound to do, standards too weak to begin with are further diluted. Oversight clearly must find additional support elsewhere.

The creation of the Federal Election Commission (FEC), following Watergate, was a weak attempt in this direction. It is a tiny agency (its enforcement staff numbers fewer than fifty); more a lapdog than a watchdog, is the word in Washington. Although in eight years (1974–82) the FEC reviewed over fourteen hundred complaints alleging violations of the election laws, most of them were technical and minor in nature. Penalties have generally been small, typically $250 to $1,000; only eight violators were assessed $10,000 or more.

The commissioners are appointed by the President. There is a deliberate balance, three Republicans and three Democrats, which means that next to nothing happens unless it suits both sides. Unlike other regulatory agencies, the FEC has no permanent chairman, but a chairmanship that rotates every year. Congress authorizes funds for the FEC one year at a time. Lee Ann Elliot, whom President Reagan appointed to the commission, is a former PAC-woman of the AMA, which itself had trouble staying within the FEC rules.

To provide the FEC with greater stature and more independence, commissioners should be appointed by the President for five-year terms, from a list, prepared by a panel of law-school deans, of persons of legal and ethical stature. Commission members should elect their own chair for a five-year term. Congress should provide multi-year authorization of funds.

Common Cause correctly called for restoration of the FEC's right to conduct random audits of candidates' and PACs' reports, an authority Congress stripped from it in 1979. Common Cause also warned that the FEC should be strengthened—rather than, as Congress was considering, abolished.

The Committee on American Legislatures of the American Political Science Association, which studied lobbying on the state level, suggested a remedy that may be applied on the federal level. (This measure assumes that there is a lobby registry, which already exists on the federal level, although its scope must be widened.) The committee recommends setting up an enforcement agency that "should have the power to suspend or revoke lobbyists' certificates of registration, to hold hearings on complaints, to report violations of the law, to examine periodically the administration of the law, and to recommend revisions. The usual rules restricting admission of outsiders to the floor should be tightened and more rigidly enforced." (The last point refers to the habit of lobbyists, especially former members of state legislatures or of Congress, to enter "the floor" and sit by legislators to prod them during voting. This unseemly maneuver opens the doors to pressure at close quarters.)

To help launch a reform drive we should return to an institution that helped the first Progressive Era: we should set up a public commission to conduct hearings on political corruption, to form recommendations for reform, and to help marshal consensus in their support. The commission should also act as a watchdog for their implementation.

A recent example of how such a commission may work comes to us from Boston. After allegations of fraud surrounded the construction of Boston University buildings, and after two Massachusetts state senators were convicted of extortion, public pressure was exerted on the Massachusetts state legislature, which then created the Special Commission Concerning State and County Buildings in 1978. Since "it was thought that an investigation into fraud and corruption, into white collar crime and malfeasance in public office, would have no credibility with the public unless the body doing the investigation was insulated from the slightest possibility of political motive or personal gain," there were no politicians on the commission, except for the elected attorney general of Massachusetts. The rest of the commission was composed of unpaid, independent professionals, appointed by the state auditor or the secretary of state upon recommendations by professional organizations, and one "President of a private College or University," appointed by the governor.

The commission found that corruption "is a way of life in Massachusetts." Political influence, especially in the form of illegal campaign contributions, is the prime criterion for doing business with the state, and shoddy work and debased standards are the norm. Although the majority of state administrators were found to be honest, "at those crucial points where money and power come together, the system is rotten." This "unholy alliance between private money and public power" is facilitated because there is no system for preventing corruption. In addition, the commission cites "skepticism, sometimes to the point of outright cynicism, about elected and appointed officials" as a contributor to corruption.

Many of the substantive suggestions of the commission were enacted into law. An inspector-general bill, which created an independent office to monitor construction, a construction-reform bill, and a commercial-bribery bill were passed. The commission also referred all evidence of fraud to the appropriate authorities so that legal action could be pursued. It would be best if the President, in consultation with Congress, would set up such a commission. But if neither will, a citizen commission of inquiry is called for. It would include prominent public leaders and help mobilize public support for the needed reforms.

The commission could pave the way to a "national summit" meeting of representatives of all the major interest groups. The purpose of the summit would be to highlight the devastating effects interest-group-politics have on the nation, and to gain—from each group— a commitment to give up some of the privileges they have accumulated, if the other groups would do the same. Each group finds it difficult to concern itself with the common good, as long as all other groups are going all out for their members. However, they may find it easier to balance their concern for their members with a concern for the republic, if all lend a hand simultaneously. Also, under these circumstances, the benefits of restraining self-interest would be much more forceful and forthcoming than they are when each group is making some concessions.

Above all, the country needs a president, like Theodore Roosevelt or Woodrow Wilson, who will endorse a new Progressive platform and instruct his attorney general to enforce the laws vigorously and to initiate new ones. (The fact that several presidential candidates for 1984 have declined to accept PAC money is encouraging from that viewpoint.)

TOO MUCH REGULATION?

Are the suggested reforms in effect largely a bunch of regulations to be slapped on top of existing regulations? Do I not realize that the public is sick and tired of big government and regulations? And does the history of reform not show that such regulations do not work?

No, these reforms are not all regulations. One pivotal building-block is public provision of the means necessary to campaign, an economic underwriting of equal opportunity to participate in public life. Nor are all regulations to be damned, certainly not those that curb political corruption. Moreover, if effectively enforced, these reforms will make for *smaller* government: the interest groups, we have seen, swell and inflate it.

Last but not least, besides the fact that the regulations tried so far were introduced without public financing of congressional elections, several of the key regulations were invalidated by the Supreme Court in 1976 and have been replaced by very few new ones. A full regimen of reform should now be tried. Indeed, the measure of corruption is such that adding limits on the role of private power in public life is fully justified. The effort to shore up the public realm must be equal to the scope of the recent erosion.

TOUGHER MEASURES

Aside from the measures listed so far, which are more or less part of the mainstream of reform, several have been suggested, or suggest themselves, that for one reason or another are much more controversial, or are difficult to attain for other reasons. They nevertheless deserve to be considered, especially if the recognition grows that the "normal" list will not suffice no matter how closely they are linked in time.

Extend the Term of House Members
from Two to Four Years

The term of office in the House should be extended from two to four years, to coincide with the term of the President. This act would sharply reduce campaign costs and shorten the time representatives spend running for office and raising funds. It would also allow them more time to get to know their duties. Currently many representatives spend more than half of their time in office running for re-election. The Senate's longer term is one reason that body, already more selective because of its smaller size and more august stature, draws a group of people who on average seem of higher caliber and less addicted to campaign fund-raising, even though they need to raise larger amounts than candidates for the House.

Those opposed to a change in the term of office see in frequent elections a guarantee of democratic representation. But people elected every two years seem not to heed their constituency better, especially since such frequent elections put them deeper in hock with PACs than less frequent elections would. True, this reasoning could lead one to the opposite extreme—say, calling for elections once a decade. Many a good argument will turn absurd if pushed to an extreme. A four-year term is by no means a radical corrective and could have significant salutary effects.

Reducing Temptation

The salary of members of Congress should be substantially increased, to at least $90,800. (This figure is based on the 1982 salary of senators plus the *maximum* of outside honoraria they are allowed to receive, according to the Senate vote of June 4, 1983.) The raise should be tied to a requirement that, in exchange, members of Congress will forgo all outside income from honoraria, vacations paid for by private interests, etc., and will turn over to charity all gifts in kind that exceed $25 in value.

Those who say that limitations like these cannot be enforced should note that such a code now covers members of the executive branch, and most abide by it strictly. Like many others before me, I have often spent time with a member of Congress, being wined and dined with him by a representative of an interest group, only to join at the next meal a federal "bureaucrat" who insists that we split the tab for a meager lunch because "it's against the law for me to accept a gift." There are exceptions, but surprisingly few members of the executive will accept gifts, let alone fees, from private interests. In short, a code *can* be formulated and made to stick. Members of Congress should be expected by the electorate to abide by the same code that governs the executive, or a similar one.

Some members of Congress say that it is unfair for them to be prevented from earning extra money from speeches while other members, who are richer, continue to receive income from their stocks and bonds. The problem is not income, however, but its sources and payoffs. If Senator X gets dividends from a thousand shares of GM (or whatever other dividend-paying company), there is very little he can do to increase his income from that source substantially.

Trading in stocks is different, especially in the stocks of smaller companies, which often do not pay dividends but whose stock prices can double and triple. Therefore, members of Congress should be required to put their stocks, bonds, and other instruments of investment in a blind trust while they are in office.

The virtue of using a blind trust, especially if the trustees are truly independent of the member of Congress, rather than kin or employees, is illustrated by the behavior of one senator, not atypical at all. Senator Steve Symms has sometimes been so busy trading commodities, engaging in as many as seven transactions in one day, that one wonders how much he was distracted from his other duties.

Much more important is the potential for conflict of interest. On December 3, 1981, Senator Symms, together with other representatives of Idaho, a silver state, demanded that the U.S. government stop selling silver from its stockpiles because this undermined the price. At the time the senator was "long" on silver, and would have benefited from an increase in its price. He was, of course, in a position to know about the demand he and his colleagues put on the government before it was issued. At the time, traders in silver pointed to the statement by the members of Congress as a reason for a rise in the price of silver on the day the statement was issued and on the following one. The senator's office, asked about the matter, stated that the Senate Ethics Committee saw nothing wrong in senators' trading. But, then, the congressional ethics committees are known for their tendency to whitewash almost anything. A general rule prohibiting such conduct would be much cleaner.

Besides reducing temptation, higher salaries and greater integrity might attract people of higher caliber to the job. Many of our strongest leaders and best minds are to be found in business and the professions (such as law and medicine), where pay scales are substantially higher. Public office has other rewards, so there is no need to match or even approximate private-sector salaries, but narrowing the gap will enhance the attraction and stature of the office.

As salaries of members of Congress are improved (in exchange for the cut-off of private fees), their *working conditions*—not life style— should also be improved. Americans think nothing of a business executive's being chauffeured in a car, flown in a private jet, backed up by all the staff his or her work requires, but members of Congress are expected to drive their own cars and fly economy. Their staffs' quarters are so crowded that many practically sit in one another's laps; some work out of converted closets. The public is not best served if, in the name of democratization, members of Congress cannot spend their travel time working, reading, or resting.

It is simplistic to argue that the best way for Congress to know "how we live" is for our elected officials to be stuck daily in the same traffic jam, or ride the same bus, as other citizens do. Yes, our senators and representatives should spend *some* time each year with the people, living among them. But the attempt to achieve this by subjecting them daily to poor transportation and unproductive working conditions simply hinders the nation's lawmakers in carrying out their duties. I do not suggest we provide them with a lavish life style. I am referring to working conditions, which include transportation to and from work, and appropriate office backup.

No Reimbursement or Deductions for Lobbying Costs

Among all the inroads corruption makes into the nation's life, little is more bizarre—or defies credibility more—than the situation whereby the public is made to pay the very people who seek to thwart its will. I ran into this first when I was the staff director of a commission investigating nursing homes. The commission, which had limited resources, had a hard time attracting top legal staff because it was paying government rates. The nursing homes, on the other hand, could retain as many lawyers as they wished and pay them private-sector rates —and add these high fees to their expenses, which were to a large extent covered by the government, even if the nursing homes were found guilty of gross abuse and corruption. A similar situation arises when corporations that receive government contracts use some of these funds to cover the costs of their Washington representatives—and these, in turn, spend much of their time lobbying.

In 1983 the Reagan administration tried to introduce rules limiting the use of federal funds for lobbying by recipients of government grants or contracts. The rules, which critics alleged were aimed at not-for-profit public-interest and human-service groups, alarmed these groups as well as some defense contractors, such as Boeing and Lockheed. Jointly, they defeated the rules. This was not a difficult task; the rules had been poorly drafted. For instance, they called for organizations to maintain separate staffs, premises, and equipment for lobbying, a requirement that, among other things, would have proved an untenable burden for small groups. This point was stressed by the coalition that defeated the rules.

As I see it, the deeper issue, though, is that the rules were not encompassing *enough* and hence were discriminatory. Such rules should encompass all businesses, whether or not they get federal funds. The reason is simple: by adding their lobbying costs to their regular business costs, corporations reduce the profits on which they pay taxes. In this way they get the government (the taxpayers) to pick up part of the tab for their lobbying. Businesses that seek to promote policy positions should pay for such messages with their *after-tax* dollars, just as citizens do.

I made this point to Michael J. Horowitz, counsel to the director, Office of Management and Budget, who spearheaded the failed effort to ban the use of federal dollars for lobbying. His response was as follows:

> I disagree profoundly with your conclusions. There is a difference between use of one's own money for the *legitimate* (and often necessary) purpose of lobbying and the use of federal monies to do so. In fact, our A-122 proposal made that distinction as between different grants/contracts. If the grant/contract was *fixed price* (e.g., $X for Y bars of soap, miles of road, etc.) the proposal was *inapplicable*. It was only in cost plus arrangements—where federal dollars "bought"—through overhead mostly—the use of specific people, facilities, etc. used for lobbying that we objected to the "buy."

What Horowitz overlooks when he writes about using "one's own" money is that as long as such expenditures are tax-deductible, they are in part reimbursed by Uncle Sam. To make them truly one's own money, lobbying costs should be made nondeductible.

That the line between business expenses (deductible) and expenditures from undistributed profits (not deducted) is currently unclear is highlighted by the following example. Mobil Oil has been running ads about PACs that are, in my judgment, extremely misleading. (Readers are not protected by truth-in-advertising codes when it comes to political information, whereas such protection is available to them when it comes to consumer goods, credit terms, or drugs.) I asked my research assistant to ask Mobil Oil if it was going to pay in full for those PAC ads—or charge them in part to the taxpayers. A Mobil representative wrote back, on July 5, 1983, saying that the status of these particular ads has not yet been fully resolved—though Mobil has been engaging in advocacy advertising for ten years.

A Special FBI Section

With the political system PACed and ethically weak, and with enforcement of anti-lobbying laws nebulous, the need to add a vector on the side of integrity outside of Congress is evident. The FEC, even reinforced, may not be enough. A more powerful antidote may be found in the FBI. Between 1978 and 1980, in an operation known as Abscam, the FBI "stung" eight members of Congress, showing, in vivid cinematic relief, that elected officials were only too quick to accept money in exchange for promises of illicit favors.

Following the FBI "sting" operation (previously employed against other groups, from johns in hot pursuit of prostitutes to art fences), there was a considerable outcry in Congress, an outcry not heard before, when other groups had been "stung." Senator John Stennis characterized the conduct of the FBI as a "national disgrace." Two sets of investigations were conducted, one chaired by Representative Don Edwards, one by Senator Charles McC. Mathias, both focusing on the way the sting had been introduced, and some misdeeds committed in the process. For example, some FBI agents were said to have bought goods from a crook serving as an intermediary between them and the members of Congress. Neither hearing paid any attention to the greater lessons to be learned about the weak ethics of many members of Congress.

It was argued that such operations entice members of Congress to crimes they would not otherwise commit, that they were entrapped.

In response, the FBI pointed out that all it was doing was creating opportunities for people to engage in criminal activity. Nobody was forced or pressured to come and deal with the imaginary sheiks (disguised FBI agents), let alone pocket the bribe money or in return promise to deliver legislative favors.

I realize, of course, that in view of several violations of civil rights by the FBI in previous decades, and the proper concern about enhancing the role of an agency that could become a national secret-police force, one turns to draw on the FBI only with great reluctance. I share that reluctance.

Nevertheless, political corruption has gotten out of hand. There are numerous constitutional, legal, and practical barriers to going after corrupt members of Congress. Boosting the FBI's role—*not its powers!* —in this area may be a step that will have to be undertaken.

The FBI might be granted the additional resources needed to set up a special division to use whatever legal means are available, including stings, to help ensure that members of Congress stay within the bounds of the law. Indeed, it is high time the FBI rounded up some lobbyists to admit, in courts of law, that they do buy specific votes, thereby removing the last vestiges of doubt from the public's mind that such ugly wheeling and dealing is common in the national capital.

The FBI, I realize, is in a difficult position. It cannot lead a drive to investigate and indict another branch of government, lest the whole constitutional structure be undermined. (Also, both its budget and its authority are set by Congress.) Hence, it was not surprising to hear O. B. "Buck" Revell, assistant director of the FBI, stress that the FBI has *no* "proactive" program to go after members of Congress. Indeed, the FBI regards Congress as a profession, the way it views, say, doctors and lawyers. Professions, even professions known to have numerous members who violate the law, are *not* to be targeted, the way the IRS, for instance, will go after waiters, who are known often to not report tips as income. Indeed, when this example is mentioned to Mr. Revell, he says, "I have trouble with the IRS on this point." The FBI, he says, focuses only on individuals, on the basis of solid information that *someone brings to it,* or on cases in which a member of Congress walks into a trap the FBI has sprung on another suspected criminal (an art dealer, in the Abscam case).

Indeed, members of Congress are better protected from wanton FBI action than all other professionals. Any FBI action against them must be approved by a high-level authority within the FBI. The higher the suspect, the higher the review required (review of senators, for instance, runs higher than that of representatives).

Even then, special caution is exercised. Mr. Revell pointed out, for example, that when Senator Pressler walked into the Abscam trap, the FBI agents first sought to verify that he understood the situation (that a fix was being offered). When he did not, no bribe was offered. (This differs from the senator's account, in which he claims that he stormed out when a bribe was offered. The actual Abscam tape leaves no doubt that the FBI version is the correct one.)

Mr. Revell sees no way the FBI would pay or could be made to pay *special attention* to corruption in Congress. Nor does he see the need for any special or additional legislative authority.

At the same time, there is no denying that the FBI has changed, over time, its focus and priorities. For instance, J. Edgar Hoover was quite reluctant to take on organized crime and had no authority to deal with drugs. Organized crime became a top priority in 1978, when William Webster became head of the FBI. Drugs were added to the FBI's responsibilities during the Reagan administration, following the merger of the Drug Enforcement Agency with the FBI. Hence, it seems reasonable to expect that a concerned president, prodded by a public outcry, could get the FBI to pay more attention, and commit more resources, to the fight against political corruption, without adding to the bureau's authority or powers.

One way this might be initiated, and symbolized, is by promoting the low-level FBI public-corruption *unit* to the higher level of *section* (now it is a unit within the white-collar-crimes section, part of the criminal-investigation *division*). Elevating the administrative level of an activity historically has been an effective way to highlight its importance and add to its resources. This was the case, for instance, when the U.S. Air Force was made a service after it had been merely a unit within the army.

A Two-Barreled Constitutional Amendment

Buckley v. Valeo left the floodgates to private money wide open. Although I hope that, when the opportunity arises, the Supreme Court will reverse itself, one must realize that the court does so only rarely. Members of Congress who have come to such a realization, ranging from Henry Reuss to Barry Goldwater, have therefore suggested that it will require a constitutional amendment to allow Congress to write laws limiting private contributions to campaign funds. Because constitutional amendments are very difficult to pass (and many people are reluctant to tamper with the Constitution), even reform groups like Common Cause do not support such an amendment. They fear it would drain energy that could yield much more progress elsewhere. However, if public financing is not to be available for congressional campaigns and the corruption of PACs continues to spread, I see little alternative but to promote such a constitutional amendment as part of a neo-Progressive platform. Even if it were not passed, it might serve as a useful educational device, because the debate it would generate would focus attention on the corruption generated by floods of private money into public life.

A constitutional amendment may be needed anyhow to establish that bribes are not covered by the constitutional protection of Congress under Article 1, Section 6, the "speech and debate" clause, to offset Supreme Court decisions that unduly widened the interpretation of this article. Here, too, there are other ways to deal with the issue: the court may reverse itself, or the House and the Senate, acting collectively, may decide to waive immunity in bribery cases or may expect individual members to waive it if they are charged with bribery. A member who refused to waive it would come before the Ethics Committee, which would be expected to recommend his ouster if he did not waive immunity. (Because it seems unclear whether either house —or only the members—have the right to waive immunity, I cover both possibilities.) But Congress has so far shown little inclination to clean its own house. Hence, I very reluctantly conclude that despite the difficulties and controversy entailed in seeking a constitutional amendment, one covering both points might be needed. Meanwhile, members of Congress should be queried by the press and their constituents as to where they stand on these matters, to prod them to act and to serve as a litmus test.

Members of Congress are fond of proclaiming that the country has gone so far to protect the rights of the criminal that those of the victim are often short-changed. On this basis, they call for tougher laws to redress the balance, to make sure more criminals will be caught and convicted. *The same point must be applied to members of Congress themselves.* Their rights are protected by the Constitution, the U.S. legal codes, and several major court cases, to the point where they can accept most bribes openly, even promise a *quid pro quo,* and still not be convicted. If they will not restrain themselves, a constitutional amendment may be necessary after all.

Back to a Reform Package

A reform package should encompass as many "standard" and "drastic" measures as possible. We saw one reason: many of the measures reinforce one another; introduced one or a few at a time, they may be insufficient, if not so weak they will soon lose their credibility and hence their staying power.

However, there is a second reason that a package is desirable. Some of the measures favor Democrats—public financing, for instance, because Republicans, *in toto,* draw much more private money. Others favor the GOP, such as increasing the role of political parties, which is discussed below. Since major reforms require the support of both major parties, a package of measures is more likely to satisfy both sides than any single measure.

But why would members of Congress agree? Don't they know on which side their bread is buttered? "True," explained a lawyer who has spent half a lifetime on the Hill, "their self-interest has become intertwined with PACs and lobbies. However, they don't like the feeling, the feeling of being like whores." Responding to such inner feeling, encouraged by a concerned president, prodded by an aroused public, Congress may well enact a package of reforms.

CHAPTER EIGHTEEN

INSTITUTIONAL CHANGES, HISTORICAL FORCES, AND YOU

THE TIME IS RIPE

Discussions of reforms—pass this bill, stick in that regulation—can be naïve, if not dangerously misleading. They may imply that if the lawmakers would put their minds to it, they could fix the political system. But in effect, progress results from a complex interplay among deliberate efforts by conscientious lawmakers, the work of active citizens and those public-interest groups concerned about the political system, and historical forces that nobody can control or orchestrate.

Reforms help; they draw on historical forces, feed into them, even advance them. Thus, when there is a ground swell for shoring up the public realm, as there was after Watergate, suitable reforms are still needed. If they are not instituted, the energy generated will be dissipated—or, worse, it will propel measures that are counterproductive.

But reforms cannot succeed on their own or be advanced against historical trends. To call for more concern with the public realm, the sector we all share in, at the height of the era of me-ism would indeed be a cry in the wilderness. Fortunately, from this viewpoint, the American society exhibits many signs that a return to civility, to caring about the social order, is very much under way. Religious revivals, greater participation in community groups, a return to structure in colleges and schools, new writing about the *common* good, are all signs of a revitalization of civic commitment. Progressive reforms, of the kind explored in the preceding chapter, will be sustained by—and will feed into—broader revitalization. Their time has come.

There are three kinds of change particularly relevant to the proper underpinning of the reforms discussed so far: the rejuvenation of the political parties; the rise of forces that encourage national unity; and an increase in individuals' personal commitment to the protection of the public realm. A closer examination of each suggests which historical forces to look for, as favorable trends to ride—and also how to contribute to their flow.

POLITICAL PARTIES:
A MAIN COUNTERVAILING FORCE

I'll turn below to what individuals can do personally, as part of the public at large and as members of a social movement, a new, progressive one. I see strong reasons, which I'll spell out, to maintain that the ultimate fate of reforms and of democracy is in the hands of individuals. But social scientists who do not share this view make a point that deserves attention. The public at large tends to blow hot and cold; it is mercurial; it tends to be mobilized by muckraking for a while, only to return soon to apathy. One must therefore use the periods of public outrage to mobilize lasting institutional changes and to build the countervailing elements that will curb special-interest groups even after the public zeal for reform is exhausted and private powers have resumed their quest to control the public realm.

The Potential of Political Parties

The most effective tools in the fight against corrupting interest groups, I hate to say, could be the political parties themselves. I realize that the two major political parties have been, at least until recently, quite unpopular. (Third parties and third-party candidates, in the last hundred years, have been helpful in raising issues and influencing the main parties, but they have not been lasting fixtures in the American political system.) Peoples' feelings about the parties are reflected in public-opinion polls which show that in 1981, 55 percent of the people agreed with the statement that the Democratic Party and its leaders "care more about special interest groups than about the majority of the people," and 57 percent said the same about the Republican Party. A significant percentage of the population felt even more strongly: 35

percent felt that the Democratic Party and its leaders "tend to be corrupt," and nearly half—49 percent—felt that way about the Republican Party.

People may grow more favorably inclined toward the political parties once they realize the pivotal role parties have played historically in curbing interest groups, especially special-interest groups. Political parties have also worked to moderate and help knit together constituency-representing organizations. Indeed, in those periods in American history—and that of states within the union—in which the parties were relatively strong and responsive to their constituents, their congressional delegations relatively unified and responsive to party direction, policy, and discipline, the parties probably contributed more than any other single force to limiting interest groups to tolerable levels.

James Q. Wilson reports:

> There are essentially two kinds of organizations that can assemble and use political power—parties and interest groups. Where political parties are strong, interest groups are likely to be weak. As parties decline in strength, interest groups are likely to become more powerful.

He provides some illuminating cases in point:

> The powerful Cook County Democratic machine has long controlled the government of Chicago; interest groups—labor unions, civic associations—have been, as a consequence, less powerful. When such groups want to get something done, they must usually do it in cooperation with the party or not at all. In New York City or Boston, by contrast, political parties are quite weak and various interest groups can play a large and independent role in policy-making.

Grant McConnell analyzed the situation in the state of California between 1905 and the early 1950s. During this period, various reforms weakened both the Democratic and the Republican parties. As McConnell puts it, "Both parties, heavily inhibited by the restrictions in the state Elections Code, consisted of little more than labels." As a result, McConnell shows, the election campaigns "fell into the hands of smaller, less comprehensive organizations, for the most part well-financed groups." The final effect: "The more important consequence . . . was that interest groups were spared the compromises that might have been imposed on them by a stronger organization within the Republican Party." McConnell focuses on the GOP because the interest groups he studied were largely those of the wealthy, whom he associates with the GOP, but the same would apply to the relations between the Democrats and, say, the labor unions. He adds, though, "Had they chosen to act through either party . . . their influence on policy would have been diluted by passage through the party medium."

McConnell points to interest groups in "weak party states" other than California. He cites a study by Roland R. Renne showing how Montana was dominated by the Anaconda Company, while the Montana Power Company, the state's three large railroads, and the sugar-refining companies played a secondary role. Another study, this one by Duane Lockard, found the dominant special interests in Maine to be those of timber companies, paper manufacturers, and developers of hydroelectric power.

On the national level, focusing on the period between 1960 and 1980, the major political parties weakened as the interest groups increased in power and simultaneously, and as a consequence, had a freer rein, although other factors were also at work. Everett Ladd observes: "As the parties thus withered, candidates for Congress and other elective offices were left to operate as independent entrepreneurs." He quotes the Committee on Political Parties of the American Political Science Association: "It must be obvious . . . that the whole development [the proliferation of interest groups] makes necessary a reinforced party system that can cope with the multiplied organized pressure."

Although there are many reasons political parties declined (egged on by interest groups, most especially by PACs, which are said to "hate" political parties), the most significant reason in my judgment is the general retreat from institutions that took place in the United States beginning in the mid-sixties, and that encompassed all institutions, from the family to labor unions, from the parties to churches. In 1966, 43 percent of adult Americans expressed a great deal of confidence in the leaders of the major American institutions, including medicine, unions, Congress, and the executive branch. (The percentage is based on an average score for nine institutions.) By 1979, only 23 percent still expressed confidence in these institutions. While the decline slowed down, and recently there have been some upswings, the measure stood at 23 percent as of November 1983. A revival of political parties is much more likely to take place within the context of a general resurgence of faith in institutions.

Several suggestions have been made to enhance the revival of the parties, ranging from deep realignment of the major parties to limited changes in election or campaign procedures. One suggestion for realignment calls for two political parties, one liberal, one conservative. (Theoretically, this could result from the uniting of liberals in the GOP and the Democratic Party, leaving the conservatives in the two parties to consummate their alliance.) The parties, it is said, would then be ideologically "cleaner" and hence more effective. One must note that since elections are often won by those who appeal to the middle ground (the more conservative liberals, or the more liberal conservatives), parties that aim to win (as distinct from "raising an issue") are under pressure to fashion an "unclear" profile, rather than represent clear ideological choices, as some social engineers recommend.

Others have called for the formation of four parties, roughly paralleling the Northern liberal Democrats, Southern conservative Democrats, liberal members of the GOP, and the right wing. But this multi-party continental model has its difficulties in Europe in forming and maintaining a governing majority. Nor is it clear whether it can be fitted into the American presidential electoral system, in which the biggest winner takes all.

Other suggested party reforms are much less far-reaching. Nelson W. Polsby, in his 1983 book, *Consequences of Party Reform,* examines various changes that have been suggested for the way primaries are now conducted, to secure a more reliable way of selecting presidential candidates representative of the party (especially among the Democrats). The problem is, here again, that reforms have had ironic consequences: it is widely held that reforms previously introduced to make the parties more democratic have in effect opened them, especially the Democrats, to capture by "media" candidates or those able to knit together a few small constituencies whose members are more likely to vote in the primaries, but not to be representative of most party members. Candidates elected that way were unable to govern (governing requires the ability to build a wide base of support). Hence the call for reforms of the previous reforms.

The issue is more important than it seems. Strengthening the parties' role in nominating candidates may well make for more "representative" candidates and leave less room for the influence of special interests. Such candidates, in turn, will be able to command more loyalty, following, and enthusiasm from party members, for themselves and for the parties—in other words, help revitalize the parties. On the other hand, if carried too far, the increased role of parties would allow factions or individuals that capture party control—"power brokers"—to impose their views on candidates for the presidency and for Congress. At this stage, though, this danger seems remote.

David Cohen, a former president of Common Cause, has suggested several measures to rebuild the parties, including giving them some control over the campaign financing of candidates, issuing *party* reports on the voting records of members of Congress (they are now issued by interest groups), and prohibiting crossovers in primaries.

In my judgment *there is nothing that in the short run would do more to restore the political parties to a more proper, vigorous role than to involve them more deeply in the financing of congressional elections.* One way this might be achieved would be for people to be allowed to check off two dollars instead of one on their income-tax returns. The first dollar would continue to be dedicated to finance the presidential election; the second, congressional elections. These funds would be turned over to the parties (minor parties included) in proportion to their polling in the most recent presidential election, *not* according to the size of party membership. (Allowing people to dedicate the second dollar to the party of their choice might favor the Democratic Party, which tends to have more mass appeal. In all but three elections from 1932 through 1980, the Democratic Party outpolled the Republican Party in votes cast for the House of Representatives. Opinion polls over the last few decades show that more people identify themselves as Democrats, by margins as high as 2 to 1. In one poll in 1982, 48 percent identified themselves as Democrats, and 26 percent as Republicans.) The parties would then be free to use these funds to provide backup for their candidates—in the form of public opinion analyses, for instance—or to turn cash over to them.

Florida, Kansas, North Carolina, and Wyoming, Herbert Alexander reports, permit unlimited contributions to the political committees of parties within their states. These party organizations, in turn, are not limited in the amount they may give candidates for election to state and local offices. In contrast, individuals and other PACs are limited in the amount they may give to these candidates. Eleven states distribute public funds to political parties.

Both approaches enhance the parties' ability to reward those who follow party policy and to exact a penalty from those who break party discipline to follow an interest group. One could go too far in that direction, making the parties dominant and stifling new candidates and independent thinking. But in the present context, with parties on their knees, overshadowed by interest groups, this is not a problem one must be concerned with. Restoring the parties is the issue for the near future.

Political scientists—for instance, Hugh L. LeBlanc—have pointed to the tension between political parties and the Progressive movement. Since I favor the revitalization of *both,* I have some explaining to do. Historically, there was a tension between the two because the Progressive movement rose, among other things, in confrontation with strong, machine-controlled, corrupt political parties. It sought to bring the people directly into politics, by referendums and initiatives, to circumvent "representation" by the corrupt parties. Now, private power and political corruption reside largely in interest groups, not in the parties. Hence, in the present environment a social movement could both involve the people more in politics and support stronger political parties, without contradicting itself.

Emergency and Reform Bipartisanship

On several occasions in recent years, bipartisan commissions have worked out thorny social-policy issues, most notably Social Security reform. When the two major parties pull together, interest groups are particularly ineffectual, just as they are particularly powerful when they can run a "bidding war" between the parties, a war in which they pit the parties against each other and get both to up the ante used to court the interest groups. When the American government seems nearly at a standstill, when differences between Democrats and Republicans and between Congress and the President seem to deadlock the whole system, it seems proper to call for emergency bipartisanship. Aside from advancing issues that have been deadlocked, such bipartisanship might also help restore public confidence in political parties as responsible agencies. At the same time, it is not a basis for running the government year in, year out, because the parties' task is to represent divergent viewpoints and "fight it out." If they become too much like two wings of one party, they will lose their representative function and distinct identities, further alienate the electorate, and short-circuit the democratic process.

Before the bipartisan temper is exhausted, there is one set of bipartisan acts that is both called for and quite unlikely to raise public opposition: shoring up the separation of public and private power via legislation to curb interest groups and reform campaign financing. Indeed, it is inconceivable that these reforms will take place if only one of the major parties supports them and the other actively opposes them.

To repeat: many of the specific reforms suggested here and elsewhere favor, or are believed to favor, one political party or the other. For example, public funding is said to favor the Democrats, because they are more strapped for funds; "deregulating" contributions to political parties is believed to favor the GOP, since it can raise more money; and so it goes. By combining items attractive to at least the two major parties, a bipartisan reform might be fashioned that is encompassing and fair to all sides, and that provides the parties with a greater role.

BUILDING UNITY

Evidence was presented above that interest groups are basically centrifugal forces, seeking to advance *their* members. Constituency-representing organizations at least moderate their group-level me-ism with a concern for the community of which they are a part. Special-interest groups are inclined to go the limit, whole-hog. To contain special-interest groups, and to sustain constituency-representing organizations' involvement in the community, the bonds that tie the plurality of groups into a national community must be constantly reinforced. This is especially the case now, after the last two decades, during which the forces of unity have diminished while those of interest groups, we have seen, have risen.

There is no simple list of select steps that might raise unity to the desired level. Scores of factors affect the level of unity, from the content and quality of education (for citizenship, say) to the volume and nature of interstate commerce, from the way the President carries out his duties (for instance, highly partisan versus "above it all") to the role of the churches. Indeed, a full study of the forces of unity versus divisiveness would amount to nothing less than a study of the American society, a monumental task.

Instead of conducting such a study here, I point to the *kinds* of change in *institutions* that would help curb interest groups and build unity, and, in turn, to the *kinds* of changes in *orientation,* in attitude, that are called for. Equipped with these two insights, one can then examine, as the need arises, other changes in institutions and orientation, to see whether they promote unity or set it back.

An Honest Tax Code

People concerned with improving the balance between the forces that build unity and those that promote segmentation should favor a *flat tax* of one kind or another. (Some policy-makers favor a completely flat tax, others would add a few exemptions—for instance, a zero tax on the first $10,000 of income, to give it a progressive touch. A bill advanced by Senator Bill Bradley and Representative Richard Gephardt closes most loopholes and taxes income at rates ranging from 14 percent to 30 percent.)

The introduction of a flat tax, even if modified by a few wide-gauged exemptions, would have a triple significance. It would reduce the interest groups' take by some $200 billion, give or take $50 billion, depending on the details. That is, by itself it would constitute a hefty diminution of the resources available for political wheeling and dealing. In addition, it would greatly help to restore confidence in the fairness and effectiveness of the political system, an important unity-enhancer. Finally, it would highlight the kind of changes in economic policy we need, changes that both are "good" in themselves and help curb interest groups.

Expose and Oppose Other Special Concessions

One must expect that if a drastic tax reform were to take place, interest groups' pressure would increase to provide them with other kinds of concessions. As it is, they pocket many benefits other than tax privileges, from credit at rates below the market to various subsidies.

Hence, the fight to curb interest groups requires, first, bringing the various concessions into the "sunshine" so that the public at large will be more aware of them and able to fight them. One example will have to stand for scores that come to mind. Sugar farmers make it seem as if they get loans from the government, for which they put up their sugar as collateral. The fiction is advanced that if the price of sugar were to rise beyond a certain level, the farmers would sell the sugar and repay their loans. In effect, that level is set so high that collateral is regularly forfeited, and the loan is a government handout in all but name. All such arrangements should be brought into the open by advocates of reform, so that their true nature and public cost will become evident. If a group is entitled to special help from the public, let it be "on" budget, an open appropriation, visible and accountable.

Second, the concessions need to be examined to see if they can be cut back. From Export-Import Bank credits to farm subsidies, examination shows that many concessions do very little for the purposes for which they are granted; they are but thinly concealed handouts to groups with clout. One example: DISC, Domestic International Sales Corporation, is not exactly a matter most voters follow closely, to put it mildly. It costs the taxpayers an estimated $1.4 billion per year, although study after study has shown that its benefits for U.S. trade are at best negligible. To gain it, all one needs is to adjust the way the corporate ledgers are kept—no change in production, export-effort, etc. Little wonder the benefits are so hard to see. Under the drumbeat of a new Progressive movement, such concessions might be cut back.

The Value of Budget Resolutions

The flat tax and the rollback of subsidies illustrate the kind of changes that must be sought in the area of public economic policy, to restore the balance between the weakened national community and the overpowering interest groups. Support for the budget resolutions concerns the way Congress manages its affairs.

I frequently encounter citizens who are quite well informed about public affairs or about how the government functions but who know little about the significance or fate of the budget resolutions. Moreover, their eyes glaze over quickly when the issue is discussed. It seems a highly technical, complex, and remote matter.

At issue, though, is an important tool to contain interest groups. And the fate of the budget resolutions is as good an indicator as one can hope for of how well interest-group segmentation is counteracted by unifying forces.

At stake is nothing less than whether any one interest group can exact its cut without having to face the effects of its take on the share of others, and the cumulative effects of the "work" of all interest groups together, on the well-being of the economy and society.

Congress, as is well known, works in committees and subcommittees, most of which are close to one or more interest groups. In the past, the needs of each group were examined independently and voted up or down, with but vague attention to the resulting overall budget. (Difficult to believe, I agree, but true.) After great difficulties, it was agreed, as of 1974, that by May 15 each year Congress will pass a budget resolution that sets targets for total expenditures and revenues and outlines a rough hierarchy of priorities by establishing specific targets for twenty functional categories, such as defense, health, and income security. The committees are supposed to work out the budget for "their" programs within these confines. A second and binding resolution, supposed to be passed by September 15, sets a ceiling above which total expenditures are not to rise and a floor below which revenues are not to fall. After this resolution is approved, Congress may not consider any bill that would result in busting the budget by either exceeding the spending limits or lowering the revenues beyond what has been agreed.

The budget resolutions thus (a) put a limit on the concessions that can be made to interest groups *in toto,* and (b) provide some kind of deliberate Congress-wide balance among the various needs and groups. However, precisely because Congress is severely tempted to accord groups more than a sensible, balanced budget would allow, and the President tends to have priorities of his own, Congress has had great difficulties in recent years in adhering to this procedure and keeping appropriations within the limits set in the budget. Those concerned with national unity should insist that their members of Congress support the budget process and adhere to its outcomes.

A United Chiefs of Staff

All the major areas in which government is involved must be examined, one by one, to unearth the inroads interest groups have made, and find ways to block them. Institutional changes in the Joint Chiefs of Staff, which enhance unity, serve to suggest not only changes badly needed in the government's most important department, that of Defense, but also the kind needed elsewhere.

Most citizens, public-opinion polls show, shy away from questions such as which weapons system the country ought to have (unless, like nuclear or chemical arms, it acquires a special emotional significance), or how the military should be organized. These are considered matters for experts to decide. But the question of how the Joint Chiefs of Staff is set up deserves public attention both because it is of extraordinary significance for the national security and because it provides a major opportunity, akin to congressional budget resolutions, to see the tension between unity and segmentation, and to support unity where segmentation is clearly winning. How unjoint the Joint Chiefs of Staff currently is was detailed earlier (Chapter 6).

The remedies required are, first, to provide the Joint Chiefs of Staff with a staff working for *joint* purposes, and recruited by, paid by, and loyal to it, rather than the rivalrous armed services. This would require either allowing staff members to make a career of service to the Joint Chiefs of Staff, or making their promotion and assignment within a service be subject to review and reversal by the Joint Chiefs of Staff.

Second, the Joint Chiefs of Staff should be authorized to render cross-service judgments, not merely "represent" their service. One way this could be achieved, according to a former chairman of the Joint Chiefs, David Jones, would be for the Joint Chiefs to be responsible for the development of war plans. These plans would be used to determine needs for forces, which, in turn, would be assigned to services according to the plans' needs, not service loyalties.

Finally, the President and Congress should demand that the Joint Chiefs of Staff represent a unified command, not "their" services. That might require that the chiefs and the heads of services not be one and the same persons, admittedly a radical step. For the time being, it would help if the authority of the "Chairman" of the Joint Chiefs of Staff were enhanced.

The 1982–84 Chairman of the Joint Chiefs of Staff, General John W. Vessey, Jr., pointed out that "Chairman" smacks of a corporation committee. He would prefer the term "Chief of Defense Staff" used in Europe. More to the point, he would make the "Chairman" part of the chain of command, between the President and the services. Now, he merely advises the President.

Even if all this were achieved, the Joint Chiefs of Staff would still be far from a centralized command, which is widely feared both as a threat to civilian control (and to the role of the President as commander-in-chief) and because of the danger it would pose of locking onto a one-sided strategy. The existing multi-service structure is so segmented that excessive unification is almost inconceivable. Indeed, the problem is that interservice rivalry, backed by congressional committees, industries, and service associations, is such that it does not "allow" a genuine Joint Chiefs of Staff.

There are numerous issues raised by the suggested modifications in the Joint Chiefs of Staff. It is not my purpose to explore those here, but to illustrate a more generic point: institutional changes can embody greater unity, enhance the capacity to integrate, to keep the parts from dominating the whole—without abolishing the autonomy of parts. Down-sizing, yes; blending, no.

A New Civility

The institutional changes suggested so far provide but an illustrative list of the kinds of change required. While they are important in their own right, many others are called for and will come to the fore, once a movement to roll back the interest groups sets in. Beyond changes in institutions, a successful reform movement must build on, and contribute to, a change of attitude. Just as the civil-rights legislation of 1964 and 1965 both reflected and advanced a new acceptance of America's blacks, similarly, the curbing of interest groups, via various reforms suggested in the previous chapter and the kinds of institutional changes suggested here, will be most effective if accompanied by a change of attitude. The change must take place in the public mentality, the "mind-set" that defines citizens' views and feelings about public life and ethics. In the late 1960s and in the 1970s, the American mentality tended toward a high level of me-ism, of withdrawal from relationships and commitment toward celebration of self. The notions of Adam Smith and *laissez-faire* conservatism were extended from the market place (where an invisible hand was expected to ensure that the effort of each to maximize self would lead to the greatest joint production for all) to the community. Such slogan books as *Being Your Own Best Friend* and *Looking Out for No. 1* became popular. The "politics of interest groups" was, from this viewpoint, me-ism raised to a group level: my group and who else?

A congressional aide effectively summarized the mood in 1979: "You cannot imagine the number of political groups now that are not interested in what's good for the nation, but what's good for me and my group. Their whole philosophy is 'if I'm aboard the ship, it's time to pull up the ladder.'"

Fred Wertheimer, now president of Common Cause, stated at the time: "The sum of the parts of this political system has become much greater than the whole."

In recent years, the resulting free-for-all, unwieldy government, and withdrawal from commitment have generated a rising yearning, indeed a demand, for a return to concern for others and community, for a new public civility. There is a renewed understanding of the paradox of the commons, that if each sets out to maximize self, no one will attend to shared needs and the community will be undercut. There is a new recognition of the need to balance self-interest with a concern for the community all parties share. The more these new attitudes take hold, the more they are advanced in schools, pulpits, and the community, the more will the needed reforms and institutional changes find the ethical underpinning that they require, and that in turn they can embody and thus help advance.

TO ENERGIZE PROGRESS

There remains one key question: What is the ultimate source of the political energy for propelling reforms, institutional change, and redirection of attitudes? The ultimate protectors of the public realm are, oddly, those usually protected by it, the public at large. It is a matter of political energy. The Constitution, democratic institutions, the autonomy of the public realm do not simply stand there once provided, a democracy carved in stone. They need to be continually shored up against eroding forces; we have seen, in some detail, where the eroding forces come from. Shoring up comes from several sources. Confrontations among special-interest groups, when they occur, help to reduce the power of each. Constituency-representing organizations help, especially the more they themselves balance their concern for their members with a commitment to the national community—and counter special-interest groups. Public-interest groups help, but most are relatively weak. Political parties can play an important role, but ultimately they themselves are dependent on commitments and efforts by the public at large.

To put it differently: the power of special-interest groups is *not* based on their ability to serve most people, via one interest group or another, but on the fact that most people, most times, are not active politically. This is the dirty little secret that allows groups representing but small segments of society to capture most of what is to be had, and to twist national policy and direction. They often do not face active, effective opposition; they march largely unopposed.

It is only when abuses by interest groups accumulate—and are dramatized by investigative commissions, hearings, investigative reporting, and public-interest groups—that large segments of the public awaken from their resigned apathy. Then the public may mobilize around effective reforms and support institutional changes, and special-interest groups may be rolled back, as they were in the first Progressive Era.

The first step of public mobilization is to place the issue on the agenda of the national town meeting which, in effect, we continually have. The media, including middlebrow intellectual publications (such as *The Public Interest, The New Yorker, The New Republic, The New York Review of Books*); newspapers (especially *The New York Times, The Washington Post,* and *The Wall Street Journal,* and in particular investigative reporting); electronic media (led by *60 Minutes* and the network news); process-oriented public-interest groups (led by Common Cause); and public figures (such as John Gardner) can trigger what I have called elsewhere a national "megalogue." In it, billions of hours are spent over dinner tables and in bars, in student halls and pulpits, at work and at home, discussing the issue of the day. Out of this often rises a consensus on what must be done.

We have had such national megalogues in the early seventies about the damage done to the environment and how it must be protected, in the early sixties about poverty and social justice, and recently (as well as in the early sixties) about the danger of nuclear bombs. Critics chastise such megalogues because often they are not scientifically precise. Rachel Carson, who helped get the environment on the national agenda, is said not to have had all the facts about DDT. Michael Harrington's book *The Other Americans,* which helped focus attention on poverty, is said to rely on erroneous data on poverty. Similarly, the muckrakers of the Progressive Era were said to exaggerate things, and these days Common Cause and Congress Watch—and Elizabeth Drew —are said to overstate the measure of political corruption. Even if this were the case, they all serve to focus attention on a new major issue and to help launch a megalogue that in turn may lead to consensus on the need to act, and what is to be done.

Such a consensus is never complete. For instance, environmentalists do not agree with one another about the importance of preserving the snail darters and other endangered species. And some segments of the public feel the United States has done too much—others too little— in response to the recognition that the environment was neglected. But these imprecisions and differences of opinion are an inevitable part of what is often a massive, society-wide, lumbering effort. It progresses, even if it oversteers first to the left, then to the right. To oppose it by pointing to such imperfections is to try to block the way society corrects itself. Excesses should be pointed out and ironed out, but they should not lead one to oppose the basic progressive thrust.

To say that the public is aroused out of its apathy is to say that an issue has been put at the top of the agenda. Just being covered by magazines and books, as one out of numerous issues, will not do. Indeed, because our national town meeting is often cluttered with many issues being explored simultaneously, special efforts are often needed to get the meeting to focus on any one. That is why drama often sets in, such as the marches led by Martin Luther King, Jr., "Earth Day," the Vietnam teach-ins, and the anti-bomb demonstrations.

As these lines are written, the invasion of the public realm by special interests is at issue for the second time in a decade. It first came up following Watergate. The resulting reforms helped somewhat, especially by the introduction of public financing of presidential elections, some limitations on contributions, and some disclosure requirements. The rise of PACs since then urgently requires refocusing on the issue: bringing it, and the discussion of what is to be done, to the forefront of the public megalogue, so we can agree with one another that the system badly needs shoring up, and how that can be done.

The next steps are quite familiar to anyone who has participated in or studied a social movement. Once people inform themselves and evolve group consensus, the time is ripe to alert others; to form more encompassing circles, associations, and organizations; to promote the needed reforms and institutional changes. Soon coalitions of such reforming groups, backed up by an alerted public, will be able to overcome the resistance of special interests and open the way to the much-overdue corrections.

In 1983 Common Cause declared a "war on PACs." (The Chamber of Commerce promised to launch a campaign in their defense.) Before the 1982 election, Common Cause stated it would "track the PACs" with its computer, and provide voters and the press with updated information on who gets how much from whom. It called on its members to ask their members of Congress to speak out against PACs; to write to local newspapers in support of reforms of campaign financing; to raise the issue in public forums; and to speak out on local radio and TV stations. Common Cause is, though, fully aware that the deeper issue is not PACs, but special interests. It is not only that their most recent, favored tool—PACs—must be checked, but that the invasion of the public realm by interest groups—whatever means they use—must be curbed.

There is no shortage of suggested reforms that informed, concerned, active citizens can support. If introduced at the same time, or in rapid succession, these reforms will shore up the protection of the public realm, the foundation of democracy. Additional reforms may surface and capture public support as the debate intensifies. What is needed now is for more individuals to spend more of their energy, time, and resources to learn the issues; involve others; organize; form coalitions of concerned groups; and act to promote the kind of reforms and changes required to sustain the democratic form of government dear to all of us.

ACKNOWLEDGMENTS

Without the disclosure laws and the work of the Federal Election Commission, this book would not have been possible. Statistical data, unless otherwise indicated, are from the FEC. Some of the analyses of these data are by Public Citizen's Congress Watch and by Common Cause; others are by the author with the assistance of Paul Jargowsky.

Numerous individuals commented on parts of the manuscript or were otherwise helpful. Many of them differed with the author on matters of interpretation or perspective. Acknowledgment of their help *is not to be construed as endorsement* on their part of any statements in this book.

On the political-science part, I benefited greatly from comments by Hugh L. LeBlanc, Professor and Chairman, Political Science Department, George Washington University, and James L. Sundquist, Senior Fellow, The Brookings Institution. On the historical part, I am indebted to spirited comments and corrections by Edward D. Berkowitz, Associate Professor of History, George Washington University, and the excellent research assistance of Barbara Shuttleworth. On specific reforms (Chapters 16 and 17), I am indebted to David Cohen, former President of Common Cause; Randy Huwa, Director, Campaign Finance Monitoring Project, Common Cause; and Joseph E. Cantor, Analyst, American National Government, Congressional Research Service, Library of Congress. Paul Reyes, Public Information Specialist, Federal Election Commission, commented on segments of Chapter 16. On defense (Chapter 6), I learned from Adam Yarmolinsky, Esq.; Richard L. Kugler, Division Director, European Forces Division, Office of the Secretary of Defense; John F. Dealy, former President, Fairchild Industries, Inc.; Albert J. Redway, retired head of the Washington, D.C., office of McDonnell-Douglas Corp.; Commander J. D. Buttinger; and Jacques Gansler, Vice President, The Analytic Sciences Corp. On constitutional law, I benefited from the wisdom of David M. Ifshin, Esq., Richard Moe, Esq., Ronald D. Eastman, Esq., C. Thomas Dienes, Professor, National Law Center,

George Washington University, and Jerry Caplan, Professor, National Law Center, George Washington University. Discussions at the Department of Justice with Craig C. Donsanto, Director, Election Crimes Branch, Public Integrity Section, and at the FBI with Buck Revell, Assistant Director, Criminal Investigative Division, were eye-opening. A once-over everything was provided by Ann MacDonald, Vicki Alexander, Oren Etzioni, and Pamela Doty. Susan J. Irving, Vice President, Committee for a Responsible Federal Budget, clarified the mystery of budget resolutions.

John W. Gardner's encouragement and the excellent advice of Marie Arana-Ward, Senior Editor of Harcourt Brace Jovanovich, Publishers, sustained my efforts. Minerva Etzioni, a professor who chose to become a homemaker, kept the home front shipshape, allowing me to wallow in the book. Mary Pockman edited the manuscript under great time pressures, and helped greatly to clarify the text. Paul Jargowsky stayed with the book from beginning to end. He provided excellent research assistance and raised numerous specific and general questions, forcing the author to rethink many a point. I am greatly in his debt.

A. E.

NOTES

QUOTATIONS

p. vii Breaux: Quoted in "Struggling to Explain Washington to the Folks Back Home," interview of Pete Earley by Joan McKinney, *Washington Post*, November 7, 1982.

vii Senate Bill 3242: *Congressional Record*, February 20, 1956, p. 2855.

PREFACE

xii Helstoski Accused: *Congressional Ethics*, 2nd ed. (Washington, D.C.: Congressional Quarterly, Inc., 1980), p. 24.

xii Laxalt and Underworld: Edward T. Pound, "Las Vegas Links—Some Backers of Laxalt, a Friend of President's, Show Up in FBI Files," *Wall Street Journal*, June 20, 1983.

CHAPTER ONE—**The New Plutocracy in America**

5 James Madison on Interest Groups: James Madison, "Number X" and "Number LI," in *The Federalist*, by Alexander Hamilton, James Madison, and John Jay (Avon, Conn.: The Heritage Press, 1973).

5 Political Action Committees (PACs) Defined: Joseph E. Cantor, *Political Action Committees: Their Evolution and Growth and Their Implications for the Political System* (Washington, D.C.: Congressional Research Service, 1981, 1982), pp. 1–6.

5 Corporate PACs: "Proliferating Political Action Committees," *National Journal*, January 29, 1983, p. 239.

5 Examples of Corporate PACs: Specific names of PACs and data regarding them are found in *FEC Reports on Financial Activity, 1981–1982, Interim Report No. 4: Party and Non-Party Political Committees* (Washington, D.C.: Federal Election Commission, 1983) (hereafter cited as *RFA*), vol. III, *Non-Party Detailed Tables (Corporate and Labor)*, and vol. IV, *Non-Party Detailed Tables (No Connected Organization, Trade/Membership/Health, Cooperative, Corporation without Stock)*.

6 Professionals' PACs: *RFA*, vol. IV, table D. AMPAC is the largest of the PACs in the Trade/Membership/Health category that represent professionals.

6 Farmers' PACs: Federal Election Commission, *Sponsor/Committee Index*, April 5, 1983, pp. 63, 133.

6 Labor PACs: "Proliferating PACs," p. 239.

6 United Auto Workers PAC: *RFA*, vol. III, table B.

6 Ideological PACs: Nonconnected PACs, not all of which are purely ideological,

accounted for only 746 out of 3,371 PACs on January 1, 1983, or 22.1 percent ("Proliferating PACs," p. 239).

6   Senator Helms's National Congressional Club: *RFA*, vol. IV, p. C-164.

6   PAC Money for 1981–82 Congressional Campaign: *RFA*, vol. I, *Summary Tables*, p. 83.

6   Corporate PACs in 1981–82 Election: *Ibid.*

6   Trade, Membership, and Health PACs in 1981–82 Election: *Ibid.*

6   Labor PACs in 1981–82: *Ibid.*

7   Senior PACs in 1981–82: Senior PAC of Washington, D.C. and Senior PAC of Salem, Oregon: *RFA*, vol. IV, p. C-224.

7   "A Major . . . Scandal . . .": Mark Shields, "The Coming Campaign Scandal," *Washington Post*, February 25, 1983.

7   "That Scandal May . . .": Elizabeth Drew, "Politics and Money—I," *The New Yorker*, December 6, 1982, p. 55.

7   Herbert Alexander: Herbert E. Alexander, *The Case for PACs* (Washington, D.C.: Public Affairs Council, n.d.).

7   Michael Malbin: Michael Malbin, "The Problem of PAC-Journalism," *Public Opinion*, December/January 1983, pp. 15–16, 59.

9   PACs Unknown Before Mid-1970s: Edward M. Epstein, "The PAC Phenomenon: An Overview," *Arizona Law Review* 22, (1980): 357.

10 Tillman Act, 1907: *Dollar Politics*, 3rd ed. (Washington, D.C.: Congressional Quarterly, Inc., 1982), pp. 10–11, 5.

10 Watergate-Era "Laundering" Corporate Contributions: *Ibid.*, p. 11.

10 Nixon and Dairy Industry: "Ervin Panel Staff Links Milk Rise to Aid to Nixon," *New York Times*, June 1, 1974; see also Anthony Ripley, "Milk, at the Least, Is Good for the Dairymen," *New York Times*, August 4, 1974.

10 Amerada Hess Corporation: *Watergate: Chronology of a Crisis* (Washington, D.C.: Congressional Quarterly, Inc., 1974), 2:286.

10 Herbert Kalmbach: *Ibid.*, pp. 133–34, 258; *Dollar Politics*, p. 11.

10 Vesco, Hughes, et al.: *Dollar Politics*, pp. 10–11.

10 Bebe Rebozo: John M. Crewdson, "Nixon's Taped Remarks on Apparent Slush Fund Called Key Evidence in Rebozo Inquiry," *New York Times*, December 9, 1974.

10 Frederick Malek's "Responsiveness" Program: John M. Crewdson, "Ervin Staff Sees White House Plot in '72 Nixon Drive," *New York Times*, June 10, 1974.

10 Campaign Reforms, 1974: *Dollar Politics*, pp. 134–35.

11 Ban on Labor PACs Lifted: *Ibid.*, p. 42.

11 SunPAC Ruling, 1975: *Ibid.*, pp. 42–43.

11 Number of Corporate PACs from 139 to 294: *Ibid.*, p. 43.

11 Number of PACs to 608: Cantor, *Political Action Committees*, p. 56.

11 Number of PACs to 3,371: "Proliferating PACs," p. 239.

11 PACs Spend $21 Million in 1974: Cantor, *Political Action Committees*, p. 83.

11 Increase of 805%: *RFA*, vol. I, p. 92.

11 Congress Gets $12.5 Million: Cantor, *Political Action Committees*, p. 87.

11 Congress Gets $83.1 Million: *FEC Reports on Financial Activity, 1981–1982, Interim Report No. 3: U.S. Senate and House Campaigns* (Washington, D.C.: Federal Election Commission, 1983), p. 92. (Hereafter cited as *RFA, Senate and House.*)

12 Lewis Lehrman: Frank Lynn, "Lehrman Is Close," *New York Times*, November 3, 1982.

p. 12   William Clements: Adam Clymer, "Campaign Funds Called a Key to Outcome of House Races," *New York Times,* November 5, 1982.

12   Mark Dayton: *RFA, Senate and House,* p. 218.

12   Twelve Senate Winners Spent Over $2 Million: Patricia Theiler, "Capitol Bowl," *Common Cause,* January/February 1983, p. 15.

12   House Median Winners and Losers: Adam Clymer, "Will Congress Pass the Buck on Campaign Financing?" *New York Times,* February 20, 1983.

12   House Campaign Funds $38.9 Million: Cantor, *Political Action Committees,* p. 77.

12   House Campaign Funds $214.1 Million: *RFA, Senate and House,* p. 89.

12   Senate Campaign Funds $23.3 Million: Cantor, *Political Action Committees,* p. 78.

12   Senate Campaign Funds $142.6 Million: *RFA, Senate and House,* p. 89.

12   1972–82 Difference Three Times Consumer Price Index: The Consumer Price Index increased 131 percent (from 125.3 to 289.1; 1967 = 100) from 1972 to 1982. House campaign costs rose 426 percent over the same period, or more than three times the CPI's percent increase. Senate costs rose even faster. (Bureau of the Census, *Statistical Abstract of the United States 1981* [Washington, D.C.: Government Printing Office, 1981], p. 467, and Bureau of Labor Statistics 1982 figures.)

12   Average Congressional Campaign Cost: Calculated from *RFA, Senate and House,* pp. 33, 37–38.

13   Rodino Campaign Cost: *Dollar Politics,* pp. 144, 152.

13   Bevill Campaign: Michael Barone and Grant Ujifusa, *The Almanac of American Politics: 1982* (Washington, D.C.: Barone and Company, 1981), p. 15.

13   Dornan Won: *Ibid.,* p. 131.

13   Tower Won: *Ibid.,* p. 1053.

13   Bell Spent $1,418,931: *Ibid.,* p. 678.

13   Weber/Ashley Campaign: *Ibid.,* p. 871. The House average that year was $107,621 (calculated from *FEC Reports on Financial Activity, 1979–1980, Final Report: U.S. Senate and House Campaigns* [Washington, D.C.: Federal Election Commission, 1982], p. 58; excludes primaries).

13   PAC Funding 15.7%: Cantor, *Political Action Committees,* p. 74.

13   PAC Funding 26.2%: Calculated from *RFA, Senate and House,* pp. 35–36, using total non-party committee contributions as a percentage of total receipts in general election campaigns. Information in footnote from Joseph E. Cantor, private communication, May 24, 1983.

14   Badham's Wife's Expenses: Kathryn Johnson, "How Lawmakers Misuse Your Campaign Donations," *U.S. News & World Report,* March 7, 1983, p. 35.

14   Rangel's Trip to Hawaii: Howie Kurtz, "Magazine Airs Campaign Gift Use," *Washington Post,* August 13, 1982.

14   McClure Speaks in Hawaii: *Congressional Ethics,* 2nd ed. (Washington, D.C.: Congressional Quarterly, Inc., 1980), p. 84.

14   Packwood's Trip to Tel Aviv: *Ibid.*

14   "If You're Chairman . . ." Martin Tolchin, "Perils Presented by Outside Income," *New York Times,* January 10, 1983.

14   $25,000 Ceiling on Honoraria: *The Outside Income Issue,* Special Report No. 97–46 (Washington, DC: Democratic Study Group, U.S. House of Representatives, June 16, 1982), p. 3.

14   $12,900 Pay Raise: *A Common Cause Study of Outside Earned Income by United States Senators* (Washington, D.C.: Common Cause, 1979), p. 3.

15   Congress Failed to Limit Honoraria: Democratic Study Group, *Special Report,* p. 3.

p. 15 $25,000 Honoraria Limit Removed: *Ibid.*

15   Speaking Fees for Dole, Garn, Cranston, Jackson: *Ibid.,* pp. 9–12.

15   Senators Get Over $25,000 each: *Ibid.,* p. 3.

15   Senate Speaking Fees Total $2.4 Million: Howard Kurtz and Mary Thornton, "15 Senators Received at Least $50,000 in Lecture Fees in '82," *Washington Post,* May 20, 1983; Mary Thornton, "Legislators' Speeches Netted Twice as Much in '82 as in '80, Study Shows," *Washington Post,* May 26, 1983.

15   House Limited Honoraria to 15%: Democratic Study Group, *Special Report,* p. 3.

15   House Made Honoraria Limit 30%: *Ibid.;* "Outside Earnings/Honoraria Limit," *Common Cause,* August 1982, p. 74.

15   Senate Lifted Honoraria Instead of Pay Raise: Tolchin, "Perils."

15   Senators Voted Pay Raise: Brooks Jackson and Edward F. Pound, "Legislative Lucre: Fees for Congressmen from Interest Groups Doubled in Past Year," *Wall Street Journal,* July 28, 1983.

16   Committee Chairmen Get Most Speaking Money: Democratic Study Group, p. 19.

16   Speaking Fees Vary According to Committee: Elizabeth Drew, "Politics and Money —I," *New Yorker,* December 6, 1982, p. 122.

16   "It Was a Senator's . . .": Tolchin, "Perils."

16   Fees for Speeches: Jackson and Pound, "Legislative Lucre."

16   Supreme Court Rules Against Independent Spending: *Buckley v. Valeo,* 424 U.S. 1 (1976), pp. 39–51.

17   Mills and Fanne Foxe: *Congressional Ethics,* p. 181.

17   Bauman's Conduct: "Bauman Charges Are Dismissed," *New York Times,* April 3, 1981.

17   George Hansen's Silver Drive: Brooks Jackson and Edward T. Pound, "Rep. Hansen's Reports to Congress Leave Out Links to Bunker Hunt," *Wall Street Journal,* July 27, 1982.

18   Hansen Indictment: "Rep. George Hansen Indicted for Failure to Disclose Profits," *Wall Street Journal,* April 8, 1983.

20   "Available Poll Data . . .": Everett Carll Ladd, "205 and Going Strong," *Public Opinion,* June/July 1981, p. 11.

21   PACs Not Mentioned in Article: John Herbers, "Is Post-Watergate Government Morality Slipping?," *New York Times,* March 29, 1983.

21   Congressional Junkets to Palm Springs, etc.: Jack Anderson, "Lobbyists Offer Junkets, Parties Liberally on Hill," *Washington Post,* January 25, 1983.

21   Gifts from Businesses: Kathryn Johnson, "The Santa Claus Syndrome on Capitol Hill," *U.S. News & World Report,* August 23, 1982, p. 32.

21   Parkinson: "U.S. Plans Inquiry into Sex-for-Vote Reports Involving 3 in Congress," *New York Times,* March 13, 1981.

22   Definition of Corruption: Joseph J. Senturia, "Political Corruption," *Encyclopaedia of the Social Sciences,* vol. 4 (New York: Macmillan, 1931), p. 449.

23   "The Rules of the Game . . .": Lester W. Milbrath, *The Washington Lobbyists* (Chicago: Rand McNally, 1963), pp. 297–98.

23   "It Certainly Looks . . ." Michael Barone, "When the Price Is Right," *Washington Post,* March 9, 1983. (Emphasis added.)

23   "In Congress, *Buy* Your Seat . . .": Emphasis added.

23   "A Government of . . .": Cantor, *Political Action Committees,* p. 192.

CHAPTER TWO—The Ways Private Power Penetrates

25 "We Came to a Decision . . .": David Rogers, "Oil Emerges as Leading Hill Patron," *Washington Post*, September 15, 1981.

25 "More than Two-Thirds . . .": "How Business Is Getting Through to Washington," *Business Week*, October 4, 1982, p. 16.

26 Helms's PAC Spending: *FEC Reports on Financial Activity, 1981–1982, Interim Report No. 4: Party and Non-Party Committees* (hereafter cited as *RFA*), vol. IV, *Non-Party Detailed Tables (No Connected Organization, Trade/Membership/Health, Cooperative, Corporation Without Stock)* (Washington, D.C.: Federal Election Commission, 1983), pp. C-167–68.

26 General Dynamics' PAC Spending: *RFA*, vol. III, *Non-Party Detailed Tables (Corporate and Labor)*, pp. A-175–76, 179–80.

26 Ideological PACs Provided 17 Percent: Calculated from *RFA*, vol. I, *Summary Tables*, pp. 90, 94.

27 PACs Provided 26.2% for 1982 Election: Calculated from *FEC Reports on Financial Activities, 1981–1982, Interim Report No. 3: U.S. Senate and House Campaigns* (Washington, D.C.: Federal Election Commission, 1983), pp. 35–36. (Hereafter cited as *RFA, Senate and House*.)

27 PACs Provided 15.7% for 1974: Joseph E. Cantor, *Political Action Committees: Their Evolution and Growth and Their Implications for the Political System* (Washington, D.C.: Congressional Research Service, 1981, 1982), p. 74.

27 Percentages House Winners Got from PACs in 1978, 1980, 1982: Adam Clymer, "PAC Money's Role in Congress Raises Suspicions," *New York Times*, January 19, 1983.

27 PAC Money for O'Neill and Jones: *Ibid.*

27 Dingell: *RFA, Senate and House*, table I.

27 Root-Canal Work: Mark Shields, "The Coming Campaign Scandal," *Washington Post*, February 25, 1983.

27 "Constant Trips . . .": As quoted in an interview with Dom Bonafede, "Textbook Candidate," *National Journal*, December 18, 1982, p. 2172.

28 Hart's Fund-Raising Strategy: Dan Balz, "Hart Presses Old Lessons into New Service," *Washington Post*, March 27, 1983.

28 D'Amato Spent $219,461: Jane Perlez, "D'Amato Leading Senate in Raising Funds for 1986 Campaign," *New York Times*, May 16, 1983.

28 Liberal PAC Raised $70,000: "PACs Try to Rescue Besieged Candidates," *Business Week*, November 8, 1982.

28 "A Tidal Wave . . .": Dennis Farney and Brooks Jackson, "GOP Channels Money into Those Campaigns That Need It the Most," *Wall Street Journal*, October 19, 1982.

28 Democrats Lost by 70,000 Votes: Elizabeth Drew, "Politics and Money—I," *New Yorker*, December 6, 1982, p. 68.

28 GOP Might Have Lost 14 House Seats: George J. Church, "Slinging Mud and Money," *Time*, November 15, 1982, p. 43.

29 "I Think the Story . . .": Drew, "Politics and Money—I," p. 68.

29 64% of Labor Candidates: "Fruits of Labor: The AFL-CIO Prepares to Call In Some IOUs from Congress," *Wall Street Journal*, November 9, 1982.

29 Chamber of Commerce Candidates: Julia Malone, "PAC Election Money Wasn't All for Nought," *Christian Science Monitor*, November 15, 1982.

p. 29 NARAL Candidates: Phil Gailey and Warren Weaver, Jr., "Briefing: Special-Interest Tally," *New York Times*, November 10, 1982.

29 Home-Builders' Candidates: "Interest Groups Rejoice—or Grieve—over Election Showings," *Wall Street Journal*, November 5, 1982.

29 "One That Would Cost . . .": Jim Mintz, "Playing the Insider's Game," *Washingtonian*, January 1983, p. 122.

29 "Wouldn't Let His Personal . . .": *Ibid.*

30 Congressmen Boggs Helped: *Ibid.*

30 Lobbyist for Mars, Inc.: *Ibid.*, pp. 123–24.

30 PAC Gifts to Incumbents: *FEC Reports on Financial Activity, 1979–1980, Final Report: Party and Non-Party Committees* (hereafter cited as *RFA, 1979-80*), vol. I, *Summary Tables* (Washington, D.C.: Federal Election Commission, 1982), pp. 109–10.

31 Ideological PACs Favored Challengers in 1980: *Ibid.*

31 Ideological PACs Gave 9%: Calculated from *Ibid.*, p. 110.

31 Total PAC Money for Incumbents: *Ibid.*, pp. 109–10.

31 PACs Favor Incumbents Even More in 1982: *RFA*, vol. I, pp. 103–4.

31 "Democrats . . . Continue to . . .": "How the PACs Are Spending Their Money," *National Journal*, October 9, 1982, p. 1730.

31 Democrats Got 52.3% PAC Money in 1980: Calculated from *FEC Reports on Financial Activities, 1979–1980, Final Report, U.S. Senate and House Campaigns* (Washington, D.C.: Federal Election Commission, 1982), p. 127. (Hereafter cited as *RFA, 1979–80, Senate and House.*)

32 Democrats Got 54% in 1982: Calculated from *RFA, Senate and House*, p. 36.

32 PACs Favored Senate GOP 2½-TO-1 for Open Seats: Calculated from *RFA, 1979–80*, vol. I, pp.105–6, and *RFA, 1979–80, Senate and House*, p. 129.

32 PACs Favored House GOP 2-TO-1 for Open Seats: Calculated from *RFA, 1979–80*, I: 107–8, and *RFA, 1979–80, Senate and House,* p. 130.

32 Independent PAC Spending Favors GOP: *Dollar Politics*, 3rd ed. (Washington, D.C.: Congressional Quarterly, Inc., 1982), p. 81.

33 84% for GOP: Calculated from *Ibid.*

33 Establishment PACs Gave 59% to GOP: *RFA, 1979–80, Senate and House*, p. 127. Figures for "establishment" PACs were calculated by combining data for corporate, trade/membership/health, cooperative, and corporation-without-stock PACs; see p. 30.

33 Labor Gave Democrats $12.4 Million: *Ibid.*

33 "Much of the Democratic . . ." Farney and Jackson, "GOP Channels Money."

34 Nineteen Democrats vs. 11 Republicans: *RFA, Senate and House*, pp. 39–40. These figures include only incumbents who sought re-election in the general election.

34 Better-Financed Candidate Won 81% of Time: *Open Seat Elections, 1980* (Washington, D.C.: Public Citizen's Congress Watch, n.d. [c. January 1981]), p. 1.

34 Campaign Funds from All Sources—1980: Calculated from *RFA, 1979–80, Senate and House*, pp. 129–30.

34 Democratic Edge Slight: Calculated from *RFA, Senate and House*, pp. 93–94, and *RFA*, vol. I, pp. 99–102.

35 Labor PAC-Money Decrease 1980–82: Calculated from *RFA*, vol. I, p. 94.

35 Labor PAC-Money Decrease 1974–78: Calculated from Cantor, *Political Action Committees*, p. 87.

35 Ideological PAC Money 1974: *Ibid.*

35 Ideological PAC Money 1982: Calculated from *RFA*, vol. I, p. 94.

p. 35   Establishment PAC Money 1974: Calculated from Cantor, *Political Action Committees*, p. 87, using "business-related" and "other" (includes dairy) categories.

35   Establishment PAC Money 1982: Calculated from *RFA*, vol. I, p.94. See note to p. 33, above, for a definition of "establishment" PACs.

35   100% ADA-Approved Got $16,919 Less: Ratings from *ADA's 1980 Voting Record* (Washington, D.C.: Americans for Democratic Action, n.d.), pp. 4–8; PAC contribution amounts from *RFA, 1979–80, Senate and House*, table I.

35   Bayh Mustered $446,000: *RFA, 1979–80, Senate and House*, table I.

35   Grassley Over Culver: *Ibid.*

35   Grassley Highest Recipient: *Ibid.*

35   Grassley $722,000, Culver $329,000: *Ibid.*

36   "Whatever Happened to . . .": Rich Jaroslovsky, "New Right Groups Find Their Favorite Issues Slip in Popular Appeal, Liberal Attacks More Effective," *Wall Street Journal*, October 20, 1982.

36   "Sea Change from 1980": *Ibid.*

37   Oil PACs: Thomas B. Edsall, "Business Tries Hand at Feeding GOP Early in Marginal Races," *Washington Post*, September 12, 1982.

37   Contributions Chart for Oil PACs: Federal Election Commission, "Committee Index of Candidates Supported/Opposed—(D) 1981–82," June 1983, for the listed PACs; size order verified in *RFA*, vol. IV, table C.

37   Archconservative PACs Raised Most Money: Calculated from *RFA*, vol. IV, table C.

37   Parties Gave 6% in 1980: Calculated from *RFA, 1979–80, Senate and House*, pp. 126–27 (using "total receipts" for comparability to 1981–82).

37   Parties Gave 6.8% in 1982: Calculated from *RFA, Senate and House*, pp. 91–92.

38   Cantor: Private communication.

38   60% Local Funds from Out of State: Xandra Kayden, "Campaign Finance: The Impact on Parties and PACs," in U.S. Congress, House of Representatives, Committee on House Administration, *An Analysis of the Impact of the FECA, 1972–78* (Washington, D.C.: Government Printing Office, 1979), p. 96. Quoted in Cantor, *Political Action Committees*, pp. 162–63.

38   Southwest Oil PACs Fight Northern Liberals: Thomas B. Edsall, "PACs Bankrolling GOP Challengers," *Washington Post*, September 14, 1982.

38   Coyne: As quoted in "PAC Inc.," by Julie Kosterlitz, *Common Cause*, August 1982, p. 12.

38   Moynihan: As quoted in "Lobbying Aides Wait, of Course, in a Lobby," by David Shribman, *New York Times*, July 2, 1982.

39   Dole: As quoted in "Politics and Money—I," by Drew, p. 147.

39   "In 1976, for Example . . ." Lloyd N. Unsell, "Business PACs: Do They Really Sway Votes?" *Wall Street Journal*, September 29, 1982.

40   Labor PACs Outspent Corporate PACs in 1974: Cantor, *Political Action Committees*, pp. 56, 87.

40   Pressure on the Job to Donate: Stephen J. Sansweet, "Political Action Units at Firms Are Assailed by Some Over Tactics," *Wall Street Journal*, July 24, 1980.

40   Mayton: William T. Mayton, "Politics, Money, Coercion, and the Problem with Corporate PACs," *Emory Law Journal* 29 (1980), pp. 375–94.

41   Hierarchy vs. Free Consent: Amitai Etzioni, *A Comparative Analysis of Complex Organizations*, rev. ed. (New York: Free Press, 1975).

41   20% Work Force Unionized: Bureau of the Census, *Statistical Abstract of the United States, 1981* (Washington, D.C.: Government Printing Office, 1981), p. 412.

p. 41   44% From Union Households Voted For Reagan: James Q. Wilson, *The 1980 Election* (Lexington, Mass.: D. C. Heath, 1981), supplement to Wilson, *American Government* (Lexington, Mass.: D. C. Heath, 1980), p. 10.

CHAPTER THREE—Retail: Buying Vote by Vote

42   Campaign Debt Figures: Maxwell Glen, "Going for Broke—A Third of House Winners End Campaigns in the Red," *National Journal*, January 8, 1983, p. 61.

44   Voluntary Plan Ineffectual: *The Government Subsidy Squeeze* (Washington, D.C.: Common Cause, 1980), p. 13.

44   "The Force that . . .": "The Swarming Lobbyists: Washington's New Billion Dollar Game of Who Can Influence Whom," *Time*, August 7, 1978, p. 14.

44   AMA Contributions: Common Cause, *Government Subsidy Squeeze*, p. 87.

44   AMPAC Contribution to Health Subcommittee: *How Money Talks in Congress* (Washington, D.C.: Common Cause, 1979), pp. 12–13.

45   AMA Contributions in 1976: *Ibid.*, p. 13

45   AMA Funds for Freshmen: *Government Subsidy Squeeze*, p. 87.

45   "It Is Not Uncommon . . .": John J. Rhodes, *The Futile System* (Garden City, N.Y.: EPM Publications, 1976), p. 22.

46   Congressmen Not Accepting PAC Money: Verified individually with their offices and with Common Cause, Press Office, May 24, 1983.

46   How Money Influences Votes (Table): *Government Subsidy Squeeze*, p. 94.

47   "Cease and Desist . . .": "Rise in Mortgage Insurance Ceiling Is Voted by House," *Wall Street Journal*, June 8, 1979.

48   NAR vs. HUD: *Ibid.; National Association of Realtors PAC Contributions Study* (Washington, D.C.: Common Cause, June 21, 1979), p. 1.

48   NAR Campaign Contributions: *More than $1 Million*, p. 2.

48   Oil PAC Money Influencing Vote: Public Citizen's Congress Watch, "Oil Industry PAC Contributions and Jones Amendment Vote," July 23, 1979.

49   Domestic Content Bill: For details concerning the domestic content bill, see "Detroit's Advocates in Congress Want to Stamp Cars with 'Made in America,'" by Gordon T. Lee, *National Journal*, July 10, 1982, pp. 1221–23.

49   Influence of UAW on Votes: *UAW PAC Contributions Study* (Washington, D.C.: Common Cause, December 18, 1982), p. 1.

49   Dairy Industry Costs $2 Billion: *An Ocean of Milk, a Mountain of Cheese, and a Ton of Money: Contributions from the Dairy PACs to Members of Congress* (Washington, D.C.: Public Citizen's Congress Watch, July 1982), p. 1.

49   530 Million Pounds of Cheese: "A Mess However It's Sliced," *Time*, January 4, 1982, p. 63.

49   1981 House Vote to Cut Subsidy: William Black, Office of Congressman Barney Frank, private communication, May 24, 1983.

49   Dairy PACs Gave $1,600 Per Yes Vote: *An Ocean of Milk*, pp. 6–8.

50   Sixteen Cosponsors of FTC Legislative Veto: *Congress Gets a Tune-up: Campaign Contributions from Car Dealers to Congress After the FTC Issued Its Used Car Rule* (Washington, D.C.: Public Citizen's Congress Watch, February 1982), pp. 1–2.

50   FTC Veto Passed: "Would You Buy a Used Car from Congress?" *U.S. News & World Report*, June 7, 1982, p. 11.

50   Moffett: *Ibid.*

50   PAC Money and Clinch Reactor Vote (Table): *Campaign Contributions Breed Subsi-*

dies for the Clinch River Breeder Reactor (Washington, D.C.: Public Citizen's Congress Watch, August 1982), pp. 1–3 (table from covering press release, August 26, 1982).

50 PAC Money and Auto-Emission Standards: *The Cash Solution to Air Pollution: Contributions from the Auto Industry to Members of the Energy and Commerce Committee on the Clean Air Act* (Washington, D.C.: Public Citizen's Congress Watch, September 1982), pp. 1, 5–6.

51 Contributions to Cosponsors: *Campaign Contributions from the Three Major Financial Institutions, PACs to Co-Sponsors of Bills to Repeal Withholding on Interest and Dividends* (Washington, D.C.: Public Citizen's Congress Watch, 1983), pp. 6–7.

51 Nuclear PACs' Influence in Senate: *The Nuclear Congress,* (Washington, D.C.: Public Citizen's Critical Mass Energy Project, April 1982), chart B.

51 PACs Lost FTC/Health Bill in 1982: Simon Lazarus, "PAC Power? They Keep on Losing," *Washington Post,* March 27, 1983.

51 $3 Million to Exempt Doctors: *AMA and ADA PAC Contributions to Current Members of the House of Representatives and Representatives' Votes on the Broyhill Amendment* (Washington, D.C.: Common Cause, December 1982), appendix B.

52 "That's Hardly Enough . . .": Mobil Corporation, "PACs—The Voice of Real People" (advertisement), *New York Times,* December 2, 1982.

52 "It Is Sheer Nonsense . . .": Robert McMillan, "We Need More PACs to Restore Faith in Political Equity," *Newsday,* October 29, 1982.

53 List of Dairy PACs: Federal Election Commission, *Sponsor/Committee Index,* April 5, 1983, pp. 63, 133.

53 Twenty-One Dairy PACs: Randy Huwa, Common Cause, private communication, September 22, 1982.

53 Dairy Funds for Jenrette et al.: *How Money Talks,* p. 53.

53 Oil PACs' Contributions: "Energy Group Political Giving Tops $3 Million," *New York Times,* July 18, 1982.

54 Jewish PACs: John J. Fialka, "Pro-Israel Politics: Jewish Groups Increase Campaign Donations, Target Them Precisely," *Wall Street Journal,* August 3, 1983.

54 Oil PACs' Funds Received by Hatch Et Al.: "Energy Group Political Giving Tops $3 Million."

54 Bankruptcy Bill Unites PACs: *Taking Credit for Bankruptcy: Campaign Contributions from the Credit Industry to Co-Sponsors of the Bankruptcy "Reform" Bill* (Washington, D.C.: Public Citizen's Congress Watch, July 1982) p. 1.

54 Fenwick Raised $14,650: Walter Isaacson, "Running with the PACs," *Time,* October 25, 1982, p. 26.

54 Wives of Commodity Traders Donating: Jerry Knight, "Commodity Traders Donate to Rep. Russo," *Washington Post,* August 1, 1981.

55 "If BIPAC . . .": Steven W. Thomas, in *Parties, Interest Groups, and Campaign Finance Laws* ed. Michael J. Malbin (Washington, D.C.: American Enterprise Institute, 1980), p. 83.

55 Opportunity List Is Lightning Rod: Paul Taylor, "Chamber of Commerce Says Nay to Democrats," *Washington Post,* October 7, 1982.

55 "Very Clearly We Will . . .": Julie Kosterlitz, "PAC Inc.," *Common Cause,* August 1982, p. 15.

CHAPTER FOUR—**Legalized Corruption**

56 "Whoever, Directly or . . .": Title 18, *United States Code,* §201(b).

56 "Whoever, Being a . . .": Title 18, *United States Code,* §201(c).

p. 57   "Holding Any Office . . .": Title 18, *United States Code,* §201.

57   "To Any Other Person . . .": Title 18, *United States Code,* §201(b).

57   "To Receive Anything . . .": Title 18, *United States Code,* §201(c).

58   Funding and Briefing Divisions: Peter Lauer, Executive Director of AMPAC, private communication, June 7, 1983.

58   "Perfectly Legal": Common Cause, "A Declaration of War" (advertisement), *New York Times,* February 6, 1983. (Emphasis in original.)

58   "Unspoken Obligation": Archibald Cox, "A Liberal Looks at the 1980's," Girvetz Memorial Lecture, University of California at Santa Barbara, January 13, 1981, p. 15.

59   "No One Here Today . . .": Testimony by Mike Synar on H.R. 4070, The Campaign Finance Reform Act of 1982, before the House Administration Committee Task Force on Elections, June 10, 1982, p. 2.

59   "The Process Has . . .": Testimony of Bob Eckhardt before the House Administration Committee Task Force on Elections, June 10, 1982, p. 8.

59   "The Legalities Are . . .": In an interview with Julie Kosterlitz and Florence Graves, "A Congressional Rising Star Calls It Quits," *Common Cause,* June 1982, p. 25.

60   "You Still Have to . . .": Michael R. Gordon, "Are Military Contractors Part of the Problem or Part of the Solution," *National Journal,* July 11, 1981, p. 1234.

60   "Obviously, We Contribute . . .": Brooks Jackson, "Doctors and Dentists Prescribe Donations for Some in House," *Wall Street Journal,* September 17, 1982.

60   "The Dairy Industry . . .": Julie Kosterlitz, "PAC Inc.," *Common Cause,* August 1982, p. 12.

60   "Before, Builders Viewed . . .": Timothy D. Schellhardt, "Builders Try to Wield Political Cash to Get Housing Aid From Congress," *Wall Street Journal,* March 25, 1982.

60   "If You Will Make . . .": Kosterlitz, "PAC Inc.," p. 15.

60   Fenwick: As quoted by Jay Angoff in testimony before the House Administration Committee Task Force on Elections, June 10, 1982, p. 4.

61   Gilman Form Letter: Albert R. Hunt, "An Inside Look at Politicians Hustling PACs," *Wall Street Journal,* October 1, 1982.

61   Mazzoli Reduces Anti-trust Restrictions: *Ibid.*

61   Bristol-Myers: Larry J. Sabato, *The Rise of Political Consultants* (New York: Basic Books, 1981), pp. 273, 296–99.

61   Dick Clark: "Single Issue Politics," *Newsweek,* November 6, 1978, as quoted in "Beyond Democracy: Interest Groups and the Patriotic Gore," by Irving Louis Horowitz, *The Humanist,* September/October 1979, p. 6.

61   Metzenbaum: Private communication.

61   "The Business PAC . . .": Lester L. Cooper, Jr., "PACs: What Claybrook and Drabble Didn't Say," *Washington Post,* October 2, 1982. (Emphasis added.)

61   "In the Mid-1970s . . .": Mark Green, "Political PAC-Man," *The New Republic,* December 13, 1982, pp. 18–19.

62   "A . . . Refreshing Concession . . .": Brooks Jackson, "Office-Machine Dealers' PAC, Unlike Most, Uses Cash to Single-Mindedly Push One Bill," *Wall Street Journal,* April 6, 1983.

62   "I'm a Seller": Dennis Farney, "Rep. Coelho Makes Money, and Waves, for the Democrats," *Wall Street Journal,* June 14, 1983.

63   Interested Party Can Get Help: Private communication.

63   Campaign Committee Raised $5.7 Million: Farney, "Rep. Coelho Makes Money."

p. 63 Staff Insist Work Done Elsewhere: Private communication.

63 "Potential Contributors . . .": Farney, "Rep. Coelho Makes Money."

63 "Among Many Democrats . . .": "Campaign Committees: Focus of Party Revival," *Congressional Quarterly Weekly Report,* July 2, 1983, p. 1347.

64 "All Things Generally . . .": Lawrence H. Tribe, *American Constitutional Law* (Mineola, N.Y.: Foundation Press, 1978), pp. 291–92.

64 U.S. v. Johnson: *Ibid.,* pp. 292–93; *Congressional Ethics,* 2nd ed. (Washington, D.C.: Congressional Quarterly, Inc., 1980), p. 169.

65 U.S. v. Brewster: Tribe, *American Constitutional Law,* p. 293.

65 "On Charges that He . . .": *Congressional Ethics,* p. 24. (Emphasis added.)

65 "The Helstoski Decision . . .": Private communication.

65 Three-year Limitation: Title 2, *United States Code,* §455.

66 "Based on the Basic . . .": Jackson, "Doctors and Dentists."

66 Luken Got $174,778: Dennis Farney, "A Liberal Congressman Turns Conservative; Did PAC Gifts Do It?" *Wall Street Journal,* July 29, 1982.

66 Luken's Contributors: *Ibid.*

67 Gary Hart Reports: Horowitz, "Beyond Democracy," p. 6.

67 Tax Law Writing Took 17 Hours: Thomas B. Edsall, "Tax-Leasing Issue Proving Costly to Business," *Washington Post,* July 11, 1982.

67 "Strong Ties . . .": *Ibid.*

67 Gorton Helped Boeing: "Airlines Split over the Tax Bill's Proposed Break for Leasing Planes," *Wall Street Journal,* August 11, 1982.

68 Oil-company Tax Break Repealed: Robert W. Merry, "Oil Provision in the Tax Bill Stirs Big Fight," *Wall Street Journal,* August 9, 1982.

68 Cochran's Error: "The Senate's Goof on Gulf's Tax Break," *Newsweek,* August 23, 1982, p. 13.

68 "Hypocrisy Poll": Jay Angoff and Jane Stone, eds., *Congressional Voting Index / Money Index* (Washington, D.C.: Public Citizen, 1981), p. 7.

68 PACs Diluted Clean Air Act: Walter Isaacson, "Running with the PACs," *Time,* October 25, 1982, p. 24.

69 "It Was Clear . . .": *Ibid.*

69 PAC Heaven: David Maraniss, "Powerful Energy Panel Turns on Big John's Axis," *Washington Post,* August 21, 1983.

69 "The 'Dirty Dozen' . . .": Kosterlitz, "PAC Inc.," p. 15.

69 "With a Little Money . . .": *How Money Talks in Congress* (Washington, D.C.: Common Cause, 1979), p. 32.

69 "If You Make Contributions . . .": Jeffrey H. Birnbaum and Brooks Jackson, "Commodity Traders' Big Donations Pay Off in Lobbying Against Fee," *Wall Street Journal,* September 15, 1982.

69 Henson Moore: Kosterlitz, "PAC Inc.," p. 12.

70 Thomas Tauke: As quoted in "Study Ties Oil Gifts to Voting in House," by Steven V. Roberts, *New York Times,* July 24, 1979.

70 "I Must Object . . .": Senator Steve Symms, letter to the editor, *Time,* November 15, 1982, p. 6.

70 Studies Show Money Made a Difference: James B. Kau and Paul H. Rubin, *Congressmen, Constituents, and Contributors* (Boston: Martinus Nijhoff Publishing, 1982); Candice J. Nelson, private communication; John P. Frendreis and Richard W. Waterman, "PAC Contributions and Legislative Behavior: Senate Voting on Trucking Deregulation," paper presented to the annual meeting of the Midwest Political

Science Association, Chicago, April 20–22, 1983; Diana Evans Yiannakis and Kirk F. Brown, papers presented to the annual meeting of the American Political Science Association, Chicago, September 1983.

71   Fowler "Is a Valuable Member . . .": Hunt, "Politicians Hustling PACs."
71   Machine Dealers Association: Jackson, "Office-Machine Dealers' PAC."
72   "That Corruption Exists . . .": Albert Finkelstein, letter dated September 22, 1982.
72   Henry B. Gonzalez: Kosterlitz, "PAC Inc.," p. 12.
72   Boggs' Personal Contributions: Paul Taylor, " 'One Stop Shopping': A Law Firm Prospers in the New Marketplace of Influence," Washington Post, August 1, 1983.
73   "Certainly, We Take . . .": As quoted in "Study Ties Oil Gifts," by Roberts.
73   "As a Matter of Policy . . .": H. David Crowther, chairman, Lockheed Political Action Committee, letter to the editor, Time, November 15, 1982, p. 6.
73   Realtors' PAC Liked 40: James M. Perry, "How Realtors' PAC Rewards Office Seekers Helpful to the Industry," Wall Street Journal, August 2, 1982.
73   Checks Delivered Personally: Ibid.
73   Phone Bank: Ibid.
73   Some Donations Counted at Lower Value: Code of Federal Regulations, Title 11, §104.13(a)(1), 106.4(g).
73   RPAC Independent Expenditures: Perry, "Realtors' PAC"; Federal Election Commission, "Committee Index of Candidates Supported/Opposed (D) 1981–82," Realtors Political Action Committee, May 17, 1983, p. 14.
74   "The Realtors Aren't . . .": Perry, "Realtors' PAC."
74   Local Realtors Involved: Ibid.
74   "Some PACs Want . . .": Quoted in an interview with Dom Bonafede, "Textbook Candidate," National Journal, December 18, 1982, p. 2172.
75   "Money, Specifically Campaign . . .": Albert R. Hunt, "The Power Brokers: Thomas Boggs Offers Full Service Lobbying for a Diverse Clientele," Wall Street Journal, March 23, 1982.
75   Chiles Limits Individual Contributions: Gene Hammel, administrative assistant to Senator Chiles, private communication, July 21, 1982.
75   Conable Refuses PAC Money Over $50: Mark Shields, "The Coming Campaign Scandal," Washington Post, February 25, 1983.
75   Kemp Limits PAC Money: Steven V. Roberts, "Moving to Limit the Impact of PACs," New York Times, August 16, 1983.
75   Rostenkowski Gifts Cancel Out: Brooks Jackson, "Lawmakers' Success with Fund Dinners Hinges on Lobbyists," Wall Street Journal, February 25, 1982.
76   "The Ability of Even . . .": Elizabeth Drew, "Politics and Money—I," New Yorker, December 6, 1982, p. 54.
77   "A Huge, Masked Bribe": "Parting Shots by Retiring Lawmakers," U.S. News & World Report, December 20, 1982, p. 24.
77   "Threatens the Very Future . . .": Paul Taylor, "Efforts to Revise Campaign Laws Center on PACs," Washington Post, February 28, 1983.
77   Sen. Thomas Eagleton: As quoted in "The Pernicious Influence of PACs on Congress," by Norman C. Miller, Wall Street Journal, February 17, 1983.
77   "There Has Been . . .": Taylor, "Efforts to Revise."
77   "I Turned Down . . .": Congressional Ethics, p. 9.
78   "What Emerges Are . . .": Hunt, "Politicians Hustling PACs."
78   "A Strong Letter . . .": George Lardner, Jr., "Black Caucus Seen Favoring, Fighting Bill to Curb PACs," Washington Post, May 2, 1983.

p. 79 "We Did Nothing . . .": *Dollar Politics,* 3rd ed. (Washington, D.C.: Congressional Quarterly, Inc., 1982), p. 48.

79 Grassley Raised $722,000 from PACs: *FEC Reports on Financial Activity, 1979–80, Final Report: U.S. Senate and House Campaigns* (Washington, D.C.: Federal Election Commission, 1982), table I.

79 Tolchins' Book: Martin Tolchin and Susan Tolchin, *Dismantling America* (Boston: Houghton Mifflin, forthcoming in 1984).

80 PACs Prevent Immigration Legislation: Robert Pear, "New Drive Under Way in Congress to Revamp U.S. Immigration Law," *New York Times,* February 22, 1983.

80 PACs Prevented Gas Deregulation: Peter W. Bernstein et al., "Zoo Time for Gasmen," *Fortune,* April 4, 1983, pp. 29, 32.

80 Law Firms Make Contributions: John J. Fialka, "Making Friends: Legal Profession Tops All Others in Financing Candidates for Congress," *Wall Street Journal,* August 18, 1983.

CHAPTER FIVE—**The Scope of Corruption: Perverting Economic Policy**

82 Reagan's Skill as Communicator: Dale Tate with Andy Plattner, "House Ratifies Savings Plan in Stunning Reagan Victory," *Congressional Quarterly Weekly Report,* June 27, 1981, p. 1127; "Tax Cut Passed by Solid Margin in House, Senate," *Congressional Quarterly Weekly Report,* August 1, 1981, p. 1371.

82 "The President Has Shown . . .": As quoted in "The Master Politician Has His Day," by Lou Cannon, *Washington Post,* August 2, 1981.

83 "By Now, Ronald Reagan . . .": Mark Shields, "Sorry, Democrats, but the Message Got Through," *Washington Post,* July 31, 1981.

83 Sugar Price Supports: Barton Gellman, "Reagan's Deal on the Budget—A Sweetener for the Sugar Industry," *National Journal,* August 8, 1981, pp. 1417–18.

83 Midwestern Farmers: "Reagan's Revised Tax Cut Plan Doesn't Come Up 'Clean,' " *National Journal,* June 13, 1981, p. 1061.

83 "There Are Half a Dozen . . .": Bill Keller, "Democrats and Republicans Try to Outbid Each Other in Cutting Taxes for Business," *Congressional Quarterly Weekly Report,* June 27, 1981, pp. 1133–36.

83 "All Savers" Certificates: "Reagan Aides Need a Scorecard," *Washington Post,* July 25, 1981.

84 Steven Ross: Elizabeth Drew, "Politics and Money—I," *New Yorker,* December 6, 1982, pp. 88–90.

84 Selling Tax Breaks: Leslie Wayne, "Tax Lease Aiding Bigger Companies," *New York Times,* November 17, 1981; Joint Committee on Taxation, *General Explanation of the Economic Recovery Tax Act of 1981* (Washington, D.C.: Government Printing Office, 1981), table V-3, note 5.

84 $8.1 Billion AT&T Provision: Robert W. Merry, "AT&T Could Get $14 Billion in Tax Breaks From Obscure Change in Write-off Rules," *Wall Street Journal,* October 7, 1981; revenue loss cited is less than quoted in article, to conform with time period covered by Reagan tax bill (figures from Howard Nestor, economist, Department of the Treasury).

84 $1.6 Billion Utilities Break: Joint Committee on Taxation, *Tax Act of 1981,* pp. 216–18; figures from table V-3.

84 $11.7 Billion to Oil and Gas Interests: *Ibid.,* pp. 316–25; figures from table V-3.

p. 84   Estate and Gift Taxes: *Ibid.,* pp. 227–76; figures from table V-3.

84   All Savers Certificates Favor Wealthy: "Tax Cuts: How You Will Be Better Off," *U.S. News & World Report,* August 10, 1981, p. 22.

84   "All Savers" Cost $3.3 Billion: Joint Committee on Taxation, *Tax Act of 1981,* pp. 187–92; figures from table V-3.

84   Total Tax Bill Cost: The principal additions and their revenue costs in billions, fiscal years 1981–86, as cited in *Tax Act of 1981,* by the Joint Committee on Taxation, table V-3, pp. 382–91 (except for AT&T—see above note to p. 84):

Indexing	48.8
Marriage penalty reduction	37.5
Leasing tax breaks	27.0
Estate and gift tax	15.4
Energy provisions	11.8
Retirement savings	8.3
AT&T retroactive reclassification	8.1
Charitable contributions	3.8
Research and development	3.3
All Savers certificates	3.3
Exclusion of foreign income	2.7
Corporate tax rates	2.2
Interest exclusion	1.8
Utilities stock reinvestment	1.6
Child-care credit	1.1
Investment credit for used property	0.6
Total:	$177.3 billion

85   1982 Tax Increase Less than Pork: House Ways and Means Committee staff, private communication, May 1983.

86   1,800 Exclusions to Tax Code: Caryl Conner, "Offering Incentives to Tax Evaders," *Wall Street Journal,* May 13, 1983.

86   One-half Personal Income Escapes Taxes: Robert E. Hall and Alvin Rabushka, *Low Tax, Simple Tax, Flat Tax* (New York: McGraw-Hill, 1983), p. 11.

86   Tax Breaks Total $327.5 Billion: "Tax Subsidies: They Just Keep Climbing," *U.S. News & World Report,* March 21, 1983, p. 75.

86   114% and 151% Higher: Data on estimated 1984 budget receipts and CPI obtained from the Statistical Office, Office of Management and Budget, April 8, 1983, and subject to revision.

86   25 Cents on Dollar Deduction: Robert J. Samuelson, "The Tax Trap," *National Journal,* April 10, 1982, p. 641.

86   High-priced Toys: "Fun and Games," *Fortune,* January 24, 1983, p. 36.

86   Maldistribution of 1982 Tax Breaks: Department of the Treasury, study done at the request of the Joint Economic Committee, September 28, 1982.

87   Corporate Taxes Cut: Leslie Wayne, "The Corporate Tax: Uneven, Unfair?" *New York Times,* March 20, 1983.

87   Commercial Banks Paid 2.7% Tax: Joint Committee on Taxation, *Taxation of Banks and Thrift Institutions* (Washington, D.C.: Government Printing Office, 1983), pp. 1–15.

87   Some Industries Got Refunds: Wayne, "Corporate Tax."

87   "If Any of Them . . .": Charles Vanik, "The Corporate Raid on the Treasury," *Washington Post,* January 23, 1983.

p. 87   Breaks for Oil Companies and Hog Farmers: *The Kindest Cuts of All* (Washington, D.C.: Public Citizen's Congress Watch, 1981), pp. 14–18.

87   AMC: "For Some It's a Tax Cut," *U.S. News & World Report,* August 30, 1982, p. 21.

87   Scott Paper Co.: *Ibid.*

87   Marriott Corp.: *Ibid.*

87   Beatrice Foods Co.: *Ibid.*

88   Athletes and Veterans: *Ibid.*

88   1,846 Tax-break Bills: Julie Kosterlitz and Jean Cobb, "Give Me a Break!" *Common Cause,* March/April 1983, p. 25.

88   Farms as Tax Shelters: Ruth Simon, "The Small Farmer: An Endangered Species," *Public Citizen,* Winter 1982, pp. 12–15.

89   Tax Could Be 19%: Hall and Rabushka, *Low Tax,* p. 23.

89   Tax Gap Tripled: Statement of Roscoe L. Egger, Jr., Commissioner of Internal Revenue, before the Subcommittee of Oversight of the Internal Revenue Service, Committee on Finance, March 22, 1982, p. 4.

89   "Underground Economy": As quoted in "Why the Underground Economy Is Booming," by Irwin Ross, *Fortune,* October 9, 1978, p. 93.

89   $87 Billion in Taxes Not Paid: As quoted in an interview, "$300 Billion That Evades Taxes—IRS on the Trail," *U.S. News & World Report,* April 11, 1983, p. 54.

89   One in Four Admit to Cheating: Otto Friedrich, "Cheating by the Millions," *Time,* March 28, 1983, p. 27.

89   Loopholes Multiply: See note to p. 86.

90   Sharp Rise in Credit: Timothy B. Clark, "Reagan's Assault on Federal Borrowing —Making Room for the Private Sector," *National Journal,* October 17, 1981, p. 1860; these figures include federally guaranteed loans, borrowing by government-created enterprises, and borrowing favored by tax exemptions, but exclude direct federal borrowing.

90   Small Businesses Pay 18%, Corporations 15%: Bureau of the Census, *Statistical Abstract of the United States 1981* (Washington, D.C.: Government Printing Office, 1981), p. 522.

91   Students Paid 5% or 9%: "Student Aid Programs by the Half Dozen," *National Journal,* July 17, 1982, p. 1263.

91   Other Government Loan Subsidies: Clark, "Reagan's Assault," p. 1862; Gellman, "Reagan's Deal," p. 1420; *Federal Credit Activities: An Analysis of President Reagan's Credit Budget for 1982,* Congressional Budget Office Staff Working Paper (Washington, D.C.: Congress of the United States, April 1981), pp. 66–67.

91   "Presumed to Be . . .": As quoted in "Trade Adjustment Assistance Program May Be Too Big for Its Own Good," by Michael R. Gordon, *National Journal,* May 10, 1980, p. 765.

91   Qualifications for Trade Adjustment Assistance: Gordon, "Trade Adjustment Assistance Program," p. 765.

91   Results of 1974 Trade Act: Ibid.; Richard S. Frank, "New Law Must Be Translated into Gains at GATT Talk," *National Journal,* January 18, 1975, p. 77.

92   "Substantial Cause": Paul Lewis, "Protecting the Talks and the Trade: A Hard Act to Follow," *National Journal,* April 17, 1976, p. 504.

92   TAA Participants Doubled: "Adjustment Assistance: Helping the Penalized Company," *National Journal,* April 17, 1976, p. 507.

92   Benefits $9 Million in 1973: Michael Reed, "The Administration Wants to Withdraw the Carrot of Trade Adjustment Aid," *National Journal,* May 29, 1982, p. 958.

p. 92   Benefits $259 Million in 1979: Gordon, "Trade Adjustment Assistance Program," p. 766.

92   TAA Cost $1.5 Billion in 1980: Reed, "Withdraw the Carrot," p. 958.

92   "Provided Handsome Cash, Education . . .": "That $1 Billion 'Surprise,' " *Washington Post,* April 10, 1980.

92   ¼ .TAA Beneficiaries Returned to Old Jobs: *Ibid.*

92   Very Few Used Retraining Program: Reed, "Withdraw the Carrot," p. 959.

92   TAA Discouraged Relocation: Robert J. Samuelson, "On Mobility," *National Journal,* August 16, 1980, p. 1366.

93   12% Americans under EDA in 1965: Cristie Backley, Public Affairs Office of the Economic Development Administration, private communication, March 11, 1983.

93   84.5% Americans under EDA by 1979: Rochelle L. Stanfield, "EDA—The 'Perfect Vehicle' for Carter's Urban Strategy," *National Journal,* June 23, 1979, p. 1034.

93   Carter Failed to Reduce EDA: *Ibid.*

93   85% Americans Still Qualify: Backley, private communication.

94   Eads's Testimony: Statement of Professor George C. Eads before the Subcommittee on General Oversight and Renegotiation, Committee on Banking, Finance and Urban Affairs, U.S. House of Representatives, March 10, 1983, especially pp. 6–7.

94   Interest Groups Prevent Congressional Studies: House Joint Resolution 599–19 (1982).

94   National Laboratories: Stanley N. Wellborn, "Why National Laboratories Are Under Fire," *U.S. News & World Report,* November 8, 1982, p. 54.

94   High-sugar Cereals: Ward Sinclair and Thomas Edsall, "Sweets: Lobbyists Add Sugary Cereal to High-Nutrition Menu," *Washington Post,* December 10, 1982.

95   Lobbyists Reduced Wheat for International Relief: Ward Sinclair, "Wheat for Famine Relief Makes Lobbyists Hungry," *Washington Post,* May 5, 1983.

95   Broadcasters Opposed Radio Marti: Ernest Holsendolph, "U.S. Lists 'Options' on Cuban Jamming," *New York Times,* May 7, 1983.

95   "Every Industry . . .": George J. Stigler, "The Theory of Economic Regulation," *Bell Journal of Economics and Management Science,* Spring 1971, quoted in "The Politics of Regulation," by James Q. Wilson, in *The Politics of Regulation,* ed. James Q. Wilson (New York: Basic Books, 1980), p. 358.

96   Wilson Pointed to Deregulation: Wilson, "The Politics of Regulation," pp. 359–60.

96   Barry P. Bosworth: As quoted in an interview with Robert J. Samuelson, "Bosworth on Inflation Fight: 'Nobody has the Answer,' " *National Journal,* September 1, 1979, p. 1452.

96   Frank Church: *Ibid.*

97   Current Cost of Farm Subsidies: Seth S. King, "Farm Price Props Expected to Rise Above '82 Record," *New York Times,* January 23, 1983.

97   Reconstituted Milk Would Save Tax Money: Patricia Theiler, "Milking the System," *Common Cause,* October 1982, p. 11.

97   Labor Lobbies for Davis-Bacon Act: Shirley Scheibla, "Powerful Lever: How the Davis-Bacon Act Jacks Up Construction Costs," *Barron's,* August 28, 1978, pp. 4–6.

97   Hansen and Hunt: Brooks Jackson and Edward T. Pound, "Rep. Hansen's Reports to Congress Leave Out Links to Bunker Hunt," *Wall Street Journal,* July 27, 1982.

98   "U.S. Steel's Pushing . . .": William P. Ashworth, *Under the Influence: Congress, Lobbies, and the American Pork-Barrel System* (New York: Hawthorn/Dutton, 1981), p. 108.

98   Rising Health Costs: Bureau of the Census, *Statistical Abstract,* pp. 111, 459.

p. 98   AMA Indicted of Violating Sherman Act: Paul Starr, *The Social Transformation of American Medicine* (New York: Basic Books, 1982), pp. 272, 305, 347.

98   AMA Opposes Cost-cutting Measures: *Ibid.,* pp. 398–408 and *passim;* Milt Freudenheim, "Doctors Battle Nurses over Domains in Care," *New York Times,* June 4, 1983; *How Money Talks in Congress* (Washington, D.C.: Common Cause, 1979), pp. 12–13.

98   Hospital Lobbyists Fought for 19% Return: Robert Pear, "Lobbyists Fight to Retain Special Medicare Aid for Some Hospitals," *New York Times,* March 22, 1983.

99   "The Soft Drink Deal . . .": "Bad Beer Business," *New York Times,* August 31, 1982.

99   Public Doesn't Form Interest Groups: William S. Peirce, "The Power and the Bureaucracy," *Wall Street Journal,* April 9, 1982.

100   Interest Groups Root of Inflation: Mancur Olson, *The Rise and Decline of Nations* (New Haven, Conn.: Yale University Press, 1982).

CHAPTER SIX—**National Security: Mangled by Interest Groups**

104   Profile of Defense Contractors: Adam Yarmolinsky and Gregory D. Foster, *Paradoxes of Power: The Military Establishment in the Eighties* (Bloomington, Ind.: Indiana University Press, 1983), pp. 56–58.

104   Defense PACs: Bob Adams, "Congressmen Who Can Help Get Helped," *St. Louis Post-Dispatch,* April 18, 1983.

104   Armed Services Committee Chairmen Prosper: *Ibid.*

104   "You Know Who Shows . . .": *Ibid.*

105   "We Actively Support . . .": Adams, "Congressmen Who Can Help."

105   White House Gets Involved: William H. Lewis, Security Policy Studies Program, George Washington University, private communication.

105   "California Has Been Built . . .": As quoted in Anthony Sampson, *The Arms Bazaar: From Lebanon to Lockheed* (New York: Viking, 1977), p. 214.

106   "Perhaps the Most Common . . .": Walter S. Mossberg, "Pork-Barrel Politics: Some Congressmen Treat Military Budget as Source for Patronage," *Wall Street Journal,* April 15, 1983.

106   $2 Billion Wasted: George C. Wilson, "It May Be National Defense, but the Pork Is Just as Sweet," *Washington Post,* September 26, 1982.

106   $296 Million Padding: Brad Knickerbocker, "Trying to Find the Pork in the Pentagon's Barrel," *Christian Science Monitor,* May 5, 1983.

106   Rivers: Robert N. Winter-Berger, *The Washington Pay-off: An Insider's View of Corruption in Government* (Secaucus, N.J.: Lyle Stuart, 1972), p. 191.

106   "Rivers Delivers": Private communication.

107   "Sir, If You Try . . .": Winter-Berger, *Washington Pay-off,* p. 192.

107   "In Most Instances . . .": Mossberg, "Source for Patronage."

107   "Congress Votes Itself . . .": *Ibid.* (Emphasis added.)

107   Senator Tower Asked Colleagues: Mary McGrory, "John Tower Knows that Even Doves Spare the Pork Back Home," *Washington Post,* February 8, 1983.

107   Rockwell, Cranston, and the B-1: *Ibid.*

107   Lockheed, Young, and the C-5B: Fred Kaplan, "The Flying Lazarus," *Washington Monthly,* February 1983, pp. 55–56.

107   "To Win the Votes . . .": Walter Isaacson, "The Winds of Reform," *Time,* March 7, 1983, p. 16.

p. 107   A-10 Is on Long Island: *Ibid.*

107   Service Associations: Gordon Adams, *The Politics of Defense Contracting: The Iron Triangle* (New Brunswick, N.J.: Transaction Books, 1982), p. 157.

107   Service-Association Membership: Bob Adams, "Socializing Seeds Defense Orders," *St. Louis Post-Dispatch,* April 22, 1983.

108   Corporations Pay for Service-Association Dinners, etc.: Private communication.

108   Trade Associations: Winter-Berger, *Washington Pay-off,* p. 190.

109   "This Country and Its . . .": Louis J. Walinsky, "Coherent Defense Strategy: The Case for Economic Denial," *Foreign Affairs,* Winter 1982–83, pp. 272–73.

109   "The United States Lacks . . .": W. Bowman Cutter, III, et al., "Budget and Policy Choices for 1983: Taxes, Defense, Entitlements," Center for National Policy, *Alternatives for the 1980's,* No. 7, p. 27.

109   Cabinet Members Wrote Reagan: Richard Halloran, "Military Spending Is Criticized Again," *New York Times,* March 27, 1983.

110   "The Arms Lobby Tends . . .": Bill Keller, "In a Bull Market for Arms, Weapons Industry Lobbyists Push Products, Not Policy," *Congressional Quarterly Weekly Report,* October 25, 1980, p. 3202.

110   "Most of the Defense . . .": Michael R. Gordon, "Are Military Contractors Part of the Problem or Part of the Solution?" *National Journal,* July 11, 1981, p. 1232.

110   "They're So Attuned . . .": Keller, "In a Bull Market," p. 3202.

110   "It Is This Network . . .": *Ibid.,* p. 3201.

111   Senator William Proxmire: As quoted in *Arms, Money, and Politics,* by Julius Duscha (New York: Ives Washburn, 1965), p. 50.

111   "Primarily Keeps Things . . .": Gordon, "Are Military Contractors," p. 1233.

111   " 'Canceling an Established . . .' ": Charles Mohr, "Congress and Intractable Military Costs," *New York Times,* February 18, 1983.

111   "History Shows That . . .": Walter S. Mossberg and Rich Jaroslovsky, "Arms and the Man: Reagan's Defense Push Draws Increasing Fire as Big Drain on Budget," *Wall Street Journal,* December 27, 1982.

111   "Flying Dump Truck": Daniel J. Balz, Richard Corrigan, and Robert J. Samuelson, "Muffling the Arms Explosion," *National Journal,* April 2, 1977, p. 503.

112   "It's John Tower's Project": Mark Green and Jack Newfield, "Who Owns Congress," *Washington Post Magazine,* June 8, 1980, p. 14.

112   "So Out of Date . . .": *Ibid.*

112   "The B-1 Program . . .": Richard B. Hoey, "Culture Clash," *Forbes,* July 19, 1982, p. 118.

113   Duplication of Missiles: Samuel P. Huntington, *The Common Defense* (New York: Columbia University Press, 1961), pp. 413–14.

113   "Fixed-wing" Rivalry: Gregg Easterbrook, "All Aboard Air Oblivion," *Washington Monthly,* September 1981, p. 16.

113   Interservice Rivalry Caused Casualties: Private communication.

113   4,900 Helicopters Lost: Easterbrook, "All Aboard," p. 19.

114   Study by Kuhn: George W. S. Kuhn, "Ending Defense Stagnation," in *Agenda '83,* ed. Richard N. Holwill (Washington, D.C.: The Heritage Foundation, 1983), pp. 69–114.

114   Military Reform Caucus: Richard Halloran, "Caucus Challenges Defense Concepts," *New York Times,* January 12, 1982.

114   General Accounting Office Report: Walter S. Mossberg, "Are Pentagon's Planes, Ships, Tanks Getting Too Complex?" *Wall Street Journal,* March 13, 1981.

114   Fallows: James Fallows, *National Defense* (New York: Random House, 1981); see also

James F. Digby, "New Weapons Technology and Its Impact on Intervention," in *The Limits of Military Intervention*, ed. E. P. Stern (Beverly Hills, Calif.: Sage, 1977).

115 Military Did Better in Recession: Richard Halloran, "Army Chief Reports a 'Renaissance,'" *New York Times*, October 15, 1982.

115 F-15 and MK86 Too Complex: Mossberg, "Too Complex."

115 "Seductiveness of High Technology": As quoted in "The American Way," by Michael R. Gordon, *National Journal*, October 23, 1982, p. 1811.

115 "Our Strategy of . . .": As quoted in Isaacson, "Winds of Reform," p. 16.

115 90% and 95% Decrease in Production: *Ibid.*, p. 12.

115 "The Procurement of . . .": *VISTA 1999*, National Guard Bureau, March 1982, p. 48.

115 Cost of A-10s: *Ibid.*

116 "The National Defense . . .": *Ibid.*, p. 35.

116 "Has Long Committed . . .": Kuhn, "Ending Defense Stagnation," pp. 69–70.

116 "We're About to Pay . . .": Curt Suplee, "Brains, Power, Money & Rocks," *Washington Post*, October 1, 1982. See also Gregg Easterbrook, "DIVAD," *Atlantic Monthly*, October 1982, pp. 29–39.

116 "It Is a Myth . . .": Private communication.

116 F-18 Serves Two Functions: "Why We Love High Technology," *Fortune*, April 4, 1983, p. 128.

116 Israeli Success with U.S. Planes: Captain Santana, Department of Defense, Public Affairs Office, private communication, June 10, 1983.

117 Israeli Success with U.S. Tanks: Kuhn, "Ending Defense Stagnation," p. 77; George C. Wilson, "Army Chooses Weapons over More Personnel," *Washington Post*, August 5, 1982.

117 14 Major Weapons Simultaneously: Wilson, "Army Chooses Weapons."

118 Chart on Defense Budget: Isaacson, "Winds of Reform," p. 13.

118 Less Maneuverable, More Vulnerable: Kuhn, "Ending Defense Stagnation," pp. 76–77.

118 "To Attract and Promote . . .": Halloran, "Caucus Challenges Defense Concepts."

119 Navy Slow to *Mayaguez:* Representative Les Aspin's press officer, private communication, July 26, 1983.

119 "Hollow Army": Halloran, "Army Chief Reports 'Renaissance.'"

119 Underestimating Weapon Costs: Isaacson, "Winds of Reform," p. 16.

121 "Weinberger . . .": "Big Defense Cuts Grow Doubtful for Now but May Come Later," *Wall Street Journal*, February 18, 1983.

121 "Money Can Be Made . . .": Private communication, name withheld by request.

121 R & D, Procurement, and Operations and Maintenance: Office of Assistant Secretary of Defense (Public Affairs), "Financial Summary, Fiscal Year 1983 Department of Defense Budget," News Release No. 50–82, February 8, 1982.

122 "Very Large Increase . . .": Jacques S. Gansler, *The Defense Industry* (Cambridge, Mass.: M.I.T. Press, 1982), pp. 32, 34.

122 Profits of Douglas Aircraft: Clark R. Mollenhoff, *The Pentagon* (New York: Putnam, 1967), p. 274, citing Senate Report No. 970, 88th Congress.

122 Avco: Douglas B. Feaver and Fred Hiatt, "Avco Fighting to Hold Turf in Army Tank Program," *Washington Post*, June 10, 1983.

122 House Prohibition Prevailed: Vernon A. Guidry, Jr., "Army Shuffles Tank Engines to Keep Production Lines Rolling," *Washington Post*, August 7, 1983.

122 Defense R & D Low Risk: Gansler, *Defense Industry*, pp. 75–76.

p. 122 Planned Obsolescence of A-7: Private communication, name withheld by request.
  122   "We Rape Them . . .": Private communication.
  123   Prime Contractors Profit, Subcontractors Don't: Gansler, *Defense Industry*, p. 146.
  124   Cozy Relationship: James Barron, "How Military Buys Its Parts," *New York Times*, September 10, 1983.
  124   Larger Corporations Tend to Form PACs: Gary John Andres, "Corporate Involvement in Campaign Finance During the 1970's," unpublished paper, Department of Political Science, University of Illinois at Chicago, 1982.
  124   Air Force Association Presidents: Air Force Association, private communication, September 14, 1983.
  124   Schenck an Executive: *Who's Who in America*, 41st ed. (Chicago: Marquis Who's Who, 1980), vol. 2.
  124   Navy League Directors and Advisory Council: Navy League, private communication, September 14, 1983.
  124   Kimball President of Aerojet: *Current Biography Yearbook, 1970* (New York: H. W. Wilson, 1970), p. 465.
  124   Carney the Board Chairman: Bath Iron Works, private communication, September 14, 1983.
  124   "You Cannot Buy . . .": Private communication, name withheld by request.
  125   Membership Dues Preclude Small Businesses: Winter-Berger, *Washington Pay-off*, p. 190.
  125   Defense Science Board: Fred Hiatt, "Defense Panel Reported Rife with Conflicts and Cronyism," *Washington Post*, August 26, 1983.
  125   "To Pay and Play": Private communication, name withheld by request.
  125   "Each Time, I Pointed . . .": Winter-Berger, *Washington Pay-off*, p. 191.
  126   "Rather Than Eliminate . . .": George C. Wilson, "Reagan Agrees . . . Panel Votes Freeze on Troop Numbers," *Washington Post*, May 4, 1983.
  126   European Security Study Report: "More Options," *Time*, May 30, 1983, p. 29.
  126   "The 'Conventional Option' . . .": Report prepared by Manfred Woerner and Peter-Kurt Wurzbach, excerpted in "Nato's New 'Conventional Option,' " *Wall Street Journal*, November 19, 1982. (Emphasis added.)
  126   Conventional Forces Stretched: Richard Halloran, "U.S. Held Unready for Show of Force," *New York Times*, July 31, 1983, and "Military Forces Stretched Thin, Army Chief Says," *New York Times*, August 10, 1983.
  126   Shortage of Ammunition: Richard Halloran, "National Security Decisions to Be Focus of Broad Inquiry," *New York Times*, June 22, 1983.
  126   "The Risk Now Exists . . .": Report by Woerner and Wurzbach. (Emphasis added.)
  128   Sen. Dale Bumpers: As quoted in "Money and Politics—I," by Elizabeth Drew, *New Yorker*, December 6, 1982, p. 147.
  129   "I Patiently Explain . . .": Dwight D. Eisenhower, *Mandate for Change, 1953–1956* (New York: Doubleday, 1963), p. 606.
  129   General Jones: Private communication.
  129   JCS Staff Service-bound: David C. Martin and Michael A. Lerner, "Why the Generals Can't Command," *Newsweek*, February 14, 1983.

CHAPTER SEVEN—**The Other Separation of Powers**

  136   Rules in European Feudal Society: T. H. Marshall, *Class, Citizenship, and Social Development*, intro. Seymour Martin Lipset (Garden City, N.Y.: Doubleday & Co.,

1964; Westport, Conn.: Greenwood Press, 1973), pp. 65–122 (page references are to the Greenwood edition).

138   Reform Act of 1832: Marshall, *Class,* p. 78.

138   Act of 1918 and Basic Shift of Rights: *Ibid.*

139   "No Principle of the Equality . . .": *Ibid.,* p. 72. (Emphasis added.)

139   "Modern Industrial Democratic . . .": S. M. Lipset, Introduction, in *ibid.,* p. x.

CHAPTER EIGHT—**From Plutocracy: The Rise of American Democracy**

141   "The Underlying Idea . . .": Kirk H. Porter, *A History of Suffrage in the United States* (Chicago: University of Chicago Press, 1918), pp. 2–3.

141   English Restriction of Vote to Freeholders: Chilton Williamson, *American Suffrage from Property to Democracy: 1760–1860* (Princeton, N.J.: Princeton University Press, 1960), p. 5.

142   "A Common Interest in . . .": *Ibid.*

142   "The Freeholders Are . . .": As quoted in *ibid.,* p. 6.

142   "As Vulnerable to . . .": *Ibid.,* p. 11.

142   "Uncompromising . . .": Porter, *History of Suffrage,* p. 7.

142   Property Requirements in Colonies: *Ibid.,* pp. 7–10.

142   Ethnic and Religious Bars: Williamson, *American Suffrage,* pp. 12–16.

142   "Desirable Elements" Only: *Ibid.,* p. 19.

142   "Free, White, Twenty-one . . .": *Ibid.*

143   Vermont's Requirements: Porter, *History of Suffrage,* pp. 22–23.

143   Maryland's Requirements: Williamson, *American Suffrage,* p. 150.

143   Maine and Universal Suffrage: *Ibid.,* p. 190.

144   1860 Universal Suffrage in All States: Porter, *History of Suffrage,.* p. 111.

145   States' Requirements for Candidates: Robert J. Dinkin, *Voting in Provincial America: A Study of Elections in the Thirteen Colonies, 1689–1776* (Westport, Conn.: Greenwood Press, 1977), p. 51.

146   Northern Chesapeake in 1700: Aubrey C. Land, "Economic Base and Social Structure: The Northern Chesapeake in the Eighteenth Century," *Journal of Economic History* 25 (December 1965): 641–42, 645.

146   Land of the Great Planters, etc.: See, for example, Leonard Woods Labaree, *Conservatism in Early American History* (New York: New York University Press, 1948), p. 3.

146   Political Appointments among Planters: *Ibid.,* pp. 3–4.

146   Powerful Families in Virginia: *Ibid.,* p. 7.

146   "One Sixth of All Virginia . . .": *Ibid.,* pp. 7–8.

146   "A Body of Uncles, Cousins . . .": *Ibid.,* p. 6.

147   Wealthy Quakers in Pennsylvania: Frederick B. Tolles, *Meeting House and Counting House: The Quaker Merchants of Colonial Philadelphia, 1682–1763* (New York: Norton, 1948), pp. 114–23.

147   New Jersey as Proprietorship: Labaree, *Conservatism,* p. 15.

147   New York "Manor Lords": Richard R. Beeman, "History of the United States," *The Encyclopedia Britannica,* 15th ed. (Chicago: Encyclopedia Britannica, Inc., 1982), vol. 18, p. 951.

147   "The American Aristocracy . . .": Arthur M. Schlesinger, *The Birth of the Nation* (New York: Knopf, 1969), p. 140.

147   The Same Top Men "Dominated *ALL* . . .": Leonard L. Richards, *Gentlemen of*

Property and Standing: Anti-Abolition Mobs in Jacksonian America (New York: Oxford University Press, 1970), p. 167.

147   "Those Who Were Recognized . . .": Richard P. McCormick, *The Second American Party System* (Chapel Hill, N.C.: University of North Carolina Press, 1960), p. 30.

147   "A Formidable Force . . .": George Thayer, *Who Shakes the Money Tree?* (New York: Simon and Schuster, 1973), pp. 26–27.

147   Manasseh Cutler: E. Pendleton Herring in *Encyclopaedia of the Social Sciences,* vol. 9 (New York: Macmillan, 1933), p. 565.

148   Excited by Democratic Ideals: See John A. Garraty, *The American Nation: A History of the United States,* 3rd ed. (New York: Harper and Row, 1975), p. 168.

148   Jefferson's Election and Popular Vote: McCormick, *Second American Party System,* p. 343.

148   Jackson's Election and Popular Vote: Thayer, *Money Tree,* p. 27.

148   "Even in Those States . . .": Richard Hofstadter, *The American Political Tradition* (New York: Knopf, 1949), p. 47.

CHAPTER NINE—Securing Democracy: The First Progressive Era

150   GNP Three Times Greater: Bureau of the Census, *Historical Statistics of the United States: Colonial Times to 1970* (Washington, D.C.: Government Printing Office, 1975), pt. 1, ser. F 3 (GNP in 1958 prices).

150   Steel, Coal, Electricity, Oil: *Ibid.,* ser. P 265, M 56, S 13, M 79.

150   "Trusts" Formed: Mark Sullivan, *Our Times* (New York: Scribner's, 1939), II: 307–08.

150   Control by Sugar Trust: John A. Garraty, *The American Nation,* 3rd ed. (New York: Harper and Row, 1975), p. 508.

151   "Became the Object . . .": Richard Hofstadter, *The Age of Reform* (New York: Knopf, 1966), p. 227.

151   "In the Earlier Nineteenth Century . . .": *Ibid.,* p. 229. (Emphasis added.)

151   Boston Railroad Compared with Government: *Ibid.*

151    $22 Billion Tied to Morgan: "The Pujo Committee on the Money Trust," in *The Progressive Movement: 1900 to 1915,* ed. Richard Hofstadter (Englewood Cliffs, N.J.: Prentice Hall, 1963), p. 160; see also Hofstadter, *The Age of Reform,* p. 230.

151   "A Single Network of Interests . . .": Hofstadter, *The Age of Reform,* p. 230; Hofstadter footnotes this statement to *Other People's Money,* by Louis D. Brandeis (New York: Frederick A. Stokes, 1914), pp. 22–23.

151   Morgan's $65 Million Loan to Treasury: Ernest R. May et al., *The Progressive Era,* Time/Life History of the United States, vol. 9 (1901–1917) (New York: Time-Life Books, 1964, 1974), p. 12.

151   San Francisco and Abe Ruef: Garraty, *American Nation,* p. 625.

152   "Golden Rule" Jones in Toledo: *Ibid.*

152   Johnson in Cleveland: Joseph Lincoln Steffens, *The Struggle for Self-Government* (New York: McClure, Phillips & Co., 1906), pp. 186, 197, 196.

152   Steffens Commendation of Cleveland: *Ibid.,* pp. 161, 183.

152   La Follette's Program: David P. Thelen, *The New Citizenship* (Columbia, Mo.: University of Missouri Press, 1972), pp. 167–70; and Garraty, *American Nation,* pp. 625–26.

152   Johnson and Progressives in California: See George E. Mowry, *The California Progressives* (Berkeley: University of California Press, 1951), chaps. I–III; see

also Alan Rosenthal, *Legislative Life* (New York: Harper and Row, 1981), p. 112.

153   Reform Administrations between 1901 and 1910: Garraty, *American Nation*, p. 626.

153   La Follette's Use of "Machine" to Stay in Power: Hofstadter, *Age of Reform*, pp. 267–68.

153   State Governments and Business Concentration: *Ibid.*, p. 231.

153   "Is J. Pierpont Morgan Greater . . .": Lewis Corey, *The House of Morgan* (New York: G. Howard Watt, 1930), quoted in *The Robber Barons,* by Matthew Josephson (New York: Harcourt, Brace & World, 1934), p. 374.

153   Roosevelt Characterizations: Sullivan, *Our Times, passim.*

154   Extreme Examples of Corrupt Practices: Garraty, *American Nation*, pp. 567–68.

154   "When I Came into Power . . .": H. A. Gibbons, *John Wanamaker* (New York: Harper and Brothers, 1926), 1:299–300, quoted in *The Politicos,* by Matthew Josephson (New York: Harcourt, Brace & World, 1938), p. 438.

154   Champion of Wealth and Industry: Hofstadter, *Age of Reform,* p. 256.

154   "Ohio Sent Oilmen . . .": William Ashworth, *Under the Influence: Congress, Lobbies, and the American Pork-Barrel System* (New York: Hawthorn/Dutton, 1981), p. 107.

154   "Early Lobbyists' Techniques . . .": *Ibid.,* p. 106.

154   "Bribery of Members . . .": *Current American Government, Spring 1982 Guide* (Washington, D.C.: Congressional Quarterly, Inc., 1982), p. 81.

155   Sherman Antitrust Act "Made No Attempt . . .": Josephson, *Robber Barons,* p. 359.

155   Sherman Antitrust Act Ignored: *Ibid.*

155   "Antirailroad Sentiment Was . . .": M. P. Rogin and J. L. Shover, *Political Change in California* (Westport, Conn.: Greenwood Press, 1970), p. 53, quoted in "Styles of Electoral Competition," by William Schneider, in *Electoral Competition: A Comparative Analysis,* ed. Richard Rose (Beverly Hills, Calif.: Sage, 1980), p. 89.

155   "Still More Widely Felt . . .": Hofstadter, *Age of Reform,* p. 225.

155   Sullivan on Mark Hanna: Sullivan, *Our Times,* II: 372.

155   Hanna's Assessments from Industrialists: Josephson, *Robber Barons,* p. 360.

155   "Men, Vote as You Please . . .": Garraty, *American Nation*, p. 588.

155   Dingley Tariff Act: Richard N. Current et al., *American History: A Survey,* 5th ed. (New York: Knopf, 1979), vol. II, *Since 1865,* p. 510.

156   Roosevelt's Prohibition on Corporate Contributions: William T. Mayton, "Politics, Money, Coercion, and the Problem with Corporate PACs," in *Emory Law Journal* 29 (1980): 376.

156   "We Bought the Son of a Bitch . . .": As quoted in *ibid.*

156   "The Fortunes Amassed . . .": As quoted in *ibid.*

156   Roosevelt, Rockefeller, and the Bureau of Corporations: May et al., *The Progressive Era,* p. 75.

157   Roosevelt's Initiatives "Encouraged Everyone . . .": Hofstadter, *Age of Reform,* p. 235.

157   "In Addition to Being Used . . .": Theodore Roosevelt, speech in January 1905, as quoted in *The Progressive Era,* by May et al., p. 76.

157   Roosevelt and the Hepburn Act: Garraty, *American Nation*, p. 636.

158   "Everything That Bears . . .": As quoted in *The Progressive Era,* by May et al., p. 102.

158   "That the People at Large . . .": As quoted in *ibid.*

158   Wilson, the Senate, and the Underwood Tariff Act: *Ibid.*

158   1913 Constitutional Amendment: Ashworth, *Under the Influence,* p. 107.

p. 158   Wilson and the Bankers: May et al., *The Progressive Era*, p. 103.

159   "Not the Rule of Wealth . . .": Carl Joachim Friedrich, "Plutocracy," in *Encyclopaedia of the Social Sciences* vol. 12 (New York: MacMillan, 1934), p. 176.

159   "It Is an Ever Recurring Phenomenon . . .": *Ibid.*

159   "Woodrow Wilson Maintained . . .": *Ibid.*, p. 177.

160   Efforts of the Progressives: Hofstadter, *Age of Reform*, p. 231.

161   "Senators Had to Go Directly . . .": *Ibid.*, p. 256.

161   Progressives Striving for Meritocracy: See, for example, Robert H. Wiebe, *The Search for Order, 1877–1920* (New York: Hill and Wang, 1967).

161   Progressives' Concentration on "Common Public Interest": Schneider, "Electoral Competition," p. 88.

CHAPTER TEN—Democracy as an Inter-class Deal

166   Median Incomes of Black and White Families: Calculated from *Statistical Abstract of the United States 1982–83,* by U.S. Bureau of the Census (Washington, D.C.: Government Printing Office, 1982), p. 432, table 713.

166   Percentages of All Income in 1981: *Ibid.*, p. 435, table 719.

166   Percentages of All Income in 1950s: U.S. Bureau of the Census, *Historical Statistics of the United States, Colonial Times to 1970* (Washington, D.C.: Government Printing Office, 1975), pt. I, ser. G 85–89; slightly revised data received from Chuck Nelson, Bureau of the Census, private communication, 1983.

168   60% of Americans Feel Alienated: Louis Harris, "Alienation," *The Harris Survey,* February 18, 1982, p. 2.

CHAPTER ELEVEN—The Case for the Interest Groups

171   "The PAC-Men: Turning Cash into Votes": Walter Isaacson, "Running with the PACs," *Time,* October 25, 1982, pp. 20–26.

172   Kuhn's Notion of "Paradigms": Thomas Kuhn, *The Structure of Scientific Revolutions,* 2nd ed. (Chicago: University of Chicago Press, 1970).

173   "From the Beginnings . . .": Harmon Zeigler, *Interest Groups in American Society* (Englewood Cliffs, N.J.: Prentice Hall, 1964), p. 33.

173   "The Criticism Exemplified . . .": *Ibid.*, p. 35.

173   Concessions to Special Interests Viewed as Undemocratic: *Ibid.*

173   "The American Press . . .": Norman J. Ornstein and Shirley Elder, *Interest Groups, Lobbying and Policymaking* (Washington, D.C.: Congressional Quarterly Press, 1978), p. 8.

173   Madison's View of Groups: *Ibid.*, p. 9.

173   Work of Bentley, Truman, Milbrath: Arthur F. Bentley, *The Process of Government* (Cambridge, Mass.: The Belknap Press, Harvard University Press, 1967); David B. Truman, *The Governmental Process: Political Interests and Public Opinion* (New York: Knopf, 1951, 1964); Lester W. Milbrath, *The Washington Lobbyists* (Chicago: Rand McNally, 1963).

173   "Tends to Portray Groups . . .": Ornstein and Elder, *Interest Groups,* p. 12.

173   "The View That Pressure Groups . . .": V. O. Key, Jr., *Politics, Parties, and Pressure Groups,* 4th ed. (New York: Thomas Y. Crowell, 1958), p. 144.

173   "Lobbying is Not a Sinister Practice . . .": Belle Zeller, ed., *American State Legisla-*

tures: Report of the Committee on American Legislatures, American Political Science Association (New York: Thomas Y. Crowell, 1954; New York: Greenwood Press, 1969), p. 214 (Greenwood ed.).

173 "Most Persons . . .": Milbrath, *Washington Lobbyists*, pp. 297–98.

174 "There Are a Few Corrupt . . .": *Ibid.*, p. 304.

174 "The Liberal and Radical . . .": Henry W. Ehrmann, "Interest Groups," in *International Encyclopedia of the Social Sciences* (New York: Crowell Collier and Macmillan, 1968), 7:490.

174 "The Latest Word Is That . . .": Aage R. Clausen, *How Congressmen Decide: A Policy Focus* (New York: St. Martin's Press, 1973), p. 152.

174 Weatherford's Views: J. McIver Weatherford, *Tribes on the Hill* (New York: Rawson Wade, 1981), p. 114.

175 Lobbyists as "Integral" to System: *Ibid.*, pp. 115–33.

175 Alexander's Defense of PACs: Herbert E. Alexander, *The Case for PACs* (Washington, D.C.: Public Affairs Council, n.d.); Paul Taylor, "Don't Pick on PACs, Corporate Unit Says," *Washington Post*, April 14, 1983.

175 Political Scientists Critical of PACs: E. E. Schattschneider, *Politics, Pressures and the Tariff* (New York: Prentice-Hall, 1935); Theodore J. Lowi, *The End of Liberalism* (New York: Norton, 1969); Mancur Olson, *The Logic of Collective Action* (Cambridge, Mass.: Harvard University Press, 1965); Robert A. Dahl, *Dilemmas of Pluralist Democracy: Autonomy vs. Control* (New Haven, Conn.: Yale University Press, 1982).

176 "Voting Conveys . . .": Karl W. Deutsch, *Politics and Government: How People Decide Their Fate*, 2nd ed. (Boston: Houghton Mifflin, 1974), p. 278.

176 "Interest Groups Articulate . . .": *Ibid.*, p. 64.

176 "Lack the Power . . .": *Ibid.*, p. 278.

176 "Lobbying Is an Activity . . .": Thomas A. Reilly and Michael W. Sigall, *Political Bargaining: An Introduction to Modern Politics* (San Francisco: W. H. Freeman, 1976), p. 81.

177 "There Is No Substitute . . .": Milbrath, *Washington Lobbyists*, p. 313.

177 "If We Had No Lobby Groups . . .": *Ibid.*, p. 358.

178 "The Doctrine Recurs . . .": Key, *Politics, Parties*, p. 163.

179 "Washington Office Staffers . . .": Gordon Adams, *The Politics of Defense Contracting: The Iron Triangle* (New Brunswick, N.J.: Transaction Books, 1982), p. 131.

179 "The Best Thing About . . .": "How the Weapons Lobby Works in Washington," *Business Week*, February 12, 1979, p. 135.

179 "Most Important, Perhaps . . .": Dell G. Hitchner and William H. Harbold, *Modern Government*, 3rd ed. (New York: Dodd, Mead, 1972), p. 139.

179 "PACs and the Interest Groups . . .": Alexander, *The Case for PACs*, pp. 29–30.

180 "Encourage Participation . . .": Joseph E. Cantor, *Political Action Committees: Their Evolution and Growth and Their Implications for the Political System* (Washington, D.C.: Congressional Research Service, 1981, 1982), p. 164.

180 "The Socialization of the Citizen . . .": Ehrmann, "Interest Groups," p. 487.

180 "Pressure Groups Frequently . . .": Zeller, *American State Legislature*, p. 214.

180 "Obviously, Organized Groups . . .": Key, *Politics, Parties*, p. 158.

181 "Legislators Could Speak . . .": *Ibid.*, pp. 158–59.

181 "The General Theme . . .": *Ibid.*, p. 142.

181 "The New Types of Interests . . .": *Ibid.*, p. 143.

182 Need for "The Rules of the Game": Truman, *Governmental Process, passim*.

CHAPTER TWELVE—**A Loss of Balance**

185 New Whigs: Amitai Etzioni, *An Immodest Agenda* (New York: McGraw-Hill, 1982), especially chap. 1.

186 "A Considerable Part . . .": Henry S. Kariel, "Pluralism," in *International Encyclopedia of the Social Sciences* (New York: Macmillan, 1968), vol. 12, p. 168.

186 "So Thoroughly . . .": *Ibid.*

186 "The Conviction . . .": Grant McConnell, *Private Power and American Democracy* (New York: Knopf, 1966), p. 5.

186 Government as "Arena" or "Umpire": William E. Connolly, "The Challenge to Pluralist Theory," in *The Bias of Pluralism*, ed. William E. Connolly (New York: Atherton, 1969), p. 8.

186 "Perhaps There Was No Such Thing . . .": McConnell, *Private Power*, p. 158.

186 Public Interest and Values as Meaningless: *Ibid.*, pp. 158–59.

187 "We Have the Strongest . . .": Adam Smith, *The Theory of Moral Sentiments*, ed. D. D. Raphael and A. L. MacFie (Oxford: Clarendon Press, 1976), p. 39.

187 Empathic Ability as Basis of Human Happiness: Garry Wills, "Benevolent Adam Smith," *New York Review of Books*, February 9, 1978, p. 40.

187 Durkheim's Views on Business Contracts: Émile Durkheim, *Suicide: A Study in Sociology*, tr. John A. Spaulding and George Simpson, ed. George Simpson (Glencoe, Ill.: Free Press, 1951).

190 "The U.S. Might Have . . .": Everett Carll Ladd, "How to Tame the Special Interest Groups," *Fortune*, October 20, 1980, p. 66.

191 Confidence Vote in 1966: "Confidence Rollercoaster," *Public Opinion*, October/November, 1979, p. 30.

191 Confidence Vote in 1980: Louis Harris, "Confidence in Institutions," *The Harris Survey*, October 22, 1981, pp. 2-3.

191 Confidence in Congress and Executive: "Confidence in Selected Institutions," *Public Opinion*, October/November 1979, p. 32.

192 Public Loss of Loyalty vs. Performance: Everett Carll Ladd, "205 and Going Strong," *Public Opinion*, June/July 1981, pp. 7–12.

192 Index of Disaffection: Louis Harris, "Alienation," *The Harris Survey*, February 18, 1982, p. 2.

192 Nonvoter Statistics: Bureau of the Census, *Statistical Abstract of the United States, 1981* (Washington, D.C.: Government Printing Office, 1981), tables 798, 824.

192 Annual Growth of GNP: *Ibid.*, table 704.

193 GNP Per Employed Worker: Council of Economic Advisers, *The Economic Report of the President, 1980* (Washington, D.C.: Government Printing Office, 1980), p. 85, table 15.

193 States Affected by Energy Prices: Jill Schuker, "The Energy Concerns of New England," in *Energy: Regional Goals and the National Interest*, ed. Edward J. Mitchell (Washington, D.C.: American Enterprise Institute, 1976), p. 13.

193 Energy Costs in Northeast: Michael J. McManus, ". . . In the Face of Dire Economic Necessity," *Empire State Report* 2 (1976): 344.

193 "The Committees Tend to Be . . .": Elizabeth Drew, "A Tendency to Legislate," *New Yorker*, June 26, 1978, p. 84.

194 Staffs of House and Senate Members: House and Senate Disbursement Offices, Private communications.

195 "I Can't Remember . . .": Meg Greenfield, "Thinking Small," *Washington Post*, April

19, 1978, as quoted in *Interest Groups, Lobbying and Policymaking,* by Norman J. Ornstein and Shirley Elder (Washington, D.C.: Congressional Quarterly Press, 1978), p. 228.

195 "Citizen Affiliation . . .": Norman H. Nie, Sidney Verba, and John R. Petrocik, *The Changing American Voter* (Cambridge, Mass.: Harvard University Press, 1976), p. 73.

195 Public Identification with Parties: Jack Dennis, "Trends in Public Support for the American Party System," *British Journal of Political Science* 5(1975): 192.

195 "More and More People . . .": Richard G. Niemi and Herbert F. Weisberg, "Are Parties Becoming Irrelevant?" in *Controversies in American Voting Behavior,* ed. Niemi and Weisberg (San Francisco: W. H. Freeman, 1976), p. 413.

196 Burnham and Converse: Walter Dean Burnham, "The Onward March of Party Decomposition," and Philip E. Converse, "The Erosion of Party Fidelity," both in Niemi and Weisberg, eds., *Controversies.*

196 Rise of Media Candidates: David B. Hill and Norman R. Luttberg, *Trends in American Electoral Behavior* (Itasca, Ill.: F. E. Peacock, 1980), especially chap. 2.

196 "As the Parties . . .": Ladd, "How to Tame the Special Interest Groups," p. 67.

196 David Adamany: David Adamany, "Political Finance and the American Political Parties," unpublished, p. 108.

CHAPTER THIRTEEN—**Special Interests Are Not Constituencies**

199 Definition Follows Others' Work: See, for example, J. La Palombara, *Interest Groups in Politics* (Princeton: Princeton University Press, 1964).

199 Almond's Typology: Gabriel A. Almond, "Introduction: A Functional Approach to Comparative Politics," *The Politics of Developing Areas,* eds. Gabriel A. Almond and James S. Coleman (Princeton: Princeton University Press, 1960), p. 33.

200 "They Are Structures . . .": Earl Latham, *The Group Basis of Politics* (Ithaca, N.Y.: Cornell University Press, 1952), p. 12.

201 McKean's Listing of Interest Groups: Dayton David McKean, *Pressures on the Legislature of New Jersey* (New York: Russell and Russell, 1967), p. 52.

201 Key's Listing of Interest Groups: V. O. Key, Jr., *Politics, Parties, and Pressure Groups,* 4th ed. (New York: Thomas Y. Crowell, 1958), p. 141.

201 Wilson's Listing of Interest Groups: James Q. Wilson, *American Government: Institutions and Policies* (Lexington, Mass.: D. C. Heath & Co., 1980), pp. 212–13.

201 "However, Some Pressure Groups . . .": Belle Zeller, ed., *American State Legislatures* (New York: Greenwood Press, 1969), p. 214.

202 Sugar Lobbies as SIGs: Anthony Marro, "Powerful Rivals Clash over Sugar Price Supports," *New York Times,* January 16, 1979.

202 Comparative Size of Interest Groups' Social Base: *Encyclopedia of Associations,* 17th ed. (Detroit: Gale Research Co., 1982), p. 1417.

202 Size of AFL-CIO: "Report of the Executive Council of the AFL-CIO," Fourteenth Convention, New York, N.Y., November 16, 1981, p. 45.

203 Difficulties in Defining "the" Public Interest: See, for example, Jeffrey M. Berry, *Lobbying for the People: The Political Behavior of Public Interest Groups* (Princeton: Princeton University Press, 1977), pp. 6–7; Irving Louis Horowitz, "Beyond Democracy: Interest Groups and the Patriotic Gore," *The Humanist,* September/October 1979, p. 4; Andrew S. McFarland, *Public Interest Lobbies* (Washington, D.C.: American Enterprise Institute, 1976), pp. 25–27.

p. 204 Estimates of Numbers of Lobbies: Alfred de Grazia, *Politics and Government,* rev. ed. (New York: Collier Books, 1962), 1:243.

205 Business Roundtable: Kim McQuaid, "The Roundtable: Getting Results in Washington," *Harvard Business Review,* May/June 1981, p. 115.

205 Chamber of Commerce: Tom Richman, "Can the U.S. Chamber Learn to Think Small?," *Inc.,* February 1982, p. 81; Richard I. Kirkland, Jr., "Fat Days for the Chamber of Commerce," *Fortune,* September 21, 1981, p. 144.

205 "Imagine a Checker Player . . .": John W. Gardner, from an unpublished speech delivered at Brown University on March 17, 1980.

205 Riesman's View: David Riesman, *The Lonely Crowd* (New Haven, Conn.: Yale University Press, 1950), pp. 244–48.

205 "Major New Problems . . .": Suzanne Berger, "Interest Groups and the Governability of European Society," *Items* 35, no. 4 (December 1981): 64 (*Items* is a bulletin published by the Social Science Research Council).

206 Effects of Change on Oil Pricing: *The Windfall Profits Tax: A Comparative Analysis of Two Bills* (Washington, D.C.: Congressional Budget Office, 1979), p. xvii.

206 Savings to Oil Industry: Steven V. Roberts, "Study Ties Oil Gifts to Voting in House," *New York Times,* July 24, 1979; *Nader Study Links Oil Contributions to Pro-Oil House Vote* (Washington, D.C.: Public Citizen's Congress Watch, 1979).

206 CROs and SIGs Contribute to Inflation: Daniel Bell, "The Revolution of Rising Entitlements," *Fortune,* April 1975, p. 100; Milton Friedman, *Capitalism and Freedom* (Chicago: University of Chicago Press, 1962, 1982), p. 23.

207 AFL-CIO Supports Wage Guidelines: "Kirkland Style," p. 77.

207 Inflation Percentages, 1979 and 1980: Bureau of the Census, *Statistical Abstract of the United States, 1981* (Washington, D.C.: Government Printing Office, 1981), table 766.

207 Percentages of Union Wage Increases: Joan D. Borum, "Wage Increases in 1980 Outpaced by Inflation," *Monthly Labor Review,* May 1981, p. 55.

207 Hospital Room Charges, 1979 and 1980: Calculated from Bureau of the Census, *Statistical Abstract,* table 157.

CHAPTER FOURTEEN—**The Public Interest**

209 "Assume Explicitly . . .": David B. Truman, *The Governmental Process: Political Interests and Public Opinion* (New York: Knopf, 1964), p. 50.

209 "Do Not Describe . . .": *Ibid.,* pp. 50–51.

209 "According to Some Classic . . .": Karl W. Deutsch, *Politics and Government: How People Decide Their Fate,* 2nd ed. (Boston: Houghton Mifflin, 1974), p. 199.

210 "It Is No Simple Task . . .": Murray L. Weidenbaum, *The Future of Government Regulation: The Public Response* (St. Louis: Center for the Study of American Business, 1979), p. 5.

210 "We Have Now Reached . . .": Irving Louis Horowitz, "Interest Groups and the Patriotic Gore," *The Humanist,* September/October 1979, p. 4.

210 "While Denying That . . .": David Vogel, "The Public Interest Movement and the American Reform Tradition," *Political Science Quarterly* 95 (Winter 1980–81): 608.

210 "PAC Supporters Object . . .": Joseph E. Cantor, *Political Action Committees: Their Evolution and Growth and Their Implications for the Political System* (Washington, D.C.: Congressional Research Service, 1981, 1982), p. 152.

p. 211 "The Public Interest Is Not . . .": Archibald Cox, "A Liberal Looks at the 1980's," Girvetz Memorial Lecture, University of California at Santa Barbara, January 13, 1981, pp. 13–14. (Emphasis added.)

211 "Special-interest Groups . . .": E. E. Schattschneider, *The Semisovereign People: A Realist's View of Democracy in America* (New York: Holt, Rinehart and Winston, 1960), p. 25.

212 NAM vs. ALACP: *Ibid.,* p. 26.

212 "One That Seeks . . .": Andrew S. McFarland, *Public Interest Lobbies* (Washington, D.C.: American Enterprise Institute, 1976), p. 40.

212 Not All PIGs Represent Public Interest: *Ibid.,* p. 41.

212 Tucker's Assessment: William Tucker, *Progress and Privilege: America in the Age of Environmentalism* (New York: Anchor Press, 1982).

212 Weidenbaum on PIGs: Weidenbaum, *Future of Government Regulation,* pp. 3–6.

212 "Conservatives Criticize . . .": McFarland, *Public Interest Lobbies,* p. 26.

212 Lichter-Rothman Survey: S. Robert Lichter and Stanley Rothman, "What Interests the Public and What Interests the Public Interests," *Public Opinion,* April/May 1983, p. 46.

213 "Many Analysts Assert . . .": "Lean Times for 'Citizens' Lobbies,' " *U. S. News & World Report,* April 19, 1982, p. 90.

214 Common Cause and "Sunshine": Tom Bethell, "Taking a Hard Look at Common Cause," *New York Times Magazine,* August 24, 1980, p. 44.

214 Factions "Sown in the Nature of Man": James Madison, "Number X," in *The Federalist,* by Alexander Hamilton, James Madison, and John Jay (Avon, Conn.: The Heritage Press, 1973), p. 56.

214 "Interest Group Activity . . .": James Q. Wilson, *American Government: Institutions and Policies* (Lexington, Mass.: D. C. Heath & Co., 1980), p. 227.

215 "It Is of Great Importance . . .": James Madison, "Number LI," in *The Federalist,* pp. 349–50.

215 "In Situation after Situation . . .": V. O. Key, Jr., *Politics, Parties, and Pressure Groups,* 4th ed. (New York: Thomas Y. Crowell, 1958), p. 166.

215 "An Important Factor . . .": Lester W. Milbrath, *The Washington Lobbyists* (Chicago: Rand McNally, 1963), p. 345.

215 "This Natural Self-Balancing Factor . . .": *Ibid.*

216 "Constituent Pressures and the Vote . . .": *Ibid.,* p. 346.

217 Schattschneider's Findings on Imports: E. E. Schattschneider, *Politics, Pressures and the Tariff* (New York: Prentice-Hall, 1935).

217 Author's View on Human Nature: This position is spelled out and documented in Amitai Etzioni, *A Comparative Analysis of Complex Organizations,* rev. ed. (New York: Free Press, 1975).

217 Presence vs. Absence of Community-Capsule: Amitai Etzioni, *Political Unification: A Comparative Study of Leaders and Forces* (New York: Holt, Rinehart and Winston, 1965). See also the discussion of self-encapsulation in *The Active Society: A Theory of Societal and Political Processes* (New York: Free Press, 1968), pp. 586 ff.

CHAPTER FIFTEEN—**Are Reforms Constitutional?**

224 Conable and Contributions: Mark Shields, "The Coming Campaign Scandal," *Washington Post,* February 25, 1983.

p. 225 Definition of Poverty in 1981: Poverty Statistics Office, Bureau of the Census, private communication, 1983.

225 1907 Law Challenged in Courts: William T. Mayton, "Politics, Money, Coercion, and the Problem with Corporate PACs," *Emory Law Journal* 29 (1980): 376.

225 U.S. v. U.S. Brewers Association: *Ibid.*, fn. 11 (citing *U.S. v. U.S. Brewers Association* 239 F. 163, 169 [W.D. Pa. 1916]).

225 "Unique Business Entity . . .": *Ibid.*, pp. 375–76.

226 First National Bank of Boston v. Bellotti: John R. Bolton, "Constitutional Limitations on Restricting Corporate and Union Political Speech," *Arizona Law Review* 22 (1980): 409–11.

226 "PACs Are Truly . . .": Mobil Corporation, "PACs—Consider the Alternatives (advertisement), *The Economist,* April 30, 1983, p. 26.

226 Solicitation of PAC Contributions: See Mayton, "Problem with Corporate PACs," pp. 383, 391; also Stephen J. Sansweet, "Political Action Units at Firms Are Assailed by Some over Tactics," *Wall Street Journal,* July 24, 1980.

227 "All Costs Associated With . . .": H. Richard Mayberry, "Business Political Action Committees: A Significant Factor in 1980 Election Results," in *The PAC Handbook* (Washington, D.C.: Fraser/Associates, 1981), p. 349.

228 Corporate PACs and 1982 Elections: Calculated from *FEC Reports on Financial Activity, 1981–1982, Interim Report No. 4: Party and Non-Party Political Committees,* vol. I, *Summary Tables* (Washington, D.C.: Federal Election Commission, 1983), pp. 90, 94.

228 Comparative Percentages of PAC Contributions: Calculated from *Ibid.*, pp. 90, 94, 119.

228 Council for a Livable World: Private communications, June 20 and 23, 1983.

229 Boeing Civic Pledge Program: Charles M. Sauvage, Common Cause (Washington State), private communication, June 21, 1983.

230 Lehrman's Campaign Funds: Frank Lynn, "Lehrman Is Close," *New York Times,* November 3, 1982.

230 David Koch's Promise to Contribute: *Dollar Politics,* 3rd ed. (Washington, D.C.: Congressional Quarterly, Inc., 1982), p. 101.

230 Fonda's Contributions to Hayden: Office of the Secretary of State, State of California, "Expenditure and Major Donor Committee" campaign statements filed by Jane Fonda for the period January 1, 1982, through March 17, 1983.

231 "A Restriction on the Amount . . .": *Buckley v. Valeo,* 424 U.S. 1 (1976), p. 19.

231 "This Is Because . . .": *Ibid.*

231 "By Contrast with a Limitation . . .": *Ibid.*, p. 20.

232 "Considering the History . . .": "The Money Game: Changing the Rules," *Time,* February 9, 1976, p. 11.

CHAPTER SIXTEEN—**What Is To Be Done?**

234 Irving Kristol: As quoted in "The Problem of PAC–Journalism," by Michael Malbin, *Public Opinion,* December/January 1983, p. 59.

235 Minish's Proposal for Reduction: Joseph E. Cantor, *Political Action Committees: Their Evolution and Growth and Their Implications for the Political System* (Washington, D.C.: Congressional Research Service, 1981, 1982), p. 189.

235 Franks's Suggestion on Raising Ceiling: Brooks Jackson, "The Problem with PACs," *Wall Street Journal,* November 17, 1982.

p. 235 Frenzel's Bill to Raise Limits: Paul Taylor, "Efforts to Revise Campaign Laws Center on PACs," *New York Times,* February 28, 1983.

236 Experience with Public Financing: *Dollar Politics,* 3rd ed. (Washington, D.C.: Congressional Quarterly, Inc., 1982), pp. 91–111, especially pp. 91–92.

237 "This System Has Worked . . .": Testimony of Fred Wertheimer, president, Common Cause, on the Federal Election Campaign Act before the Committee on Rules and Administration of the United States Senate, January 27, 1983, p. 13.

238 "A Unique Freedom . . .": *How Money Talks in Congress* (Washington, D.C.: Common Cause, 1979), p. 20.

238 State-by-state Limits on Campaign Spending: *Dollar Politics,* pp. 91–92.

238 Public Financing in Michigan and New Jersey: Joseph F. Sullivan, "Turning Off Party Machines Turned On the Candidates," *New York Times,* March 8, 1981.

240 1982 Total Congressional Campaign Spending: *FEC Reports on Financial Activity, 1981–1982, Interim Report No. 3: U.S. Senate and House Campaigns* (Washington, D.C.: Federal Election Commission, 1983), p. 91.

240 Ward on Whether Costs Are Excessive: Testimony of Gregg Ward, Sheet Metal and Air Conditioning Contractors' National Association, Committee on House Administration's Task Force on Elections, June 10, 1982, p. 9.

240 McHugh and Conable: Jonathan Fuerbringer, "Bill Would Alter Some Tax Credits," *New York Times,* August 3, 1983.

241 List of Reasons for Objections: Douglas Caddy, *How They Rig Our Elections: The Coming Dictatorship of Big Labor and the Radicals* (New Rochelle, N.Y.: Arlington House, 1975), appendix I.

241 Supreme Court on Public Financing of Campaigns: *Buckley v. Valeo,* 424 U.S. 1 (1976), pp. 92–93.

242 Surplus Funds in Election Campaigns: Bill Hogan, Diane Kiesel, and Alan Green, "The New Slush Fund Scandal," *The New Republic,* August 30, 1982, p. 21.

242 Inouye's Use of Funds: Bill Hogan, Diane Kiesel, and Alan Green, "The Senate's Secret Slush Funds," *The New Republic,* June 20, 1983, p. 14.

242 Study on Improper Use of Surplus Funds: Hogan, Kiesel, and Green, "The New Slush Fund Scandal," and "The Senate's Secret Slush Funds."

243 Rhodes's Use of Funds: "The New Slush Fund Scandal," p. 22.

243 Badham's Use of Funds: Kathryn Johnson, "How Lawmakers Misuse Your Campaign Donations," *U.S. News & World Report,* March 7, 1983, p. 35.

243 Taylor's Use of Funds: "The New Slush Fund Scandal," p. 22.

243 Williams's Use of Funds: Hogan, Kiesel, and Green, "The Senate's Secret Slush Funds," p. 14.

243 Congressional Exemption in Fund Limitations: Hogan, Kiesel, and Green, "The New Slush Fund Scandal," p. 25.

243 House Rule Prohibition: Mark Elam, counsel for the House Committee on Standards, private communication, May 1983.

243 Senate Ruling on Defraying Extra Costs: Ann Miskovsky, press officer, Senate Ethics Committee, private communication, May 1983.

243 Wilson's Violations and House Ethics Committee: *Congressional Ethics,* 2nd ed. (Washington, D.C.: Congressional Quarterly, Inc., 1980), pp. 32–35; "Rep. Charles H. Wilson Censured by House for Violation of Its Rules," *New York Times,* June 11, 1980.

244 Korean Influence-peddling Investigation: *Congressional Ethics,* p. 21.

244 Senate Ethics Committee's 370 Advisory Opinions: Private communication.

244 Senate Ethics Committee's Rulings Misused: Floyd Norris, "Capitol Transactions:

How Members of Congress Handle Their Own Money," *Barron's,* June 13, 1983, pp. 11, 38.

244   Senator Paula Hawkins: "All in the Family," *Common Cause,* July/August 1983, p. 22.

244   Representative Norman Lent: Michael Isikoff, "Phone Firm Hires Wife of Lawmaker on Key Committee," *Washington Post,* October 25, 1983; Michael Isikoff, "Rep. Lent Told to Decide If Conflict Exists," *Washington Post,* October 27, 1983.

244   Five-year Statute of Limitation in Criminal Law: Department of Justice, "Federal Prosecution of Election Offenses," October 1982, p. 42.

245   1976 Supreme Court Ruling on Campaign Funds: *Buckley v. Valeo,* 424 U.S. 1 (1976).

246   Hayakawa's Suggestion on PAC Money: As quoted in "Parting Shots by Retiring Lawmakers," *U.S. News & World Report,* December 20, 1982, p. 24.

246   Leach's Suggestion to Limit Contributions: Cantor, *Political Action Committees,* p. 186.

246   Limits before 1976 Supreme Court Ruling: *Buckley v. Valeo,* 424 U.S. 1 (1976), p. 44.

246   Independent-Expenditure Limit for Presidential Candidates: *Federal Election Commission v. Americans for Change* 455 U.S. 129 (1982).

247   Obey-Railsback Bill: Cantor, *Political Action Committees,* pp. 191–94.

247   1983 Bipartisan Bill: Office of Congressman David R. Obey, *Bipartisan Coalition Introduces Bill to Limit Spending by Political Action Committees,* April 11, 1983; Jim Drinkard, "House Members Propose Public Campaign Financing," *Associated Press,* April 11, 1983.

248   "The Candidate who Chooses . . .": Drinkard, "Public Campaign Financing."

248   Malbin's Objections to Limits: Malbin, "The Problem of PAC-Journalism."

249   Democratic Campaigning Period: James R. Dickenson, "Politics Is Endless in This Country," *Washington Post,* April 17, 1983.

249   Winograd and Hunt Commissions: Nelson W. Polsby, *Consequences of Party Reform* (New York: Oxford University Press, 1983), pp. 173–74, p. 251 note 18.

249   Former President Ford: Juan Williams, "Carter Says Congressmen Are Hurdle to Higher Voter Registration," *Washington Post,* October 1, 1983.

249   "A Precisely Calculated Amount . . .": R. W. Apple, Jr., "Campaigning in Britain: No Frills and No Glamour, Just $6,633.72," *New York Times,* June 9, 1983.

250   1973 Limits on Mailing: *Congressional Ethics,* pp. 98–100.

250   Free Airtime for Candidates: Mark Green, "Political PAC-Man," *The New Republic,* December 13, 1982, p. 24.

250   "A Dime per Citizen": *Ibid.*

251   Lobbyists and Visibility: "How the Weapons Lobby Works in Washington," *Business Week,* February 12, 1979, p. 135.

252   Sunshine Act of 1976: *Shadows over the Sunshine Act* (Washington, D.C.: Common Cause, 1977), pp. 5–7.

252   1954 Supreme Court Interpretation of "Lobbying": Richard C. Sachs, *Lobby Act Reform* (Washington, D.C.: Congressional Research Service, 1981), p. 1.

252   AT&T Drive: Monica Langley, "Ma Bell's Shepherds: AT&T Sends a Horde of Lobbyists to Fight a Phone-Bill Proposal," *Wall Street Journal,* November 4, 1983.

253   Disclosure Laws and Record-keeping: *Dollar Politics,* pp. 136–37.

254   AJC and Disclosure on Arms: Stephen Grover, "Jewish Group Asks 23 Firms to Disclose AWACs Lobby Funds," *Wall Street Journal,* February 24, 1983.

p. 254 Effect of Revised Proxy Rule: Philip R. O'Connell, "The Tightening of Proxy Rules: Legitimate Voices Will Still Be Heard," *New York Times,* September 4, 1983.

CHAPTER SEVENTEEN—**More Bite: Beyond "Routine" Reforms**

255 Federal Corrupt Practices Act of 1925: *Dollar Politics,* 3rd ed. (Washington, D.C.: Congressional Quarterly, Inc., 1982), pp. 3–4.

255 American Enterprise Institute Report: *Proposals to Revise the Lobbying Law* (Washington, D.C.: American Enterprise Institute, 1980), p. 20.

255 Common Cause Study: *The Power Persuaders* (Washington, D.C.: Common Cause, 1978), pp. ii–iii.

256 1946 Act Deprived of Power: James Q. Wilson, *The 1980 Election* (Lexington, Mass.: D.C. Heath, 1981), supplement to Wilson, *American Government* (Lexington, Mass.: D. C. Heath, 1980), p. 227.

256 "A Check of the Records . . .": *Congressional Record—Senate,* December 11, 1981, p. S 15140.

256 Creation of FEC: FEC Press Office, private communication, July 28, 1983.

256 Violations of Election Laws and Penalties: David R. Spiegel, "Our Toothless Watchdogs," *Newsweek,* November 1, 1982, p. 18.

256 FEC Administration: Herbert E. Alexander, *Financing Politics,* 2nd ed. (Washington, D.C.: Congressional Quarterly Press, 1980), p. 38.

256 Congress Authorizes FEC Funds: *Ibid.*

256 Elliot Appointed to FEC: Elizabeth Drew, "Politics and Money—II," *New Yorker,* December 13, 1982, p. 101.

257 Common Cause Call for Random Audits: Testimony of Fred Wertheimer, president, Common Cause, on the Federal Election Campaign Act before the Committee on Rules and Administration of the United States Senate, January 27, 1983, pp. 14–15.

257 CAL Remedy: Belle Zeller, ed., *American State Legislatures* (New York: Greenwood Press, 1969), p. 238.

257 Massachusetts Commission in 1978: *The Final Report to the General Court of the Special Commission Concerning State and County Buildings* (Office of the Massachusetts Secretary of State, December 31, 1980), pp. 23–24.

258 "Commission Findings": *Ibid.,* pp. 1–4, 20.

258 Commission Suggestions Made Law: *Ibid.,* p. 25.

259 1984 Candidates Declined PAC Money: Martin Schram, "Mondale, Hart Bar PAC Funds in '84 Primaries," *Washington Post,* February 9, 1983; Martin Schram, "Askew to Reject Funds from PACs," *Washington Post,* February 10, 1983.

261 Symms and Silver: Floyd Norris, "Capitol Transactions: How Members of Congress Handle Their Own Money," *Barron's,* June 13, 1983, pp. 11, 38.

263 Defeat of Reagan-Administration Rules: Michael Wines, "Lobbyists Unite to Lobby Against OMB's Proposed Curbs on Lobbying," *National Journal,* February 19, 1983, pp. 370–72; Kathleen Teltsch, "Lobbying with U.S. Money: New Rules Stir Protests," *New York Times,* March 1, 1983.

263 "I Disagree Profoundly . . .": Michael J. Horowitz, private communication, June 1983.

264 Mobil Oil and PAC Ads: H. B. Olsen, Jr., Public Relations Department, Mobil Oil Corporation, private communication, July 5, 1983.

p. 264   FBI Abscam Operation 1978–80: FBI Press Office, private communication, June 17, 1983.

264   Stennis Criticism: James Q. Wilson, "The Real Issues in Abscam," *Washington Post,* July 15, 1982.

264   Congressional Investigations and Hearings: Mary Thornton, "Former Justice Official Defends Abscam Probe," *Washington Post,* June 4, 1982; Leslie Maitland, "Senate Panel Begins Review of Abscam-Type Inquiries," *New York Times,* July 21, 1982; private communication.

265   FBI Response to Argument of Enticement: See Gerald M. Caplan, *Abscam Ethics: Moral Issues and Deception in Law Enforcement* (Cambridge, Mass.: Ballinger Press, 1983).

265   Revell Comment on Monitoring Corruption: O. B. Revell, assistant director of the FBI, private communication.

266   The Senator's Account: *Congressional Ethics,* 2nd ed. (Washington, D. C.: Congressional Quarterly, Inc., 1980), p. 9.

266   Drugs and FBI: FBI Press Office, private communication, July 28, 1983.

267   Suggestions that Constitutional Amendment May Be Required: Joseph E. Cantor, Congressional Research Service, private communication, July 28, 1983.

CHAPTER EIGHTEEN—**Institutional Changes, Historical Forces, and You**

270   Public Sentiment on Parties: "Sizing Up Political Parties," *Public Opinion,* August/September 1982, p. 32.

271   Polls on Corruption and Parties: *Ibid.*

271   "There Are Essentially . . .": James Q. Wilson, *American Government* (Lexington, Mass.: D. C. Heath, 1980), p. 207.

271   "The Powerful Cook County . . .": *Ibid.,* pp. 207–208.

271   "Both Parties, Heavily . . .": Grant McConnell, *Private Power and American Democracy* (New York: Knopf, 1966), p. 179.

272   McConnell Citations of Studies: *Ibid.,* pp. 180, 382.

272   "As the Parties . . .": Everett Carll Ladd, "How to Tame the Special Interest Groups," *Fortune,* October 20, 1980, p. 67.

272   "It Must Be Obvious . . .": *Ibid.,* p. 72.

272   Reasons Political Parties Declined: Larry J. Sabato, *The Rise of Political Consultants* (New York: Basic Books, 1981), p. 274.

272   Confidence Polls: "Confidence in Institutions," *Public Opinion,* October/November 1979, p. 30.

272   1983 Confidence Polls: Louis Harris, "Confidence in Institutions Rises Slightly," *The Harris Survey,* November 17, 1983.

273   Polsby's Suggested Reforms: Nelson W. Polsby, *Consequences of Party Reform* (New York: Oxford University Press, 1983).

274   Cohen's Suggested Reforms: David Cohen, "Reviving the Political Parties," *In Common,* Fall 1979, pp. 19–22.

274   Parties and House Votes, 1932 through 1980: "Election '82 Preview," *Public Opinion,* August/September 1982, p. 28.

274   Party Identification in Last Decades: "A Republican Revival? Too Early to Tell," *Public Opinion,* April/May 1981, pp. 30–31.

274   Party Identification in 1982: Gallup survey, June 25–28, 1982, reported in "Party Identification," *Public Opinion,* August/September 1982, p. 29.

p. 274 Alexander Report on Contribution Limitations: Herbert E. Alexander, *Financing Politics*, 2nd ed. (Washington, D.C.: Congressional Quarterly Press, 1980), p. 129.

274 Eleven States Give Funds to Parties: *Ibid.*, p. 137.

277 Bradley-Gephardt Tax Bill: "Capital Wrapup," *Business Week*, April 18, 1983, p. 141.

278 DISC Costs and Benefits: Philip M. Stern, "What Corporate Tax?" *New York Times*, February 17, 1983.

279 September 15 Resolution: Committee for a Responsible Federal Budget, "The Congressional Budget Process: Review and Assessment," paper presented at Symposium on Proposed Changes in the Budget Act and Process, Arkadelphia, Arkansas, January 1982, pp. 2–3; see also "Defending the Budget Process," *Business Week*, May 9, 1983, p. 146.

280 Jones's Comment on Joint Chiefs: Private communication.

280 General Vessey: Richard Halloran, "Reshaping the Joint Chiefs by Way of Persuasion," *New York Times*, June 29, 1983.

281 "You Cannot Imagine . . .": Eleanor Randolph, "American Politics Joins the 'Me' Generation," *Boston Globe*, November 13, 1979.

281 "The Sum of the Parts . . .": *Ibid.*

284 Common Cause "War on PACs": Common Cause, "A Declaration of War" (advertisement), *New York Times*, February 6, 1983.

284 Common Cause Plan against PACs: "What You Can Do," *Common Cause*, August 1982, p. 19.

INDEX